Demystifying the DSM

Demystifying the DSM

A TOOL FOR SCHOOL COUNSELING STUDENTS AND PRACTITIONERS

REVISED FIRST EDITION

Edited by
M. Ann Shillingford, Ph.D. and
Tiphanie Gonzalez, Ph.D.

Bassim Hamadeh, CEO and Publisher
Amy Smith, Senior Project Editor
Abbey Hastings, Production Editor
Emely Villavicencio, Senior Graphic Designer
Stephanie Kohl, Licensing Coordinator
Natalie Piccotti, Director of Marketing
Kassie Graves, Vice President of Editorial
Jamie Giganti, Director of Academic Publishing

Printed in the United States of America.

BRIEF CONTENTS

DETAILED CONTENTS

CHAPTER TWO

Specific Learning Disorder 23

Jon Borland and Whitney Hanley

CHAPTER THREE

Attention Deficit Hyperactivity Disorder (ADHD) 33

Christopher Belser and Dalena Dillman Taylor

CHAPTER FIVE

Bipolar Disorder 59

Erika Cameron, Lauren Flynn, and Matt Dahlman

CHAPTER SIX

Eating Disorders 75

M. Ann Shillingford, Lèa Herbert, and Vikki Gaskin-Butler

CHAPTER SEVEN

Oppositional Defiant Disorder 91

Jason Duffy

CHAPTER EIGHT

Conduct Disorder 103

Dana Griffin and Nicole S. Helton

CHAPTER TEN

Obsessive-Compulsive Disorder 131

Carrie Lynn Bailey and Christie Jenkins

CHAPTER ELEVEN

Separation Anxiety Disorder 143

Pamela Harris and Amy E. Williams

CHAPTER SIXTEEN

Grief and Bereavement 209

Naomi J. Wheeler and Autumn Cabell

CHAPTER SEVENTEEN

Selective Mutism 221

Jung H. Hyun and Tiphanie Gonzalez

INTRODUCTION

This book has been written as a guiding tool for counselors in training, particularly school counselors in training, as well as practitioners who are interested in learning more about common diagnoses among children and youth. Although counselors do not diagnose, they are charged with working with all students within the school environment. Each diagnosis mentioned in this text was selected in consultation with experienced practicing school counselors. Although these diagnoses are not by any means exhaustive to the experiences of children and youth, they represent prevalent symptomatic concerns in this population.

Each academic year, school counselors are confronted with many students who begin the school with a diagnosis or exhibit behaviors that may warrant a diagnosis. While school counselors are on the front line when it comes to supporting all students, many are not equipped to address the unique needs of students living with social, emotional, behavioral, and/or learning disabilities or disorders. In fact, many, if not most, graduate school counseling programs do not include a course on diagnosis and treatment as part of their student academic plan of study. This knowledge and skill deficiency can significantly hinder the ability of school counselors to contribute effectively as multidisciplinary team members. We hope that the information shared in this book will fill this knowledge gap and build on the professional efficacy of school counselors when they are faced with a student with questionable behaviors.

Structure of the Book

There are 17 chapters listed in this text. Each chapter is formatted to address knowledge, skills, and awareness of common diagnoses among children. Each chapter (a) begins with a vignette to set the stage for learning, (b) includes course objectives for reflective learning, (c) provides core information related to the identified diagnosis, and (d) offers strategies for school counselors, teachers, and parents. In addition, each chapter ends with two case examples with questions related to each case. Although these basic structures are followed within each chapter, each is unique in its own way with supplemental information based on the prevalence of the diagnosis, information available in the literature, and strategies that are practical to the role, training, and resources of school counselors.

Ethical and Legal Considerations

With each chapter presented, readers should keep in mind that ethical and legal considerations drive the ultimate decisions they make in how best to support students, how to engage teachers and administration, and how to include caregivers in the process. Confidentiality of student information should be upheld as with other counseling protocols. When consulting with teachers and administrators, counselors should be mindful of how much and what type of information is shared so not to breach the confidential nature of the counseling relationship. For example, a teacher may ask for an update on a student's progress and your response should be, *"I see that you are concerned about Bobby. We are continuing to work on making more positive choices."*

You may also be confronted by parents who want to know more about what you and their child are discussing in session. An appropriate response would be, *"Jadira and I are continuing to work on appropriate ways of communicating. You may want to ask her how she thinks our sessions are going and what has been most helpful to her."* Other ethical and legal practices to keep in mind include avoiding (a) engaging in hallway and teacher lounge room conversations about students, (b) therapeutic conversations with students outside of the privacy of the counseling setting, and (c) use of the student's full name in email communications and certainly avoid including the personal nature of the student's concerns.

Cultural Considerations

As you explore the different diagnoses that P–12 students may be experiencing in your schools, you must consider student cultural diversity. As we saw with the *Diagnostic and Statistical Manual of Mental Disorders, Fifth Edition* (*DSM-V*) updates, there was an expansion on the discussion around cultural considerations when working with client mental illness. In addition to highlighting diagnoses that were unique to specific communities with examples given for mental illnesses that occur largely within or among persons from Latin America, the Caribbean, across Asia, or the United States, there is also a continued discussion about cultural diversity throughout the manual (American Psychiatric Association, 2013a).

Along with the updated cultural considerations by chapter, the *DSM-V* has adopted a guide for counselors to build consideration of client culture using the Cultural Formulation Interview published in the *DSM-V's* Appendix E (American Psychiatric Association, 2013b).

It is important to note that counselors are charged with building an understanding of diversity among client populations with continued education expanding counselor multicultural competence. In 2015, the Association for Multicultural Counseling and Development updated its multicultural counseling competencies (Sue et al., 1992) and published the Multicultural Social Justice Counseling Competencies (Ratts et al., 2015). These competencies also serve as a guide for working with client populations from diverse backgrounds in addition to exploring the role of the counselor both with clients and as change agents in the world.

For you as a school counselor, often the student body of your school is a direct reflection of the community in which it is housed. School counselors should be aware of the individual intersectional identities of students, their families, and the overarching diversity of the school community. Finally, you must consider your own intersectional identities, including how they play a role in who you are as an individual and who you are as a counselor as you engage with others in your school community; how your areas of privilege and oppression directly affect your worldview, how your students' intersectional identities play a role in the way they view the world in addition to where they are developmentally in age and understanding as they are growing up, and how even if you are in the same space at the same time, your worldviews may not align.

Special Education Services

As you read each chapter, there are certain terms that may come up more frequently than others, so let us talk about each of these terms before moving forward.

Through thorough evaluative assessments, students may be determined to qualify for special education services and/or accommodation plans. Determining eligibility for special education services must be a two-pronged decision. The evaluation team must decide (1) whether the student has a disability and (2) if the student needs support from special education and related services to be successful, usually, these needs are then outlined into a student's individual education program (IEP) as dictated by the Individuals with Disabilities Education Act (IDEA) of 2004. Note that the title of the evaluation team may vary by state and school district. Some more popular terms include multidisciplinary team, school instructional team, and child study team.

The IDEA of 2004 is a set of federal guidelines used to govern special education. The six principals of IDEA are as follows:

1. **Free Appropriate Public Education (FAPE).** Students with disabilities are entitled to attend public school and are provided FAPE services to meet their individual needs.
2. **Least Restrictive Environment (LRE).** To the "maximum extent appropriate," students with disabilities are educated with their nondisabled peers. LRE involves a continuum of places from the least restrictive (general education classroom) to most restrictive (separate school). While mainstreaming (dated term) and inclusion are not terms in IDEA, inclusion refers to educating students with disabilities in the general education classroom with special education supports.
3. **IEP.** The IEP includes a statement about the student's current level of performance, measurable goals, how progress will be evaluated, where and how services will be provided, and who will provide services as written in the IEP.
4. **Procedural Safeguards.** Federally regulated guidelines to protect parents' and students' rights under IDEA.
5. **Appropriate Evaluation.** Nondiscriminatory evaluations should be conducted by a team of knowledgeable and trained evaluators. Evaluations must be done in a timely manner and used to determine a child's eligibility for special education and/or related services.
6. **Parent Participation.** Parents (and children) have the right to be active and equal participants in the decision-making process.

IEP

The IEP is designed to meet the unique needs of students with disabilities. This legally binding document guides the delivery of specially designed instruction and services to students with identified disabilities that fall under one of the 13 categories under the IDEA of 2004. Although IEP documents may look different based on state regulations, each document should include annual goals to assist the student in advancing toward academic success, related special education services (e.g., occupational therapy, speech therapy), and measurable progress. The U.S. Department of Education (2019) highlights the following steps toward eligibility:

1. The student is identified as potentially in need of services.
2. The student is evaluated.
3. The student's disability eligibility is determined.
4. The student's qualifications for special education services is determined.
5. An IEP meeting is scheduled.
6. An IEP meeting is held, at which point an IEP is written.
7. Special education services are provided.
8. Student progress is measured and reported to caregivers.
9. The IEP is reviewed annually.
10. The student is reevaluated at least every 3 years.

Section 504 Plan

Section 504 of the Rehabilitation Act is a nondiscrimination law and civil rights mandate. Section 504, enacted in 1973, was developed by the Office of Civil Rights to protect students with disabilities from discriminatory practices. Students who are determined to have a disability but do not qualify for an IEP, as described earlier, may qualify for a Section 504 plan. This plan denotes that school districts provide FAPE to qualifying students with physical or mental impairments that limit one or more major life activities, such as learning, walking, talking, or seeing). Physical and mental impairments may include diseases (e.g., cancer), chronic illnesses (e.g., diabetes, asthma), and injuries (e.g., broken limb that affects the ability to write). Similar to determining eligibility for an IEP, students must be identified with a disability that falls under Section 504 before initial placements; then an individualized plan with accommodations will be developed. Section 504 plans differ from the IEP because the IEP provides individualized education for students through a special education service provider, such as a special education teacher, speech-language pathologist, occupational therapist, or physical therapist. Students on 504 plans simply require accommodations and modifications to access the general education and school environment. However, the district- and school-level administrations are primarily responsible for Section 504 plans, not the special education teachers.

Response to Intervention (RTI)

RTI is a framework for addressing the needs of students with academic or behavior issues using three tiers of intervention that are focused on addressing academic deficiencies. RTI is a multitiered process that is also used to identify students with learning disorders more accurately (Vaughn & Fletcher, 2012). The key components of the RTI process include (a) universal screening, (b) continuous progress monitoring, (c) continuum of evidence-based interventions, (d) data-based decision making and problem solving, (e) implementation fidelity, (f) high-quality instruction, and (g) intervention tiers that increase with intensity (Fuchs & Deshler, 2007; Jimerson et al., 2016; Sanetti & Collier-Meek, 2015; Utley & Obiakor, 2015). Using a team approach, the RTI protocol has been found to be beneficial in identifying students in need of more in-depth psychological evaluations and, ultimately, relevant interventions. Key professionals in the RTI collaborative team may include the following individuals: student's guardian(s), students' general education teachers, school psychologists, school counselors, and speech-language pathologists.

Multi-tiered System of Support (MTSS)

MTSS (a federal initiative) is a data-driven, problem-solving framework that was developed to provide a more systematic way of addressing academic, behavioral, social, and emotional concerns among school-aged children. MTSS follows three tiers of support: (1) determination of needs of all students through universal screening processes; (2) determination of support for identified students in need of intensive interventions, either individually or through small group settings; and (3) determination of more specialized services for students in need of more intensive and individualized services. It should be noted that participation in the MTSS is not a school counselor role, but the school counselor should be an integral member of the team. Other stakeholders include administrators, teachers, parents, and other professionals who can provide expertise related to the student needs.

Positive Behavior Interventions and Supports (PBIS)

PBIS enhances a positive school climate to promote more successful learning environments. PBIS is a preventative measure that focuses on optimistically teaching children more positive behavior while at the same time reducing the need for reactive disciplinary actions.

Social-Emotional Learning (SEL)

SEL promotes school success through critical thinking, conflict resolution, developing skills for emotional regulation, and positive decision making. According to Collaborative for Academic, Social, and Emotional Learning (CASEL, 2019), there are five key SEL competency components that promote social and emotional learning: (1) self-awareness (e.g., personal strengths and limitations), (2) self-management (e.g., impulse control and stress management), (3) self-awareness (e.g., understanding diversity between self and others), (4) relationship skills (e.g., effective communication), and (5) responsible decision making (e.g., making appropriate choices).

References

American Psychiatric Association. (2013a). *Cultural concepts in DSM-5.*

American Psychiatric Association. (2013b). *Diagnostic and statistical manual of mental disorders* (5th ed.).

Collaborative for Academic, Social, and Emotional Learning (CASEL). (2019). What is SEL? https://casel.org/what-is-sel/

Fuchs, D., & Deshler, D. D. (2007). What we need to know about responsiveness to intervention (and shouldn't be afraid to ask). *Learning Disabilities: Research & Practice, 22,* 129–136.

Jimerson. S. R., Burns, M. K., & VanDerHeyden, A. M. (2016). *Handbook of response to intervention: The science and practice of multi-tiered systems of support.* Springer Publishing.

Ratts, M. J., Singh, A. A., Nassar-McMillan, S., Butler, S. K., & McCullough, J. R. (2015). *Multicultural and social justice counseling competencies.* Multicultural Counseling Competencies Revisions Committee. http://www.counseling.org/docs/default-source/competencies/multicultural-and-social-justice-counseling-competencies.pdf?sfvrsn=20

Sanetti, L. M. H., & Collier-Meek, M. A. (2015). Multi-tiered implementation support for educators. *Psychology in the Schools, 52,* 815–828.

Sue, D. W., Arredondo, P., & McDavis, R. J. (1992). Multicultural counseling competencies and standards: A call to the profession. *Journal of Counseling and Development, 70*(4), 477–486. https://doi.org/10.1002/j.1556-6676.1992.tb01642.x

U.S. Department of Education. (2019). A guide to the individualized education plan. https://www2.ed.gov/parents/needs/speced/iepguide/index.html

Utley, C. A., & Obiakor, F. E. (2015). Special issue: Research perspectives on multi-tiered system of support. *Learning Disabilities: A Contemporary Journal, 13,* 1–2.

Vaughn S., & Fletcher, J. M. (2012). Response to intervention with secondary students with reading difficulties. *Journal of Learning Disabilities, 45,* 241–253. https://doi.org/10.1177/0022219412442157

CHAPTER ONE

Autism Spectrum Disorder

Kara Ieva and Stacy Walkowitz

THE CASE OF ZAYED Zayed is a 7-year-old boy who attends first grade at a Title 1 public school. He was diagnosed on the autism spectrum at the age of 19 months. As such, Zayed received multiple services through early intervention, outpatient, and inclusive preschool prior to entering the public school in kindergarten. Those services included developmental instruction, speech therapy, occupational therapy, and physical therapy. Simultaneously, Zayed was also diagnosed with general anxiety disorder and is currently taking medication. Overall, Zayed is a happy student who loves to learn and play with select peers. Recently, his teachers (inclusion setting) have noticed an increase in levels of frustration in class, specifically during the time of day in which he is asked to write. The classroom teachers have taught Zayed strategies to use when he is frustrated, and for the most part, he had been using those strategies until the past 2 weeks. On his communication log that gets sent home, he typically receives all "smiley faces" and either one "meh" or a "sad" face. The sad faces come during writing and gym times. The parent calls the school counselor to see if she is willing to speak to the student and gauge what might be causing his frustrations. Mom indicated that he responds to visual connections and play as opposed to tenants of cognitive behavioral therapy (CBT). She also explains that she does the best to support him, but culturally, specifically with her spouse, this diagnosis is not accepted and that his behaviors would typically be elicit some type of punishment. She is working on educating the family, but they are still trying to understand, so she feels pretty isolated.

Introduction to the Chapter

Zayed is one of numerous children diagnosed with *autism spectrum disorder* (ASD) who have difficulties in school because of the fact that educational systems are ill equipped to support students like him who might understand language and rules in the more literal sense. In addition, since Zayed is academically able to function in an inclusive or general education setting (not always the case), behavioral and social expectations generally remain similar to his peers. These implicit expectations add a lot of pressure on ASD students who already feel like they are different or that they don't fit in when walking into schools. ASD students receive numerous mixed messages all day, both implicit and explicit, that make it hard to make meaning of those messages, as the rules they may understand don't apply. This leaves ASD students to internalize feelings that include feeling like they are not in control of themselves (physically and emotionally), the environment, or those around them. It is essential for school counselors and educators to have a clear understanding of ASD so that they can support the social-emotional awareness and development needs of ASD students, which is critical to their success in school and beyond.

Learning Objectives

By the end of this chapter, readers will accomplish the following:

- Understand an overview and uniqueness of those students diagnosed on the autism spectrum.
- Understand how ASD is connected to comorbid physical and mental health diagnoses.
- Understand the best strategies when promoting the academic and social-emotional development of students on the autism spectrum.

Insight on ASD

Before you continue reading this chapter, it is important to note that while you may know, have met, or worked with someone who has been labeled with the *ASD* diagnosis, no two individuals with the diagnosis are the same, and, therefore, supporting these students in schools is individually tailored to their strengths and deficits. The uniqueness is well represented in Figure 1.1, featuring the *autism ribbon,* made up of unique and colorful (red, blue, yellow, and green) puzzle pieces, which is the international symbol for autism awareness. As such, each student will require their own treatment plan and support in schools to address their social and academic development. Approaching ASD students from a strengths-based position is ideal and can make the difference in supporting students' social-emotional development and preventing mental health concerns. While the case of Zayed will be infused throughout the chapter, it is only one representation of a high-functioning ASD student with verbal communication and therefore not generalizable. This chapter is meant to highlight all of the potential nuances that could exist for just one individual.

FIGURE 1.1. The Infinity Symbol for Autism

> ***If all you see is Autism, then you miss out on loving, kind, creative, extraordinary, generous, honest, sweet, loving, uniquely observant, intelligent, and inspiring.***
>
> — Raising an Extraordinary Person

ASD Defined

Just like the uniqueness of each individual diagnosed, there have been numerous labels that have defined autistic conditions. In the previous edition of the *Diagnostic and Statistical Manual of Mental Disorders, Fourth Edition* (American Psychiatric Association [APA], 2000), *autism disorder* fell under the label of *pervasive developmental mental disorder*, which also included the term *Asperger's disorder*. However, in the *Diagnostic and Statistical Manual of Mental Disorders, Fifth Edition* (APA, 2013), both of those labels have been omitted and combined under one term: ASD. The "spectrum" is the key word to keep in mind. The spectrum indicates the range of impact from mild to pervasive, allowing for a wide range of abilities among those who are diagnosed. To add to the complexity of terms, the federal definition outlined in the Individuals with Disabilities Act (IDEA) and used in the educational context is *autism*. The term "disorder" has a negative connotation, and when speaking about students, we ask that you use "students who are (diagnosed) on the autism spectrum." Some adult students refer to themselves as an autistic as a part of their identity. However, for the purpose of this chapter, ASD, the medical diagnosis, will be used as the term to describe those who are diagnosed.

ASD (APA, 2013) is defined as the umbrella label that describes a set of impairments in social communication and social interaction across multiple contexts and some level of repetitive patterns of behavior, interests, or activities that persist throughout the life span. According to the federal definition provided by IDEA,

> autism means a developmental disability significantly affecting verbal and nonverbal communication and social interaction, generally evident before age three, that adversely affects a child's educational performance. Other characteristics often associated with autism are engagement in repetitive activities and stereotyped movements, resistance to environmental change or change in daily routines, and unusual responses to sensory experiences. (U.S. Department of Education, 2018, Regulations Section, 300.8 C1)

In examining the range on the spectrum, students can be mildly impacted while others can be severely disabled. Specifically, students with ASD might not have language or communication skills, might live in their own worlds, and may not be able to emotionally connect. On the contrary, other students with ASD are able to function in general education and inclusion classes with or without support, often displaying strong academic knowledge and skills, having minimal to moderate social skills, and/or present as "quirky." Although the range is vast in abilities, there are some central characteristics that are at the core of the diagnosis, such as difficulties with social skills, language, and restricted interests and/or repetitive behaviors (Auger, 2012).

Initial signs and symptoms of ASD are typically apparent in the early developmental period; however, social deficits and behavioral patterns might not be recognized as symptoms of ASD until a child is unable to meet social, educational, occupational, or other important life-stage demands (APA, 2013). In other words, people can be diagnosed at any age across the life span.

Prevalence

While currently 1 in 6 children in the United States have a developmental disability, ranging from mild disabilities, such as speech and language impairments, to serious developmental disabilities, such as intellectual impairments, cerebral palsy, and autism, the current rate of those diagnosed with ASD in the United States is 1 in 59 and climbing each decade (Centers for Disease Control and Prevention [CDC], 2014). This equates to about 1.7% of all children across all gender, racial, ethnic, and socioeconomic groups (Baio et al., 2018). Some states have higher rates, with New Jersey as the highest at 1 in 35 by the age of 4, which equates to about 3% of all children in schools within the state, a 43% increase in a 4-year span. In addition, children are diagnosed at different ages. Even though 85% of the parents mention developmental concerns by 3 years old, only 42% had a comprehensive evaluation by that age (Baio et al., 2018), resulting in the median age of diagnosis as 4.3 years old (52 months). The differences in prevalence rates and age of diagnosis can be explained by regional differences in diagnostic practices and access to services.

Autism and Demographics

There are multiple disparities with diagnosis and certain demographics. For example, boys are 4 times more likely to be diagnosed than girls (CDC, 2014). While there are numerous factors that contribute to this, it is harder to recognize the social deficits in girls at a younger age unless they present with language difficulties. Historically, non-Hispanic white children were more likely to be diagnosed than black and Hispanic children (Baio et al., 2018). However, in recent years, the gap has been narrowing among black and Hispanic children, as they are approaching a similar percentage to their white peers (CDC, 2014). This may be related to concentrated outreach efforts for early diagnosis in minority communities.

Moreover, there is an intellectual range among those who are diagnosed: 44% have IQ scores that fall in the average to above average range in intelligence (i.e., IQ > 85), 25% fall in the borderline range (IQ 71–85), and 31% fall in the intellectual disability range (IQ < 70; CDC, 2014). The spectrum of abilities is one of the reasons, along with financial resources, that schools struggle with appropriate school placements and settings (e.g., out-of-district placements, life skills classrooms, self-contained, inclusion, or general education classrooms). Sometimes, because of special education labels, schools put students, regardless of intellectual abilities, in self-contained rooms, which does not reflect the *least restrictive environment*. The goal for each student is to provide as many inclusion opportunities as possible so that students feel like they are a part of their peer group, the school, and the community.

Screening

A comprehensive developmental evaluation is a thorough review of how a child plays, learns, communicates, acts, and moves and whether those characteristics have changed over time. A range of professionals, including teachers, social workers, nurses, psychologists, doctors, and speech-language pathologists, can conduct developmental evaluations. Specialists, such as developmental pediatricians, often use the results of a developmental evaluation to determine if a child has ASD and make the official diagnosis.

Equity in Autism

While autism effects all gender, racial, ethnic, and socioeconomic groups, there are still some disparities for those who are diagnosed. For example, to get a diagnosis, families must have access to health care. ASD is a medical diagnosis and, therefore, must be given by a developmental pediatrician or a neurologist. This may limit low socioeconomic families from seeking evaluation and, therefore, children will not be able to receive treatments for early intervention through the medical community prior to 3 years old, which has proven to be the most successful intervention for children diagnosed with ASD (Autism Speaks, 2017. Regional differences in diagnostic procedures and geographic locations (e.g., urban, rural, suburban) also present access difficulties to medical care, period, but specifically specialists who can evaluate and diagnosis ASD.

Complexity of the Diagnosis

Since ASD is a medical diagnosis, school counselors are not allowed to diagnose and, therefore, even mention that students display symptoms of autism with teachers or families; rather, they can only offer a description of observable behaviors. However, it is important for school counselors to be aware that symptoms begin in early childhood, even if they go unrecognized, and they can persist to the point of interfering with daily living. There are specialized health-care providers who assess symptom severity using a scale that reflects how much support a person needs for daily function, which may be useful information to have when working with the students, educators, and families. The following are some common symptoms that are visible at any age at home, in school, and in the community at large and can lead to greater psychological impact.

Sensory Issues

Many people with autism have sensory issues. These typically involve over- or under-sensitivities to sounds, lights, touch, tastes, smells, pain, and other stimuli. Depending on the scope of sensitivity to these things, this can lead to limited spaces for ASD students to feel comfortable, restricted diets, and a multitude of exhibited behaviors that may stem from sensory difficulties.

Behaviors

Stimming

The word stim is short for self-stimulation. While it is most commonly associated with autism, all people have a stim. For example, one might twirl their hair, bite their nails, bite their lip, suck their teeth, or even crack their knuckles. The following may be some reasons that students diagnosed with ASD stim.

- **Overstimulation.** Stimming can help block out excess sensory input.
- **Understimulation.** Stimming helps provide extra sensory input when needed.
- **Pain Reduction.** Repeated banging of the head or body actually reduces the overall sensation of pain.
- **Management of Emotions.** Both positive and negative emotions may trigger a burst of stimming, including joy or excitement, such as jumping, touching, or hand flapping. Frustration or anger may intensify a stim to the point that it becomes destructive.
- **Self-Regulation.** Some stims serve the purpose of soothing or comforting. An example is when babies learn to suck their thumbs to relax themselves.

Scripting

Scripting is the repetition of words, phrases, intonation, or sounds of the speech of others, sometimes taken from movies but also taken from other sources (e.g., favorite books or something someone else has said). People with ASD often display scripting in the process of learning to talk (Autism Society Baltimore-Chesapeake, 2019).

Repetitive and Restricted Behaviors

Restricted and repetitive behaviors vary greatly across the autism spectrum. The following are some behaviors that may present (Autism Speaks, 2019):

- Repetitive body movements (e.g., rocking, flapping, spinning, running back and forth)

Zayed has limited sensory issues that bother him. His most intensified sensory is to smell and texture of food. Therefore, he is limited in his diet to pizza (a very specific frozen brand), pancakes, occasionally McDonald's chicken nuggets, and Hazelnut sandwiches. This presents a problem in school, where they are not required to heat food that he would eat unless stated in his individualized educational plan (IEP). In addition, there are two sounds that cause him to display behaviors. The first is a baby crying. It is very persistent to his ears, and he covers them and screams for them to stop. The second is when entering an auditorium. Zayed is able to take in all sounds at once, and this can be very intrusive. Therefore, he uses strategies to cover his ears upon entering and slowly removes his hands until he can ease into all of the sounds. These are two types of sensory issues that early intervention professionals were able to provide strategies for before Zayed entered public school.

In the case of Zayed, when the teacher indicated that he becomes frustrated with writing, he tends to stim. Stimming for Zayed is touching (no slapping or punching) his paraprofessional repetitively. The teacher also indicated that he stims when he is excited to play with his friends; therefore, he stims when he is happy and angry.

Zayed's early intervention speech therapist and parents noted that when attempting to engage in conversation and language development, he would use quotes from movies and TV shows that he watched. While it was repeated language, the speech therapist noticed it was also in the correct context, so she did not want to limit his scripting. He was comfortable communicating that way prior to fully grasping spoken language.

Zayed's family indicated that even prior to his diagnosis, they were constantly on the go without a set routine and that didn't seem to bother him. To reduce his anxiety levels (he could not be officially diagnosed until age 5), *visual schedules* were presented the day before and the day of, and he could be in control by checking off/crossing out items as each thing was accomplished. The schedules didn't have to be the same routine, but he needed to have the information to know what to expect. This would take place both at home and at school.

- Repetitive motions with objects (e.g., spinning wheels, shaking sticks, flipping levers)
- Staring at lights or spinning objects
- Ritualistic behaviors (e.g., lining up objects, repeatedly touching objects in a set order)
- Persistent repetition of words or phrases (echolalia)
- Narrow or extreme interests in specific topics
- Need for unvarying routine/resistance to change (e.g., same daily schedule, meal menu, clothes, route to school)

Social Connectedness

Children and adults with ASD have difficulty with verbal and nonverbal communication. In addition, sometimes processing speeds are slower than nondiagnosed children and can sometimes present as awkward. Figure 1.2 depicts a visual that captures what could be happening to slow the process and make it difficult to connect. This visual displays the multiple processes at play when ASD children are

FIGURE 1.2. Autism and Communication by the Little Black Duck

TABLE 1.1 Social Connectedness Communication Barriers

NON-VERBAL DIFFICULTIES	VERBAL DIFFICULTIES
Gestures	Receptive language is not processed, just sounds
Facial Expressions	Spoken expressions taken literally
Eye Contact	Expressing Emotions
Tone of Voice	Seeking emotional comfort from others (can also be sensory related)
Recognizing Emotions and Intentions in Others	Taking turns in conversations
Recognizing one's own emotions	Miscomprehending sentences with words that have more than one meaning
Feeling Overwhelmed in social situations	Limited vocabulary
Gaging personal space	

interacting. The authors believe the visual can give nonassociated ASD people greater insight into *social burnout*, also referred to as *autistic burnout*. Autistic burnout is a state of physical and mental fatigue, heightened stress, and diminished capacity to manage life skills, sensory input, and/or social interactions, which comes from being severely overtaxed by the strain of trying to live up to demands that are out of sync with society's needs (Barton, 2019). This does not mean personality traits (e.g., introvert vs. extrovert) but rather the mental exhaustion of program attending and processing, which are discussed further in this chapter. Ask yourself how you would feel if you had to do that much thinking all day long and with every interaction with academics and people? Simultaneously, this also highlights the intellect, cognitive ability, and stamina needed to operate in this way.

There are a variety of behaviors and characteristics that also make it hard to connect socially. At the core is the ability to understand and express verbal and nonverbal language. ASD children also have difficulties understanding and processing emotions that can be a barrier to connecting socially with peers. Table 1.1 outlines these difficulties.

Comorbid Diagnoses and the Psychological Impact

A number of medical and mental health issues frequently accompany ASD. Statistically, 83% of ASD students are diagnosed with the co-occurrence of one or more non-ASD developmental diagnoses (Pratt, 2018), and 10% co-occur with one or more psychiatric diagnoses. Figure 1.3 outlines the many physical (sleep disorders, immune dysfunction, gastrointestinal issues, feeding), neurological (epilepsy, language disorders, dyslexia, dysgraphia, attention-deficit/hyperactivity disorder, sensory processing disorders), and mental complications (anxiety, depression, obsessive-compulsive disorder (OCD), mood disorders) that are frequently diagnosed in ASD populations. To further complicate the myriad of potential diagnoses, many diagnoses overlap in symptoms and run the risk of misdiagnoses and numerous attempts at medication to address potential ailments. This process of trying to figure out, prescribe, and repeat the pattern can further cause trauma to children with ASD. This perpetuates limited trust in doctors and medical professionals.

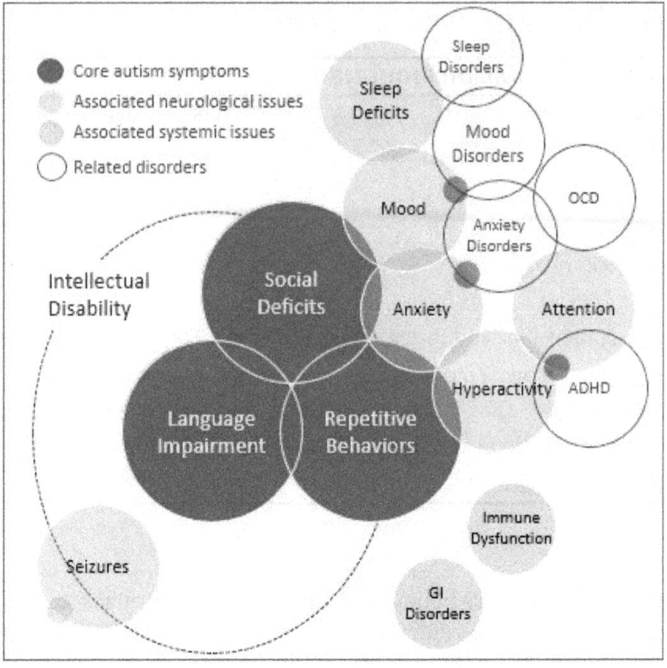

FIGURE 1.3. Comorbid Diagnoses and Complications Associated With ASD

Zayed's medical records indicate that he has also been diagnosed with *receptive and expressive language disorder and generalized anxiety disorder.* In further conversation with his mom, she indicated that he also has a sleep disorder and is unable to "shut down" at night. Therefore, he is currently taking medication to help him sleep, as well as medication, since he was 4, to treat the anxiety. Both have made significant changes in his mood and willingness to participate in school and home activities. This is why the mom is concerned about the writing triggers, as that behavior has not been present in a year. It might indicate that there is something more going on with Zayed.

Psychological Impact

As previously mentioned, those who are diagnosed with autism have an 83% chance of receiving a comorbid diagnosis (Pratt, 2018). Students with ASD often feel like outcasts, both at home and school. The consistent redirection and inability to understand and express what is happening in the world around them is extremely debilitating. This leaves ASD students to have low self-esteem and internalize negative thoughts and feelings. This is extremely important, as 40% of those diagnosed with ASD also have a co-occurring anxiety disorder, which is the most common comorbid diagnosis. Because of the inability to potentially function as a result of anxiety, recognizing it early and treating properly is critical for students' well-being.

Symptoms of anxiety are often characterized in two categories. *Behavioral* issues (aggression, irritability, self-injurious behaviors), which are linked to the core *repetitive behaviors and compulsivity.* These symptoms are especially a concern for those with intellectual disabilities and language difficulties; as the manners in which these children express emotions can be harmful. The other category is classified as *internalizing symptoms*, such as depression and anxiety, which students with ASD, especially those labeled with "high-functioning autism," may develop as a result of their insight but continued awareness of a lack of *social communication skills.* To further complicate the psychological effect, students who have ASD are 4 times more likely to be diagnosed with depression than the general population (Hudson et al., 2018) and 5 times more likely to attempt suicide (Croen et al., 2015). This poses an immediate concern for intervention and medication, as there is an extreme risk of self-harm and suicide. One of the limitations is that diagnosing depression in ASD children is difficult because of shared symptoms between both disorders, and there are currently no psychometric assessments for detecting depression in ASD patients. Moreover, as students age, there are additional factors, such as cultural aspects, multiple identities, and adolescent angst that complicate the mental health of those with ASD.

Family Systems

Although there might be one person in the family diagnosed with ASD, it is a lifestyle diagnosis for the entire family. The child, the siblings, and the caregivers are affected in their own ways. Divorce rates are generally high for families with students with disabilities; however, the risk further increases with the ASD diagnosis (Hartley et al., 2010). This can leave a single parent to attend to all accommodations needed in the home, financial worry, and limited self-care, which can result in emotional exhaustion, fatigue, anxiety, or depression in the parent. Having a support system is essential for the caregiver to continue to provide care for their ASD child.

Treatments and Therapies for the ASD Individual and Family Systems

While there are many therapies and interventions needed and available to treat the complicated physical, cognitive, and behavioral characteristics of ASD students, the main goal is to improve social communicative functioning and reduce the effect of repetitive behaviors on learning (National Institute for Health and Care Excellence [NICE], 2015). Table 1.2 displays treatment approaches for early educational and behavioral interventions. "Early intervention" is the term used to describe the services and supports that are available to babies and young children with developmental delays and disabilities and their families until they reach the age of 3 (CDC, 2014). These are publicly funded programs available in every state that can provide services for free or at reduced cost for any child who is eligible. Some of those therapies include speech therapy, physical therapy, and other types of services based on the needs of the child and family. Early intervention can have a long-term significant effect on a child's ability to learn new skills and overcome challenges (Reichow & Wolery, 2009). This can increase success in school and life; however, it is critical that children are diagnosed before the age of 3 when, by law, school districts are responsible for students, even if they do not have a preschool on-site.

Strategies for School Counselors Working With ASD Students and the School Community

As part of delivering a multi-tiered system of support (Goodman-Scott et al., 2019) through a comprehensive school counseling program (American School Counselor Association [ASCA], 2019), school counselors are tasked with working with all stakeholders. Therefore, there are multiple ways to support ASD students. Working with the school community, school counselors have the ability to promote the academic and social-emotional development of all students. School counselors use multiple roles to work with and on behalf of ASD students. They work individually with ASD students, provide education and awareness for students and staff, and consult with teachers, parents, and student support specialists to create plans and interventions that attend to students' social-emotional development and, therefore, promoting their academic success.

TABLE 1.2 Treatments for ASD Children and Their Families

POTENTIAL TREATMENT	EXPLANATION
Applied Behavior Analysis (ABA)	A type of therapy that focuses on improving specific behaviors, such as social skills, communication, reading, and academics, as well as adaptive learning skills, such as fine-motor dexterity, hygiene, grooming, domestic capabilities, punctuality, and job competence.
ASD/Inclusive Preschool Program	Preschool programs that have a mix of abilities in a setting that has two teachers: a general education and special education teacher, along with other classroom support to promote optimal learning and more small-group attention.
Early Start Denver Model	A behavioral therapy for children with autism between the ages of 12–48 months, based on ABA. Parents and therapists use play to build positive and fun relationships to boost language, social, and cognitive skills. It can be used in many settings, including at home, at a clinic, or in school. Therapy is also provided in both group settings and one-on-one.
Pharmacology Therapy	There are classes of different pharmacological agents that are found to be effective in improving behavioral symptoms of ASD, such as neurotransmitter reuptake inhibitors, antidepressants, anticonvulsants, atypical antipsychotics, to name a few.
Picture Exchange Communication Systems (PECS)	A modified ABA program designed for early nonverbal symbolic communication training. It is not a program designed to teach speech, although this is encouraged indirectly, and some children begin to use speech spontaneously while enrolled in the PECS program. Treatment occurs during typical activities within the natural settings of the classroom and the home.
Hormones, Diet, and Alterative Options	Using specific hormones, changing diets to be organic and gluten free and incorporating natural supplements to address the symptoms experienced by ASD children.
Music Therapy	Uses music and the interactions between teachers and children to teach specific skills. Although, there are many different types of music therapy, with ASD individuals, music therapy uses interactive musical activities to improve social and communication skills.

POTENTIAL TREATMENT	EXPLANATION
Equine Therapy	Horses are used by physical, speech, and occupational therapists to reach their patients on a personal level through what is referred to as "hippotherapy." Children with autism also benefit from equine therapy because of the motor, emotional, and sensory sensations that come with riding a horse. Horses are used to create an emotional bond. By learning to care for the horse, they associate the care they provide with feelings and an emotional bridge is constructed that can lead to increased social and communication skill production with others.
CBT	Used for treating anxiety disorders and OCD in youth with ASD, especially in those with high-functioning and adequate verbal skills. Components involve psychoeducation about anxiety and cognitive and behavioral strategies.
Mindfulness-Based Therapy	Mindfulness-based programs are centered in the Buddhist traditions of mindfulness meditation and adjusted to mental health care based on the Western science of psychology. Participants train to pay attention to the present moment, on purpose and with a nonjudgmental, openhearted, and curious attitude. The enhanced attention and awareness of experiences such as bodily sensations, feelings, thoughts, and senses help with impulsivity control.
Social and Vocational Skills Programs	Vocational training can focus on skill sets and hands-on learning in a simulated work environment and allows students to develop skills that can be used in the workplace. Classes would prepare the autistic student for a specific trade or career area that emphasizes hands-on learning and the application of knowledge.
Systemic Autism-Related Family Enabling (SAFE)	A new type of family therapy created specifically for families with children who are diagnosed with ASD. There are multiple uses of therapeutic activities, such as drawing, clay modeling, and role-playing to help families and their children explore aspects of ASD and improve problem-solving and coping strategies. SAFE therapy sessions generally last for 3 hours and take place in the home and with other families. The efficacy of SAFE is currently being evaluated, and it is most common in the United Kingdom. (McKenzie et al., 2019)

Creating a Neurodiverse Culture

Creating a *neurodiverse* culture is the foundation for building a community that celebrates all students' (ASD and non-ASD) unique gifts and abilities and what they bring to the table but also promotes empathy and normalizing some of the stigmatized behaviors associated with ASD.

Specifically, students with ASD who are included in regular classrooms develop more positive views of themselves, form friendships with their peers, and are able to be more successful academically (Armstrong, 2012). The following are some suggestions for school counselors to address the whole school community.

Awareness and Training

School counselors can create professional development for all school staff, parent workshops, and classroom lessons to promote the need and rational for celebrating neurodiversity. These presentations as a whole should be interactive, promote empathy, and understand the gifts that ASD students have to offer in classroom settings and beyond. Included in those trainings should also be the bus drivers, members of the lunch staff, and paraprofessionals. Training for all should include how to communicate with ASD students effectively rather than shaming them.

When working with the entire student population, school counselors already deliver classroom lessons on bullying prevention and can easily add neurodiversity to the instruction and case scenarios/examples. The more non-ASD students understand that some behaviors are not necessarily in ASD students' control, the more likely they are to accept their ASD peers and further cultivate friendships.

Neurodiversity Programming

School counselors can also include neurodiverse programming into their comprehensive counseling programs (ASCA, 2019). One way would be to create a peer mentoring program. School counselors can train peers to serve as role models who interact positively with ASD students on a regular basis. This can promote empathy in the mentors and self-esteem and acceptance in ASD students and, therefore, decrease potential mental health concerns (Kasari et al., 2012). In addition to the mentoring program, school counselors can also deliver group counseling to ASD and non-ASD students to promote social skills within the same context. Further, school counselors can sponsor a Neurodiversity Club that supports those diagnosed with a number of neurological and mental health diagnoses in conjunction with allies (similar to a gay-straight alliance). Lastly, school counselors can use the morning announcements to promote other neurodiverse celebrities (e.g., actors, musicians, painters, scientists, engineers) and share how their diagnoses and characteristics allowed them to thrive and succeed, displaying the need for neurodiversity in the world.

Individual Counseling

School counselors can create a safe space (both physical and emotional) in the school counseling office with a "Brain Break Corner." This is space for all students, regardless of age and grade level (yes, high school too!) that can also be created in each classroom in the building that can normalize the frequent need for ASD students to have time to themselves and reduce school anxiety. This space can be used for physical and emotional safety. The following are some potential items that can be used in the space.

- Calming items (e.g., art, music, meditation cards/recordings)
- Sensory items (e.g., squish balls, sequence pillows, blankets, fidget spinners)
- Physical activities (e.g., blocks, puzzles, games, Legos, yoga cards with visual poses)

Once students have transitioned from a "brain break," whether it is in your office or the classroom, ASD students may be more open to individual counseling. As mentioned, because of the varying needs and abilities, school counselors may focus on a variety of topics and interventions. Table 1.3 provides an overview of some common areas to focus on in sessions. There are many approaches that school counselors may use to reach students. From a theoretical orientation, cognitive behavioral frameworks and mindfulness-based techniques have demonstrated effectiveness with ASD students who understand verbal communication (Ridderinkhof et al., 2018; Speck et al., 2013; Wood et al., 2009). To ease anxiety, and to help students focus, school counselors should use games, masks, puppets, music, art supplies, and any other manipulatives or creative expression to engage in play across all age groups. Table 1.3 presents an array of topics and skills that could be developed when working with ASD students.

TABLE 1.3 Key Concepts for Counseling ASD Students

TOPICS	EXPLANATION	OTHER POSSIBLE DELIVERY METHODS
Social Skills	These can range from how to have a conversation, how to take turns in a game, how to make friends, how to ask for help, to how to display empathy. There are many social skills, and each skill will need to be modeled, taught, and named in language and positively reinforced. School counselors can provide the space to develop social skills in a safe setting.	Small-group counseling Classroom lessons
Executive Functioning Skills	Executive function and self-regulation skills are the mental processes that enable us to plan, focus attention, remember instructions, and juggle multiple tasks successfully. The eight key executive functions are impulse control, emotional control, flexible thinking, working memory, self-monitoring, planning and prioritizing, task initiation, and organization.	Small-group counseling Classroom lessons
Self-Advocacy Skills	Teach students to speak up for themselves to address wants or needs and to ask for help.	Peer sessions
Self-Awareness	Physical self-awareness in proximity to boundaries and personal space. Using a strength-based approach to understanding strengths and limitations and learning how to use strengths to address some deficits. Also, students gain self-awareness in taking responsibility for actions.	Peer sessions
Self-Regulation	Help students understand feeling words and vocabulary and how they connect to their physical and emotional responses. Assist students in recognizing and managing their behavioral challenges with appropriate strategies and coping skills.	Individual only

Social Stories

Social stories are the most frequently used strategy to address the communication, social, and behavioral deficits of ASD students (Gray, 2015), particularly in schools. "Social story" is a broad term used to describe a visual, story-based approach to "facilitate a wide range of social, behavioral, and communication functions in preschool and school-age children and adolescents with ASD who vary widely in their cognitive and linguistic profiles" (Hutchins, 2012, pp. 313–314). There are trademarked and authored social stories that can be purchased just like curricula. Similarly, anyone (e.g., parents, teachers, educational support professionals) can author social stories (Goodman-Scott & Carlisle, 2014); however, school counselors have the competency and insight to intersect skill development with the emotional connection (Auger, 2012). At the core, social stories use simple language with visual representation to describe feelings and others' perspectives. They take a complex situation and developmentally scaffold it into a simple story, describing concepts (e.g., taking turns in game play), situations (e.g., waiting in line), and skills (e.g., academic organization) through the inclusion of 10 criteria (Gray, 2013; Gray, 2015). For more information on how to create and implement social stories, please see the resources section (Goodman-Scott & Carlisle, 2014 Gray, 2015).

Video Self-Modeling

Another evidence-based intervention that increases social interaction and preferred behaviors is video self-modeling (Victor, Little, & Akin-Little, 2011). This technique requires resources and functional knowledge to use technology (e.g., iMovie) in session. Auger (2012) described video self-modeling as a form of "feed forward" (as opposed to feedback). More specifically, students watch videos of themselves that are edited and erased of negative behavior and present the student engaged in appropriate or prosocial behavior in a setting where the negative behaviors typically occur. Allowing students access to watch the video prior to the school day, or before transitioning to the setting where the negative behavior is exhibited, can promote the use of prosocial strategies modeling (Victor et al., 2011).

Working With Teachers, Parents, Support Professionals, and the Local Community

Consultation is one of the roles of the school counselor (ASCA, 2019). School staff, teachers, and parents seek guidance when they have trouble reaching students. The following section will discuss some strategies to suggest and/or use when consulting with the teachers, parents, support professionals, and the larger community. *These concepts are also applied when school counselors provide individual, small-group, and classroom guidance lessons.*

Strengths-Based Communication

Positive redirection and reinforcement can help build a positive self-image of the student. The use of verbal redirecting can amplify negative responses in ASD students if they already feel overstimulated and overprocessed. In those situations, the use of pictures to demonstrate what is expected can be beneficial (Autism Speaks, 2019). For example, if teaching a student to respond to directions (e.g., taking a paper out of their folder), then show them a picture of that exact request, and repeat with verbal language. If they comply, then give encouragement or positive praise about the specific behavior, in this case, following instructions. Supporting ASD students with praise helps contribute to successful interactions and the willingness to repeat prosocial behaviors.

Communication can be difficult for students who are overstimulated, overwhelmed, or feeling anxious. When ASD students are overwhelmed, having to process language becomes difficult (as depicted in Figure 1.2). Therefore, nonverbal communication (e.g., flashing a picture or showing a written note on a Post-It) is helpful for a student to comply with a request rather than a verbal command. When a student reads the note, or sees the flashing picture, they process the information in their head as if they are giving themselves the request (metacognition) and, therefore, remove the emotional response. All of the behavior exhibited by an ASD student is communication. Stimming may help the student self-regulate their emotions. Some stimming includes tapping a pencil, shaking a leg, doodling, etc. Allow the student to stim if they are not hurting themselves, and if needed, find a classroom-acceptable stimming technique that doesn't interfere with the learning process (e.g., fidget, sensory toys). As a reminder, stimming is as important as scratching an itch in order to continue to move on.

Instructional Strategies

As previously mentioned, lots of language, both verbal and written, can make an ASD student anxious. Table 1.4 highlights important academic strategies that can help ASD students focus and feel successful completing academic assignments, further building their academic confidence.

TABLE 1.4 Classroom and Group Counseling Instructional Strategies

STRATEGY	DESCRIPTION
Highlighting	Highlighting the important words or phrases in both the directions and assignments help ASD students focus to complete tasks and assignments.
Workload Reduction	Once an ASD student masters a concept, repetition can cause emotional distress. Therefore, reducing the work after mastery is suggested. ASD students are literal, and once they have proved that they can do something, they become bored and frustrated, which can lead to behaviors. Students might enjoy an extension or a puzzle.
Chunking Information and Language	Chunking refers to an approach for making more efficient use of short-term memory by grouping information. Chunking breaks up long strings of information into units. The resulting chunks are easier to commit to memory than a longer uninterrupted string of information. If possible, have fewer written passages with separate paragraphs or less written language on a page so that students don't get overwhelmed attempting to process a lot of language. Some ASD students prefer graphic novels for the same reasoning.
Wait Time	Teachers and school counselors are trained in using wait time as a strategy for all students. However, it is exceptionally important for ASD students who process language differently.

(Continues)

TABLE 1.4 *(Continued)*

STRATEGY	DESCRIPTION
Visual Aides for Instruction	We can't stress this enough: *visuals are key*, specifically in regard to ASD students' first and native languages. Visuals promote quicker processing time and can help with expectations and task completion. This can be applied to specific assignments and directions. It can also be applied to classroom norms and systems (e.g., organize desk, end project, expectations for entering the classroom). Further, the use of graphic organizers with visuals can help with planning out thoughts.
Visual Aides for Self-Advocacy	To increase self-advocacy, the use of visual coping strategies in the room or on their own desks, can keep students from drawing negative attention and then internalizing those emotions. For example, an index card with a picture of a student getting a drink in the hallway and returning to the class within a certain time frame can reduce risk. In other words, when a student is overwhelmed, they may need a break and not be able to ask for what they need. Therefore, a colored index card with a positive coping strategy listed can be beneficial.
Transitions/Brain Breaks	Staying focused in school all day is physically and emotional draining for ASD students. One of the reasons is that their brains process differently and take an added exertion of mental energy, which also effects ASD students' physically. Further, there are multiple transitions in lessons that require ASD students to exert even more mental energy than their peers. This is what makes transitions so hard for these students. Therefore, providing "brain breaks" when transitioning during lessons is a great tool. Short video clips are useful, as they allow students to zone out. More videos with limited language are preferred—for example, a video of shapes moving to music, watching dominoes fall, or marbles moving through mazes.
Thinking Outside the Box	Teachers and school counselors tend to be creative individuals. Don't limit your strategies to a specific set. For example, students might be more successful when listening to music and writing or pacing while thinking and processing information.

Working With Families

Living with ASD children can be exhausting for families. Remaining present and nonjudgmental while conveying empathy is key to maintaining an open line of communication with families. ASD students require consistency both at home and at school in the areas of language, rules, schedules, and norms to maintain positive communication and behaviors. In addition, there is limited support post-early intervention for families. Providing access to parent workshops and parenting support groups as part of the comprehensive school counseling program can support the individual child and family from a systemic perspective. As families and caregivers become overwhelmed, they might consult with the school counselor for assistance. School counselors will need to operate from the standpoint that the parent/guardian is the expert on their child unless they state otherwise. School counselors can collaborate with other stakeholders internal and external to the school to provide parents with support in various topics.

Understanding What You Have Read: Comprehension Questions

Directions: Refer to what you have learned in this chapter to answer the following questions.

1. Why might autism present as a challenge in schools?
2. What is the school counselor's role in supporting students on the autism spectrum?
3. What are some types of support that you can provide across the educational continuum for those who are diagnosed with ASD?
4. What are ways in which you might be able to advocate for students with ASD?
5. What are some ethical and multicultural considerations when working with students with ASD?

Case Examples

Case Example One

As you read the case about Grady, reflect on the strategies that we discussed earlier in the chapter. Following the case, we have provided questions related to the student's behavioral symptoms and accompanying responses.

Grady is a 10-year-old boy in an inclusive fourth-grade classroom in an urban setting. He is currently classified with sensory processing disorder and a specific learning disability. Recently, Ms. Moody, one his classroom teachers, asked for all of the students to get in line, as it was time to go to the monthly special assembly in the auditorium. As the class lined up, students were talking, rushing, pushing, shoving, and laughing. Ms. Moody indicated that she was waiting for everyone to be calm and orderly to walk down the hallway. After 3 minutes of waiting, Grady begins to tap on Elijah (the student standing next to him who is humming and singing). Elijah then starts kicking Grady. So, Grady removes himself from the line, only to hear Ms. Moody say, "Grady, we are waiting. Get back in line!" Listening to the teacher, Grady goes back in line, but states, "I can't take this anymore. I need a break." Ms. Moody responds (while sucking her teeth), "Just get back in line, Grady, we are almost ready to go!" After another 2 minutes, Grady walks out of line and screams, "AHHHHHH," while placing his hands over his ears and running around the classroom. Ms. Moody reprimands Grady and asks a student to walk him to the principal's office. The principal is currently in the auditorium waiting for the classes to arrive, so the secretary brings the student into your office, still screaming.

Case Example One: Questions for Processing and Reflection

Directions: Use what you have learned in this chapter to respond to Grady's case.

1. What type of space would you provide, or what strategies do you think would help regulate Grady?
   - We would allow Grady to use the space in the counselor's office that might be called the *Chill Out Zone* or *Brain Break Space* (a location for students to use sensory-appropriate or calming manipulatives) without having to process language. We might consider handing out the deep breathing cards with visuals that Grady might use to physically calm down. When Grady seems calmer, we would praise him for advocating for himself and allow him to draw or tell in his own words what took place. We would follow-up using a social story that might help Grady sort through some of his emotions and incorporate new strategies he might use in the future with his teacher if something like this happens again—for example, example, color-coded index cards that he can raise his hand to show his teacher to indicate that he "needs a break."
2. How might you communicate with the parents about what occurred? What would be your follow-up?
   - We would call the parents to inform them of what occurred, paying close attention to Grady's sensory needs, and his positive attempt to remove himself from the situation. We would invite the parents to share strategies they use at home or in the community. We would present ideas on strategies we would like to implement with the teacher and receive their feedback. In addition, we would send home a list of the strategies so that they can potentially use them at home.
3. How might you help support Grady with the strategies you would give to his teacher(s)?
   - As mentioned, we would attempt to implement the color-coded index cards to show his teachers to limit language interaction in those moments.
     - Red might indicate "I need a break, and I am going to use the chill out space."
     - Blue might indicate "I need some assistance when you get a chance."
     - Yellow might indicate "I need to get up and walk around or need physical stimulation. I am not just getting out of my seat" (more as needed).

     The index cards might be useful to both the teacher and Grady communicate with limited language use. For Grady, this allows him to be more self-aware and to self-advocate. For the teacher, it translates the underlying causes to behavior and reduces the "acting out" behaviors in class.
4. What are some ways in which you might support Grady by working with his peers?
   - There are multiple ways we might work with Grady in addressing his peers. Some suggestions include delivering a classroom guidance lesson to promote neurodiversity and peer allies, using a peer in a counseling session to role-play new strategies regarding sensory issues, and facilitating small-group counseling focused on social skills with peers.
5. With whom might you consult, and what would you say/do?
   - There are a variety of people to potentially consult with regarding Grady. If he has an IEP, we might consult with his case manager and/or the school psychologist for further strategies or support and communicate what occurred. In addition, we might consult with the occupational therapist, who might be able to suggest specific strategies to help alleviate some sensory issues that might present in the future.

Case Example Two

As you read the case about Finley, reflect on the strategies that we discussed earlier in the chapter. The questions that follow the case relate to the student's behavioral symptoms and accompanying responses.

Finley is a 14-year-old girl in the ninth grade who is very passionate about drawing. Her functional language (e.g., greeting, introducing oneself, asking for or giving advice, explaining rules, apologizing, or agreeing and disagreeing) is on grade level. However, she is unable to identify and understand figurative language (e.g., metaphors, similes, hyperboles). Her thinking is operationalized in black-and-white areas, without the ability to see the "gray" and weigh different options. Finley has trouble relating to her peers. Because of her lens of thinking, she is a rule follower and tends to be impulsive when speaking to her peers. For example, if students are talking at her table when the teacher is explaining directions, she raises her hand and states, "I can't hear you because Kate and Destiny are talking, which we are not supposed to do." When Kate and Destiny begin to make faces and call her names, she is upset and yet not sure why this is happening. Her teacher gives her permission to go to your school counseling office. She arrives in tears, and her face is bright red as if she is angry. She keeps repeating herself, "Why are they mean? I just don't understand! I just don't understand!"

Case Example Two: Questions for Processing and Reflection

Directions: Use what you have learned in this chapter to respond to Finley's case.

1. What type of space would you provide, or what strategies do you think would help regulate Finley?
2. How might you communicate with the parents about what occurred? What would be your follow-up?
3. How might you help support Finely with the strategies you would give to her teacher(s)?
4. What are some ways in which you might support Finley by working with her classmates?
5. With whom might you consult, and what would you say/do?

Chapter Summary

This chapter focused on the nuances associated with the communication, behaviors, and underlying co-occurring diagnoses and symptoms related to ASD in children. The authors present comprehensive strategies and interventions to create a school climate that celebrates neurodiversity, to counsel from a strengths-based approach, and to consult with teachers, educational staff, and families. ASD can be harmful if not treated from a systemic approach, as it can lead to major episodes of anxiety, depression, and suicide. School counselors play a pivotal role in the balance of providing interventions, practical strategies, and supporting the system of caregivers who shape the development of ASD students.

Additional Recommended Readings and Resources

17 Children's Books About Autism: https://www.huffpost.com/entry/17-childrens-books-that-promote-understanding-of-autism_n_5ade4580e4b036e7aeb58a64?ncid=engmodushpmg00000003

Autistic Brain Video: https://youtu.be/RbwRrVw-CRo

Autism Speaks: www.autismspeaks.org

Auger, R. W. (2012). Autism spectrum disorders: A research review for school counselors. *Professional School Counseling.* https://doi.org/10.1177/2156759X12016002S02

Goodman-Scott, E., & Carlisle, R. (2014). School counselors' roles in creating and implementing social stories to serve students with autism spectrum disorder. *Professional School Counseling.* https://doi.org/10.1177/2156759X0001800108

Gray, C. (2013). What are social stories? Retrieved from https://carolgraysocialstories.com/

Gray, C. (2015). *The new social story book: 15th anniversary edition.* Future Horizons.

Sensory Overload: https://vimeo.com/52193530

Little Black Duck: Visual Aids to Support Emotional Development https://www.thelittleblackduck.com.au/

References

American Psychiatric Association (APA). (2000). *Diagnostic and statistical manual of mental disorders* (4th ed., text revision).

American Psychiatric Association (APA). (2013). *Diagnostic and statistical manual of mental disorders* (5th ed.).

American School Counselor Association (ASCA). (2019). *The ASCA national model: A framework for school counseling programs* (4th ed.).

Armstrong, T. (2012). *Neurodiversity in the classroom: Strength-based strategies to help students with special needs succeed in school and life.* ASCD.

Auger, R. W. (2012). Autism spectrum disorders: A research review for school counselors. *Professional School Counseling.* https://doi.org/10.1177/2156759X12016002S02

Autism Society Baltimore-Chesapeake. (2019). Scritping. https://www.baltimoreautismsociety.org/glossary/term/scripting/

Autism Speaks. (2017). Strategies for supporting social skill development. *School Community Toolkit.* https://www.autismspeaks.org/tool-kit-excerpt/strategies-supporting-social-skill-development

Baio, J., Wiggins, L., Christensen, D. L., Maenner, M. J., Daniels, J., Warren, Z, Kurzius-Spencer, M., Zahorodny, W., Rosenberg, C. R., White, T., Durkin, M. S., Imm, P., Nikolaou, L., Yeargin-Allsopp, M., Lee, L-C., Harrington, R., Lopez, M., Fitzgerald, R. T., Hewitt, A., Pettygrove, S., et al. (2018). Prevalence of autism spectrum disorder among children aged 8 years—autism and developmental disabilities monitoring network, 11 sites, United States, 2014. *MMWR Surveillance Summaries, 67*(SS-6), 1–23. http://dx.doi.org/10.15585/mmwr.ss6706a1

Barton, J. (2019). *Autistic burnout or regression: Individuals on the autism spectrum* [Paper presentation]. South Carolina Speech-Language-Hearing Association Annual Convention, Greenville, SC, United States. https://www.scsha.net/assets/handouts/Austic%20burnout_SCSLHA_2019.pdf

Centers for Disease Control and Prevention (CDC). (2014). *Autism spectrum disorder: Data & statistics.* www.cdc.gov/ncbddd/autism/data.html

Croen, L. A., Zerbo, O., Qian, Y., Massolo, M. L., Rich, S., Sidney, S., & Kripke, C. (2015). The health status of adults on the autism spectrum. *Autism: The International Journal of Research and Practice, 19*(7), 814–823. https://doi.org/10.1177/1362361315577517

Goodman-Scott, E., & Carlisle, R. (2014). School counselors' roles in creating and implementing social stories to serve students with autism spectrum disorder. *Professional School Counseling.* https://doi.org/10.1177/2156759X0001800108

Goodman-Scott, E., Donahue, P., & Betters-Burbon, J. (2019) *Multi-tiered systems of support for school counselors.* Routledge.

Gray, C. (2013). What are social stories? https://carolgraysocialstories.com/

Gray, C. (2015). *The new social story book: 15th anniversary edition.* Future Horizons.

Hartley, S. L., Barker, E. T., Seltzer, M. M., Floyd, F., Greenberg, J., Orsmond, G., & Bolt, D. (2010). The relative risk and timing of divorce in families of children with an autism spectrum disorder. *Journal of Family Psychology: JFP: Journal of the Division of Family Psychology of the American Psychological Association (Division 43)*, 24(4), 449–457. https://doi.org/10.1037/a0019847

Hudson, C. C., Hall, L., & Harkness, K. L. (2018). Prevalence of depressive disorders in individuals with autism spectrum disorder: A meta-analysis. *Journal of Abnormal Child Psychology.* https://doi.org/10.1007/s10802-018-0402-1

Hutchins, T. L. (2012). Social stories. In P. A. Prelock & R. J. McCauley (Eds.), *Treatment of autism spectrum disorders: Evidence-based intervention strategies for communication & social interaction* (pp. 313–343). Paul H. Brookes Publishing Company.

Kasari, C., Rotheram-Fuller, E., Locke, J., & Gulsrud, A. (2012). Making the connection: Randomized controlled trial of social skills at school for children with autism spectrum disorders. *Journal of Child Psychology and Psychiatry, 53*, 431–439.

McKenzie, R., Dallos, R., Stedmon, J., Hancocks, H., Vickery, P. J., Ewings, P., Barton, A., Vassallo, T., Myhill, C., et al. (2019). SAFE, a new therapeutic intervention for families of children with autism: study protocol for a feasibility randomised controlled trial. *BMJ Open*. https://doi.org/10.1136/bmjopen-2018-025006

National Institute for Health and Care Excellence. (2015). *Challenging behaviour and learning disabilities: prevention and interventions for people with learning disabilities whose behaviour challenges.*

Pratt, C. (2018). *Increasing incidence of autism spectrum disorders in Indiana. The Reporter, 22*(11). https://www.iidc.indiana.edu/pages/incidence-of-autism-spectrum-disorders-in-indiana

Reichow, B., & Wolery, M. (2009). Comprehensive synthesis of early intensive behavioral interventions for young children with autism based on the UCLA young autism project model. *Journal of Autism and Developmental Disorders, 39*(1), 23–41.

Ridderinkhof, A., Bruin, E. I., Blom, R., & Bögels, S. M. (2018). Mindfulness-based program for children with autism spectrum disorder and their parents: Direct and long-term improvements. *Mindfulness, 9*(3), 773–791.

Speck, A., van Ham, C., & Nyklíček, I. (2013). Mindfulness-based therapy in adults with an autism spectrum disorder: A randomized controlled trial. *Research in Developmental Disabilities, 34*(1), 246–253.

U.S. Department of Education . (2018). Building the Legacy: IDEA 2004, Federal regulations Section 300.8: Child with a disability. Retrieved from http://idea.ed.gov

Victor, H., Little, S. G., & Akin-Little, A. (2011). Increasing social engaged time in children with autism spectrum disorders using video self-modeling. *Journal of Evidence-Based Practices for Schools, 12*, 105–124

Wood, J. J., Drahota, A., Sze, K., Har, K., Chiu, A., & Langer, D. A. (2009). Cognitive behavioral therapy for anxiety in children with autism spectrum disorders: A randomized, controlled trial. *Journal of Child Psychology and Psychiatry, and Allied Disciplines, 50*(3), 224–234. https://doi.org/10.1111/j.1469-7610.2008.01948.x

CHAPTER TWO

Specific Learning Disorder

Jon Borland and Whitney Hanley

THE CASE OF QUINN Quinn is a third-grade student at Fairbanks Elementary School. This is Quinn's first year at Fairbanks. She was transferred to the school in December from an elementary school out of state. When speaking with Quinn about her experience so far at Fairbanks, Quinn often expresses feeling alone and not having friends. Quinn is quiet and reserved and rarely participates in class discussions. Although the school is waiting on Quinn's complete academic record, when she enrolled, her parents shared that she had been receiving speech and language services and struggled with reading and understanding grade-level text. Quinn's teacher, Ms. Fleischmann noticed that she often struggles with vocabulary and has difficulties with spelling, expressing details from a story, and organizing sentences. In math, she struggles with basic calculations and applied concepts, such as counting money and reading an analog clock. Ms. Fleischman referred Quinn to the school counselor as she has noticed her starting to withdraw from her peers and hiding under her desk during reading time.

Introduction to the Chapter

According the U.S. Department of Education (2018), approximately 14% of all public school students meet the eligibility requirements for special education services under the Individuals with Disabilities Education Act (IDEA). Among those students receiving services, 34% are designated as having a specific learning disability (SLD), making it the most common eligibility category (U.S. Department of Education, 2018). Because of the high number of students who qualify for services, the American School Counselor Association (ASCA, 2016) encourages school counselors to remain informed of best practices for serving students with unique abilities to ensure their inclusion in a comprehensive counseling program.

The school counselor is a crucial point of contact for students, parents, and other stakeholders (Buckley & Mahdavi, 2018; Kushner et al., 2011). School counselors possess specialized training and knowledge that is relevant to ensuring the achievements of students with unique abilities, making them an important part of the identification and evaluation process (Buckley & Mahdavi, 2018; Lambie et al., 2019). This chapter sets out to provide an overview of IDEA, the identification and evaluation of students, and the working definitions of SLD. Further, we will discuss ways in which school counselors can support students identified with SLDs, effectively collaborate with parents and teachers, and advocate for the needs of students with unique abilities.

Learning Objectives

By the end of this chapter, readers will accomplish the following:

- Understand the risk factors associated with the determination of SLD.
    - Recognize and describe the four steps of the determination process.
    - Understand how the use of response to intervention (RTI) is central to the identification process.
- Develop increased knowledge of the educational and social effects of SLD on adolescents and youth.
- Understand best practice strategies for supporting students diagnosed with SLD.
    - Learn how to best use a team-based paradigm when supporting youth with SLD.

The definition of SLD, more commonly referred to as learning disability, is written in the federal regulations of IDEA as follows:

> A disorder in one or more psychological processes. It affects an individual's ability to function at the level of their same-age peers in the area of thinking, speaking, reading, writing, spelling, or mathematical calculations. It also includes disabilities such as brain injury, minimal brain dysfunction, dyslexia, and development aphasia. It is important to note, the learning difficulties whose primary origin is that of a visual, hearing, motor impairment, intellectual disability, emotional disturbance, or of environmental, cultural, or economic factors, can be served in other disability categories of IDEA or through programs such as Title I. (United States Code 20 U.S.C.§1401[30], 2006)

Educational History

Public education for students with disabilities has been influenced by a legislative history of challenging inequalities for individuals who are different. Requirements of education and support for students with disabilities was influenced by the landmark case *Brown v. Board of Education* (1954). The *Brown v. Board of Education* decision challenged the separate but equal standard and required schools to make "good faith effort" to desegregate with "all deliberate speed." Twenty years after the Brown decision, *Mills v. the District of Columbia Board of Education* (1972) expanded the decision to integrate schools to students with mental, behavioral, physical, or emotional disabilities. The case was fought on behalf of more than 10,000 children with disabilities who were being excluded from public education. The ruling stated that no child can be denied a public education based on "mental, physical, behavioral or emotional deficiencies" (*Mills v. the District of Columbia Board of Education*, 1972). Shortly afterward, the Education for All Handicapped Children Act (1975) was signed into law. This legislation required public schools to provide students with a broad range of disabilities with a "free appropriate public education." It also called for school districts to provide such schooling in the "least restrictive environment" possible. This law stipulated zero rejection of, and total service delivery to, students with disabilities (Education for All Handicapped Children Act, 1975).

The Education for All Handicapped Children Act was reauthorized in 1990, and 1997, it was renamed IDEA. IDEA elaborated on what constitutes an appropriate education as it pertains to the delivery of services for individuals with disabilities. The reauthorization replaced the term "handicap" with "disability" and included mandating that individuals with disabilities be assigned to small classes with teachers who were specially trained and provided lessons that were tailored to individual student needs. Although IDEA's goal were to create an equitable system of education for a range of learners, it misaligned with *Brown v. Board of Education* (1954) (Artiles et al., 2010). With the passage of IDEA, there was an increase in students from culturally and linguistically diverse backgrounds being placed in special education simultaneous with their enrollment in previously all white schools (Blanchett, 2009).

According to Artiles et al. (2010), this also altered the relationship parents from minority groups, especially African American, had with their children's schools and lessened their ability to advocate on behalf of their children regarding disproportionate identification. The 1997 reauthorization of IDEA focused on accurate assessment of student behavior. This is where the role of the functional behavior assessment is addressed. The requirement for educators to be explicit with their identification of disruptive, aggressive, or violent behaviors and critical information within the description of the behavior was determined as necessary to support students. The law also focused on positive behavior interventions.

Before the reauthorization of IDEA 2004 (IDEIA, 2004), the protocol for testing and diagnosing a student with an SLD was termed "wait to fail." The "wait to fail" method was the result of the language used in the original mandate (IDEA, 1997). IDEA 1997 stated that a student must have a severe discrepancy in IQ (ability) and one of the following: oral expression, listening comprehension, written expression, basic reading skills, reading comprehension, mathematics calculation, or mathematics reasoning. The "wait to fail" method increasingly became a problem, resulting in misidentification or late identification of students from culturally or linguistically diverse backgrounds, English language learners, and students living in poverty.

In 2002, the No Child left Behind Act (2001) was signed into law. The No Child Left Behind Act was a reauthorization of Lyndon B. Johnson's implementation of the Elementary and Secondary Education Act (1965). This act required that if states are to receive federal funding for schools, they must develop assessments in basic skills to be given to all students in certain grades. Standards for achievement were to be set by each individual state. With a focus on academic standards and testing on the rise, in 2004, IDEA was reauthorized and titled the Individuals with Disabilities Education Improvement Act (IDEIA, 2004). This reauthorization mandated schools to monitor the academic outcomes of vulnerable populations and ignited the growth in implementation of RTI models. Both aimed to improve the historically poor outcomes of minority students by increasing accountability. This included disaggregated statewide testing, early intervention, and classroom adoption of research-based interventions.

In 2015, President Obama signed the Every Student Succeeds Act (ESSA, 2015) into law. ESSA addresses assessment to meet the needs of diverse student populations. Within this act is the regulation of states to offer the appropriate accommodations when assessing all students. In addition to this, highlighted is the use of the universal design for learning principle, which helps diversify the way in which students are required to demonstrate their knowledge and, therefore, promotes the individualization of learning for students, especially those with disabilities.

ESSA requires schools and districts to develop a multi-tiered system of support (MTSS) to respond to students' academic and behavioral needs, whereas IDEA allows schools to use "a process based on a child's response to scientific, research-based intervention" as part of the procedure to determine whether a student has a specific learning disability. The language and terms used to refer to this multi-tiered process differs based on the practitioner. Some refer to the process as RTI and others as MTSS. Review the introductory chapter to gain more familiarity with these interventions.

Specific Learning Disorder and the *DSM*

So far in this chapter, we have presented SLD as a learning disability within the educational settings. SLD is also noted in the *Diagnostic and Statistical Manual of Mental Disorders, Fifth Edition* (*DSM-5*) as a clinical disorder. In fact, the *DSM-5* describes SLD as a type of neurodevelopmental disorder that affects students' academic abilities in certain areas, such as reading and writing (e.g., SLD with impairment in written expression). According to the *DSM-5*, for a clinical diagnosis of SLD, an individual must meet four specific criteria:

> Criteria A: There must be ongoing challenges in the school-aged years in at least one of the following areas: reading fluency, math facts, and written expression. In addition, evidence should be shown that despite quality interventions by a trained specialist for at least 6 months, these difficulties continue to exist. So let's say that in the earlier vignette, Quinn has been experiencing difficulties with reading, and although her teacher has been working with her, her parents have hired a tutor, and they all have been working with her for over 6 month, she still shows no improvement in reading fluency. We would say that she has met the first criteria for a clinical diagnosis of SLD.
>
> Criteria B: Standardized assessments are administered to evaluate the individual, and the results indicate performance at a lower level than their average peers. Quinn's parents decide to take her to a clinical psychologist who assesses her and reports that she is performing below expectations for her developmental level.
>
> Criteria C: The individual's academic challenges have been observed or at least have been of concern since elementary grades. The *DSM-5* does note that exceptions may be present when a student in high school, for example, begins to show signs of academic difficulties as the rigor of coursework increases. In Quinn's case, reading difficulties have been noted since elementary school. Now, suppose Quinn was able to maintain an average to slightly below average performance in reading in elementary school, but as she moved into the more advanced grades and the coursework became more arduous, without the necessary interventions, Quinn may begin to struggle significantly.
>
> Criteria D: Consideration should be given for differentiated diagnosis; that is, other possible reasons need to be ruled out. Suppose Quinn was constantly absent in previous grades. The gaps in instruction as the possible cause of Quinn's reading difficulties and not necessarily a clinical diagnosis should be taken into consideration.

Comparatively, as you review the processes of RTI and MTSS, you will see that there are marked similarities between the process of identification of a learning disability by educational definition and a specific learning disorder as defined in the *DSM-5*.

Effects on Children and Adolescents

Despite the mode of identification, research shows that learning disabilities can present various issues that may challenge a student's development. In fact, Tarver-Behring et al. (1998) noted that students identified with a disability often experience more obstacles and may require more support from the school counselor than their unidentified peers. Academically, students with SLDs may struggle with executive functioning skills, thus affecting their ability to organize, study, or effectively manage time. Others may struggle to organize their thoughts, perform simple math calculations, or comprehend what they read (Lambie & Milsom, 2010). According to Hen and Goroshit (2014), students with SLDs are found to have lower academic self-efficacy and higher rates of absences from school.

Along with the potential effect on academic success, students with SLDs may also exhibit a range of emotional and behavioral concerns (Buckley & Mahdavi, 2018; Pullen et al., 2011). Prior to identification, many students identified with SLDs may be seen as discipline problems, unmotivated, or liars, thus diminishing their self-esteem (Rodis, et al., 2000). Once identified, students might often feel different or isolated from their peers, further affecting their self-concept (Lambie & Milsom, 2010). Furthermore, Rodis and colleagues (2000) observed that students with SLDs often do not have a clear understanding of their disabilities, thus creating a sense of confusion about what they experience, particularly when they compare themselves to their peers.

Research has shown that students with SLDs struggle with social and emotional competence (Buckley & Mahdavi, 2018; Elksnin & Elksnin, 2004). They grapple with communication skills, understanding social behavior, social information processing, and relationships with family and friends (Elksnin & Elksnin, 2004; Lambie & Milsom, 2010). Heinrichs (2003) suggested that students identified with a disability do not always isolate themselves but are often rejected by their peers and teachers, and their disabilities often make them targets of bullying. All of these issues can lead to further frustration, anxiety, and depression, which if not appropriately addressed can lead to drug use, dropping out of school, poor health, and lack of future employment (McGrady et al., 2000). Students with SLDs can and do learn successfully with the right support and strategies implemented by their school teams.

Strategies for School Counselors

Working With Students

It is essential to understand that students identified with SLDs are no different than their unidentified peers. However, because the degree of disability differs for each person, students will have their own unique needs (Lambie & Milsom, 2010). Thus it is crucial for the school counselor to first seek to understand the student and build a relationship before implementing any support. Rodis and colleagues (2000) found that many students with disabilities desire for someone to focus on their strengths and the things they have done well. Using unconditional positive regard is one technique that can help a school counselor build that relationship with a student. Students who feel valued and supported by their school counselors are more likely to share their concerns and explore their feelings (Buckley & Mahdavi, 2018). Opening the door to social-emotional learning helps the school counselor to work on emotional regulation, social problem solving, empathy, and nonverbal communication.

Academically, school counselors can help students with SLDs develop executive functioning skills, such as studying, organization, time management, and decision making. Students also benefit from learning to self-advocate (Buckley & Mahdavi, 2018). Teaching students to ask for help or advocate for their IEP accommodations can provide them with a sense of control over their learning. Likewise, educating students about their unique learning needs, aiding them in recognizing their strengths and setting goals, and providing them an active role in the IEP process are all important factors in developing practical self-advocacy skills and an understanding of their disabilities (Lambie & Milsom, 2010; Woods et al., 2013). Self-advocacy skills will also help to bolster their self-confidence, as well as make academic and life transitions (e.g., middle school to high school) more manageable (Hatch et al., 2009).

Many students with SLDs exhibit lower career maturity (Castellanos & Septowski, 2005) and are often influenced to pursue vocational training instead of college (Lambie & Milsom, 2010). Career development for a high school student with SLD is hindered by several factors, such as inadequate academic skills, poor self-awareness, limited career resources, and diminished autonomy (Buckley & Mahdavi, 2018; Chen & Chan, 2014). School counselors can aid in a student's career development by educating the student about appropriate professional soft skills, such as how to interview and build a resumé, as well as communication, time management, decision making, and self-motivation. In addition, school counselors can provide the student and their family with adequate career information and resources, help the student to translate their strengths into words, and work with the IEP and individualized transition plan teams.

Further support may be needed for students planning to attend college. School counselors may need to work with students and their families on college testing preparation, requesting testing accommodations for the ACT/SAT, contacting the university's disability center for future assistance, and helping families and students understand that the safety net they are used to in high school gets thinner as they move through academia and life. School counselors may need to role-play with students on how to broach the topic of their disabilities and needs to faculty and future employers, thus providing opportunities for students to hone their advocacy skills, which is a significant key to their future success.

Working With Families

When collaborating with the parents of a student the team identifies as having SLD, one of the most important steps is to help them learn about the disability (Trolley et al., 2009). The more knowledge the parents have about the disability, the better prepared the family is to support the student at home. School counselors can be instrumental in helping parents understand how their child learns best so that they can encourage learning outside of school. Further, providing tips on how to implement interventions and accommodations at home can provide continuity between school and home, as well as help to ease the stress surrounding homework.

Parents should continue to work on their student's social and emotional competence too. Work with the parents to focus on the student's strengths. Providing praise for and focus on their student's strengths can help combat negative thoughts and feelings (Buckley & Mahdavi, 2018; Trolley et al., 2009). In addition, connectedness to parents and peers can also help decrease a student's emotional distress. Encourage parents to find out what their child enjoys doing, such as clubs, sports, art, or technology, and allow the student to pursue these activities. Undertakings that bring joy to the student can be an outlet and an opportunity for them to socialize with peers away from academics.

Working With Community and Advocacy

School climate issues are critical for those identified with a disability because of the amount of bullying or other insensitive behavior that they could experience. Assessing school climate issues for students with SLDs is one way that school counselors can address behavior concerns (Buckley & Mahdavi, 2018). A school climate assessment can provide detailed insight into the attitudes, biases, and behaviors of the students and faculty, addressing the building environment through appropriate alterations.

School counselors may further advocate for students identified with disabilities through classroom guidance lessons, consultation, and in-service training (Buckley & Mahdavi, 2018; Lambie & Milsom, 2010). Classroom guidance lessons related to learning disabilities and special education can help students gain compassion for their peers. Some teachers may feel unprepared to work with students with SLDs, or they may not have an understanding of the social-emotional implications a disability can have on a student. Consulting with teachers or working with the administration and exceptional education teachers to provide in-service training can help to curb such attitudes.

Understanding What You Have Read: Comprehension Questions

Directions: Refer to what you have learned in this chapter to answer the following questions.

1. What are some risk factors teachers may observe that should signal the need for a referral for the determination of eligibility for a student having an SLD?
2. Why do you think it is important to have the school psychologist and counselor as part of the prereferral process in addition to the classroom teacher, special education teacher, and parents?
3. Why is it important to implement MTSS with fidelity and evidence-based interventions?
4. What possible effects can an SLD diagnosis have on a child's academic and social-emotional development?
5. What are some ways you can help a student learn about their disability?
6. What career and college resources would you provide a student identified with an SLD and their family?
7. How can you advocate for a student identified with an SLD?

Case Examples

Case Example One

As you read the case about Malcolm, reflect on the strategies that we discussed earlier in the chapter. The questions that follow the case relate to the student's behavioral symptoms and accompanying responses.

Malcolm's seventh-grade teacher has assigned the class to complete several math problems for homework. Malcolm spent 2½ hours working on the math problems but failed the math quiz the next day. Even after the quiz was over and the teacher was reviewing the problems, he struggled to answer any questions that came up during the class discussion. Malcolm's teacher assumed he did not review the assignment the night before; however, upon further discussion with Malcolm, it became clear to the teacher that he had indeed attempted the homework problems and had spent way longer than most of his classmates trying to solve them. As the school counselor, you recognize Malcolm, as you have conducted several study skills lessons with each grade level, including Malcolm's class. You too are concerned that he is struggling academically, even with the tools you have shared with him.

Case Example One: Questions for Processing and Reflection

Directions: Use what you have learned in this chapter to respond to Malcolm's case.

1. Based on the information you've read, what might be some plausible reasons for Malcolm's struggles?
   a. Malcolm may be struggling because of difficulties processing and recalling information.
   b. Based on the scenario and his performance on the assessment, as well as during class discussion, Malcom may need more support using strategies for remembering information.
   c. Malcolm needs more guidance in choosing what information to study, depending on the complexity of the math problems.
   d. Malcolm may also struggle with using basic facts to solve multistep problems.
   e. Malcolm may be experiencing issues with his vision.

2. How might the school counselor support Malcolm?
    a. The school counselor could check in with Malcolm about how he is doing and how he feels he is doing in seventh grade. You should also address areas of strength and limitation, especially if Malcolm is unwilling to bring up the subject of his academic struggles.
    b. The school counselor could work with Malcolm on remembering the study skills strategies that were taught earlier in the year.
    c. The school counselor should check with Malcolm's caregivers to determine if there have been any changes at home that might be affecting him.
    d. The school counselor could check with other teachers to determine if Malcolm is struggling in their subjects.

Case Example Two

As you read the case about Gage, reflect on the strategies that we discussed earlier in the chapter. The questions that follow the case relate to the student's behavioral symptoms and accompanying responses.

Gage has been struggling with fourth-grade writing assignments for the first two grading reports. He is often off task during independent work and struggles to write legibly in all subject areas. Gage's parents notice that he gets frustrated with an assignment that requires written expression responses and often avoids homework unless it permits him to work collaboratively and present his work orally. When answering multistep word problems, Gage often struggles and turns in incomplete work. His desk space is not well organized, and he has several assignments that are missing. Gage's parents are concerned that he is falling further behind in school.

Case Example Two: Questions for Processing and Reflection

Directions: Use what you have learned in this chapter to respond to Gage's case.

1. What could be the possible reasons for Gage's struggles?
2. What areas should Gage's teacher monitor?
3. How might the MTSS process be helpful in addressing Gage's needs?
4. What would be your role as a school counselor in the MTSS process?

Chapter Summary

SLD is the most commonly identified eligibility category under IDEA. It can affect a student's ability to think, read, speak, write, spell, or perform mathematical calculations, thus affecting their capability to succeed in an academic setting. Students who are identified as struggling academically are entered into a process of scientific evaluation to determine if they have a disability. If identified with SLDs, students are placed on an IEP and provided with academic accommodations to help them achieve academic success.

In their school communities, students identified with SLDs frequently exist at the margins. They experience many challenges with school, peers, and their self-concept. This population of students tend to feel isolated, shameful, and frustrated more than their unidentified peers. Many are inclined to drop out of school and abuse substances, and others are victims of bullying. School counselors can help to address these issues by collaborating with the student, parents, and IEP team. Establishing a meaningful relationship in which the student feels heard and accepted can offer school counselors insight into their needs and provide them with the tools to be effective advocates.

Additional Recommended Readings and Resources

Rehabilitation Act of 1973. If a student has a disability that does not affect their educational performance, that student is not eligible for services under IDEA 2004 but would be protected under Section 504 of the Americans with Disabilities Act. Section 504 protects those students from discrimination and ensures that they enjoy equal access to education, including appropriate accommodations.

IDEA 2004: https://sites.ed.gov/idea/

Parent Rights IDEA 2004: https://www.parentcenterhub.org/parental-rights/

https://www.ncld.org/wp-content/uploads/2014/11/IDEA-Parent-Guide1.pdf

National Center on Student Progress Monitoring: https://rti4success.org/resource/student-progress-monitoring-what-means-your-child

National Center on Response to Intervention: https://www.rti4success.org/

National Center on Intensive Interventions: https://intensiveintervention.org/

References

American School Counselor Association (ASCA). (2016). *The school counselor and students with disabilities.* https://www.schoolcounselor.org/asca/media/asca/PositionStatements/PS_Disabilities.pdf

Artiles, A., Kozleski, E., Trent, S., Osher, D., & Ortiz, A. (2010). Justifying and explaining disproportionality, 1968–2008: A critique of underlying views of culture. *Exceptional Children, 76*(3), 279.

Blanchett, W. J. (2009). A retrospective examination of urban education: From Brown to the resegregation of African Americans in special education—it is time to "go for broke." *Urban Education, 44*(4), 370–388.

Brown v. Board of Education, 347 U.S. 483 (1954).

Buckley, M., & Mahdavi, J. (2018). Bringing children from the margins to the page: School counselors supporting students with learning disabilities. *Journal of School Counseling, 16*(23). Retrieved from http://www.jsc.montana.edu/articles/v16n23.pdf

Castellanos, P., & Septeowski, D. (2005). Career development for persons with learning disabilities. In S. Burhardt, F. E. Obiakor, & A. F. Rotatori (Eds.), *Current perspectives on learning disabilities: advances in special education* (Vol. 16, pp. 157–181). JAI Press.

Chen, C., & Chan, J. (2014). Career guidance for learning-disabled youth. *International Journal of Vocational Guidance, 14*, 275–291.

Education for All Handicapped Children Act of 1975, Pub. L. No. 94–142, § 89 Stat. 773 (1975).

Elementary and Secondary Education Act of 1965, § 1208(3) (1965).

Elksnin, L., & Elksnin, N. (2004). The social-emotional side of learning disabilities. *Learning Disabilities Quarterly, 27*, 3–8.

Every Student Succeeds Act of 2015, Pub. L. No. 114–95 § 1177 (2015).

Hatch, T., Shelton, T., & Monk, G. (2009). Making invisible visible: School counselors empowering students with disabilities through self-advocacy training. *Journal of School Counseling, 7*(14), 1–19.

Hen, M., & Goroshit, M. (2014). Academic procrastination, emotional intelligence, academic self-efficacy, and GPA: A comparison between students with and without learning disabilities. *Journal of Learning Disabilities, 47*, 116–124.

Individuals with Disabilities Education Act of 1990, Pub. L. No. 101–475, § 104 Stat. 1142 (1990).

Individuals with Disabilities Education Act of 1997, Pub. L. No. 105–17, 111 § Stat. 37 (1997).

Individuals with Disabilities Education Act, 20 U.S.C. §§ 1401 et seq. (2006).

Individuals with Disabilities Education Improvement Act of 2004, Pub. L. No. 108–446, § 118, Stat. 2647 (2004).

Kushner, J., Maldonado, J., Pack, T., & Hooper, B. (2011). Demographic report on special education students in postsecondary education: Implications for school counselors and educators. *International Journal of Special Education, 26*(1), 175–181.

Lambie, G., & Milsom, A. (2010). A narrative approach to supporting students diagnosed with learning disabilities. *Journal of Counseling & Development, 88*(2), 196–203.

Lambie, G., Stickl Haugen, J., Borland, J., & Campbell, L. (2019). Who took "counseling out of the role of the professional school counselors? *Journal of School-Based Counseling Policy and Evaluation, 1*(3), 51–61.

McGrady, H., Lerner, J., & Boscardin, M. (2000). The educational lives of students with learning disabilities. In P. Rodis, A. Garrod, & M. L. Boscardin (Eds.), *Learning disabilities & life stories* (pp. 177–193). Allyn & Bacon.

Mills v. Board of Education of District of Columbia, 348 F. Supp. 866 (D.D.C. 1972).

No Child Left Behind Act of 2001, Pub. L. No. 107–110, § 115, Stat. 1425 (2002).

Pullen, P., Lane, H., Ahsworth, K., & Lovelace, S. (2011). Learning disabilities. In J. Kauffman & D. Hallahan, (Eds.), *Handbook of special education* (pp. 187–197). Routledge.

Rodis, P., Garrod, A., & Boscardin, M. L. (2000). *Learning disabilities and life stories.* Pearson Pub

Tarver-Behring, S., Spagna, M., & Sullivan, J. (1998). School counselors and full inclusion for children with special needs. *Professional School Counseling, 1*, 51–56.

Trolley, B., Hass, H., & Campese Patti, D. (2009). *The school counselor's guide to special education.* Skyhorse.

U.S. Department of Education, National Center for Education Statistics. (2018). Table 204.30: Children 3 to 21 years old served under Individuals with Disabilities Education Act, Part B, by type of disability. https://nces.ed.gov/fastfacts/display.asp?id=64

Woods, L., Martin, J., & Humphrey, M. (2013). The difference a year makes: An exploratory self-directed IEP case study. *Exceptionality, 21*, 176–189.

CHAPTER THREE

Attention Deficit Hyperactivity Disorder (ADHD)

Christopher Belser and Dalena Dillman Taylor

THE CASE OF RHETT Rhett is an energetic, 8-year-old boy in the third grade. He has a late spring birthday and, therefore, is younger than most of his peers. Rhett is described by his parents as full of life and curious. Rhett is the middle of three children; he has an older sister by 2 years and a young brother by 4 years. All members of Rhett's family live together. Rhett's teachers in the first grade identified him as above average, although he did not qualify as gifted. This year, Rhett has consistently been getting into trouble for not following directions, being easily distracted, and overly fidgety. During the initial consult with the school counselor, his parents explained that Rhett has always exhibited as a more hyperactive child; however, they viewed his behaviors as a by-product of him being bored in class because of his intellect. The school counselor processed with his parents the negative side of his behaviors, especially as he advances through school.

Introduction to the Chapter

Rhett's circumstances are not uncommon. Some signs point to possible hyperactive and problematic behaviors, whereas other signs point to him not being challenged enough in class. Which perspective is more accurate in this case? Without more information, determining whether Rhett's struggles stem from boredom in class or from a possible diagnosable disorder would be very difficult. Attention deficit hyperactivity disorder, or ADHD, is certainly not a new disorder showing up in schools, but diagnosis rates have been on the rise. Moreover, diagnostic changes between the *Diagnostic and Statistical Manual of Mental Disorders, Fourth Edition, Text Revision* and the *Diagnostic and Statistical Manual of Mental Disorders, Fifth Edition* (*DSM-5*) can create confusion and misconceptions about what ADHD actually is. This chapter seeks to address some of those issues.

Learning Objectives

By the end of this chapter, readers will accomplish the following:

- Understand the signs and symptoms of ADHD.
- Increase knowledge of the potential effects that a diagnosis of ADHD can have on children and adolescents.
- Gain information on best practices for working with students, parents/caregivers, and teachers who are affected by students' diagnosis of ADHD.

Prevalence of ADHD

Recent studies have estimated that more than six million children have received an ADHD diagnosis from a health-care provider in their lifetimes (Centers for Disease Control and Prevention [CDC], 2019; Danielson et al., 2018; Visser et al., 2014). This number represents approximately 11% of school-aged children in the United States, with 1 in 5 high school boys and 1 in 11 high school girls having a diagnosis of ADHD (CDC, 2019). According to surveyed parents, the average age that children were first diagnosed was 7, with more severe cases of ADHD typically diagnosed earlier. Of those with current ADHD diagnoses, nearly 62% took medication, just fewer than 50% had received behavioral treatment, and approximately 23% had not received either type of treatment (Danielson et al., 2018).

In addition to a general rise in ADHD diagnosis rates, discrepancies in diagnosis rates exist based on demographic factors and location. Children from families making less than 2 times the federal poverty level have an increased risk of diagnosis, and males have nearly 3 times the risk of diagnosis (Visser et al., 2014). Getahun and colleagues (2013) observed increases in diagnosis rates among white, black, and Hispanic children, with the largest increase reported with black females. Regionally, the South and Midwest lead the nation in diagnoses, with 12.6% and 12.1% of children, respectively, having received a diagnosis (Visser et al., 2014). Kentucky, Arkansas, Louisiana, Indiana, and South Carolina have the highest rates of ADHD diagnoses (CDC, 2019), whereas South Carolina, Louisiana, and Alabama have the highest rates of medication treatment for ADHD (Express Scripts, 2014). One of these states (Louisiana) commissioned a team to investigate the diagnosis and medication rates of ADHD, and their findings showed that geographic region of the state seemed to be a better predictor of ADHD prescription rates than race or gender demographics, and these regional discrepancies may have been the result of specific medical providers within high-rate regions (Louisiana Department of Health and Hospitals [LDHH], 2015). With ADHD diagnosis and medication rates on the rise around the country, school counselors are positioned in a way that necessitates that they be aware of signs and symptoms of ADHD, potential dual diagnoses and misdiagnoses, and how members of the school community perceive ADHD.

Signs and Symptoms of ADHD

ADHD diagnoses are based on criteria found in the *DSM-5* (American Psychiatric Association [APA], 2013). For a formal clinical diagnosis, a child must display "a persistent pattern of inattention and/or hyperactivity that interferes with functioning or development" that has been observed for at least 6 months and must be present in at least two settings, such as home, school, or extracurricular activities (APA, 2013, p. 59). Medical providers should specify one of three subtypes when making a diagnosis: (1) predominantly inattentive type, (2) predominantly hyperactive/impulsive type, or (3) combined type (CDC, 2019). To warrant either the inattentive or hyperactive/impulsive type, the child must present with at least six of the associated symptoms listed in the *DSM-5* for that type for at least 6 months; if the child presents with at least six symptoms from *both* categories, a diagnosis of the combined type is warranted.

The predominantly inattentive type has more commonly been observed in females than in male students (APA, 2013). This type could be described as the child who consistently day-dreams during class, regularly forgets to complete routine tasks, and quickly loses focus. You may have also experienced this child as the one who frequently starts a task but gets distracted or sidetracked easily, resulting in unfinished work. This child may also have difficulty staying organized, which can lead to problems with handling sequential tasks; issues with managing time; trouble with keeping schoolwork, lockers, or backpacks organized; and a tendency to lose materials and possessions. The next section will highlight other potential misdiagnoses that are assigned to children exhibiting symptoms of this type of ADHD, but parents, school counselors, and teachers should pay particular attention so that legitimate symptoms are not written off as conscious off-task behavior. Because this type can present without hints of hyperactivity, parents and teachers can easily overlook these inattentive ADHD symptoms or mislabel them as apathy, defiance, laziness, aloofness, or boredom. These potential misinterpretations make it critical for professionals making diagnoses to consider the degree to which symptoms adversely impact social and academic functioning and the number of settings where symptoms are usually present.

More commonly diagnosed in male students, the predominantly hyperactive/impulsive type is probably easier to observe and recognize because the symptoms relate more to a mixture of elevated motor activity and hasty decision making (APA, 2013). You may have experienced this child as the boy who frequently fidgets and wriggles in his desk, the girl who repeatedly leaves her desk without even realizing, or the child who seems to be powered by a motor. This child may also struggle to engage in play activities or classwork quietly or may talk constantly despite efforts to reduce stimuli. The hyperactivity and impulsivity can result in the child talking out of turn, not waiting in line, and interrupting others' conversations and activities. Because this type is marked by externalized behaviors, frustrated teachers and parents may be more likely to refer children exhibiting the hyperactive/impulsive type for further evaluation, for counseling, or for disciplinary consequences. As with the inattentive subtype, professionals have an imperative to consider whether symptoms merit an accurate diagnosis or if other issues, such as trauma, other disorders, or environmental concerns at home or school, may relate to the child's functioning.

Misdiagnosis and Societal Perceptions

ADHD is a term that is thrown around regularly within our society, similar to the way in which "crazy" is used. However, little is known about the criteria for a student to actually meet this diagnosis. Many of the symptomology within the ADHD diagnosis is common across neurotypical children and many childhood mental health diagnoses, thus creating many gray areas in the understanding of what actually constitutes an accurate ADHD diagnosis. Earlier, we discussed the actual criteria for ADHD. In this section, we attempt to tease apart possible comorbidities and differential diagnoses to provide substance to the catchy term "ADHD."

Normal challenges are dependent on development and may play a factor in understanding the root of the child's behavior as opposed to a quick diagnosis. Children typically have short attention spans, high activity levels, and are impulsive (Sparrow & Erhardt, 2014). Two important considerations to determine if symptoms are related to ADHD are (1) assessing whether the behavior is excessive for the child's age and gender and (2) determining if significant impairment is due to the symptomology. For example, 8-year-olds tend to exhibit high levels of energy and activity, and they tend to test limits more often—these behaviors are neurotypical, and without developmental understanding of various ages, the student could be misdiagnosed with ADHD. Therefore, it is critical for school counselors to review child development prior to referring a child for behavioral testing or assessment. We suggest school counselors keep the book *Therapist's Guide to Child Development: The Extraordinarily Ordinary Years* on hand for easy reference (Ray, 2016).

Nearly 80% of children diagnosed with ADHD are also diagnosed with another disorder. According to Willcutt and Bidwell (2011), common comorbid disorders are oppositional defiant disorder (ODD; 30%–60%), conduct disorder (CD; 20%–50%), learning disorders (20%–40%), anxiety disorders (15%–30%), and depression (15%–30%), indicating that ADHD is not an easy diagnosis to conclude. It is important to note that much consideration is necessary and to not jump to conclusions because a student is presenting with hyperactivity. Most important is to understand the context of that behavior or the intention behind it prior to making a quick decision. Sparrow and Erhardt (2014) outlined a helpful example in their book regarding compliance. If a student is compliant during a task but struggles with verbal directions, it may be more helpful to receive additional assessments related to receptive language disorder as opposed to ADHD. Whereas if a student is compliant when paying attention but noncompliant when not paying attention, the student is a likely candidate for an ADHD diagnosis. Therefore, it is critical to ask yourself what is the *basis* for this behavior? Take into consideration the child's context and the precursor events leading to noncompliance or misbehavior.

In our experience, one of the most common misdiagnoses is assessing for ADHD when context alludes to a trauma-related disorder. Many times, the symptomology appears similar, and the context for the behavior is not considered. Hypervigilance, a symptom of trauma-related disorders, may manifest in some as hyperactivity and/or distractibility. When a student is distracted in class, teachers may presume that the child has ADHD when in fact that child is scanning the room for threats based on prior history. Behaviors at face value look similar yet tell us very little when we are trying to grasp the complex nature of trauma. A helpful distinction when attempting to differentiate between the two is the onset of symptoms. If symptoms began prior to a trauma event, then ADHD is still a candidate; whereas if symptoms began post-trauma, then ADHD is not likely. If you are concerned about a student's behavior, ask questions, get to know the student better, and learn their story. Details can provide much depth to the surface behaviors exhibited by the student. As Adler stated, all behavior is purposeful (Dinkmeyer & Sperry, 2000). So what is this student attempting to communicate through their behavior?

We devised a go-to chart that references the multiple possibilities for diagnoses other than ADHD (Table 3.1). We encourage school counselors to use it as a preliminary reference and check the *DSM-5* or consult with a mental health professional to confirm the hypothesized diagnosis.

Other considerations are important to mention. Children with neurocognitive issues (e.g., brain injury, seizures, brain tumor, genetic disorders) may present with ADHD-like symptomology. Similar to trauma-related disorders, it is important to determine the chronology of events. Did the symptoms appear prior to or post-injury? Was the onset sudden? A medical professional may need to rule out neurocognitive issues prior to a diagnosis of ADHD. In addition, certain situations, environments, or cultures can play a role in children presenting with symptomology consistent with ADHD. For example, I (DDT) conducted a teacher consultation with a student who was referred to me for ADHD. Upon entering the classroom, I felt empathetic to my client, as I began to exhibit signs of distraction and inattentiveness. I noted this to the teacher by commenting; "I am feeling a little overwhelmed and distracted by all the pictures and artwork. I wonder if it's a lot for my client to take in during the day." Each square inch of her room was covered with pictures, posters, inspirational sayings, and more. Her intention was to provide an inviting space and show excitement for the artwork developed by her students; however, there can be too much. How can we help teachers find a balance and create a safe that is inviting while not distracting?

TABLE 3.1 Differential Diagnoses for ADHD

DIFFERENTIAL DIAGNOSIS	COMMON SYMPTOMOLOGY	DOES NOT MEET ADHD DIAGNOSIS IF ...	NEXT STEPS
Intellectual Disability*	Inattentiveness, impulsivity	Child's attention, activity levels, and impulse control are proportionate with the level of cognitive functioning	Cognitive testing and understanding of neurotypical development can confirm
Language Disorders*	Inattentiveness	Child's responsiveness increases when demonstration and visual cues of instruction increase and language decreases	Consult with a speech-language evaluator
Autism Spectrum Disorder*	Inattentiveness, high activity levels, irritability, executive deficits, fine motor impairment, sleep problems	Nonverbal communication is less evident, pervasive deficits in social understanding, social motivation is absent, more likely to be content in solitary pursuits, stereotyped or idiosyncratic language, limited imaginary play skills, cognitive rigidity	Refer for a thorough assessment from a trained mental health professional on the nuances of autism spectrum disorder
Specific Learning Disorders*	Inattentiveness	A pattern of difficulty is evident in one academic area but not others, there are specific academic struggles without the pairing of impairment in social or community settings, and the onset of ADHD-like symptomology is concurrent with school entry	Cognitive and academic testing
Motor Disorders*	High levels of activity, outbursts	Repetitive and fixed movements as opposed to general restlessness and fidgeting	Observation over a period of time to determine the presence of these behaviors (formulaic vs. general, variable)
Depressive Disorders*	Irritability, difficulty with concentration, poor frustration tolerance, psychomotor agitation	Common features co-occur with sadness and/or anhedonia (loss of interest/pleasure), distractibility is secondary to rumination/upsetting thoughts or feelings, loss of interest in all activities, change in behavior for at least 2 weeks	Refer for assessment to determine the onset of the symptomology

(*Continues*)

TABLE 3.1 *(Continued)*

DIFFERENTIAL DIAGNOSIS	COMMON SYMPTOMOLOGY	DOES NOT MEET ADHD DIAGNOSIS IF ...	NEXT STEPS
Anxiety Disorders*	Inattentiveness, restlessness, fidgeting, procrastination	Inattention is related to worry; restlessness presents with a fretful, agitated quality compared to overstimulation found in ADHD; ADHD-like symptoms are limited to anxiety-provoking situations	Observation over a period of time to determine the quality of the symptomology
Trauma- and Stressor-Related Disorders	Inattentiveness, hyperactivity, distractibility, recklessness, irritable/aggressive behavior	History of trauma, chronology of events—onset of behaviors is after a traumatic event	Refer for treatment for trauma (e.g., play therapy)
Disruptive, Impulse-Control Disorders and CD	Hyperactivity, impulsivity	CD—pattern of ***intentional*** antisocial behavior is present, destruction is deliberate, intention to deceive others or escape an obligation, rule violations are severe ODD—annoys others deliberately, acts spiteful/vindictive, task refusal is pervasive across situations, intentional decisions to defy instructions	Refer for treatment for CD or ODD (e.g., play therapy)

*Note: * indicates disorders can be comorbid with ADHD.*

Contributing Factors and Risk Factors of ADHD

Now that you know more about what ADHD is and is not, we will turn our attention to understanding the contributing factors and risk factors of ADHD. At present, we do not have a clear and definitive understanding of the root causes of ADHD, but research studies have helped provide information about associated factors and contributing factors. Through studies of twins and adopted children, researchers have determined that ADHD has a large genetic component, indicating that children have a higher risk of developing symptoms of ADHD if their parents have an ADHD diagnosis or a predisposition to inattentive or hyperactive behaviors (Faraone et al., 2005; Russell et al., 2014; Thapar et al., 2013). Whereas the environment in which a child is raised also plays a part in the development of ADHD, the best explanation of contributing factors might be an interaction between genetic predispositions and factors present in the home environment while the child is in utero, such as smoking during pregnancy, alcohol exposure, and nutrition (APA, 2013; Thapar et al., 2013). Researchers have found correlations between ADHD diagnoses and parenting styles/family interactions during childhood, but the evidence is still inconclusive about whether these factors cause ADHD or if they can exacerbate symptoms of ADHD (APA, 2013; Russell et al., 2014).

Although the research is not totally clear on what causes ADHD, other studies have been clearer about outcomes that can occur for individuals with ADHD. Social outcomes for the child can include peer rejection, fewer friendships, and poor social skills (Ros & Graziano, 2018). For the family, having a child with ADHD can lead to increases in family stress, time away from work for parents, and childcare costs (Russell et al., 2014). Academic outcomes include increased risk of being retained, decreased likelihood of graduating on time, less positive relationships with teachers, and increased likelihood of disciplinary exclusion from class (Balazs & Kereszteny, 2014; Bussing et al., 2010; Bussing et al., 2012). With many of these risks playing out in the school setting, school counselors may be prime candidates to intervene.

Strategies for School Counselors

The CDC (2019) reported nearly two million (11% of the population surveyed) children were diagnosed with ADHD from 2003 to 2016. Nearly two thirds of these children with ADHD diagnoses presented with comorbidity. However, Panksepp (2007) noted a common belief that only 4% of children are born with ADHD, while other children develop the disorder based on environmental influences, reflecting a "cultural illness" (i.e., lack of playtime). Therefore, the schools are a perfect environment to begin mitigating this issue through the incorporation of play. See Allee-Herndon et al. (2019) for a comprehensive overview of how school counselors can incorporate play into elementary schools. We will outline a few suggestions in the next sections.

Assessment

A common misperception is that a single assessment can diagnose or rule out ADHD as the primary concern. However, as outlined in the differential diagnoses table earlier, many factors are at play: overlap of symptomology, cultural considerations, early childhood experiences, genetic factors, and environment. We encourage school counselors to take a conservative approach to screening and assessment, considering all factors prior to taking action. According to the guidelines established by the American Academy of Pediatrics (AAP), individuals assessing for ADHD should at a minimum include interviews of relevant parties, teacher and parent rating scales, and cognitive testing. If the child's medical provider sends you a rating scale to complete on the child, ensure that educators with ample firsthand knowledge of the student complete it; you as the school counselor should only complete one after directly observing the student for a sustained period of time. Based on the differential diagnoses noted earlier, we would highly encourage child observations within classroom settings to rule out other possibilities, as well as gather information regarding the student's developmental history and current presentation. The AAP also concluded that a qualified clinician should review all assessment results. Therefore, school counselors are encouraged to develop an assessment team of individuals in the community to refer students to for assessment, consultation, and services. School counselors can draw from their training in multicultural competence when working to guard these assessment plans and procedures from implicit or explicit biases. Climie and Mastoras (2015) encouraged educators to also include interviews and rating scales to identify students' strengths and areas of interest, which can help in developing intervention plans and promoting resilience.

Individual Interventions

Because school counselors typically have large caseloads, individual interventions may not always be the most time-sensitive format; however, there are lots of ways that school counselors can support individual students who have an ADHD diagnosis. As noted earlier, conversations about students with ADHD can tend to center on problematic behaviors and deficits. School counselors, however, can use strengths-based activities to help students also become more aware of their unique attributes, which can help them build more confidence and self-efficacy. Mumbauer and Kelchner (2017) noted that children do not always fully understand their mental health concerns and recommended bibliotherapy as a strategy to help students begin to understand their diagnosis. I (CTB) found bibliotherapy, as well as psychoeducation, to be quite useful in helping students better comprehend their ADHD diagnosis. In such conversations, school counselors should remember to process feelings that students have about their diagnosis and their experiences based on that diagnosis (e.g., embarrassment, shame, apathy). For teens, Breaux et al. (2018) emphasized the importance of developing strong working alliances with both the student and the parents, as these alliances can increase the likelihood of positive outcomes. Other potential interventions for students with ADHD include check-in/check-out systems, positive behavior contracts, cognitive-behavioral techniques, and social skills training.

Group Interventions

Helping students better understand their interests and strengths can also be helpful when working with groups of students. Particular to students with ADHD, the group format can help them learn to leverage their strengths and interests to overcome social skills deficits and develop social capital with their peers (Climie & Mastoras, 2015). Such groups can also provide students a space in which they can share their experiences with teachers and parents, strategies that have worked for them in navigating these situations, and encouragement for other members. Manualized skill-based curricula may also be helpful in structuring, implementing, and evaluating group interventions. Group interventions for students with ADHD can also provide some opportunities for creative interventions. For example, I (CTB) worked in a middle school that did not provide recess for students; as the school counselor, I implemented several creative activities within my small groups that (a) allowed students to go outside for at least a short period of the day, (b) provided students with visual and/or kinesthetic activities to help them think through their diagnosis, and (c) gave students a chance to converse with each other about the stigmas surrounding ADHD. Finally, Kamali & Looyeh (2013) described a small group intervention that was very well grounded in narrative-based group work.

Play Therapy

Play therapy is a developmentally responsive approach to counseling children (Allee-Herndon et al., 2019; Association for Play Therapy [APT], 2018). Children use the natural language of play within a supportive, nurturing environment to overcome struggles and challenges that are present because of circumstances, prior events, or diagnoses. Within play therapy, children, typically ages 3–10, develop self-esteem, self-control, and increased coping skills. However, adaptations to play therapy have been developed and well-researched to demonstrate similar benefits for preadolescents and adolescents (Ojiambo & Bratton, 2016). Similarly, the use of play aligns with the neurobiology of intervening within the right/emotional brain to uncover hidden events and feelings. Play therapy is effective for children presenting with ADHD, as well as other diagnoses. The APT lists all registered play therapists (RPTs) on their website. School counselors can search their local areas for qualified play therapists or become school-based registered play therapists (SB-RPTs) through additional training and qualifications. If you are interested in providing play therapy services to children in schools beyond play-focused activities, we highly encourage school counselors to review the criteria for becoming an SB-RPT on the APT's website under the SB-RPT guide and application sections.

Strategies for Working With Parents/Guardians

Because of the importance of play on children's development, we encourage parents to incorporate free play at home, as it often reduces the expression of ADHD symptoms. Many children are overscheduled and overtired, which exasperates symptoms of ADHD. Therefore, school counselors are encouraged within their meetings with caregivers to help provide insight into the busy schedules their children lead. Awareness can be key to begin the process of developing an environment to mitigate their child's symptomology. For example, I (DDT) worked with one family in which every night of the week was packed with extracurricular events, and the children were not getting home until after 9:00 p.m. The youngest was 2 years old. Needless to say, the children, because of a lack of sleep, were struggling at home and school with behavioral problems. I worked with the caregivers to eliminate many of the extracurricular activities for a semester to see the impact. Behaviors decreased dramatically over the course of several weeks. Although this suggestion is not a one-size-fits-all approach, it can be an important first step.

As caregivers try new approaches, I (DDT) encourage the rule "be the thermostat, not the thermometer" (Landreth & Bratton, 2019). Thermostats tend to regulate the temperature of the room, whereas thermometers react to the temperature. Therefore, patience is critical for new strategies to work. As parents attempt new ways to handle their child's behavior, they are likely to be more successful if entering the situation with patience and a calm presence, recognizing that overnight successes are highly unlikely. Students with ADHD are not likely to "overcome" their symptoms but develop coping skills to handle situations that may be more difficult because of their diagnosis. Therefore, changes take time and encouragement.

One strategy can be practicing multistep tasks. If tasks are age appropriate, they can be modified for any age. A sixth grader entering middle school may find the new freedom daunting. Parents can practice multistep tasks the summer prior to the student entering sixth grade, with the understanding that much of what occurs in middle school relates to the self-responsibility of getting from class to class with all necessary items for each class. For example, parents may want to start small, asking their child to (a) get dressed, (b) eat breakfast, and (c) brush their teeth by 8:00 a.m. every morning. If the child has difficulty remembering to do those three tasks because other things distracted them, then parents can schedule a family meeting to discuss strategies to improve focus. Parents should solicit strategies from the child, as well as present suggestions. Discuss the pros and cons of each. For instance, write down the tasks and cross off items once completed for that day. We believe counselors should place importance on the process, modeling for the child to reevaluate when something is not working and not getting stuck on trying to do the same thing. This process also models for the child that all suggestions are considered and that their opinion matters too. Shillingford et al. (2007) discussed parent trainings as a means for helping parents learn how to implement strategies such as self-monitoring, self-talk, and social skills; moreover, incorporating teachers in these conversations can increase continuity across settings.

As you reflect on the families and students that you work with, what other strategies have you found helpful when working with children with ADHD?

Strategies for Working With Teachers and Other Educators

In many schools, the school counselor may be the only person or one of a few people with any training in mental health. As such, the school counselor can help provide professional development for school staff about ADHD and other disorders that manifest in school settings. Such professional development workshops could include an overview of what ADHD actually is, which can dispel myths and misconceptions that teachers might have. School counselors can also stress the importance of avoiding stigmatizing and potentially harmful language, such as, "He's so ADHD," or "Did you take your meds today?" As a school counselor, I (CTB) frequently found myself educating teachers on the different presentations of ADHD, informing them of structures that lead to the overdiagnosis or underdiagnosis of ADHD within some populations, and providing verification that ADHD is, in fact, a real disorder.

School counselors can also provide professional development and consultation services related to strategies that teachers can use to support students with ADHD. Such considerations may include the physical layout of the classroom, teachers' operating rules and classroom procedures, and strategies for communicating with students. Specifically, school counselors can help teachers begin to recognize what they may be doing that may be ineffective or even counterproductive in supporting these specific students, such as inconsistent class structure or procedures or fast-paced lessons that can leave students behind. At the classroom and school levels, teachers and school counselors can collaborate on identifying methods to promote positive behavior reinforcement rather than just relying on punishment-based strategies. Because students with ADHD can try teachers' patience, school counselors can aid teachers in building a positive classroom culture that allows students to be more than their past behavior issues.

A final area that school counselors can aid teachers in is with building collaborations with parents and caregivers. Teachers should not be using diagnostic language around ADHD ("I think your child may have ADHD.") or language that communicates medical advice ("Have you ever thought of medicating her?" Or, "Have you ever had him tested for ADHD?"), as these are operationally outside the teacher's scope of practice and training. As an alternative, school counselors can work with teachers to develop more effective and less stigmatizing methods of communicating concerns about a child's behavior and performance in class. Similarly, school counselors can stress to teachers the importance of staying in communication with parents not only when students are having problems but also when they are experiencing successes. I (CTB) once sat in on a teacher-parent conference in which teachers went around the room talking about the negative behaviors of the child, leading the mother to ask, "Does anyone have anything good to say about him?" Only hearing from teachers when something is going wrong can disenfranchise the parent or leave them feeling hopeless, which is contrary to the goal of promoting student success.

Understanding What You Have Read: Comprehension Questions

Directions: Refer to what you have learned in this chapter to answer the following questions.

1. What is ADHD?
2. What are the determining factors for a diagnosis of ADHD?
3. What are the characteristics of each of the three subtypes of ADHD?
4. What modalities or strategies can you use as a school counselor to support students who have an ADHD diagnosis?
5. What myths or misconceptions did you have about ADHD that may show up in your colleagues?
6. How can you support the parents/caregivers and teachers of students with ADHD?
7. What are some ethical and multicultural considerations you will be faced with when working with a student with ADHD?

Case Examples

Case Example One

As you read the case about Sarah, reflect on the strategies that we discussed earlier in the chapter. The questions that follow the case relate to the student's behavioral symptoms and accompanying responses.

Sarah is an 8-year-old girl at a suburban elementary school. She is an active, energetic child. Because she has exhibited higher energy levels than her peers for several years now, her parents have enrolled her in several physical activities, such as tae kwon do and soccer. Their hope was that increasing activities would help her focus while at school. However, the teacher recently reached out to the school counselor for help with Sarah. Over the past several months, her focus has waned, and her activity level within the classroom has increased. The teacher has tried several strategies to help Sarah, such as assigning her the job of class helper so that she could pass out papers and supplies throughout the day to increase her activity in a positive way and including movement activities as part of her lessons so that all students can engage in big physical movements. Yet Sarah is continually off task, not focused, and confused by her work. She is falling behind, and at the start of the second half of the year, she is no longer on track to successfully complete second grade.

Case Example One: Questions for Processing and Reflection

Directions: Use what you have learned in this chapter to respond to Sarah's case.

1. What symptoms of ADHD is Sarah showing her teacher and counselor?
    - Higher levels of energy than her peers
    - Recent decrease in focus and increase in activity level
    - Off task
    - Confusion over coursework, falling behind academically
2. Would you rule out any other diagnosis before making a plan? If so, what symptoms are leading you to think of something else?
    - Absolutely! We would refer to the chart in this chapter to determine if other diagnoses could explain her behavior. For instance, we would want to explore with Sarah's mother if any recent traumatic events have occurred given that her behaviors seemed to have increased in severity recently. Sarah's cumulative file may also provide some further information about her educational, behavioral, and/or medical history.
3. What is your next step when working with Sarah?
    - We would conduct parent and teacher consultations to understand the patterns of Sarah's behaviors, especially when and where the behaviors are occurring. We would also meet with Sarah to understand her perspective of the behavioral changes. Because of her age, we are likely to implement play-based interventions and, if trained, conduct an initial play therapy session to gather additional information.
4. What assessments would you select?
    - Given that many misdiagnoses occur because of self-report only, we recommend classroom observations of Sarah's behavior. Observations can provide context and additional information that the reporting party (i.e., parent, teacher) will be likely to miss. If ADHD rating scales are introduced, we advise using them as a *supplement* to observation, not as a stand-alone assessment.
5. With whom within the school would you collaborate/? Explain why.
    - We would elect to collaborate with the teacher. Sarah's teacher is already implementing helpful ideas to support Sarah. We would work with this teacher to expand on her interventions and to tailor them more effectively based on the results of the assessments. Because of Sarah's age, we would recommend including her in some conversations with her teacher to ensure that her voice is heard. Whereas we would certainly recommend including older students in developing action plans, we would caution that school counselors working with younger students consider the student's developmental level when making that call.

6. What are the benefits of working with Sarah's parents when building a plan for Sarah?
    - When all parties involved in Sarah's life are on the same page, Sarah's success is more likely. Therefore, we would work with her parents to implement strategies at home, some of which are outlined in this chapter, to help Sarah practice successfully planning and organizing.
7. How would you collaborate with her teacher when building a plan for Sarah?
    - We would meet with the teacher regularly to develop an intervention-based approach tailored to Sarah's needs. We would ask the teacher to inform us of what has worked in the past and what has not. This process can eliminate repeating failed attempts and increasing success. We would check in regularly with the teacher to evaluate how the intervention is working and make changes according to what is not working. If Sarah received a formal diagnosis of ADHD, we would work with Sarah's teacher and other educators from the school to determine if an individual accommodation plan (i.e., a 504 Plan) is warranted.

Case Example Two

As you read the case about Mitch, reflect on the strategies that we discussed earlier in the chapter. The questions that follow the case relate to the student's behavioral symptoms and accompanying responses.

Mitch is a 10-year-old boy at an urban elementary school. Compared to other children Mitch's age, he appears to be less focused, distracted, and overly active. Up until about 6 months ago, Mitch's parents described him as the go-with-the-flow kid who is organized and always willing to help out, even asking for an organization system for his room for his last birthday. However, Mitch's behaviors have shifted, and his teacher is growing concerned. He is falling behind in his studies because of his inability to focus and stay on task. His school counselor recently met with his parents after they reached out because of their concern over his failing grades. They reported to the school counselor that Mitch's grandma, who lived with them since he was a baby, suddenly died. They explained that Mitch observed the paramedics attempting to revive her before taking her away in an ambulance late one night.

Case Example Two: Questions for Processing and Reflection

Directions: Use what you have learned in this chapter to respond to Mitch's case.

1. What symptoms of ADHD is Mitch showing his teacher and counselor?
2. Would you rule out any other diagnosis before making a plan? If so, what symptoms are leading you to think of something else?
3. What is your next step when working with Mitch?
4. What assessments would you select?
5. With whom within the school would you collaborate? Explain why.
6. What are the benefits of working with Mitch's parents when building a plan for Mitch?
7. How would you collaborate with his teacher when building a plan for Mitch?

Chapter Summary

This chapter focused on the signs and symptoms of ADHD in children and adolescents. The authors shared information about the prevalence of ADHD, means of appropriate diagnosis, and related diagnoses that could also be in play. Next, the authors provided strategies for school counselors to work directly with students, with parents, and with teachers. With ADHD diagnosis rates on the rise, school counselors have an imperative to provide services and programming that promote optimal development and the well-being of these students and to ensure that the school environment is safe and supportive.

Additional Recommended Readings and Resources

ADDitude Magazine: http://www.additudemag.com

Centers for Disease Control and Prevention. (n.d.). *ADHD in the classroom*. https://www.cdc.gov/ncbddd/adhd/school-success.html

Attention Deficit Disorder Association: http://www.add.org

Children and Adults with Attention-Deficit/Hyperactivity Disorder (CHADD): http://www.chadd.org

Hamblett, E.C. (2017). From high school to college: steps to success for students with disabilities. Council for Exceptional Children.

Cook, J. (2008). *It's hard to be a verb.* National Center for Youth Issues.

Cook, J. (2006). *My mouth is a volcano.* National Center for Youth Issues.

School-Based Registered Play Therapist Guide: https://cdn.ymaws.com/www.a4pt.org/resource/resmgr/Credentials/SB-RPT_Guide_Dec_2017.pdf

Taylor, J. F. (2006). *The survival guide for kids with ADHD.* Free Spirit Publishing.

Miller, K. (2018). *Thriving with ADHD workbook for kids: 60 fun activities to help children self-regulate, focus, and succeed.* Althea Press.

Understood.org (Helpful resource for parents): http://www.understood.org

Miller, C. (n.d.). *What's ADHD (and what's not) in the classroom.* Child Mind. https://childmind.org/article/whats-adhd-and-whats-not-in-the-classroom/

References

Allee-Herndon, K. A., Dillman Taylor, D., & Roberts, S. K. (2019). Putting play in its place: Presenting a continuum to decrease mental health referrals and increase purposeful play in classrooms. *International Journal of Play, 8*(2), 186–203. https://doi.org/10.1080/21594937.2019.1643993

American Psychiatric Association (APA). (2013). *Diagnostic and statistical manual of mental disorders* (5th ed.).

Association for Play Therapy (APT). (2018). *Why play therapy?* http://www.a4pt.org

Balazs, J., & Kereszteny, A. (2014). Subthreshold attention deficit hyperactivity in children and adolescents: A systematic review. *European Child & Adolescent Psychiatry, 23*, 393–408. http://doi.org/10.1007/s00787-013-0514-7

Breaux, R. P., Langberg, J. M., McLeod, B. D., Molitor, S. J., Smith, Z. R., Bourchtein, E., & Green, C. D. (2018). The importance of therapeutic processes in school-based psychosocial treatment of homework problems in adolescents with ADHD. *Journal of Consulting and Clinical Psychology, 86*(5), 427–438. http://dx.doi.org/10.1037/ccp0000300

Bussing, R., Mason, D. M., Bell, L., Porter, P., & Garvan, C. (2010). Adolescent outcomes of childhood attention-deficit/hyperactivity disorder in a diverse community sample. *Journal of the American Academy of Child and Adolescent Psychiatry, 49*(6), 595–605. http://doi.org/10.1016/j.jaac.2010.03.006

Bussing, R., Porter, P., Zima, B. T., Mason, D., Garvan, C., & Reid, R. (2012). Academic outcome trajectories of students with ADHD: Does exceptional education status matter? *Journal of Emotional and Behavioral Disorders, 20*(3), 131–143. http://doi.org/10.1177/1063426610388180

Centers for Disease Control and Prevention (CDC). (2019). *What is ADHD?* http://www.cdc.gov

Climie, E. A., & Mastoras, S. M. (2015). ADHD in schools: Adopting a strengths-based perspective. *Canadian Psychology, 56*(3), 295–300. http://dx.doi.org/10.1037/cap0000030

Danielson, M. L., Bitsko, R. H., Ghandour, R. M., Holbrook, J. R., Kogan, M. D., & Blumberg, S. J. (2018). Prevalence of parent-reported ADHD diagnosis and associated treatment among U.S. children and adolescents, 2016. *Journal of Clinical Child & Adolescent Psychology, 47*(2), 199–212. http://doi.org/10.1080/15374416.2017.1417860

Dinkmeyer, D., Jr., & Sperry, L. (2000). *Counseling and psychotherapy: An integrated, individual psychology approach* (3rd ed.). Merrill.

Express Scripts. (2014). *Turning attention to ADHD.* https://corporate-site-labs-prod.s3.us-east-2.amazonaws.com/2019-08/ADHD_March2014_ExpressScripts.pdf

Faraone, S. V., Perlis, R. H., Doyle, A. E., Smoller, J. W., Goralnick, J. J., Holmgren, M. A., & Sklar, P. (2005). Molecular genetics of attention-deficit/hyperactivity disorder. *Biological Psychiatry, 57*(11), 1313–1323. http://doi.org/10.1016/j.biopsych.2004.11.024

Getahun, D., Jacobsen, S. J., Fassett, M. J., Chen, W., Demissie, K., & Rhoads, G. G. (2013). Recent trends in childhood attention-deficit/hyperactivity disorder. *JAMA Pediatrics, 167*(3), 282–288. http://doi.org/10.1001/2013.jamapediatrics.401

Kamali, K., & Looyeh, M. Y. (2013). Narrative intervention: A school-based counseling strategy for students with attention-deficit/hyperactivity disorder. *Intervention in School and Clinic, 48*(5), 307–312. http://doi.org/10.1177/1053451212472728

Landreth, G. L., & Bratton, S. C. (2019). *Child-parent relationship therapy (CPRT): An evidence-based 10-session filial therapy model* (2nd ed.). Routledge.

Louisiana Department of Health and Hospitals (LDHH). (2015). *Response to senate concurrent resolution no. 39 of the 2014 regular session.* http://ldh.la.gov/assets/ADHD/ADHD_DHH_RspnseRsltn39.pdf

Mumbauer, J., & Kelchner, V. (2017). Promoting mental health literacy through bibliotherapy in school-based settings. *Professional School Counseling, 21*(1), 85–94. http://doi.org/10.5330/1096-2409-21.1.85

Ojiambo, D., & Bratton, S. C. (2016). Effects of group activity play therapy on problem behaviors of preadolescent Ugandan orphans. *Journal of Counseling & Development, 92*(3), 355–365. http://doi.org/10.1002/j.1556-6676.2014.00163.x

Panksepp, J. (2007). Can play diminish ADHD and facilitate the construction of the social brain? *Journal of the Canadian Academy of Child & Adolescent Psychiatry, 16*(2), 57–66.

Ray, D. (2016). *A therapist's guide to child development: The extraordinarily normal years.* Routledge.

Ros, R., & Graziano, P. A. (2018). Social functioning in children with or at risk for attention deficit/hyperactivity disorder: A meta-analytic review. *Journal of Clinical Child & Adolescent Psychology, 47*(2), 213–235. http://doi.org/10.1080/15374416.2016.1266644

Russell, G., Ford, T., Rosenberg, R., & Kelly, S. (2014). The association of attention deficit hyperactivity disorder with socioeconomic disadvantage: Alternative explanations and evidence. *Journal of Child Psychology and Psychiatry, 55*(5), 436–445. http://doi.org/10.1111/jcpp.12170

Shillingford, M. A., Lambie, G. W., & Walter, S. M. (2007). An integrative, cognitive behavioral, systemic approach to working with students diagnosed with attention deficit hyperactive disorder. *Professional School Counseling, 11*(2), 105–112.

Sparrow, E. P., & Erhardt, D. (2014). Essentials of ADHD assessment for children and adolescents. John Wiley & Sons.

Thapar, A., Cooper, M., Eyre, O., & Langley, K. (2013). What have we learnt about the causes of ADHD? *Journal of Child Psychology and Psychiatry, 54*(1), 3–16. http://doi.org/10.1111/j.1469-7610.2012.02611.x

Visser, S. N., Danielson, M. L., Bitsko, R. H., Holbrook, J. R., Kogan, M. D., Ghandour, R. M., Perou, R., & Blumberg, S. J. (2014). Trends in the parent-report of health care provider-diagnosed and medicated attention-deficit/hyperactivity disorder: United States, 2003–2011. *Journal of the American Academy of Child & Adolescent Psychiatry, 53*(1), 34–46. http://doi.org/10.1016/j.jaac.2013.09.001

Willcutt, E. G., & Bidwell, L. C. (2011). Etiology of ADHD: Implications for assessment and treatment. In B. Hoza & S. W. Evans (Eds.), *Treating attention deficit hyperactivity disorder* (pp. 6-2–6-18). Civic Research Institute.

CHAPTER FOUR

Major Depressive Disorder

M. Ann Shillingford, Tiphanie Gonzalez, and Bethany Russell

THE CASE OF JENNY Jenny is a seventh-grade student at a Title I school. She is an intelligent yet introverted student and is loved by her friends. Jenny lives with her parents and one older sister. Jenny has been sent to see the school counselor a few times by her teachers because she was overly emotional in class (crying frequently). Jenny confided in the counselor that her parents were going through a divorce and that things were really tense at home. She reported feeling down often and did not always want to come to school or hang out with her friends. This had been going on for about 1 month. During one counseling session, Jenny shared with her school counselor that she sometimes felt hopeless and that she would be better off dead. Upon completing a suicide assessment, Jenny revealed that she would overdose on painkillers that were available at home. The counselor explained to Jenny that she was concerned about her safety and needed to contact her parents. Jenny's parents reported that Jenny sometimes used Tylenol for stomachaches but would never hurt herself. In fact, her dad shared that Jenny was just looking for attention because he and her mom were separating.

Introduction to the Chapter

Students like Jenny may present as quiet, sometimes even withdrawn, and continue to perform well academically and, moderately so, socially. Jenny remained slightly below the radar for a student in distress. Depression is often underdiagnosed in youth, particularly because counselors are trained to observe for depressive symptoms in adults and not necessarily adolescents. Misdiagnosis among youth is an ongoing concern that has played a significant role in interrupting the quality of life for many young people, especially between ages 10–18. Developmentally, this is also the age when youth are expected to experience mood swings, irritation, and, sometimes, restlessness. Unfortunately, because of these expectations, depression in youth is sometimes not discovered until they have harmed themselves or others.

Learning Objectives

By the end of this chapter, readers will accomplish the following:

- Learn to identify symptoms of depression in school-aged youth.
- Understand how to create a plan when working with youth living with depression.
- Develop knowledge of the appropriate resources when collaborating with teachers, counselors, and families.

Although the median age of onset for depression is 32.5 years old, someone can be diagnosed at any age, this includes a significant number of adolescents here in the United States. Thus a professional school counselor working at any grade level is likely working with a student living with depression (National Institute of Mental Health [NIMH], 2019). This is particularly true for middle school and high school counselors. According to the NIMH (2019), "An estimated 3.2 million adolescents aged 12 to 17 in the United States had at least one major depressive episode. This number represented 13.3% of the U.S. population aged 12 to 17" (para. 7). The percentage of adolescents diagnosed with depression goes up year to year, with 4.8% of 12-year-olds living with the diagnosis to 18.5% of 17-year-olds (NIMH, 2019). When working with children living with depression, there is also an increased possibility of suicidal ideation, although how much of an increase is unclear. Kodish et al. (2016) stated that although suicide is the third leading cause of death, as reported by the Centers for Disease Control and Prevention (CDC), they also reported that 20%–60% of suicidal youth have clinical levels of depression. Mental health illness, such as depression, also accounts for an increased number of students ages 15–24 who are engaged in substance use and abuse (Fischer, 2014). School counselors must be prepared to break confidentiality in the event of imminent risk.

Signs and Symptoms of Major Depressive Disorder

Mood disorders commonly diagnosed in children and youth fall into two categories, depressive and bipolar, according to the *Diagnostic and Statistical Manual of Mental Disorders, Fifth Edition* (*DSM-5*) Depressive disorders may include major depressive disorder, persistent depressive disorder (dysthymia), and other specified and unspecified mood disorders. Bipolar disorder will be covered in Chapter 5 of this book. In this chapter, we will focus on the general symptoms of major depressive disorder. A child can be depressed and/or display depressive symptoms. Depressive symptoms may mimic a diagnosis of depression but are short term and may be caused by some externalizing factor, such as a failed test or family problems. Depression can also be seasonal, otherwise known as seasonal affective disorder (Seligman & Reichenberg, 2007). That is, the observed behaviors occur around the same time each year, generally beginning in the fall and continuing through the winter. For some individuals, it may be reversed: their symptoms are noticeable during the spring through the summer. If the child is constantly anxious or exhibits symptoms of generalized anxiety disorder (GAD), that may foster depressive episodes. We will discuss GAD in Chapter 9.

Seligman and Reichenberg (2007) distinguished symptoms into five different categories that shed light on the topic from a developmental standpoint. These five categories are explained in Table 4.1.

TABLE 4.1 Signs and Symptoms of Major Depressive Disorder

SYMPTOM	DESCRIPTION
Emotional symptoms	Anxiety, anger, hostility, irritability, agitation, social distress. This child has been having angry outbursts in class and at home. Adults have a difficult time with this student as their level of emotional arousal is quite disturbing.
Behavioral symptoms	Crying, neglect of appearance, withdrawal, dependence, lethargy, reduced activity, poor social skills, psychomotor agitation. This student cries constantly, comes to school in the same clothes multiple days per week, falls asleep in class, and is not interested in engaging with their peers in normal activities.
Attitudinal symptoms	Pessimism, helplessness, thoughts of death or suicide, low self-esteem. This student sees the glass half empty, expresses that there is no use in doing any work or just being. This student shares that their life is meaningless, and they would be better off dead.
Cognitive symptoms	Reduced concentration, indecisiveness, distorted thinking. This student has a difficult time staying on task and completing assignments. They are unable to make a decision about relatively minor issues and are constantly putting themselves down.
Physiological symptoms	Sleep disturbances, loss of appetite, gastrointestinal difficulties, muscle pains, headaches. This student's parents report that their child is very picky about their diet and wakes up during the night, unable to go back to sleep. At school, the student complains constantly about stomach pains and other ailments.

Source: Seligman and Reichenberg (2007, p. 181)

Misdiagnosis and Societal Perceptions

Let us break down these symptoms a bit more for understanding. Table 4.2 presents nine symptoms associated with depression that school counselors can observe. Keep in mind that according to the *DSM-5*, these behaviors would have occurred over at least 2 consecutive weeks, nearly every day, with at least two of the symptoms being *depressed mood* and *loss of interest*. With each symptom, we have added societal misconceptions that have sometimes clouded the judgment of adults in particular.

If we were to look at these symptoms through a qualitative lens, we would think that these students were extremely lazy, moody attention seekers. Interestingly enough, isn't that how some folks have described millennials? In fact, the cover of a 2013 edition of the *Times* magazine reads, "The Me Me Me Generation: Millennials Are Lazy, Entitled Narcissists Who Still Live With Their Parents." Another journal, Axios, highlighted millennials as *spoiled* and *lazy*. It is no wonder that students are misdiagnosed or left to fend for themselves socially and emotionally.

TABLE 4.2

SYMPTOM	MISCONCEPTION
Mood Moodiness, particularly over a period of days	The student is just being a typical moody teenager. They need to get over it.
Interest Lowered interest level, no interest in engaging in regular daily activities	That student is just being lazy or feels bored. Kids these days have too much time on their hands.
Weight Significant weight gain or loss. Increase or decrease in appetite	The student is going through a growth spurt. The kid is just being greedy.
Sleep Difficulty sleeping or sleeps too much	The student is lazy or stayed up too late watching television or playing video games.
Psychomotor activity Appears restless	The student is being a busybody. Maybe this student needs to be tested for ADHD.
Fatigue Increased fatigue	The student is good at being lazy. These kids just know how to avoid work.
Self-worth Feelings of worthlessness or inappropriate guilt	These students are looking for attention in any way they can.
Concentration Difficulty concentrating or making decisions	This student is so lazy; he cannot even think for himself.
Suicide Thoughts of suicide, with or without a plan or attempt	There goes another attention seeker. Give her time, and she will get over it.

Risk Factors and Depression

Research suggests that there are varying risk factors that may contribute to the likelihood of a child experiencing depression. Risk factors include an increase in competition among youth, loss of free play opportunities, and dysfunction in family systems.

Competition

Competition is one factor that has contributed to depression in youth and young adults. Students compete over grades, athletic performance, and even romantic relationships. Competition can foster stress to perform better and/or be perceived as better. When expectations are not met, students become discouraged, and the likelihood of developing mental health issues increases (Posselt & Lipson, 2016). Posselt and Lipson determined that increased levels of competition resulted in a positive relationship with depression. Imagine the high school or even middle school student who is embraced as the strong athlete on the school campus. The bar is set, and that student needs to excel at all costs. School counselors and teachers may observe this student practicing excessively, not completing homework, acting overwhelmed, or having high emotional reactions. This student is at a vulnerable stage and may be in danger of depressive episodes if social needs are not met.

Psychological Effects From Decrease in Opportunities for Free Play

The decline in play has been linked to the decrease in the mental health of children. Free play enhances a sense of self-control, decision making, contentment, and emotional regulation (Gray, 2011).

Over the past decades, children's opportunities to play, particularly outdoor free play, have diminished significantly. Gray attributes these changes to societal influences, such as parental fear of abduction of their children, increase in community violence, and increase in the availability of technology. Here we see that a lack of opportunities to participate in free play can have diminishing effects on children's well-being.

Family Systems

Family dysfunction is another factor that has been related to depression in children and youth (Cote et al., 2009). Cote and colleagues deduced that maternal depression, maternal low self-efficacy, and poor family interactions were significant predictors of depression in young children. Philbrook et al. (2018) compared the trajectory of adolescent adjustments with marital conflict in the home. The authors reported increased levels of internalizing behaviors (e.g., pessimism, low self-worth, helplessness) among youth 16–18 years old when higher levels of marital conflict were present in the home. Similarly, girls age 8–10 were found to display higher depressive symptoms when marital conflict was present (El-Sheikh et al., 2013).

Strategies for School Counselors

School counselors functioning within the bounds of the school community do not diagnose. However, children may sometimes come to school already diagnosed or with a new diagnosis from another professional. Regardless of whether the student is already diagnosed or is suspected of having a diagnosis of depression, school counselors have a duty to address the symptoms that affect the academic, personal/social/emotional, and career development of these students. Children with mood disorders, such as depression, are at a higher risk for suicidal ideation (Reichenberg & Seligman, 2016). Based on the increased risk, as well as additional physical and psychological effects of depression, it is critical for school counselors to provide appropriate services to these students. The interventions listed in the following sections are offered as practical strategies that can be performed with the scope of available resources and training.

Fischer (2014) discussed several useful interventions. First, *develop a therapeutic relationship*. Students diagnosed with depression are often in need of individuals who believe in them and are willing to enhance their self-worth. These students also benefit from genuine, nonjudgmental relationships with adults who are willing to accept them for who they are. Second, Fischer recommended *using positive rather than punitive approaches*. School counselors should understand that the behavioral and emotional changes experienced by children diagnosed with depression cannot always be managed, and these children do not want to experience low moods or disinterest. The reality is that sometimes the students may be doing the best they can considering their situation. Third, collaborate with other stakeholders to *provide necessary accommodations* for assignments and related tasks. Individualized educational plans and/or Section 504 plans may be adjusted as needed, including extra time to complete assignments, breaks as needed, and possibly reduced assignments.

Assessments

School counselors should be instrumental in assessing students who are in their therapeutic care. Assessments should include gathering information from both parents

The SLAP Method

Specific Plan. Here you are gathering information to determine what plan the student has made by asking questions such as the following: "Have you had thoughts of killing yourself?" "How are you planning on killing yourself?" "What are you planning on using (gun, pills, etc.)?" "When are you planning on killing yourself?" Although these are difficult questions to ask, they are necessary for the ultimate safety of the student.

Lethality. The counselor is hoping to determine how deadly the plan is. Is the student thinking about shooting themself, but they do not have access to a gun? Is there a gun at hand? Is the student planning on taking a couple of Tylenol versus a bottle of Xanax? Although each of these scenarios is important, the lethality of the plan still needs to be considered.

Availability. Does the student have access to a bottle of Xanax? Is that student able to easily get access to what they need to complete the suicide plan?

Proximity. Is the student planning to go to a location where help is easily accessible? Is the student's plan to complete suicide when his mother, who uses Xanax, is at work and no one else is home?

These are all extremely crucial points to cover with the student regardless of whether the school counselor is comfortable with the questions or not. It is also important to note that different school districts may have specific suicide assessment protocols; therefore, it would be beneficial to find out what the school protocol entails and the school counselor's role in the process.

and teachers on students' academic and psychological performance. Assessment is especially important for students who may be experiencing suicidal ideations. The school counselor is often the first and possibly the only individual who may be faced with a student during a suicidal crisis. Research has shown that it is common for school personnel to feel inadequate regarding suicide assessments and addressing children or adolescents who are at risk of suicide (Shannonhouse et al., 2017). To complete a suicide assessment, school counselors should follow the SLAP method.

Another variable that is essential to include in the assessment of students is the possibility that other factors may be at play. Does the child have a medical history of illness that may be manifesting as symptoms of depression or fostering depressive episodes? Recently, there was an adolescent who was diagnosed with mitochondrial disease. For months, she was depressed because of her constant need to sleep and her lack of energy to do things in everyday life. With time and a myriad of tests, it was found that there was a biological reason for her symptoms. Once an assessment is complete and all variables are considered, then identifying the intervention for the student is critical. It is also important to consider that depression may coexist with other mental health or medical conditions. Hence an overall holistic approach to assessing students is important to avoid misdiagnosis.

Individual Counseling

Through collaborative assessments, school counselors should determine the best mode of therapeutic services for students who need psychological help. Research suggests that cognitive behavioral therapy (CBT) is beneficial when considering efficacious individual treatment for children and adolescents experiencing depression (Weersing et al., 2017). Seligman and Reichenberg (2007) also highlighted the effectiveness of CBT with depression. In fact, a combination of CBT and medication was found to be advantageous in reducing depressive symptoms. CBT can be used in individual counseling, as well as small groups. It should be conveyed that adolescents with cognitive delays and expressive language disorders may find limited benefits to individual therapy that uses conversation as the medium to process information (Reichenberg & Seligman, 2016). When talk therapy is not developmentally appropriate, it is critical that the counselor either use a modality that is suitable or refer the student out to someone who can provide the proper mental health intervention. Although there are significant benefits to individual sessions with students, we would like to focus this chapter on other modalities, especially those centered on small counseling group sessions.

Group Counseling

Group counseling has been shown to relieve depressive symptomatology in both children and adolescents. Specifically in children, child-centered group play therapy was shown to impact depressive symptomatology significantly (Baggerly, 2004). In the case of adolescents, many studies have been conducted using different curriculum-based treatments for depression and show that in the immediacy of the group process, depressive symptoms decrease but then resurface between 3 to 12 months following the group experience. While the group process has limitations, it does decrease symptomatology. In addition, it has been shown to further support the effect of medication, specifically selective serotonin reuptake inhibitors, in reducing symptomatology of adolescents diagnosed with depression (Weersing et al., 2017). Another approach, bibliotherapy, has been noted as an effective method for addressing depression in children and youth. One book, *The Turning Hour* by Shelley Fraser, has been used by school counselors in particular to address suicide in youth. PBS provides numerous lesson plans on depression based on its TV series *In the Mix* that school counselors may find useful. The lesson plans titled "What Is Depression" and "Suicide Prevention" are both accompanied by an excellent video, *Depression: On the Edge*. The links for these videos can be found in the recommended materials list at the end of this chapter.

Other Treatment Modalities

There has been a recent surge in research related to mindfulness and yoga in the past decade. Although some researchers have reported no significant correlation between childhood depression and yoga/mindfulness in reducing depression symptomatology (Kallapiran et al., 2015; McNamara et al., 2016), others have written in support of this ancient practice. In a study published by the National Institute of Health (2010), the reports supported the benefits of mindfulness and yoga as sources of relaxation, decreased anxiety and depressive symptoms, and increased positive effects. Interestingly enough, the CDC noted the health-promoting benefits of mindfulness and relaxation techniques and their role in decreasing the symptoms of depression. Other important sources included maintaining a healthy diet, participating in physical activities, and getting the required hours of sleep. School counselors can support students experiencing the symptoms of depression by using a holistic approach to wellness (Shillingford et al., 2013). Wellness activities such as the ones listed earlier may be conducted in small groups, individual growth sessions, school-wide wellness activities, and even parental training sessions.

Strategies for Working With Caregivers

When working with parents and guardians, there are several factors that professional school counselors should be mindful of. As mentioned earlier, family dynamics, particularly dysfunctional family systems, can have a direct effect on a child's mental health. While working with children living with depression, we must pay special attention to patterns of communication, such as spoken and unspoken familial rules and body language. Despite potentially challenging family situations, family involvement is crucial to the school-home partnership (Shillingford et al., 2018). Counselors may find balancing confidentiality of the content from counseling sessions versus parents' legal right to access information (if the student is under the age of 18) to be challenging at times. Parents/guardians who are strongly engaged in their children's educational experience will want information regarding services being offered at school.

So, how can the professional school counselor balance student confidentiality and parental communication?

1. **Be Transparent.** Talk to your student's parent/guardian about the importance of confidentiality for building rapport and creating an environment in which the student feels safe to share (American School Counselor Association [ASCA], 2018).
2. **Create a Plan.** It is important to work together with both the student and parent/guardian. What will the counseling experience look like for the student? What are the rules of communication for everyone involved (ASCA, 2018)?
3. **Offer Encouragement.** Students who have active and healthy parental involvement often do better in school (ASCA, 2008, 2018).
4. **Provide Education.** Although some parents may be aware that their child has a diagnosis of depression, they may not always understand what that means or how the symptoms of depression

may be affecting their child's academic and social performance. Educating the parents/guardians about what depression is and does may serve as a stepping-stone to developing a collaborative relationship between school and home. When providing educational support to parents, school counselors may want to also consider helping parents determine the right questions to ask their child's doctor. Some parents may not know how to ask certain questions appropriately or how to express their concerns in relation to their child. Review questions/statements with the parents, such as the following: "I am really worried about my child not sleeping enough at night. Is that a side effect of his medication?" "What behavioral changes should I expect from my child over the next few days/weeks/months?"

Confidentiality

Confidentiality is another area that school counselors need to consider when consulting with parents. The ASCA standards clearly discuss the student's right to confidentiality that should not be broken unless there is an eminent and foreseeable risk. However, less clear is what this means when considering the age, development, and maturity of the youth (Smith, 2015). School counselors also need to remember to identify the legal guardian. Do not make assumptions. Even if you often see an adult with your student, they may not have the legal right to attain information, not even if they are a biological parent or grandparent.

Strategies for Working With Teachers, Parents, and Other Stakeholders

Relationships between school counselors, teachers, and administrators are important in building the village to support students in the school environment. School counselors often need to navigate these relationships while maintaining the confidentiality of the client. When working with teachers and administrators in one of their many roles performed in the school setting, it is important for the school counselor to clearly identify and understand their duties.

According to the ASCA national model, the school counselor is responsible for one-on-one counseling, group counseling, classroom guidance, and program development. So how does the counselor balance these roles?

1. **Communication.** Discuss with teachers, administrators, parents, and other stakeholders your role as a school counselor. It is appropriate to highlight any training or certificates that you have earned to enhance your skills in working with children with mental health concerns.
2. **Consultation.** Consult teachers, administrators, parents, and other stakeholders about the needs of your student. Remember, when consulting with other professionals, do so in a safe space with the door closed. According to Fischer (2014), some key areas to address during consulting are (a) what depression is and looks like, (b) if the student has officially been diagnosed by a medical professional, (c) if the student is being treated with medication and taking medication consistently, (d) any potential side effects of medication that the school needs to know about, (e) services that the school counselor can provide, and (f) boundaries of confidentiality.
3. **Collaborate.** When visiting classrooms for guidance lessons, it is important to respect the space of the teacher. This is a great opportunity to collaborate with the teacher on lesson planning. Teachers and school counselors can both deliver classroom lessons on topics such as building self-esteem, suicide and suicidal ideations, building positive friendships, and empathy for others. Additional collaborators may include the school nurse, who may be able to provide an additional safe space for the student. Furthermore, if there is an external mental health provider involved

with the student's care, collaborating with this professional to discuss symptoms and treatment planning is appropriate to coordinate consistent services at school and in private sessions. In addition, school counselors and school nurses may seek parental permission to communicate with the student's physician regarding symptomatology and medication control. These collaborative efforts may prove to be an important step in building a strong plan for the student at school and at home.

4. **Education.** School counselors can play a role in educating teachers and other stakeholders about the signs of depression. As indicated earlier in this chapter, adults often make assumptions related to students' behaviors. Education related to the affective, academic, and behavioral effects of depression may elevate teachers' awareness and support of students who are experiencing depressive symptoms. School counselors can provide educational resources for teachers, administrators, parents, and other stakeholders through professional development workshops, parent consultations and training sessions, grade-level meetings, and the school counseling website or newsletter.
5. **Advocate.** School counselors can serve as advocates for students. Advocacy includes speaking up for the rights of students, particularly when injustice or unfairness exist. Depression can manifest in many ways. At times, students may not be able to fulfill classroom requirements and assignments. Students may need to miss several days of school, whereby attendance becomes a concern. For example, a student who is experiencing moderate to severe physiological and emotional effects, such as fatigue, may not be able to complete a required test or quiz in the time allotted by the teacher. The school counselor can serve as an advocate for special services to support the student.

Understanding What You Have Read: Comprehension Questions

Directions: Refer to what you learned in this chapter to answer the following questions.

1. What is depression?
2. What are the determining factors for a diagnosis of depression?
3. What modalities of support can school counselors extend to students?
4. How might you as a future counselor support a student who has experienced depressive episodes during your clinical sessions?
5. How might your personal experiences affect your ability to support students like Jenny who was presented in the case vignette?
6. What are ethical and multicultural considerations when working with a student with depression?

Case Examples

Case Example One

As you read the case about Danny, reflect on the strategies that we discussed earlier in the chapter. The questions that follow the case relate to the student's behavioral symptoms and accompanying responses.

Danny is a 15-year-old student in the seventh grade at an urban school. In elementary school, Danny was an easygoing student who was loved by many friends and teachers. In his first 9 weeks of middle school, Danny was brought to the administrative office for fighting with another student. The student expressed that he was only trying to get Danny's attention by tapping him on the shoulder, and Danny pounced on him. Upon consultation with Danny's guardians, they reported that he had been very irritable at home and had gotten into disagreements with his siblings daily for the past 2 months. Danny had been sleeping more than usual and did not want to go to his football games where he served as the team's quarterback. His parents reported that Danny does not have any health conditions. Danny met with the school counselor and expressed that he did not care about the future and didn't care if he got in trouble. Danny did not admit to having suicidal thoughts but expressed that he was worthless to others and did not want to speak about the future.

Case Example One: Questions for Processing and Reflection

Directions: Use what you have learned in this chapter to respond to Danny's case.

1. What symptoms are being displayed by Danny that *might* indicate that he may be experiencing depression?
   a. Danny has lost interest in activities that he once loved (football).
   b. Danny's mood has changed. He is more irritable and has a sense of worthlessness.
   c. Danny is sleeping more often than usual.
   d. Danny has recurring thoughts of helplessness (although no suicidal thoughts).
   e. Danny has been experiencing these symptoms for more than 2 weeks.
2. What information do you have regarding Danny's situation?
   a. He does not have any known medical conditions that could account for his behavior.
   b. His parents are aware of his negative behavior and are concerned.
   c. Danny has a strong sense of helplessness and a lack of interest in the future.
   d. A suicide assessment (SLAP).
   e. Descriptions of behavioral and academic changes from teachers.
   f. Date Danny was last seen by his physician
3. How would you address concerns related to Danny?
   a. Individual sessions to extend support in a safe and nonjudgmental format.
   b. Parent consultation to discuss what external supports are available (e.g., mental health counseling services).
   c. Interdisciplinary team meeting to determine the best course of action to support Danny.
   d. Small counseling group support (if applicable).

Case Example Two

As you read the case about Emily, reflect on the strategies that we discussed earlier in the chapter. The questions that follow the case relate to the student's behavioral symptoms and accompanying responses.

Emily is a 9-year-old girl in the fourth grade. She is from a small rural town, and there are only 45 other children in her fourth-grade class. You have noticed that Emily has started to withdraw from her friends, and the normally chatty and bubbly child has become quiet; in fact, you rarely see her speak at all. While working lunch duty, you take the opportunity to sit with Emily, who has separated herself from her peers. You try and start a conversation, but she ignores you. After lunch, you speak with her teacher, who is also concerned. He tells you that Emily has not only stopped talking, but she doesn't show interest in activities that she used to enjoy, and she doesn't eat lunch every day. She simply shrugs and will say she isn't hungry. He has also noticed a major difference in her body language. She walks with her head down and shoulders slumped; when at her desk, Emily lays her head on the table but never falls asleep. He has called her home, but her parents never answer his calls. He is at a loss as to what to do and asks you for advice about the next steps. What do you tell him?

Case Example Two: Questions for Processing and Reflection

Directions: Use what you have learned in this chapter to respond to Emily's case.

1. What symptoms of depression is Emily showing her teacher and counselor?
2. What is your next step when working with Emily?
3. Would you use the SLAP plan in your assessment? What would these steps entail?
4. With whom within the school would you collaborate? Explain why.
5. What are the benefits to working with Emily's parents when building a plan for Emily?
6. How would you collaborate with her teacher when building a plan for Emily?

Chapter Summary

This chapter focused on symptoms and behaviors related to depression in children and youth. The authors presented relatable descriptors of the varying behaviors that may be observed in a child who either has been diagnosed with depression or may be experiencing depressive episodes. Strategies have been provided for school counselors on best practices in first understanding this diagnosis and then supporting students through collaborative strategies with teachers, parents, and other stakeholders. Depression is harmful to the overall well-being of children and youth. If left untreated, it may lead to self-harm and/or suicide. School counselors, while functioning within the bounds of their unique roles, are qualified to provide systematic services to students dealing with depression.

Additional Recommended Readings and Resources

"What Is Depression?": http://www.pbs.org/inthemix/educators/lessons/depression1/

"Suicide Prevention": http://www.pbs.org/inthemix/educators/lessons/depression2/

Suicide Prevention Hotline: 800-273-8255

Gillihan, S. J. (2018). *Cognitive behavior therapy made simple: 10 strategies for managing anxiety, depression, anger, panic, and worry.* Althea Press

Phifer, L., Crowder, A., Elsenraat, T., & Hull, R. (2017). *CBT toolbox for children and adolescents.* PESI Publishing & Media.

Pipher, M., & Gilliam, S. (2019). *Reviving Ophelia* (anniversary. ed.). Riverhead Books.

Serani, D. (2015). *Depression and your child: A guide for parents and caregivers.* Rowman & Littlefield Pub.

References

American School Counselor Association (ASCA). (2018). *The school counselor and confidentiality.* https://www.schoolcounselor.org/asca/media/asca/PositionStatements/PS_Confidentiality.pdf

Baggerly, J. (2004). The effects of child-centered group play therapy on self-concept, depression, and anxiety of children who are homeless. *International Journal of Play Therapy, 13*(2), 31.

Cote, S. M., Boivin, M., Liu, X., Nagin, D. S., Zoccolillo, M., & Tremblay, R. E. (2009) Depression and anxiety symptoms: Onset, developmental course and risk factors during early childhood. *Journal of Analytic Psychology, 50*(10), 1201–1208

El-Sheikh, M., Hinnant, J. B., Erath, S., & Dyer, W. (2013). Marital conflict and growth in children's internalizing symptoms: The role of autonomic nervous system activity. *Developmental Psychology, 49*, 92–108. https://doi.org/10.1037/a0027703

Fischer, M. (2014). Students with depression. Help them find their way. *ASCA School Counselor*. http://www.schoolcounselor.org/asca/media/asca/ASCAU/M

Gray, P. (2011). The decline of play and the rise of psychopathology in children and adolescents. *American Journal of Play, 3*, 443–463.

Kallapiran, K., Koo, S., Kirubakaran, R., & Hancock, K. (2015). Effectiveness of mindfulness in improving mental health symptoms of children and adolescents: A meta analysis. *Child and Adolescent Mental Health, 20*(4), 182–194. https://doi.org/10.1111/camh.12113

Kodish, T., Herres, J., Shearer, A., Atte, T., Fein, J., & Diamond, G. (2016). Bullying, depression, and suicide risk in a pediatric primary care sample. *Crisis, 37*(3), 241–246.

McNamara, C., Johnson, M., Read, L., Vander Velden, H., Thygeson, M., Liu, M., & McNamara, J. (2016). Yoga therapy in children with cystic fibrosis decreases immediate anxiety and joint pain. *Evidence-Based Complementary and Alternative Medicine, 2016*. https://doi.org/10.1155/2016/9429504

National Institute of Health (2010). *Yoga as a complementary therapy for children and adolescents: A guide for clinicians*. https://www.ncbi.nlm.nih.gov/pmc/articles/PMC2945853/

National Institute of Mental Health. (2019). *Depression*. https://www.nimh.nih.gov/health/statistics/major-depression.shtml

Philbrook, L. E., Erath, S. A., Hinnant, J. B., & El-Sheikh, M. (2018). Marital conflict and trajectories of adolescent adjustment: The role of autonomic nervous system coordination. *Developmental Psychology, 54*(9), 1687–1696.

Posselt, J. R., & Lipson, S. K. (2016). Competition, anxiety, and depression in the college classroom: Variations of student identity and field of study. *Journal of College Student Development, 57*, 973–989.

Reichenberg, L. W., & Seligman, L. (2016). *Selecting effective treatments: A comprehensive, systematic guide to treating mental disorders*. Wiley.

Seligman, L., & Reichenberg, L. W. (2007). *Selecting effective treatments: A comprehensive, systematic guide to treating mental disorders*. Jossey-Bass.

Shannonhouse, L., Lin, Y. W. D., Shaw, K., & Porter, M. (2017). Suicide intervention training for K–12 schools: A quasi experimental study on ASIST. *Journal of Counseling & Development, 95*(1), 3–13. http://doi.org/10.1002/jcad.12112

Shillingford, M. A., Oh, Seungbin, &, Finnell, L. (2018). Perceptions of parents of color towards STEM professions: A school counselor leadership engagement. *Professional School Counseling, 21*, https://doi.org/10.1177/2156759X18773599

Shillingford, M. A., Trice-Black, S., & Butler, S. K. (2013). Wellness of minority female counselor educators. *Counselor Education & Supervision Journal, 52*, 256–269.

Smith, L. J. (2015). Minors' right to confidentiality: Addressing the issue of bullying and the ethical obligation to prevent harm. *Journal of Human Behavior in the Social Environment, 25*(7), 746–755.

Weersing, V. R., Jeffreys, M., Do, M. C. T., Schwartz, K. T., & Bolano, C. (2017). Evidence base update of psychosocial treatments for child and adolescent depression. *Journal of Clinical Child & Adolescent Psychology, 46*(1), 11–43. https://doi.org/10.1080/15374416.2016.1220310

CHAPTER FIVE

Bipolar Disorder

Erika Cameron, Lauren Flynn, and Matt Dahlman

THE CASE OF JOSHUA Joshua is a sixth-grade student who has been sent to the counselor by his teachers periodically throughout the school year as a result of increased disruptive classroom behaviors. His teachers noticed a decline in his academic performance and a shift in his behaviors from previous school years. His disruptive behaviors began about 3 months ago when he started to occasionally display high levels of energy, talkativeness, irritability, and an inability to focus in class for periods of several days at a time. Joshua explained to his counselor that during these periods of time, he often has so much energy that he does not sleep at night. Prior to the start of these behaviors, he identified experiencing multiple weeks of constant tiredness and unhappiness before he "suddenly" started to feel better again.

Introduction to the Chapter

Approximately one million American children and teenagers struggle with bipolar disorder (BD), most of them undiagnosed and untreated (Merikangas et al., 2010). BD is typically diagnosed after the age of 16, but research is finding that an increasing number of children are meeting criteria for BD at an earlier age and are being misdiagnosed with anxiety, attention deficit hyperactivity disorder (ADHD), oppositional defiant disorder, and depression, meaning children are not getting the support they need for their diagnosis. Children with BD are at higher risk for school failure, substance abuse, and suicide (Goldstein, 2009). Yet children who are stable and have the right support can thrive in school and develop satisfying peer relationships. It will be the school counselor's role to both identify the signs and symptoms of BD across developmental stages to refer students to appropriate medical professionals for diagnosis and to treat students with BD to support them in the many areas of their lives affected by the disorder. It is also imperative for the school counselor to ensure that the students are receiving the support they need rather than being punished in school for behaviors connected to their disorder.

Because of the potential risks associated with BD, it is important that school counselors be knowledgeable of the range of symptoms and how they may present differently in their students. In the case of Joshua, his declined classroom performance, the periodic nature of his behavior changes and sleep patterns, and his reference to a previous depressive episode all indicate a possible diagnosis of BD and warrant referral to a medical professional for assessment.

Learning Objectives

By the end of this chapter, readers will accomplish the following:

- Understand the symptoms of BD and bipolar spectrum disorders among children and adolescents.
- Describe the risk factors and psychological effects of pediatric BD.
- Learn strategies and interventions for supporting students diagnosed with BD.

Overview of BD and Bipolar Spectrum Disorders

Signs and symptoms of BD, while most commonly diagnosed in adults, often start in adolescent years and can become apparent in as early as elementary school aged children. Pediatric bipolar disorder (PBD) is currently diagnosed using the fifth edition of the *Diagnostic and Statistical Manual of Mental Disorders* (*DSM-5*; American Psychiatric Association, 2013). PBD presents differently in children and adolescents than adults. The cycles are shorter and less defined; there is prominent irritability and higher rates of comorbidity (e.g., ADHD and Oppositional Defiance Disorder) (West & Weinstein, 2017.) The likelihood of BD increases as children grow older. The reported rate of youth diagnosed with bipolar disorder I (BD I and bipolar spectrum disorders) is 1.8% globally (Van Meter et al., 2011). For adults who have been diagnosed with BD, 10% reported symptoms before age 10, and 60% reported having symptoms before age 20 (Diler, 2007; Kozloff et al., 2010; Perlis et al., 2009).

TABLE 5.1 Four Basic Subtypes of BD

SUBTYPE	DESCRIPTION	EXAMPLE
BD-I	Meets the full criteria for a manic episode and commonly has met full criteria for a major depressive disorder. In addition, the symptoms of mania and depression can be co-occurring.	Having episodes of mania that last at least 7 days or with symptoms of mania severe enough for hospitalization. Oftentimes, there are depressive episodes lasting at least 2 weeks.
BD-II	Full criteria have been met for past/present major depressive disorder and past/present hypomania episodes.	The hypomanic episodes should be at least 4 consecutive days. Hypomania symptoms are similar to mania but are not as severe and would not require hospitalization.
Cyclothymic Disorder	History of at least 1 year (2 years in adults) of numerous periods of hypomanic symptoms and numerous periods of depressive symptoms that do not meet the full criteria for major depressive disorder or mania.	Continuous episodes of depression and mania for at least 1 year in adolescents and children.
BD-NOS	History of significant symptoms of mania and depression that do not meet intensity, duration, or frequency thresholds for a full mood episode by *DSM-5* criteria.	Shorter episodes of hypomania, 4 days consecutively and 4 hours or less in length.

With the increasing prevalence of BD in children, there is a coinciding increase in the need to recognize and understand it to help these children succeed. Children diagnosed with BD have higher rates of morbidity and mortality and are at a greater risk for suicide (Diler & Birmaher, 2019). According to the National Institute of Mental Health (2016), BD, as defined by the *DSM-5*, has four basic different subtypes (Table 5.1): BD-I, BD-II, cyclothymic disorder, bipolar disorder not otherwise specified (BD-NOS).

Children who have BD-I or BD spectrum disorders have an increased risk of comorbidity with ADHD, anxiety disorders, and disruptive behavior disorders. Thus it is imperative that professional school counselors recognize the signs and symptoms of BD as early as possible to be instrumental in the success of children living with BD. BD is a chronic lifetime condition that can be managed, but not cured, with medication and lifestyle changes. With early intervention in cases like Joshua's, he would be able to receive support specific to his needs to manage his symptoms and improve his functioning in school and at home.

Signs and Symptoms of BD and BD Spectrum Disorder

BD often involves both manic and depressive episodes where each subtype includes changes in mood and activity levels (NIMH, 2016). Manic episodes are defined by the *DSM-5* as "a distinct period of abnormally and persistently elevated, expansive, or irritable mood and abnormally and persistently increased activity or energy level lasting at least 7 consecutive days and present most of the day, nearly every day" (Diler & Birmaher, 2019, p. 3). Table 5.2 describes symptoms of manic and depressive episodes that can occur in children experiencing BD-I and BD spectrum disorders.

Misdiagnosis

BD is frequently misdiagnosed in children because the symptoms associated with this disorder can be difficult to differentiate from age-appropriate behavior in youth. Symptoms of manic episodes, including elation, grandiosity, and increased goal activity, are often difficult to identify within a child's developmental stage because they are frequently associated with normative youth behavior (Birmaher, 2013). For example, without proper insight, Joshua's manic symptoms may be discounted

TABLE 5.2 Signs and Symptoms of a Manic/Depressive Episode

SIGNS AND SYMPTOMS OF CHILDREN/ ADOLESCENTS EXPERIENCING A MANIC EPISODE	SIGNS AND SYMPTOMS OF CHILDREN/ ADOLESCENTS EXPERIENCING A DEPRESSIVE EPISODE
• Acting inappropriately for their developmental age • Inability to focus • Increased energy levels • Acting irritable or angry • Inability to sleep • Having racing thoughts and speech patterns • Having feelings of grandiose thinking and behavior • Engaging in risky behavior	• Decreased energy levels • Inability to focus • Changes in sleep patterns: not enough or too much • Feeling fatigued • Displaying a lack of motivation • Changes in appetite and eating habits • Feeling sad, down, or hopeless • Thoughts of suicide or self-harm

as the normal behavior of a highly energetic child his age. For this reason, it is important for professional school counselors to have a thorough understanding of the normative behavioral and cognitive development, as well as cultural norms, of the students they are working with. A working knowledge of a student's stage of development will assist the professional school counselor in deciphering whether a behavior is normative or pathological.

An additional obstacle to diagnosing BD accurately is the broad range of possible symptom presentations. Youth with BD can exhibit both externalizing and internalizing symptoms, making for a variety of psychopathology that can be easily mistaken for other disorders (Diler & Birmaher, 2019). BD is most commonly misdiagnosed as disruptive behavior disorder and ADHD because of the presence of chronic irritability and behavior problems (Diler & Birmaher, 2019). In considering the overlap of Joshua's symptomatology with ADHD and understanding that youth-aged males are the most frequently diagnosed with ADHD, Joshua's behaviors could be misconstrued and misdiagnosed by the untrained eye (Holland et al., 2017).

In addition, the increased sense of grandiosity that is characteristic of manic episodes is common in children with oppositional defiant disorder (Birmaher, 2013). Children initially exhibiting signs of BD may be misdiagnosed with a form of psychosis, such as schizophrenia, because their first episode of mania may present with hallucinations and thought disorders (Diler & Birmaher, 2019). Although BD can persist with or without depressive episodes, the depressive episodes are also difficult to identify because children and adolescents exhibit these symptoms differently.

Psychological Effects

Childhood experiences of trauma and abuse have been commonly reported among adults with BD (NIMH, 2016). Although traumatic and stressful events can trigger an episode of BD, episodes can occur without a clear direct cause. The lack of control over their episodes, moods, and behaviors can cause children severe distress. In addition, the social stigmatization associated with a mental health diagnosis can be especially troublesome for those diagnosed with BD. One reason is that the term "bipolar" has been frequently misused in conversation to refer to anyone with fluctuating moods or anything behaving unpredictably. This misuse of the term negatively normalizes the diagnosis, resulting in the belittling and simplifying of the individual's experience of BD. Furthermore, although BD can be properly managed through medications, it is a lifelong diagnosis that the child will grow to live with. The child's perceived lack of immediate control over their symptoms and lack of long-term control over their diagnosis, in addition to social stigmatization, can have a negative effect on their psychological health, self-concept, and self-esteem.

Risk Factors

BD is referred to as a biosocial disorder because it is a result of a combination of biological and social factors.

Biological Factors

Children with BD have a biological vulnerability that predisposes them to developing the disorder. This vulnerability includes a temperament that is emotionally reactive and lacks emotional control, making the child easily triggered and difficult to return to their emotional baseline (Diler & Birmaher, 2019). Children who have an immediate family member with BD, such as a parent or sibling, are more likely to develop the disorder. In addition, youth who present symptoms that do not quite meet the criteria for a diagnosis are at higher risk of developing BD-I and BD-II (Birmaher, 2013).

Research also suggests that individuals with BD can have structural and functional changes in the areas of the brain that control emotional regulation and impulse control (NIMH, 2016). It is unclear if these changes are risk factors for BD or caused by the disorder. The cognitive and behavioral effects of these changes can negatively influence a student's classroom behavior and academic performance. The structural and functional differences in the brains of children with BD manifest in symptoms commonly associated with ADHD.

Using brain imaging, Deng and associates (2019) found that BD affects cognition in a number of ways. Children were found to have trouble paying attention, remembering and recalling information, being able to think critically, and organizing information, as well as lacking problem-solving skills. In addition to the cognitive deficits, children are also reported to be impulsive, talkative, distractible, withdrawn, unmotivated, and/or difficult to engage. Even if a child is taking medication for their BD, the side effects of medications can affect the student's learning and energy. For example, some of the side effects include sleepiness, slurred speech, memory loss, nausea, and excessive thirst. It is important that professional school counselors work with a well-coordinated student support team composed of parents, teachers, special education specialists, school social workers, school psychologists, occupational therapists, speech therapists, school nurses, and building administrators to provide the right support and accommodations.

Social Factors

The primary social factor for developing BD for a child is being raised in an invalidating environment. If a child does not grow up in an environment that validates the intense emotions they experience, they do not learn to regulate their emotions effectively (Diler & Birmaher, 2019). Rather, they develop unhealthy ways of coping with their feelings. Children who are unable to regulate their emotions lack the ability to recognize, monitor, and adapt their emotions appropriately according to a situation. An inability to regulate emotions can affect youth in a variety of ways, including negatively affecting their family and peer relationships, as well as their academic success (Li, 2019). The effect on the family may be observable through strained parent-child relationships as a result of frequent tantrums and emotional outbursts. A student with BD may demonstrate increased anxiety, anger, aggression, and withdrawn behaviors that can interfere with their peer relationships, making it harder for the student to develop and maintain friendships. In addition, a student's inability to regulate their emotions may be predictive of poor academic performance as a consequence of their diminished ability to mediate anxiety and focus through academic tasks and evaluations (Li, 2019). In working with Joshua, it would be important to explore not only his change in academic performance and classroom behavior but also the effect of his mood changes and disruptive behaviors on his family and peer relationships.

Strategies for School Counselors

According to the American School Counseling Association (ASCA), the essential roles of a professional school counselor are counseling, educating and advocating, consulting, and leading and coordinating. The primary responsibility of the school counselor is to "support the development and implementation of school counseling programs based upon the identified needs of the students in the individual school building, district or state" (ASCA, 2019, p.1). To achieve this goal, Dollarhide and Saginak (2017) developed the domains/activities/partners (DAP) model, which outlines how professional school counselors can intentionally collaborate with students, parents/caregivers, school colleagues, community colleagues, and other stakeholders in a comprehensive school counseling program. Students with BD have unique needs and struggles, and they will require additional school supports throughout their education. In Table 5.3, you will find that we applied the DAP model to examples of how a school counselor can provide a comprehensive counseling program for a student diagnosed with BD.

TABLE 5.3 DAP Model Applied to a Student With BD

		DOMAINS				
		ACADEMIC DEVELOPMENT	**CAREER DEVELOPMENT**	**PERSONAL/ SOCIAL DEVELOPMENT**		
PROFESSIONAL SCHOOL COUNSELORS'ROLE	**Counseling**	Academic counseling with student	Career counseling with student	Personal/social counseling with student	Counseling parent/caregiver about their child's BD diagnosis as appropriate and then referral	Counseling teachers who may be struggling or frustrated by a student with BD and then referral
	Educating and Advocating	Educating students about how BD can affect their academic performance. Teach them coping strategies	Educating students about careers that may match their mental health needs	Education students about personal/social issues that can occur as a result of living with BD	Educating parents and caregivers about BD and advocating on behalf of students and the school	Educating colleagues in the school about BD and strategies to help students to feel included and supported
	Consulting	Consulting with students about academic issues (i.e., how to manage their moods to be able to focus while taking a test)	Consulting with students about career issues (i.e., how to talk to a boss about BD and accommodations needed at work)	Consulting with students about personal/social issues (i.e., how to get along better with family members)	Consulting with parents and caregivers about students with BD (e.g., academics, behavior, social connection, medications, moods)	Consulting with colleagues in the school to help provide accommodations to students with BD (e.g., extra time on tests, periodic breaks, schedule changes, routines)
	Leading and Coordinating	Leading and coordinating academic events for students who may be struggling with a mood disorder	Leading and coordinating career activities for students with BD (i.e., job shadowing a mentor who has BD)	Leading and coordinating personal/social activities for students with BD (i.e., serving as an advisor of a student group that may engage these students)	Leadership in making the school a respectful place for parents and coordinating activities for parents (i.e., parent support group on supporting a child with a mood disorder)	Leadership in making the school a respectful place for colleagues and coordinating activities for colleagues in the school (i.e., teacher support group on teaching students with mood disorders)
		Student			**Parents and Caregivers**	**Colleagues in School**
					PARTNERS IN THE PROCESS	

Assessments and Identification

While diagnosing and assessing for BD is not within the scope of responsibilities for a school counselor, it is important for school counselors to be able to recognize the symptoms of BD mentioned earlier in the chapter to be able to intervene in a student's life proactively, provide support for the student at school, and help parents to locate community resources (e.g., medical professionals, mental health professionals, and support groups for students and parents/guardians).

Counseling

Students with BD face tough challenges navigating the many pressures of a typical school day. Their neurologically based mood disorder affects emotion, behavior, cognitive skills, and social interactions. Bipolar students can easily be overwhelmed and oftentimes have a lower tolerance to manage stress. To help them reduce exposure and build their coping skills, school counselors can provide therapeutic support in individual counseling sessions using cognitive behavioral therapy (CBT). CBT has been found to help a student with BD "self-monitor mood state, recognize and label feelings, and develop coping skills to manage expansive, negative, and irritable moods" (West & Weinstein, 2017, p. 103)

To further support students with BD, school counselors can coordinate resources, adjust class schedules, and work with teachers to provide a supportive and flexible environment to help students with bipolar stay in control when any difficulties arise. The most important factor to ensuring students' success is the ways adults at school respond to and work with students. A school counselor who is resourceful, caring, and calm and knows how to work positively with students' shifting moods and cognitive weaknesses would be able to support students diagnosed with BD more effectively. For example, when a student with BD is having an episode, the school counselor can use praise, encouragement, and key words to elicit positive behaviors. In addition, the school counselor's office can be a safe space to help the student direct energy productively with hands-on projects and increased activity.

In the following section, the emphasis will be on strategies and interventions for prevention and interventions that have proven to be efficacious in school for the concerns commonly associated with BD in children and adolescents. Many of the strategies can be directly used in individual sessions. In addition, some of the strategies could be used by a classroom teacher and supported by the school counselor or are preventative plans that are put in place to support the student in school.

Social Stories

Similar to children with other neurologically based disorders (i.e., autism spectrum disorder (ASD), ADHD), students with BD have difficulty in social situations and often have trouble behaving appropriately in school. When given some sort of structure or script, however, they are far more successful. Social stories, which have been used by children with ASD, prepare the child in advance for a given situation so that they can respond appropriately when that situation occurs. Social stories can be simple, such as talking through and role-playing how to perceive various situations. The story can be a jumping-off point for discussing "what if" scenarios so that the student has a chance to practice appropriate reactions for different outcomes. School counselors can involve the student in creating the story, either by coming up with what the child might say or by illustrating it.

Tension Feedback Scale

The escalation into rage when a student is in an episode is preventable in the dysphoric phase. Dysphoria is when the student is having a serious depressive episode accompanied by a manic psychosis. School counselors may use the following strategies to reverse the dysphoria so that the student

TABLE 5.4 Tension Feedback Scale

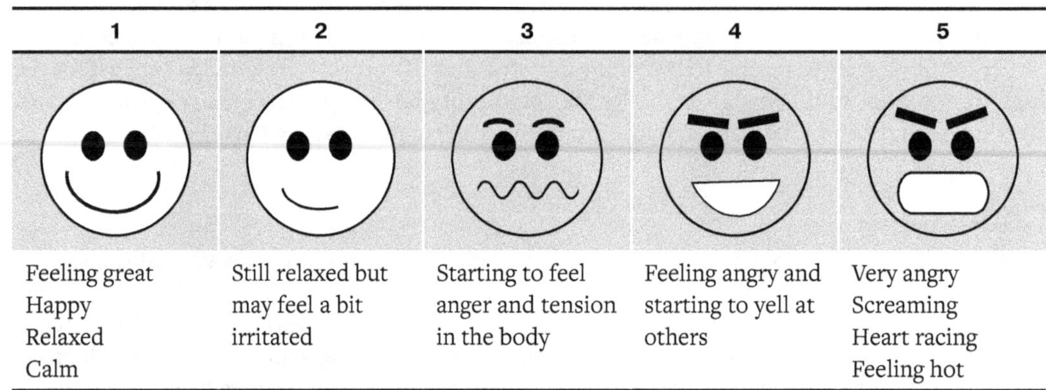

1	2	3	4	5
Feeling great Happy Relaxed Calm	Still relaxed but may feel a bit irritated	Starting to feel anger and tension in the body	Feeling angry and starting to yell at others	Very angry Screaming Heart racing Feeling hot

can experience a sense of relaxed, pleasant focus and a happy state of mind. In school, counselors must have a way to communicate with the child about the buildup of dysphoria and rage. The first step is to agree on a scale to measure buildup when the student is in a problem-solving mood. A tension feedback scale (refer to Table 5.4) is designed to communicate with the student about the buildup of tension.

School counselors discuss with the student examples of the rage-related behavior that occurs at each point on the scale. For young children, it is recommended to use a color range. For example, white means calm, yellow means heating to rage, orange means rage at the early onset stage, red means fully enraged. A tension feedback scale can be a vehicle for students to stay more aware of their own experiences and be able to enhance their ability to regulate their emotions and the response to those emotions.

Redirection and Stress Reduction

To prevent a bipolar-related rage, school counselors could plan preventative supports that help to redirect the student's focus and energy while also reducing the stress that is triggering the episode. Focusing on redirection gives the student time to de-escalate and meets their need for stimulation in a positive, nondestructive way. To start, the student needs to be separated from the stressful social situation. A school counselor can ask the teacher to pay attention to when they see the student warming up. For instance, the teacher may see the student beginning to get into a disagreement with a classmate. The teacher can intervene and suggest separate activities. If possible, the teacher can negotiate a resolution to the issue without being too obtrusive. Next, the student needs to be distracted toward a positive, enjoyable pastime involving exercise or physical movement. Exercise is an important way to discharge stress and the muscular dysphoria that contributes to rage. The teacher can send the student to the school counselor for an "energy break." Some suggested activities include running or walking around the school track, playing basketball in the gym, and jumping on a mini trampoline, to name a few. Lastly, the school counselor can invite the student to have a snack or a drink of water to aid the body's detoxification of the buildup of toxins, which is positively correlated with depression and dysphoric mood.

Have a Response Plan

At school, the rage of a student with bipolar may come out of nowhere (unpredictable). As a school counselor, you may not be able to always implement preventative measures. It is a good idea to have a response planned ahead of time to keep all students and staff safe. It is important to enforce the rules of the school that are most necessary in the moment and negotiate the rest. When rage erupts at school, there should be a clear plan outlined that indicates which adult will be in charge of the situation and who will be a backup. For example, the principal could be in charge and the school counselor can be a backup. The adult in charge is key to getting the student to move to a safe location and helping the student calm down. The backup would be used as a mediator and second set of eyes and hands to help support both the adult and student through the process.

Reflection

To help a student learn from their experience, school counselors can reflect statements they might make about their feelings concerning the event. Use these questions to frame that discussion: What behavior did they believe were problematic? What was their concern or need? What set things off? What could we all do if this situation comes up again? This is an opportunity for reflection and to help the student to make corrective changes so that they have more control of their behavior in the future.

Neuro-linguistic Programming Therapy

Neuro-linguistic programming (NLP) therapy uses language- and sensory-based interventions and behavior modification techniques to help improve the student's self-awareness, communication skills, and social actions. NLP helps the student to understand that the way they view the world affects how they operate in the world. In addition, it gives the student the opportunity to change the thoughts and behavior patterns that have not proven beneficial in the past. For example, when a student with bipolar becomes enraged, their thought processes speed up and assume the fight-or-flight mode. They stop thinking rationally and start seeing everyone around them as enemies. For a student to interrupt the process and calm down, they need to be able to have greater control over their thought processes. Using NLP can help students to change self-defeating inner dialogue and imagery.

To begin, the school counselor would teach NLP to the student during a period of mood stability, when they are feeling confident enough to learn new skills to deal with their self-defeating behavior and/or rage. The school counselor would start by asking the student to remember a time when they had a bad rage attack. Once they have brought the scene to mind, the school counselor would have them describe the incident in detail and the feelings they experienced. When the student has finished, the school counselor would ask the following questions:

1. Do you see yourself in color or black and white?
2. If there are other people in the image, are they bigger or smaller?
3. If you can describe your feelings as a color that surrounds the image in your mind, what color would you give these feelings?
4. Where in your internal imagery do you see the image? If you were to look at the memory as a picture floating above a flat landscape in your mind, is the picture of yourself right or left or in the middle? Is it high or low on the horizon?

When the student has done this, ask them to set the image in place to the left in their mind. Next, the school counselor will ask the student to recall another incident. But this time, the student will describe a time when they were to the point of rage but were able to hold their temper. Using the same questions noted above, ask the student to describe the incident. When they have done this, ask them to set that image to the right in their head. Finally, ask the student to imagine a bridge between this image and that of their rage incident. Ask the student to transport all the details from the image in which they behaved successfully over the bridge to the image in which they were enraged. As each detail is transferred across the bridge, ask the student to begin to gradually change the rage image to look like the positive image. Give the student a brief opportunity to quietly focus on the positive image. Once the student has completed the image transfer, ask them to take the negative image and begin making it smaller and dimmer. When they have done this, they should see the positive image vividly. Ask the student to focus on the positive image. To debrief, remind students that they can remember this positive image when they are feeling themselves going into a rage. They can use the intervention to calm and control themselves.

Consultation, Collaboration, and Advocacy

School counselors are in a prime position to collaborate with school and community stakeholders to both prevent and respond to the challenges experienced and exhibited by students with BD. As outlined in the DAP model (Dollarhide & Sagniak, 2017), a school counselor needs to collaborate with partners in the process effectively. To do so, school counselors need to engage in consultation, collaboration, and advocacy to support students diagnosed with BD effectively.

When a student is stable, the team needs to build the student's skills that lead to appropriate reactions and behavior, including emotion labeling, empathy, anger management, social rules, nonverbal communication, and making amends. Those who work with students diagnosed with BD need training in nonviolent crisis prevention, focusing on verbal de-escalation techniques to avoid crises. In addition, they need to reward positive behavior with praise and privileges. It is important to make sure that programs reward students for positive behavior; punishing negative behaviors sets the student up for failure and thus raises the student's stress, which could result in an episode. Punishing a student with BD for a fit of anger is much like punishing an asthmatic student for having an asthma attack.

Collaborating With Parents

It is critical to work closely with the child's family to understand the symptoms and course of the illness. Parents should identify patterns in behavior that could signal a change in the illness and help school staff brainstorm better ways of handling specific situations. Teachers and school personnel also need to know about changes in the child's home life or medication to work around them constructively at school. Good communication between home and school is essential. Contact should be frequent, timely, and focused on facts and solving problems (rather than blame). The school needs to inform parents regularly about how the student is performing. This can be done via a notebook that goes back and forth to school with the child or a daily chart or email that records successes, progress, difficulties, and mood information. Parents can then reinforce and support the teacher and the child. Parents can also spot trends in the child's illness and respond before problems reach a crisis. They should inform teachers of any unusual stressors at home and changes in medication. One of the challenges of working with a student with bipolar is that even tried-and-true strategies may not work consistently because of the frequent mood shifts the student experiences.

Consultation With Teachers

Providing teachers with interventions and behavior management strategies is an essential resource that school counselors can provide. Some skills and interventions that could be provided to teachers would include the following:

- Be flexible with adapting assignments, curriculum, and presentation style as needed.
- Be patient and ignore minor negative behaviors.
- Encourage positive behaviors and provide positive behavioral choices.

- Stay calm and be a model of desired behavior.
- Provide good conflict management skills to resolve conflicts in a nonconfrontational, noncombative, and safe manner.
- Have a plan for unstructured time or lulls in the day.
- Schedule the student's most challenging tasks at a time of day when the student is best able to perform.
- Flood the student with praise. A good rule of thumb is to praise the student at least once every 5 minutes or provide 12 positive comments for every negative statement.
- Be firm and consistent, and give the student acceptable, positive choices.
- Try to ignore inappropriate, attention-getting behaviors as much as possible.

As the school counselor, supporting teachers is best achieved when you are regularly meeting with the teacher and popping into the classroom to observe and intervene as needed. Scheduling student support team meetings to provide consultation to share specific resources based on the child's developmental age and abilities can be useful for the teacher to use in their classroom.

Advocacy for Students

Students with BD may need several or all of the following schedule accommodations: permission to arrive later and, when necessary, a shorter school day; scheduling difficult tasks for a time of day when the student is best able to perform; warnings before a change in activities; more time for turning in homework or large projects; extra time for tests; breaking tests or assignments into shorter segments with breaks scheduled; stimulating courses early in the day to get interest flowing; and periodic checks on progress during an assignment to ensure that the student is on schedule. For instance, a BD student in a depressed state can find it extremely hard to wake up on time for school, particularly at certain times of the year. They should not be penalized for tardiness that is biologically based. Many factors affect the way children with BD experience time, including difficulties with sleep, concentration, memory, and moods, plus medication side effects and a tendency to hyperfocus. School counselors have the ability to advocate for the student's needs with teachers and administrators to ensure a successful learning environment for the student and to help aid in the reduction of stressors that could trigger an episode.

Understanding What You Have Read: Comprehension Questions

Directions: Refer to what you learned in this chapter to answer the following questions.

1. What factors (academic, career, social/emotional, and behavioral) do school counselors have to consider when working with and supporting a student who has BD?
2. What are potential resources that you can use as a school counselor to assist students diagnosed with BD and their families?
3. How will your knowledge of PBD affect your future work with students?
4. How would you support a teacher who has a student with BD in their classroom?
5. What developmental factors do you need to consider when providing interventions for students struggling with BD?

Case Examples

Case Example One

As you read the case about David, reflect on the strategies that we discussed earlier in the chapter. The questions that follow the case relate to the student's behavioral symptoms and accompanying responses.

David is a 17-year-old high school senior in a rural area. He is well liked around school and in the community. He is an above-average student but has gone through a few periods of time where he struggled to keep up with his activities. David has already been diagnosed with BD-II. He has been prescribed lithium and has been taking it for about 1 year. David comes to you before school one day because he is concerned about himself. He says that he recently has been experiencing side effects of lithium, such as nausea, dry mouth, and dizziness. He has not taken his prescription for the last 3 weeks because he thought he could manage his BD without the medication, and the side effects were bothering him. Since he stopped taking his medication, he has had trouble managing his emotions and behaviors. David's teachers have also started to notice a difference in his behavior in class. He had a week where he was extremely high energy and distracting to other students. He has also had 2 weeks of showing little to no interest in school. During this time, David says he has had a hard time even getting out of bed each day. Over the last school year until recently, David's grades have improved, and he has been actively applying for college. Now in your office, David expresses that college is not realistic for him anymore.

Case Example One: Questions for Processing and Reflection

Directions: Use what you have learned in this chapter to respond to David's case.

1. How would you address David's concerns?
   a. Engage in individual counseling that focuses on reducing David's stress and helps him to reflect on his behavior.
   b. Provide a safe, caring, nonjudgmental space for David to feel supported, understood, and validated.
   c. Provide psychoeducation on the importance of taking prescribed medications as directed.
   d. Role-play with David on how he will speak to his physician about his concerns related to the medication's side effects.
2. In what ways would you involve team members in supporting David?
   a. Schedule a meeting with the school nurse and parents/guardians to discuss David not taking his medication.
   b. Consult with his teachers to see what interventions and accommodations can be used while David is in his episodes.
   c. Get consent to speak with David's prescribing medical or mental health professional to discuss the concerns and behaviors that are currently being displayed at school.
   d. Create a safety plan with the administrator to determine what steps will be taken if one of David's episodes turn into a rage.
3. In what ways can you keep David on the college track and future oriented?
   a. When his mood stabilizes, revisit his feelings about attending college and assist him in adjusting his plans if applicable.
   b. Work with teachers to provide David with academic accommodations while he works through his episodes and medication management so that his grades do not suffer, thus hurting his chances to attend college or adding more stress to David, ultimately triggering more episodes.

c. Help David to redirect his attention and reduce his stress to help him calm himself. Being able to be calm himself down will allow him to think rationally about his future and not impulsively while in an episode.

Case Example Two

As you read the case about Ashley, reflect on the strategies that we discussed earlier in the chapter. The questions that follow the case relate to the student's behavioral symptoms and accompanying responses.

Ashley is a 15-year-old high school sophomore in an urban area who has always been a good student and generally pretty quiet in classes, although she is isolative at times. Recently, over the first 2 months of the school year, her behavior has started to raise concerns from her teachers and classmates. She is sent to your office by her homeroom teacher because the teacher is worried about her elevated and distracting affect. When you sit down and talk with Ashley, she explains that she feels amazing and goes on to describe how well she is doing in school, even describing herself as the most intelligent person in her grade. Her recent grades reflect that she has been struggling in her classes so far this year. While talking with Ashley, you have a hard time keeping up with the pace of her speech and rapid change in topics. When you call home to speak with her parents, they say that they are very concerned about Ashley. They say she has been sleeping only 2 or 3 hours a night and is seemingly filled with energy. They are worried that she is sneaking out of the house at night and getting into drugs and other risky behaviors. This pattern has been happening for more than 6 months but recently has become worse.

Case Example Two: Questions for Processing and Reflection

Directions: Use what you have learned in this chapter to respond to Ashley's case.

1. Students experiencing BD I manic symptoms often are at risk of dangerous or high-risk behaviors. How can you as a school counselor assess the safety of this student and assist her guardians with keeping her safe?
2. How can you assist this family with these concerning behaviors at school and at home?
3. What support can you offer a family with a student experiencing these symptoms with no diagnosis?

Chapter Summary

BD exists in children and has the potential to be a severely impairing illness that affects all areas of children's lives. Although our knowledge is evolving, many uncertainties and questions remain. Best practices guide school counselors to (1) stay abreast of the evolving research; (2) focus on the problematic or challenging behaviors and needs of each individual child to best provide appropriate interventions in the school setting; (3) consult with teachers to support their needs in working with children with BD; (4) consult with parents to support their needs in parenting and dealing with educational issues of students with BD; (5) collaborate with the child's medical professionals, including pediatricians, psychiatrists, psychologists, and/or counselors/therapists; and (6) evaluate the effectiveness of intervention efforts. School counselors who proactively apply these skills will successfully support the needs of this unique population of children with BD.

Additional Recommended Readings and Resources

Books

Anglada, T. (2004). *Brandon and the bipolar bear: A story for children with bipolar disorder.* BPChildren.

Anglada, T. (2008). Turbo Max: A story for siblings and friends of children with bipolar disorder. BPChildren.

Cheney, T. (2011). *The dark side of innocence. Simon and Schuster.*

Faedda, G. L., & Austin, N. B. (2006). Parenting a bipolar child: What to do & why. New Harbinger Publications.

Jamison, K. R. (2009). *An unquiet mind: A memoir of moods and madness. Knopf Doubleday.*

Thompson, J. (2006). *Sugar and salt.* Author House.

Websites for Students

The Storm in My Brain Booklet for children describing how it feels to have a mood disorder: www.bpkids.org

Websites for Parents

Medication Guide for Parents: https://www.aacap.org/App_Themes/AACAP/docs/resource_centers/resources/med_guides/parentsmedguide_bipolar.pdf

Educational Issues Facing Children with Bipolar Disorder: https://www.jbrf.org/page-for-families/educational-issues-facing-children-with-bipolar-disorder/

The Ultimate Guide for Parents of Kids with Mental Health Challenges: www.bphope.com

How Bipolar in Kids Can Affect the Entire Family: www.bphope.com

Your Guide to Navigating the Mental Health System Maze: www.bphope.com

Monthly mood chart to track mood, sleep, and medication changes: http://www.cqaimh.org/pdf/tool_edu_moodchart.pdf

Websites for Teachers

The Student with Bipolar Disorder: An Educator's Guide: https://bpchildren.com/teachers

Resources for Teaching Students with Bipolar Disorder: https://www.bpchildren.com/teachers

Videos

Day for Night DVD for teens about mood disorders: www.depressedteens.com

How to Combat Myths of Bipolar Disorder: A Survival Guide: www.bphope.com

The Essential Guide to Helping Teens with Bipolar Transition to College: www.bphope.com

When You Feel "Stuck" with a Bipolar Diagnosis: Learning from the Pros and Cons: www.bphope.com

References

American Psychiatric Association (APA) (2013). *Diagnostic and statistical manual of mental disorders* (5th ed.).

American School Counselor Association (2019). The essential role of school counseling directors/coordinators. Retrieved from https://www.schoolcounselor.org/asca/media/asca/Careers-Roles/WhyDirectorCoord.pdf

Birmaher, B. (2013). Bipolar disorder in children and adolescents. *Child and Adolescent Mental Health, 18*(3), 140–148. https://doi.org/10.1111/camh.12021

Deng, W., Zhang, X., Zou, W., Zhang, B., Cheng, X., Guan, L, Lin, Y., Lao, G., Ye, B., Li, X., Yang, C., Ning, Y., & Cao, L. (2019). Abnormal degree centrality associated with cognitive dysfunctions in early bipolar disorder. *Frontiers in Psychiatry, 10*, 140.

Diler, R. S. & Birmaher, B. (2019). Bipolar disorders in children and adolescents. In Rey, J. M. & Martin, A. (Eds.), JM Rey's *IACAPAP e-Textbook of Child and Adolescent Mental Health:* International Association for Child and Adolescent Psychiatry and Allied Professions.

Dollarhide, C., & Saginak, K. (2017). *Comprehensive school counseling programs: K–12 delivery systems in action* (3rd ed.). Pearson.

Goldstein T. R. (2009). Suicidality in pediatric bipolar disorder. *Child and Adolescent Psychiatric Clinics of North America, 18*(2), 339–viii. https://doi.org/10.1016/j.chc.2008.11.005

Holland, K., Riley, E., & Krucik, G. T. (2017). *ADHD numbers: Facts, statistics, and you*. A.D.D. Resource Center. https://www.addrc.org/adhd-numbers-facts-statistics-and-you/

Kozloff, N., Cheung A. H., Schaffer A., Cairney, J., Dewa, C. S., Veldhuizen, S., Kurdyak, P., & Levitt, A. J. (2010). Bipolar disorder among adolescents and young adults: Results from an epidemiological sample. *Journal of Affective Disorders, 125*, 350–354.

Li, P. (2019). *The science of emotional regulation*. Parenting for Brain. https://www.parentingforbrain.com/self-regulation-toddler-temper-tantrums/

Perlis, R. H., Dennehy, E. B., Miklowitz, D. J., DelBello, M. P., Ostacher, M., Calabrese, J. R, Ametrano, R. M., Wisniewski, S. R., Bowden, C. L., Thase, M. F., Nierenberg, A. A., & Sachs, G. (2009). Retrospective age at onset of bipolar disorder and outcome during two-year follow-up: Results from the STEP-BD study. *Bipolar Disorders, 11*, 391–400.

Merikangas, K. R., He, J.P., Burstein, M., Swanson, S.A., Avenevoli, S., Cui, L., Benjet, C., Georgiades, K., & Swendsen, J. (2010). Lifetime prevalence of mental disorders in U.S. adolescents: Results from the National Comorbidity Survey Replication-Adolescent Supplement (NCS-A). *Journal of American Academy of Child Adolescent Psychiatry, 49*(10), 980–989.

National Institute of Mental Health (NIMH). (2016). *Bipolar disorder.* Retrieved July 16, 2019, from https://www.nimh.nih.gov/health/topics/bipolar-disorder/index.shtml#part_145404

Van Meter, A. R., Moreira, A. L., & Youngstrom, E. A. (2011). Meta-analysis of epidemiologic studies of pediatric bipolar disorder. *Journal of Clinical Psychiatry, 72*, 1250–1256.

West, A., & Weinstein, S. (2017). Bipolar disorder. In C. Flessner & J. Piacentini (Eds.), *Clinical handbook of psychological disorders in children and adolescents* (pp. 94–121). Guilford Press.

CHAPTER SIX

Eating Disorders

M. Ann Shillingford, Lèa Herbert, and
Vikki Gaskin-Butler

THE CASE OF ALEX Alex is a high school junior in the gifted program at her school. Alex's guardian has reported her concerns to the school counselor several times. She has stated that Alex comes home crying at times and has decided that she does not want to be in the gifted class any longer. Alex shared that she is teased by her peers who call her horrible names because of her weight. Alex's Mom believes the students are jealous because Alex is gifted, and they use every opportunity to tease her. At home, Alex seems to find comfort in eating, especially when she feels saddened by something that has happened at school. Mom is fretful about Alex's weight gain and her eating habits.

Introduction to the Chapter

Eating disorders (ED) have commonly been associated with college-aged students and adults; however, EDs are increasingly prevalent among children and adolescents. Conditions such as anorexia, binge eating, and bulimia, are of significant concern for parents, school personnel, and mental health counselors. In 2005, Keca and Cook-Cottone wrote that 30% of girls and 16% of boys would develop some type of ED. Eight years later, approximately 55% of high school girls and 30% of boys reported symptoms of an ED (Sim et al., 2013). An overall 6% of youth are diagnosed with some form of ED annually. In cases such as Alex's, being considered overweight or obese plays a key role in the development of an ED. In Alex's case, an ED may begin as a coping mechanism because of pressure from peers, as well as low self-image. In fact, the National Center for Health Statistics reported that at least 16% of children and youth ages 6–19 are overweight and, sadly, may be at the beginning phase of developing an ED.

Several other factors are associated with an increased likelihood of developing an ED, including, bullying and other at-school victimizations, biology and genetics, low self-esteem, societal influences such as the media, and childhood trauma. In this chapter, we will address the signs and symptoms of anorexia, binge eating, and bulimia. Strategies for school counseling interns and school counseling practitioners will be presented, as well as relevant resources to support students and families impacted by EDs.

Learning Objectives

By the end of this chapter, readers will accomplish the following:

- Understand the signs and symptoms of Eds.
- Understand the difference between anorexia, binge eating, and bulimia.
- Understand risk factors, as well as protective factors.
- Understand best practices related to supporting children and youth affected by an ED.
- Develop increased knowledge about integrating family systems into their counseling practices when working with children and youth affected by EDs.

Signs and Symptoms of EDs

Anorexia nervosa (AN), bulimia nervosa (BN) and binge eating disorder (BED) are EDs that can exist in subtle ways within a school system. Recent research has aided in informing the language, treatment, social factors, and protective recovery factors relating to EDs (Herpertz-Dahlmann et al., 2008; Polivy & Herman, 2002). Common factors related to the sources of EDs are media and peer influences, family enmeshment, and criticism, low self-esteem, and body dissatisfaction (Minuchin & Rosman, n.d.; Polivy & Herman, 2002). Cognitive and biological aspects are also a crucial component of EDs.

AN, BN, and BED are difficult to track. Realistically, clinical prevalence estimates are limited because of a few factors: often there is familial secrecy concerning Eds, and screening procedures are not wholly integrated into primary care and educational settings. Despite such confounding influences, the incidences of anorexia are an estimated 3% to 10% of individuals aged 15 through 29 (Polivy & Herman, 2002). There are higher incidences of reported cases of bulimia, so much so that for every patient diagnosed with anorexia, two patients are diagnosed with bulimia (Polivy & Herman, 2002). Interestingly, in a study conducted by Ogden and Steward (2000), it was found that mothers with a pattern of making critical comments about an adolescent's body or eating habits have a higher influence on the onset of an ED (AN, BN, and binge eating) in adolescents than weight and self-esteem concerns (Ogden & Steward, 2000).

Similarly, family dynamics affect both the onset and the development of EDs in youth (Polivy & Herman, 2002). Psychologist Minuchin stressed that families carry a sense of identity that has deep influences on trust building and feelings of safety in disclosing the presence of an ED within the family system (Minuchin & Rosman, n.d.). In his clinical observations, Minuchin noticed a correlation among families with patterns of negating individual emotional needs, helicopter parents, and hostilities with youth who develop EDs. Personal and family functioning are greatly disrupted by the onset of disordered eating; therefore, a systems approach is highly recommended in pushing the needle toward ED recovery and, most importantly, prevention. It is important for providers and advocates to remember that with patience and education, families can be the best allies in treatment.

Diagnostic Criteria

This section focuses on diagnostic criteria and features of anorexia, binge eating, and bulimia. According to the *Diagnostic and Statistical Manual of Mental Disorders, Fifth Edition* (*DSM-5*) (American Psychiatric Association [APA], 2013).

AN

AN manifests in two subtypes: restrictive type (i.e., skipping meals and/or counting calories) or binge eating/purging type (i.e., self-induced vomiting or the misuse of laxatives, diuretics, or enemas).

Anorexia is characterized by the following:

- The relentless pursuit of thinness
- An intense fear of fatness
- Significantly underweight
- Amenorrhea (missed menstruation) for at least 3 consecutive menstrual cycles (Harrington et al., 2015; Polivy & Herman, 2002).

Physiological features include anemia, low estrogen, and osteoporosis, as well as behavioral components, such as an obsession with food, binge eating, laxative/diuretic abuse, depression, social isolation, and increased physical activity. For an individual to receive an AN diagnosis, the specific symptoms mentioned earlier must occur over the duration of 3 months.

BN

The *DSM-5* criteria for bulimia include

- frequent episodes of consuming large amounts of food followed by behaviors to prevent weight gain (vomiting, laxative abuse, and excessive exercise),
- uncontrollable binge eating episodes, and
- obsessions relating to body weight and shape.

For an individual to receive a BN diagnosis, symptoms must occur over the duration of 3 months. Bulimia is a daily and weekly occurrence. Physiological features include enamel loss, salivary gland enlargement with frequent purging, and systolic murmur. Behavioral components include the disappearance of large amounts of food in short periods of time or lots of empty wrappers and containers, indicating consumption of large amounts of food, frequent trips to the bathroom after meals, signs of vomiting, and the presence of wrappers or packages of laxatives or diuretics. Treatment of bulimia centers on short-term cognitive-behavioral psychotherapy. Intensive and structured care that is usually successful includes psychotherapy, nutrition counseling, and psychiatric visits.

An important classification to be made is that anorexia is different from bulimia in several respects. The resolute refusal of normative eating is a key factor in anorexia. A helpful teaching tool is to link anorexia to avoidance when explaining the phenomenon to youth. Anorexia is the avoidance of fat intake. Whereas the marked intensity of impulsive eating is a key factor in bulimia (Herpertz-Dahlmann et al., 2008; Polivy & Herman, 2002).

Binge Eating

The *DSM-5* criteria for binge ED includes

- addictive binge eating;
- peculiar eating habits, such as eating when not hungry and eating to the point of discomfort; and
- intense feelings of strong shame regarding binge eating.

Like most EDs, BED is closely linked to the idea of being thin. Physiological features include difficulty concentrating, stomach cramps, constipation, and acid reflux; whereas behavioral components may include the development of lifestyle schedules to make time for binge sessions, fluctuations in weight, and low self-esteem. For an individual to receive a BED diagnosis, the symptoms listed previously must occur for 3 months.

The predominant focus of treatment is reducing eating binges, shame, and poor self-image and achieving healthy eating habits. Realistically, EDs rarely ever exist in solitude; often comorbidities present themselves. Common comorbidities include anxiety and depression disorders, substance abuse, and, in some cases, mood disorders (Harrington et al., 2015; Herpertz-Dahlmann et al., 2008; Polivy & Herman, 2002). Screening and integrated care are recommended to address coexisting conditions related to EDs to best improve the chances of stability. The chances of a full recovery are greatly enhanced by early intervention.

Characteristics of Increased Risk Factors

What are the risk factors for EDs? How can affected families and students gain the skills of improved eating? Education about risk factors and symptoms of EDs can be a source of acknowledgment for students and youth who often suffer in silence. This section presents risk factors of anorexia, binge eating, and bulimia and evidence-based prevention strategies for EDs in adolescents. This knowledge can be used as an educational resource to help offset the risk behaviors associated with EDs. Teachers, counselors, and school administrators can use this information to target multiple sociocultural influences relating to EDs, as well as educational material for students and parents.

According to the National Eating Disorders Association (2019), risk factors related to EDs can be categorized as (a) biological, (b) psychological, and (c) social. For a closer look at each of these factors, see Table 6.1.

TABLE 6.1 Risk Factors Related to Eating Disorders

RISK FACTORS	DESCRIPTORS
Biological	1. Close relative with ED 2. Close relative with a mental health disorder 3. History of dieting 4. Type 1 diabetes (insulin dependent) 5. Negative energy balance caused by growth spurts, illness, athletic training
Psychological	1. Perfectionism 2. Dissatisfaction with body image 3. History of anxiety disorder 4. Inflexibility in behaviors
Social	1. Stigma related to weight 2. Being bullied and/or teased 3. Internalizing the ideal body 4. Acculturation into a new system 5. Lack of social network 6. History of trauma

In the case of Alex, each of these factors plays a significant role in her developing an ED if she does not receive the necessary support services.

Strategies for School Counselors

Best Practice Approaches

Several prevention and intervention approaches have been identified for addressing EDs. Adelman and Taylor (2005) suggested a three-tiered model of addressing mental health services in schools that promotes prevention and care. Giles and Hass (2008) further highlighted these tiers, keeping in mind the limited resources and availability of intensive care services in schools. Giles and Hass viewed body image dissatisfaction as a social and psychological component that contributes to EDs. The following section introduces the three-tiered approach, which may be beneficial to school counselors and other mental health counselors in schools.

Tier-One: Prevention

It is important that preventative measures are a focus for school counselors. Prevention practices should begin as early as elementary school (Giles & Hass, 2008). Approaching topics such as body image and self-esteem may help reduce risk factors associated with EDs and increase protective factors. Early practice also builds on assisting students in developing critical thinking skills so that they are not easily influenced by peer pressure and inaccurate media portrayals of healthy bodies. Prevention strategies can include the following:

- ***Create School-Wide Programs.*** School counselors can work with teachers to promote healthy lifestyle choices. Examples include physical education or health education teachers highlighting the importance of healthy nutritional choices and the benefits of exercising. Math teachers could infuse healthy lifestyle language in their teaching, such as using fractions and ratios to determine appropriate food portions per student.
- ***Create a School Counselor Health Education Curriculum.*** This curriculum includes information related to the effects of factors such as bullying, teasing, and potential abuse (Keca & Cook-Cottone, 2005).
- ***Promote School-Community Partnerships.*** School counselors can solicit the guidance and involvement of the community, such as health agencies, community leaders, and family members, to promote prevention practices within the school setting.
- ***Educate and Collaborate With Parents and Families.*** This collaboration reduces stigma related to EDs, delivers healthy lifestyle strategies, and presents ways for parents to address their children's issues. Examples include counselor information nights, webinars, and newsletters.

Tier Two: Onset Intervention

For students who may already be demonstrating early signs and symptoms of an ED, school counselors can play a significant role in addressing the needs of these students.

- Discuss with the student the need to include the caregivers in the discussion to provide basic information as a team approach. This counselor-parent-student discussion should include the next steps for school-based interventions as needed and appropriate.
- Individual counseling sessions may address internal risk factors, such as the effect of abuse, low self-esteem, distorted thoughts related to food and eating (obsessions with food), and external factors such as distorted body image. Relaxation through guided imagery has been noted as a positive strategy for addressing these topics. Furthermore, according to Keca and Cook-Cottone (2005), it is important to focus on establishing healthy habits and positive skill building rather than weight management.

- Small-group counseling: School counselors may consider groups such as body image groups, self-esteem, self-awareness, and other topics that would help increase students' positive thoughts and feelings related to self.

Tier Three: Intervention

For those students who, despite best efforts through prevention measures, have developed an ED, school counselors can take various steps to lend support.

- It is imperative that school counselors fully recognize the signs and symptoms of EDs. School counselors should also understand what supports are needed, including making appropriate referrals for treatment.
- School counselors can consult with health professionals on best practices to address the needs of students within the school community who are experiencing the effects of an ED (e.g., nurses, doctors, psychologists, social workers).
- Counselors can build confidence in their ability to communicate with families of students who show signs of EDs. Developing consultation skills can be fostered through school counselor peer supervision, consultation with counseling faculty at a neighboring university, and professional development training.
- School counselors should understand the treatment phases. The three-phase plan includes (1) working to restore the student to a healthy weight and eating habits; (2) changing the student's thoughts, feelings, and behaviors toward themselves; and (3) implementing strategies in the case of relapse (Bardick et al., 2004). School counselors can aid in students' recovery process by consulting and collaborating with family, as well as the outside specialist working with these students.

Other Best Practice Strategies

Keca and Cook-Cottone (2005) highlighted additional prevention and intervention strategies that school counselors can embrace to support students: *ensuring that students' involvement in school activities is not regulated based on weight or body type.* These implicit practices may further create discomfort and anxiety for students already struggling with body image concerns. School counselors should *have a plan established with a list of appropriate resources and procedures* for other stakeholders within the school who may suspect or be concerned about a student having an ED. This information should be shared and revisited during the school's faculty and staff meetings at the beginning, middle, and toward the end of the academic year. Through collaborative efforts with cafeteria staff, school nurses, parent/teacher association members, and other team members, *school lunch and vending machine options should be assessed* to ensure that healthy choices are available, such as healthy juices, snacks, and water. Through these collaborative efforts, these preventative measures may serve to model for student's appropriate choices, as well as increase advocacy for student wellness.

Consultation and Intervention

School counselors who suspect that a student has an ED should take steps to first address the situation with the student and then the student's parents. The question may be asked, "How do I address such a sensitive topic with a student?" The following section describes steps for consultation.

- ***Step One.*** Meet with the student. Carney et al. (2012) recommended using open-ended questions to connect with the student: "I've noticed that you have been skipping lunch, and I am concerned about you." "You don't seem like yourself lately. How can I help you?" "Your friend mentioned to me that you are concerned about the way you look. How can I help you?" It is important to note that students may be uncomfortable sharing their personal thoughts and experiences; therefore, like other counseling platforms, building the therapeutic relationship, particularly trust, will be extremely important.
- ***Step Two.*** Based on the initial consultation with the student, the school counselor decides the next course of action. Does the student appear to have an ED or a body image issue? (Refer to signs and symptoms of EDs noted earlier.) If the student is suspected of having an ED (based on *DSM-5* criteria), the school counselor should solicit a consultation with another expert, such as the school psychologist, school or licensed social workers (as available), or other licensed clinicians. Knowledge related to the student's observed and reported behaviors should be shared to make a more accurate determination of care.
- ***Step Three.*** Parents/guardians are included in the picture to gather additional information and to offer referral services, as necessary. Parents should be made aware of the nature of the recommended referrals, such as in-school services or referrals for outside services (e.g., mental health counselor, primary care physician). In communicating with parents/guardians, a suggested statement by Carney et al. (2012) is, "I am concerned about your child's health and well-being and recommend further assessment and therapeutic interventions." Note that this statement is nondiagnostic.
- ***Step Four.*** The student should be informed of the next steps. If the school counselor is to work with the student, then a positive relationship should be established. The counselor should be aware that the student may be defensive and may even resist services. It is strongly encouraged that counselors focus on relationship building, trust, unconditional positive regard, and support. If the student is to be seen by an outside professional, then the school counselor can support the parent in processing this information with the student to dispel any misconceptions or address any anxieties the student may be experiencing.
- ***Step Five.*** If it is determined by the consultant, parents, and school counselor that in-school services are adequate, individual and small-group counseling sessions may be appropriate methods of support. It would also be beneficial for the school counselor to provide parents with resources on EDs and other pertinent topics so that the parents can provide additional support at home. Appendix A at the end of the chapter presents an example of a 4-week, small-group counseling segment.
- ***Step Six.*** For students who require more intense care, including hospitalization, reintegration into the school setting will be important (Carney et al., 2012). School counselors may serve as advocacy mediators between parents, school administrators, external clinicians, students, and teachers so that the student's transition back into the school is a positive one. School counselors should serve as advocates to ensure that homebound students are rightfully assigned the time and credit hours earned while receiving services. Adjustments may be needed in certain academic and extracurricular areas, such as gym class, lunch, and class scheduling. The school counselor may also consider introducing a Section 504 plan to address the student's continued needs in the school.

Although the strategies presented are not exhaustive, they should serve as guides for school counselors who may encounter a student or students who are experiencing the symptoms of an ED. It is of vital importance to remember that the school counselor cannot and should not attempt to serve these students alone. A systemic approach that includes parents and other experts on EDs (in school and out) is the best practice.

Understanding What You Have Read: Comprehension Questions

Directions: Refer to what you learned in this chapter to answer the following questions.

1. What are the signs and symptoms of anorexia, bulimia, and BEDs?
2. How are these three-EDs similar and different?
3. What strategies can school counselors use to support students with EDs?
4. What are the common risk factors associated with EDs?
5. How might school counselors engage families and the community in supporting students with EDs?

Case Examples

Case Example One

As you read the case about Brenna, reflect on the strategies that we discussed earlier in the chapter. The questions that follow the case relate to the student's behavioral symptoms and accompanying responses.

Brenna is one of your middle school students who is on the soccer team. She has been at your school since sixth grade, and you have included her in several of your small counseling groups on self-esteem. This academic year, you have decided to start a body image group for girls at your school. You have a few students with whom you have worked in the past that you think would benefit from this group. Although you have worked with Brenna, you do not think she needs to be in your group; however, her eighth-grade teacher hears about your group and recommends Brenna. Upon inquiring about the teacher's rationale for this referral, you find out from the teacher that at the last parent/teacher conference, Brenna's grandmother expressed concerns about Brenna's eating habits and weight loss. You now must determine if Brenna would benefit from this group after all.

Case Example One: Questions for Processing and Reflection

Directions: Use what you have learned in this chapter to respond to Brenna's case.

1. What about Brenna might indicate that she could possibly have an ED?
   a. Brenna has low self-esteem.
   b. Brenna's grandmother is concerned about her weight and eating habits.
   c. Brenna is an athlete.
2. What would your next course of action be?
   a. Meet with Brenna to observe for weight loss and to speak with her about her eating habits.
   b. Observe Brenna in the cafeteria during lunch.
   c. Speak with Brenna's grandmother about her observations and concerns.
3. Based on the information that you receive from these multiple sources, what might your diagnosis for Brenna be?
   a. Remember, school counselors *do not diagnose*!
   b. Provide community resources to Brenna's grandmother for further assessment, if applicable.
   c. Include Brenna in your small group, if applicable.
   d. *Do not diagnose* Brenna.

Case Example Two

As you read the case about Stephen, reflect on the strategies that we discussed earlier in the chapter. The questions that follow the case relate to the student's behavioral symptoms and accompanying responses.

Stephen has been attending the high school where you work for the past 3 years. He is a quiet, reserved, gifted student. His twin brother, Silas, is the captain of the school's football team. Silas is muscular and energetic; whereas Stephen is slender and meek. You, the school counselor, are delivering a classroom guidance lesson in Stephen's class on college preparation. The students are moving around to different career stations that you have set up. As Stephen nears you, he tumbles over and appears to be unconscious. You immediately call 911, and the paramedics arrive along with the school nurse. They are able to revive Stephen, and he is been sent home. The next day, you receive a call from Stephen's stepfather who shares that Stephen has been sent to a rehabilitation center for individuals with EDs. He has been diagnosed with an ED. Unbeknownst to all, Stephen had been experiencing extreme anxiety related to the way he looked compared to his brother. He had been binge eating and working out excessively so that he could be as muscular as his twin brother. Stephen's health is in jeopardy because of these habits.

Case Example Two: Questions for Processing and Reflection

Directions: Use what you have learned in this chapter to respond to Stephen's case.

1. What are the signs and symptoms that indicate that Stephen has an ED?
2. Would you say Stephen is anorexic, bulimic, or a binge eater?
3. Once Stephen returns to school, how might you as the school counselor support him?
4. What in-school and community agencies might the school counselor use to support Stephen?
5. As a school counselor, what professional development training might you pursue to prepare for working with students like Stephen?

Chapter Summary

EDs have traditionally been recognized as primarily affecting females (girls and women). In fact, EDs affect all kinds of people, regardless of gender, race, ethnicity, or socioeconomic status. EDs, commonly, anorexia, bulimia, and binge eating, are complex in nature and may not be easily recognized because of varying social factors. There are numerous risk factors linked to these disorders, but the existence of these factors does not necessarily foretell the development of an ED. School counselors, although not diagnosticians, must be vigilant in recognizing the signs and symptoms of EDs so that they can lend systemic support to students and families.

Appendix A. Small-Group Counseling

Contributed by Antoanette Gonzales Torres, Katelyn Stiles, Sharon Quackenbush, and Parinaz Fard-Aghaie

If small-group counseling is deemed appropriate, the following is a four-session example that school counselors may find helpful in supporting students with an ED, such as anorexia. These are only examples and may need to be extended or revised based on the age and developmental level of your clients. This brief group curriculum uses the wishes, outcomes, obstacles, plans (WOOP) approach developed by psychologist, Gabriele Oettingen (2015). WOOP is motivationally based to support individuals who are experiencing various life challenges, including EDs. You can find more information about this approach in her book listed in the resource section.

Session 1: Introductions and Identifying "WOOP"

Goals and Objectives

The goal of this session is to build relationships and a supportive community for members presenting with anorexia. This session will provide knowledge of the purpose of the group, group expectations, and the limitations and value of confidentiality as evidenced through discussion. In this session, group members will work together to form rules for the group, learn about the WOOP method, and begin to explore their goals related to anorexia recovery.

Materials

The materials needed include chart paper, pens, and markers.

Icebreaker

The group leaders initiate this session with a short introduction and welcome everyone to the group. During this time, the group leaders will discuss the purpose of the group; group rules, including maintaining confidentiality; their role as group facilitators; and the importance of goal setting. Introductions are then followed by an icebreaker to help group members get to know one another. In this icebreaker, each member of the group is given a sheet of paper with prompting statements, such as, "The first thing I do every morning ...," "If I have an extra 30 minutes to myself, I ... ," "My favorite outfit to wear is: ...," "I never miss a TV episode of ...," and "The last thing I do before going to bed ..." Group members are told that they can share as much or as little as they wish and that sharing is not mandatory but helps build connections within the group. Group members are invited to answer a series of unfinished phrases included in the handout. Once the group has completed the handout, group members are invited to introduce themselves and share their responses.

Alex **WISHES** that she would not revert to eating when she is anxious or stressed.

Anticipated **OUTCOME:** Alex would like to develop better coping habits when stressed.

Potential **OBSTACLE:** Alex's friends may continue to tease her about her weight.

PLAN: Alex will develop positive self-image strategies with the help of her counselor.

Psychoeducation

Group leaders will introduce the concept of WOOP. The WOOP process contains four steps. The first step has an individual determine what it is they want or "wish." The second step includes exploring what the outcome of that wish could look/feel like in that individual's life. The third step is determining possible obstacles that have or may potentially get in the way of achieving the wish, and the last step is to create a plan of action to determine how to move forward in achieving the goal. The group leader may need to give examples of these steps to best guide the group.

Conclusion

The group leader encourages each group member to share new knowledge about themselves that they have gathered from this first session.

Session 2: Identifying Wishes and Outcomes

Goals and Objectives

The goal of this session is to guide group members with developing *specific, measurable, attainable, realistic, and time-based* (SMART) goals (wishes and outcomes) based on the WOOP method. These goals will be directed toward the effects of anorexia.

Materials

The materials needed for this group session will include crafting supplies, such as crayons, markers, paper, scissors, glue, playdough, and other items. The leaders will also provide a set of index cards and pens. Group members will be given the *Costs and Benefits* handout for homework. Chairs will again be set up in a circle facing each other and the rules from the previous week will be posted on a wall visible to the entire group.

Icebreaker

The group leaders welcome members and ask them to each draw a picture that represents their journey living with anorexia. Each person will be allowed the opportunity to discuss their picture with a partner before sharing it with the entire group. This activity will allow the group leader to determine each group member's perspective on their experience with anorexia.

Psychoeducation

The group leaders review the parts of "WOOP" and explain in this session each group member will work on "wishes and anticipated outcomes" for combating anorexia. Leaders explain this goal/wish should be *"SMART."* Examples of this concept should be provided to the group. Using a pen and an index card, group members are asked to review the picture from the icebreaker and then write out at least one wish for overcoming anorexia, as well as an expected outcome. Group leaders may ask clarifying questions to help members create more concise, attainable, and measurable goals. Each member can then identify how the group may help them reach that goal through accountability or support. The group will take time to process each goal and use skills such as restating, linking, and summarizing to help members shape their own goals and understand each other's goals.

Alex **WISHES** to change the way she thinks about her body.

Anticipated **OUTCOME:** Alex would like to feel good about herself and look forward to going to school every day.

Potential **OBSTACLE:** Alex's irrational thoughts may continue to affect her self-image.

PLAN: Alex will attend a positive body image group for young girls.

Conclusion

The group leader encourages each group member to share new knowledge about themselves that they have gathered from this first session.

Session 3: Addressing Obstacles and Automatic Thoughts

Goals and Objectives

The goal of this session is to allow each group member to explore potential obstacles that may prevent them from achieving their desired goals. They practice identifying negative automatic thoughts and replacing those thoughts with neutral or more healthy thinking. The group members recognize harmful eating behaviors in themselves and create a plan for recognizing triggers and avoiding relapse behaviors through homework and discussions.

Materials

The materials needed for this group session include index cards and pens or markers.

Icebreaker

The group leaders will lead the group into the "Two Truths and a Lie" activity. The leader will explain that each member is to identify and share two statements about them that are true and one that is not. Each member will share, and determinations will be made by the group as to which statements are truths and which are lies.

Psychoeducation

The group leader explains that the group will explore the "obstacles" part of "WOOP" in this session. Although the "Two Truths and a Lie" activity is designed to connect the group and build relationships, it may also serve as a useful way to demonstrate that there are many messages people may use to deceive others or to deceive themselves. An example of this is *automatic thoughts.*

The group leaders ask the group members what the word "automatic" means to them. Then the group leader informs the participants that thoughts can control how people feel about themselves and the world around them. These thoughts can be positive or negative and can lead to healthy feelings or unhealthy feelings and actions. The leaders add that sometimes thoughts happen so quickly that a person may fail to notice the thoughts exist, yet these thoughts still affect a person's mood. These are called *automatic thoughts* and can stand as obstacles to more positive life outcomes. The leaders will explain that, often, automatic thoughts are negative or irrational, and identifying these negative automatic thoughts and replacing them with new healthy or rational thoughts can improve our moods and positively affect behaviors.

The group works through a series of scenarios to identify automatic thinking. For each scenario given, the members must first identify one or more immediate negative thoughts that come to mind. Then the members must work to write a replacement thought—one that is a neutral or less negative thought (if possible, group members can even strive for a positive thought)—for the automatic thought. The group leaders model using an example, such as, "Sarah makes a mistake at work." Sarah's first thoughts might be, "I am probably going to be fired. I always mess up. This is it. I am not good at my job." The group must work together to replace this thought with a more positive thought, such as, "I messed up, but mistakes happen. I am going to work through this like I always do." Examples of other scenarios that can be addressed within dyads may include "I avoided eating today, and when confronted about it, I lied to my friends," and "I had been doing really good with healthy eating for months, but I felt really lonely and ugly yesterday, so I purged again."

This activity is first modeled by the leaders with the whole group, and then paper and pens are given out and a few more scenario examples are done in dyads to practice. The dyads then share with the group. After it is apparent that the group members understand how to identify automatic thoughts in scenarios, they are given another piece of paper and each group member is asked to write down one event that happened recently, the automatic thoughts they had about that event, and a possible replacement thought. They are invited to share with the group.

Conclusion

The group leader reminds the group members of the termination of sessions. The group leaders lead the group through a relaxation activity to close the session. Members are encouraged to use this strategy if/when obstacles or automatic thoughts begin to appear.

Alex **WISHES** to think more positively about her body.

Anticipated **OUTCOME:** Alex will be able to use positive self-talk when she feels anxious.

Potential **OBSTACLE:** There may be moments of fear that may cause automatic thoughts.

PLAN: Alex will continue to use positive self-talk for self-empowerment.

Session 4: Making Plans and Gathering Resources

Objectives and Goals

Upon completing this session, group members will have coping skills and resources to support their psychological growth.

Materials

The materials needed for this session include a hat, whiteboard and markers, index cards, and pens.

Icebreaker

The group leader welcomes the group and reminds the members that this is their last session together. This session's icebreaker is called *Fears and Hopes in the Hat.* This activity invites members to anonymously write one of their fears on a slip of paper and place it into a hat. After everyone has placed their "fear" in the hat, a leader selects the fears at random and then reads them aloud to the group. The group shares their thoughts about the fears presented, and the group leaders link and reflect on feelings as the fears are shared.

Psychoeducation

The group members are invited to give an overview of the past sessions and answer the question, "What have you learned about yourself?" Leaders may ask more directed questions such as, "What are some negative thinking strategies you have used in the past, and what do you now know about the effect of more positive thoughts?"

Activity—Positive Activities for Behavioral Activation

Each group member is given a sheet of paper and invited to create a list of coping activities that they find rewarding. Leaders ask them to rate each activity in two categories: (1) how easy the activity is to complete and (2) how rewarding it is (with 10 being very easy or rewarding and 1 being difficult or not at all rewarding). The group leaders should assist members in brainstorming ideas for their list. Examples may include, relaxation exercises, healthy meal plans, and family engagement activities. When the exercise is complete, each member has created a list of activities. They will draw a star next to the activities that they believe may help them to achieve their goals and discuss how these activities may be helpful in those pursuits. Group members are reminded of SMART goals and are then asked to write at least one personal goal for each of the top-five coping strategies that they have identified.

Conclusion

The group leaders set aside time for this final session of "WOOP" so that the group members can have time to process the ideas and their plans. Leaders give the group members a list of resources for referrals to add to their plans for when the members become stuck, are in crisis, or need additional help. The resources should also include information for caregivers.

Additional Recommended Readings and Resources

American Obesity Association (AOA): www.obesity.org/subs/childhood/prevention.shtml

AOA provides resources, statistics, research, and advocacy information on preventing and treating obesity in adults and children.

National Eating Disorders Association (NEDA): www.kidsource.com/nedo

NEDO's mission is to eliminate EDs and body dissatisfaction through education, referral and support services, advocacy, training, and research.

NEDA Helpline: 1 (800) 931-2237

Books

Armstrong, S. C. (2009). *Not all black girls know how to eat: A story of bulimia*. Lawrence Hills Books.

Charaipotra, S. (2016). *Tiny pretty things*. HarperTeen.

Dessen, S. (2008). Just listen. Speak. Penguin.

Mattocks, B. (2013). *Please eat ... : A mother's struggle to free her teenage son from anorexia*. Creative Copy.

Mitchell, A. (2015). *It was me all along: A memoir*. Clarkson Potter.

Oettingen, G. (2015). *Rethinking positive thinking: Inside the new science of motivation*. Current Publishing.

Movies

Dying to Dance (2001)

For the Love of Nancy (1994)

I am a Child Anorexic (2006)

I am a Boy Anorexic (2007)

References

Adelman, H. S. & Taylor, L. (2005). *The school leader's guide to student learning supports: New directions for addressing barriers to learning*. Corwin Press.

American Psychiatric Association (APA). (2013). *Diagnostic and statistical manual of mental disorders* (5th ed.).

Bardick, K. B., Bernes, K. B., McCulloch, A. R. M., Witko, K. D., Spriddle, J. W., & Roest, A. R. (2004). Eating disorder intervention, prevention, and treatment: Recommendations for school counselors. *Professional School Counseling, 8*, 168–175.

Carney, J., Scott, M., & Lewy, H. (2012). Eating issue sin schools: Detection, management, and consultation with allied professionals. *Journal of Counseling & Development, 90*(3), 290–297.

Giles, M. & Hass, M. (2008). Fostering a healthy body image: Prevention and intervention with adolescent eating disorders. *Journal of School Counseling, 6*(13), Retrieved from https://files.eric.ed.gov/fulltext/EJ894784.pdf ss

Harrington, B. C., Jimerson, M., Haxton, C., & Jimerson, D. C. (2015). Initial evaluation, diagnosis, and treatment of anorexia nervosa and bulimia nervosa. *American Family Physician, 91* (1), 46–52.

Herpertz-Dahlmann, B., Wille, N., Hölling, H., Vloet, T. D., Ravens-Sieberer, U., ... Bella Study Group. (2008). Disordered eating behavior and attitudes, associated psychopathology and health-related quality of life: Results of the BELLA study. *European Child & Adolescent Psychiatry, 17* (1), 82–91.

Keca, J., & Cook-Cottone, C. (2005). *Eating disorders: Prevention is worth every ounce.* National Association of School Psychologists. www.nasponline.org

Minuchin, S., Rosman, B. L., & Baker. L. (1978). *Psychosomatic families: Anorexia nervosa in context. Harvard University Press.*

National Eating Disorders Association (2019). Risk factors. Retrieved from https://www.nationaleatingdisorders.org/risk-factors

Oettingen, G. (2015). Rethinking positive thinking: Inside the new science of motivation. Current Publishing.

Ogden, J., & Steward, J. (2000). The role of the mother-daughter relationship in explaining weight concern. *International Journal of Eating Disorders, 28* (1), 78–83.

Polivy, J., & Herman, C. P. (2002). Causes of eating disorders. *Annual Review of Psychology, 53*(1), 187–213.

Sim, L. A., Lebow, J., & Billings, M. (2013). Eating disorders in adolescents with a history of obesity. *Pediatrics*, 132(4), e1026–e1030. http://pediatrics.aappublications.org/content/early/2013/09/04/peds.2012-3940.full.pdf+html

CHAPTER SEVEN

Oppositional Defiant Disorder

Jason Duffy

THE CASE OF THOMAS Thomas is a fifth-grade student who lives primarily with his dad, Bill, since his parents separated when he was in the second grade. According to Bill, Thomas sees his mother, Sandy, one weekend a month. Bill shared that Thomas has been getting in "trouble" and "making stupid decisions in school" since he started kindergarten because he "constantly refuses to do what teachers ask him to do when he doesn't want to do it." Just last week, Thomas's science teacher asked him to work with his assigned student work group during class to complete a project on the Milky Way and the Solar System, and Thomas said, "Hell no," folded his arms, and then stared coldly at the teacher. When the teacher told Thomas that the assignment would count for 20% of his second-quarter average, he responded, "I don't give a shit about this dumbass class or you." When the teacher asked Thomas to leave the room because of his language and attitude, he laughed and said, "Whatever." He didn't get out of his seat at first, and then when he finally stood up, he knocked over a stack of papers as he walked out of the room. Once out of the room, Thomas stared through the door's small window at the teacher and just laughed before wandering down to the main office. The next morning when the teacher entered the room, Thomas was already in the room and had mixed together all of the teacher's supplies into one box. When she asked him why he'd done that, he just smirked and said, "Do I really need to answer that?" He then giggled and asked, "Am I in trouble?" In addition, Thomas has been acting out at school (e.g., bully other students, yell obnoxiously) whenever he doesn't immediately know how to answer a question, complete a task, or get what he wants when he wants it. Teachers have commented about how they can visibly see him becoming angry (e.g., face turns red, mumbling to himself, breaking a pencil) when he is unable to do something immediately.

Introduction to the Chapter

Although this vignette may seem extreme or, perhaps, tame to some readers, this behavior and attitude are very common in children and adolescents diagnosed with oppositional defiant disorder (ODD), a specific disorder listed under the umbrella term disruptive behavior disorders in the *Diagnostic and Statistical Manual of Mental Disorders, 5th Edition* (*DSM-5*; American Psychiatric Association [APA], 2013). Put simply, ODD is characterized by a consistent display of irrationally rebellious behavior and anger at authority figures over an extended period. It is not uncommon, however, for ODD to be misdiagnosed, as some of the diagnostic features are also found in attention deficit hyperactivity disorder (ADHD), various anxiety and depressive disorders, substance-related and addictive disorders, trauma- and stressor-related disorders. In addition, situational issues (changes at home, social issues, organic/biological issues, etc.), as well as developmental changes (e.g., puberty), can bring about changes in a child's emotions, thoughts, and behaviors that peers and authority figures find alarming. Finally, children like Thomas may act fine in certain contexts and then struggle with ODD-related symptoms in others, confounding people who are trying to understand what is going on during the emotional and behavioral seesawing. However, those children and adolescents who meet the criteria for ODD need research-validated, multisystemic assistance. This chapter will lay out the signs and symptoms related to ODD and strategies to support students with this disorder, specifically in the school context.

Learning Objectives

By the end of this chapter, readers will accomplish the following:

- Understand the signs and symptoms of ODD.
- Develop an increased knowledge of the educational and social effects of ODD on adolescents and youth.
- Understand the best practice strategies for supporting students diagnosed with ODD.

First introduced in 1980 as oppositional disorder in the *DMS-III* (1980), ODD is a disorder diagnosed in children and adolescents that is characterized by aggression, defiance toward authority figures, and disruptiveness that results in persistent problems at home, school, work, and in social activities (2014). It is estimated that up to 11% of children and adolescents will meet the criteria for this disorder at some point prior to adulthood (2014). Research indicates that most symptoms (the first indications) associated with ODD appear during the preschool years and that symptoms only seldomly begin later than this developmental period. The symptoms of ODD can be isolated to one setting (e.g., the home) or may be present in two or more settings (e.g., home, school, daycare, with other family members). Although the cause of this disorder is not entirely known, most research points to a combination of nature and nurture, with a higher prevalence in families with a history of ADHD, substance use disorders, or mood disorders, such as depression or bipolar disorder. Although research indicates that ODD may occur more readily in lower socioeconomic groups, ODD affects families of all backgrounds (AACAP, 2009).

Signs and Symptoms of ODD

As most educators and school professionals know, even the most well-behaved students can, at times, be difficult. But students who display a continual pattern of tantrums, arguing, and angry or disruptive behaviors toward teachers, parents, or other authority figures may have ODD. Table 7.1 lists the diagnostic criteria for the disorder noted in the DSM-5 (APA, 2013), as well as examples based on the vignette of Thomas (beginning of chapter) that illustrates what this may look like in a school setting. Students *must* meet the criteria set forth in sections A, B, and C. In addition, the student's behavior needs to be conceptualized by the observer in regard to what is normal behavior based on factors such as developmental level, gender, and culture. According to the DSM-5, the diagnostic criteria for ODD is:

TABLE 7.1 Information From the *DSM-5*

Angry/Irritable Mood (see section A)	*How This Might Manifest in Students* At school, Thomas will begin to yell obnoxiously whenever he doesn't immediately know how to answer a question, complete a task, or get what he wants when he wants it. Teachers have commented about how they can visibly see him becoming angry (e.g., face turns red, mumbling to himself, breaking a pencil) when he is unable to do something immediately.
Argumentative/Defiant Behavior (see section A)	*How This Might Manifest in Students* Thomas's science teacher asked him to work with his assigned student group during class to complete a project on the Milky Way and the Solar System and Thomas said, "Hell no," folded his arms, and then stared coldly at the teacher. When the teacher told Thomas that the assignment would count for 20% of his second-quarter average, he responded, "I don't give a shit about this dumbass class or you."
Vindictiveness (see section A)	*How This Might Manifest in Students* The next morning when the teacher entered the room, Thomas was already in the room and had mixed together all of the teacher's supplies into one box. When she asked him why, he just smirked and said, "Do I really need to answer that?" He then giggled and asked, "Am I in trouble?"

A. A pattern of angry/irritable mood, argumentative/defiant behavior, or vindictiveness lasting at least 6 months as evidenced by at least four symptoms from any of the following categories, and exhibited during interaction with at least one individual who is not a sibling.

Angry/Irritable Mood

1. Often loses temper.
2. Is often touchy or easily annoyed.
3. Is often angry and resentful

Argumentative/Defiant Behavior

4. Often argues with authority figures or, for children and adolescents, with adults.
5. Often actively defies or refuses to comply with requests from authority figures or with rules.
6. Often deliberately annoys others.
7. Often blames others for his or her mistakes or misbehavior

Vindictiveness

8. Has been spiteful or vindictive at least twice within the past 6 months

Note: The persistence and frequency of these behaviors should be used to distinguish a behavior that is within normal limits from a behavior that is symptomatic. For children younger than 5 years, the behavior should occur on most days for a period of at least 6 months unless otherwise noted (Criterion A8). For individuals 5 years or older, the behavior should occur at least once per week for at least 6 months, unless otherwise noted (Criterion A8). While these frequency criteria provide guidance on a minimal level of frequency to define symptoms, other factors should also be considered, such as whether the frequency and intensity of the behaviors are outside a range that is normative for the individual's developmental level, gender, and culture.

B. The disturbance in behavior is associated with distress in the individual or others in his or her immediate social context (e.g., family, peer group, work colleagues), or it impacts negatively on social, educational, occupational, or other important areas of functioning.
C. The behaviors do not occur exclusively during the course of a psychotic, substance use, depressive, or bipolar disorder. Also, the criteria are not met for disruptive mood dysregulation disorder.

The bottom line in section B is that the student's behavior is having a marked effect on the student and/or others in their environment (home, school, childcare, team, etc.). The bottom line in section C is that the student's behavior is happening because of ODD rather than drug use, a current issue in the student's life, or because of another mental health issue/diagnosis.

Misdiagnosis and Societal Perceptions

As stated earlier, various diagnostic characteristics associated with ODD are also found in other diagnoses. For example, students with ADHD often struggle with impulsive behaviors, such as being disruptive in a classroom setting (e.g., talking out of turn, touching/hitting other students, moving around when they are supposed to be still, out-of-proportion anger and frustration) (Frick & Brocki, 2019). For example, some students with ADHD can become easily frustrated and angry when they are unable to maintain their concentration during assignments or class-based activities that require students to focus for long periods of time or perform multilayered tasks, such as those found in math or English Language Acquisition (ELA) (Singh, 2011). To add to the complexity of diagnosing ODD, children with ODD often have co-occurring disorders, such as ADHD, anxiety disorders, mood disorders, learning disorders, and various language disorders (Frick & Nigg, 2011). Research indicates that of all co-occurring disorders, ADHD is the most common (Singh et al., 2015).

Many of the symptoms of ODD can also manifest in students who are using substances, such as nicotine or tetrahydrocannabinol. These two substances have become readily available and easily usable through the "juice" cartridges that can be loaded into e-cigarettes, vaping pens, JUULS, and other technology that have become more accessible and grown exponentially in popularity among many students in recent years (Morse et al., 2015). For example, it is estimated that 2.1 million middle and high school students were e-cigarette users in 2017, and that number has been steadily increasing (Gentzke et al., 2019). These drug-delivery devices deliver high levels of nicotine and other substances, making the product extremely addictive. One study clearly linked problematic school behaviors, such as lethargy, increased aggressiveness, lack of focus, lower frustration tolerance, and several others, to the use of nicotine and marijuana by students (Gentzke et al., 2019).

It is also not uncommon for teachers, school counselors, and other school-based personnel to label kids demonstrating ODD symptoms as "bad" kids and simply see them as a disciplinary issue. For example, the first author has heard comments such as the student chooses this behavior to get attention (to act "cool"); she wants to get out of working in class; she acts this way because she has bad or neglectful parents and, as we all know, the apple doesn't fall far from the tree! Now, to be sure, a student who meets the criteria for ODD may have a problematic home life, might consciously make questionable choices, may be a bit lazy, etc.; however, this does not mean the student does not also have ODD, which can be treated using a plethora of strategies and interventions.

Risk Factors

As researchers continue to learn about human development, it is clear that we cannot always pinpoint the exact cause of psychological and behavioral issues (Biglan et al., 2012). Based on current research, it appears that many mental health disorders evolve through an interaction of a person's biological predispositions (genes) and the environment (e.g., parenting style, peer interactions, living conditions, such as poverty) (Duncan et al., 2014). Even this, however, is an oversimplification, as current thinking posits that our gene expression (whether certain genes are activated or not and to what extent) is affected by environmental stimuli, and we also know that we have an effect on the environment. Regardless of these complexities, there are risk factors that research and anecdotal evidence have shown do increase the likelihood of a child manifesting the diagnostic criteria for ODD (Canino et al., 2010):

- A history of abuse or neglect
- A parent or caretaker who has a mood disorder (e.g., bipolar disorder, major depressive disorder, generalized anxiety disorder) or who abuses alcohol or drugs
- Exposure to violence
- Inconsistent discipline and/or supervision
- Exposure to toxins when young
- Instability in the family, such as divorce, multiple moves, and changing schools frequently
- Poor nutrition
- Mother who smoked during pregnancy
- Financial problems in the family/poverty
- Parents who have or have had ODD, ADHD, or impulse control and/or behavioral problems

As stated previously, the listed risk factors raise the probability of a child developing ODD or another mental health issue; however, it is far from a given. Many children, for instance, have experienced the risk factors listed and do not develop ODD. Yet these risk factors do represent a consistent set of environmental factors that appear in nearly all diagnosed with ODD. For this reason, taking these risk factors into account when exploring a potential diagnosis of ODD is important and will assist in developing a treatment plan, as we will explore shortly.

Assessment

School counselors are in an ideal position to assist in identifying children who meet the diagnostic criteria for ODD and other mental health issues (Fazel et al., 2014). School counselors are able to gather information, such as academic performance, cognitive and emotional testing conducted by the school psychologist, and anecdotal reports from faculty and staff that can aid in the process of assessing whether a child does meet the necessary criteria for ODD, as well as to examine the contextual elements that may have brought about and sustained the diagnosis of ODD (Fazel et al., 2014). As mentioned previously, those diagnosed with ODD typically begin to show symptoms in the early school years; therefore, with school attendance a compulsory activity for all children in the United States, the school context represents a place where problematic behaviors are often first noticed and addressed. Although the diagnosis of ODD will not necessarily come from a school-based mental health professional, the information gathered for a diagnosis will nearly always involve the school context and aid the pediatrician or outside health-care provider in reaching a diagnostic conclusion. In addition, the school will typically assist in implementing strategies and interventions.

Treatment

There are various modalities that school counselors can use or recommend for treating ODD.

Development of an Individualized Education Plan and/or 504 Plan

Under the Individuals with Disabilities Education Act (IDEA, 2004), schools are legally bound to provide appropriate services and accommodations for students with disabilities. ODD is one of the two behavioral disorder diagnoses that are covered under IDEA and, therefore, can serve as the impetus for an individualized education plan (IEP) or 504 Plan. Not all parents/guardians, school counselors, or other stakeholders are aware of this, and, therefore, it is important for school personnel to be informed that ODD is certainly a reason to convene a committee on special education meeting to create an IEP to ensure that a student is receiving the necessary support to be successful in school. Such planning may include the school counselor and other stakeholders developing a behavioral intervention plan for the student that helps the classroom teachers understand how to react appropriately and consistently when the student is being disruptive and how to track such occurrences to help gauge whether certain interventions are working and/or need to be changed or adjusted. For example, a student might have a behavior sheet in which each teacher signs at the end of class after providing a behavior score (e.g., Likert from 1 to 5) for the student. The student then checks in at the end of each day with the school counselor to review the sheet and make some simple goals for the next school day. Such a plan can also involve creating a scheduled time each week for a student to meet with a school counselor, school social worker, or school psychologist for various purposes, such as learning and practicing coping skills to better develop emotional regulation.

Individual Counseling

The use of individual counseling by school counselors is an integral part of helping students diagnosed with ODD learn how to better manage their emotions and behavior (Khanbani et al., 2011). Typically, individual counseling will involve helping a student become more aware and educated about the struggles they are having and why such struggles occur. A student can also work with the school counselor—in addition to any outside health-care providers—to develop more adaptive cognitive problem-solving skills, such as learning positive ways to react in anxiety-provoking situations. For example, a second-grade student may be given the choice to quietly go to a designated area in the classroom to color in a coloring book for a specific amount of time (e.g., up to 5 minutes) when she begins to feel emotionally dysregulated.

Individual counseling also provides a place where the student can form a relationship with a trusted and stable adult who can assist them in navigating and addressing specific situations occurring in or out of school (for example, an ongoing custody battle between two parents). Of course, the counseling will need to be uniquely tailored to the developmental level, specific issues, and contextual factors of the student involved. This person, many times, will serve as the case manager and, therefore, work with the pediatrician, outside mental health providers, parents/guardians, and school personnel to ensure that a holistic, multisystemic approach is being used and monitored.

Family Therapy and Family-Management Training

Although not always the purview of the school counselor, family counseling and training are also necessary to bring about positive and long-lasting change for those with ODD (Miller-Slough et al., 2016). This family-based work is meant to assist caregivers in better understanding the diagnosis of ODD and how to treat it in the family context. Typically, this therapy will work with the family system to diagnose family dynamics that have contributed to the child's behavior, continue to sustain the behavior, and trigger problematic behavior. In addition, caregivers are taught strategies that they can use consistently, such as the use of positive reinforcement, to bring about positive changes in the student. For example, a single parent may be taught by the school counselor how to create a visual chart to hang in the kitchen that tracks a particular behavior (e.g., the child slamming her door when angry) and then reward the child with an addition to her daily allowance when there is a decrease in that behavior. Perhaps the plan allows for an additional allowance increase if the child uses a more appropriate strategy when angry (e.g., deep breathing, a quick body scan, or yelling into a designated pillow).

Parents and caregivers can be encouraged to examine all aspects of the student's life to see what may assist the child in better controlling their behavior, cognitions, and emotions. For instance, children who are more physically active through free play or sports show decreased amounts of anxiety, depression, and other mood-based disorders (Stonerock et al., 2015). Research over the past several decades has indicated that children who have exposure to natural settings (grass, fields, lakes, streams, and natural sunlight) tend to be better behaved and feel better about themselves (Louv, 2008). In addition, and as previously stated, the nutritional intake of the child may also play a role in the manifestation of ODD-connected symptoms, and this is something that can be discussed and managed as part of family therapy.

Medicinal Interventions

Although there are currently no FDA-approved treatments for ODD, many children are treated off-label for the disorder (Zito et al., 2008). For example, many children and adolescents with ODD demonstrate measurable improvement with low doses of atypical neuroleptics (i.e., antipsychotic drugs), such as Abilify, Risperdal, and Seroquel (Gleason et al., 2007). Although the school counselor will not be responsible for the prescription of such medications, checking in to ensure that the use of any medications is happening consistently at home and reporting to outside stakeholders about any behavioral changes in the school after the student begins medicinal treatment will be valuable. For example, if the child's doctor prescribed 20 milligrams of a selective serotonin reuptake inhibitor (e.g., Lexapro) to be taken once a day because of anxiety and behavioral problems, it will be important for the school to have a mechanism (e.g., the school counselor getting behavior reports from each teacher weekly) to provide feedback for the parents/guardians and/or outside providers to evaluate the medication's effectiveness, adjust the dosage, etc.

Understanding What You Have Read: Comprehension Questions

Directions: Refer to what you have read to answer the following questions.

1. What is ODD?
2. What are the diagnostic criteria (symptoms) for a diagnosis of ODD?
3. What modalities/types of support can school counselors (and the school in general) extend to students?
4. How might you as a future counselor support a student who presents with a diagnosis of ODD during your clinical experience?
5. How might your personal experiences affect your ability to support students like Thomas (opening vignette)?
6. What are the ethical and multicultural considerations when working with a student like Thomas?

Case Examples

Case Example One

As you read the case about Marcus, reflect on the strategies that we discussed earlier in the chapter. The questions that follow the case relate to the student's behavioral symptoms and accompanying responses.

Marcus is a seventh-grade student at an urban school and lives with his maternal grandmother, Kelly. His parents never married (pregnancy was not planned); his dad lives out of state, and his mom has been in and out of rehabilitation for the past decade for opioid addiction. As early as preschool, Marcus was considered a "wild child" who would not sit still and would look right at adults and then do exactly what he was told not to do, according to his grandmother. For example, in second grade, Marcus's teacher asked him to sit down, and rather than do as he was told, he looked at the teacher and then stood up on his chair. Marcus was diagnosed with ADHD in second grade and has been taking Adderall once a day since that time with mixed results, according to parents and teachers. Other than the diagnosis of ADHD, Marcus is a healthy young man, according to his grandmother. But the school is not sure what to do at this point because Marcus has been assigned detention three times over the past month for being disrespectful toward his teachers and was just recently suspended for 5 days after refusing to leave the room when a teacher told him to go to the main office. Marcus has also become more isolated this school year because of the fact that many kids are starting to distance themselves from him because of his, as one student put it, "shitty and disrespectful" attitude and behavior toward adults in the building, as well as some of his peers.

Case Example One: Questions for Processing and Reflection

Directions: Use what you have learned in this chapter to respond to Marcus's case.

1. What symptoms are being displayed by Marcus that *might* indicate a diagnosis of ODD?
   a. Marcus has been experiencing symptoms since a very young age (preschool).
   b. Marcus is disrespectful and defiant toward some adults/authority figures (teachers).
   c. There have been problematic transitions and issues related to Marcus's family of origin (drug use, lack of attachment to biological parents).
   d. Marcus's behavior has and continues to get him in trouble with school and with peers.
   e. There is no evidence that Marcus's behavior is due to an organic cause or substance issues (nicotine, etc.).
   f. Marcus has a diagnosis of ADHD, which has a high level of comorbidity with ODD.
2. What information do you have regarding Marcus's situation?
   a. Lives with his maternal grandmother
   b. No evidence of a relationship with his biological parents
   c. Lives in an urban environment
   d. Long history of problematic behavior at school
   e. Very few friends
   f. Diagnosed with ADHD since second grade—taking Adderall since that time
3. What additional information might you still need?
   a. Do the problematic behaviors happen in other contexts (e.g., home, when with friends outside of school, in the neighborhood)?
   b. What dosage of Adderall is Marcus on, and has it been adjusted over the years based on his weight, age, etc.?
   c. What are the teachers' specifically seeing in the classroom? What tends to trigger his behavior? How often does it happen? Does it happen more at different times of the day?

   d. When was Marcus last seen by a pediatrician?
   e. How are Marcus's sleep and nutritional intake?
   f. What does Marcus have to say about all of the things discussed in the case example? Why does he think this stuff happens?
   g. Is Marcus using any substances that could be leading to or exacerbating his symptoms?
   h. Examine Marcus's scoring on standardized tests to determine if there is an underlying academic issue or if there is a potential need for the school psychologist to do any testing. Has any testing been done in the past?
4. How would you address concerns related to Marcus?
   a. Provide individual sessions to extend support in a safe and nonjudgmental format.
   b. Recommend that Marcus's grandmother takes him in to see his pediatrician.
   c. Gather specific information from teachers regarding Marcus's behavior.
   d. Meet with the interdisciplinary team meeting (school social worker, administrators, teachers, school psychologist) to determine a plan to support Marcus and to create a consistent way of dealing with problematic behaviors and rewarding positive behaviors.
   e. See if Marcus has a strong connection to any adults in the building. If not, see if getting him an adult mentor in the building is possible.

Case Example Two

As you read the case about Sophia, reflect on the strategies that we discussed earlier in the chapter. The questions that follow the case relate to the student's behavioral symptoms and accompanying responses.

Sophia is an eight-year-old girl in third grade who lives with her biological mother and father. She is from a small rural town, and there are only 13 other children in her entire third-grade cohort. Over the past 6 months, her teacher has been reporting to you and the principal that Sophia has been coming to class looking disheveled (hair not kept, greasy and unshowered looking) and acting in a "hyperactive way." On several occasions, she has been asked to stop making noises during quiet time, and she has responded by saying things like "whatever" and "try to make me." On most occasions, Sophia does stop the problematic behavior, but this has been an ongoing issue for nearly the whole school year (school has been in session for about 7 months). When you—as the school counselor—think about Sophia, you remember that she has had issues with bad behavior during the few past years; however, this year seems more extreme. When you call home, mom says that she is not surprised and that life at home has been tough since Mark, Sophia's father, lost his job about a year ago. However, mom also reports that she feels like Sophia has always been a bit of a "little snot" when she doesn't get her way and often is in trouble at home. One issue that Sophia's mom mentions is that since Mark has been home, the rules and structure have gone out the window: "He is like having another kid at home."

Case Example Two: Questions for Processing and Reflection

Directions: Use what you have learned in this chapter to respond to Sophia's case.

1. What symptoms are being displayed by Sophia that *might* indicate a diagnosis of ODD?
2. What information do you have regarding Sophia's situation?
3. What additional information might you still need?
4. How would you address concerns related to Sophia?

Chapter Summary

This chapter focused on the diagnostic criteria and behaviors related to ODD in children and youth, specifically in terms of its manifestation in the school context. The authors presented the information delineated in the *DSM-5* and then used relatable language and examples to further illustrate the diagnosis and its presentation. In addition, strategies were provided to assist school counselors in identifying students struggling with ODD and then collaboratively designing an appropriate plan to support students in the school context. Although school counselors will not be responsible for diagnosing a child with ODD, their unique input, ability to help design a holistic and collaborative approach to treatment, and ability to case manage and provide counseling in the school context are invaluable.

Additional Recommended Readings and Resources

Barkley, R. A., & Benton, C. (2013). *Your defiant child: 8 steps to better behavior* (2nd ed.). Guilford Press.

eAACAP. (2009). *ODD a guide for families by the American Academy of Adolescent Psychiatry.* American Academy of Child and Adolescent Psychiatry. www.aacap.org

Kazdin, A. E. (2008). *The Kazdin method for parenting the defiant child: With no pills, no therapy, no contest of wills.* Houghton Mifflin Company.

Louv, R. (2008). *Last child in the woods: Saving our children from nature-deficit disorder.* Algonquin Books of Chapel Hill.

Phelan, T. (2016). *1-2-3 magic: Effective discipline for children 2–12.* Sourcebooks LLC.

Riley, D.A. (2008). *What your explosive child is trying to tell you: Discovering the pathway from symptoms to solutions.* Houghton Mifflin Harcourt.

References

AACAP. (2009). Practice parameter for the assessment and treatment of children and adolescents with attention-deficit/hyperactivity disorder. *Journal of the American Academy of Child & Adolescent Psychiatry, 46*(1), 894–921.

American Psychiatric Association (APA) (2013). *Diagnostic and statistical manual of mental disorders* (5th ed.).

American Psychiatric Association (APA) (1980). *Diagnostic and statistical manual of mental disorders* (3rd ed.).

Biglan, A., Flay, B., Embry, D., & Sandler, I. (2012). The critical role of nurturing environments for promoting human well-being. *American Psychologist, 67*(4), 257–271.

Canino, G., Polanczyk, G., Bauermeister, J., Rohde, J., & Frick, L. (2010). Does the prevalence of CD and ODD vary across cultures? *Social Psychiatry and Psychiatric Epidemiology, 45*(7), 695–704.

Duncan, L., Pollastri, A., & Smoller, J. (2014). Mind the gap: Why many geneticists and psychological scientists have discrepant views about gene-environment interaction (G × E) research. *American Psychologist, 69*(3), 249–268.

Fazel, M., Patel, V., Thomas, S., & Tol, W. (2014). Mental health interventions in schools in low-income and middle-income countries. *Lancet Psychiatry, 1*(5), 388–398.

Frick, M. A., & Brocki, K. C. (2019). A multi-factorial perspective on ADHD and ODD in school-aged children: What is the role of cognitive regulation, temperament, and parental support? *Journal of Clinical and Experimental Neuropsychology, 41*(9), 933–945. https://doi.org/10.1080/13803395.2019.1641185

Frick, P., & Nigg, J. (2011). Current issues in the diagnosis of attention deficit hyperactivity disorder, oppositional defiant disorder, and conduct disorder. *Annual Review of Clinical Psychology, 8*(1), 77–107.

Gentzke, A., Creamer, M., Cullen, K., Ambrose, B., Willis, G., Jamal, A., & King, B. (2019). Vital signs: Tobacco product use among middle and high school students—United States, 2011–2018. *Morbidity and Mortality Weekly Report, 68*(6), 157–164.

Gleason, M., Egger, H. L., Emslie, G. J., Greenhill, L. L., Kowatch, R. A., Lieberman, A. F., Luby, J. L., Owens, J., Scahill, L. D., Scheeringa, M. S., Stafford, B., Wise, B., & Zeanah, C. H. (2007). Psychopharmacological treatment for very young children: Contexts and guidelines. *Journal of the American Academy of Child & Adolescent Psychiatry, 46*(12), 1532–1572.

Khanbani, M., Mohammadi, M., Jafari, N., Farid, S., & Chit, P. (2011). Effect of play therapy on behavioral problems of mal-adjusted pre-school children. *Iranian Journal of Psychiatry, 6*(1), 37–42.

Louv, R. (2008). *Last child in the woods: Saving our children from nature-deficit disorder.* Algonquin Books of Chapel Hill.

Miller-Slough, R., Dunsmore, J., Ollendick, T., & Greene, R. (2016). Parent-child synchrony in children with oppositional defiant disorder: associations with treatment outcomes. *Journal of Child and Family Studies, 25*(6), 1880–1888.

Morse, M., Benson, K., & Flory, K. (2015). Disruptive behavior disorders and marijuana use: The role of depressive symptoms. *Substance Abuse: Research and Treatment, 9*(1), 69–76.

Singh, A., Yeh, C., Verma, N., & Das, A. (2015). Overview of attention deficit hyperactivity disorder in young children. *Health Psychology Research, 3*(2), 2115.

Singh, I. (2011). A disorder of anger and aggression: Children's perspectives on attention deficit/hyperactivity disorder in the UK. *Social Science & Medicine, 73*(6), 889–896.

Stonerock, G., Hoffman, L., Smith, B., & Blumenthal, M. (2015). Exercise as a treatment for anxiety: Systematic review and analysis. *Annals of Behavioral Medicine, 49*(4), 542–556.

Zito, J., Derivan, A., Kratochvil, C., Safer, D., Fegert, J., & Greenhill, L. (2008). Off-label psychopharmacologic prescribing for children: History supports close clinical monitoring. *Child and Adolescent Psychiatry and Mental Health, 2*(1), 24.

CHAPTER EIGHT

Conduct Disorder

Dana Griffin and Nicole S. Helton

THE CASE OF MASON Mason is an 8-year-old, white male student in the third grade. He lives with his grandmother, who raised him since birth. His birth mother moved back into the area, but Mason does not see her often. Mason's birth father is unknown. Prior to the third grade, Mason was frequently suspended for violent physical attacks against others in his previous schools. For the first 6 weeks at a new school, Mason was doing well. He received only minor infractions for his behavior. However, 6 weeks into the year, Mason became more violent toward his peers. Mason would kick his classmates at recess or throw sand at teachers. As the weeks progressed, Mason would increase this behavior to punching teachers and throwing chairs. Most days, he would be suspended before 11:00 am. The school counselor, school psychologist, and school social worker could not determine any triggers for Mason's behavior and concluded that he was being manipulative. Upon consultation with Mason's grandmother, she confirmed that this behavior was not new or unusual for him and has been persistent. Mason expresses that he enjoys hitting people and likes to spit on them. When his grandmother tries to process the violent attacks, he shows no remorse for his actions.

Introduction to the Chapter

Students like Mason, although rare, are enrolled in our schools, and they present many challenges to the teachers, counselors, administrators, and other school staff members who must work with them. As in the case study, many of these students end up being frequently suspended or expelled from school, which leads to lower academic achievement and graduation rates. Without obtaining the intense help they need, students like Mason are at extreme risk for being caught in the criminal justice system, where they will unlikely receive the help they need. Indeed, it is reported that jails house a number of mentally ill inmates (Shatkin, 2015). Therefore, the purpose of this chapter is to provide a school-family-community partnership approach to working with kids diagnosed with conduct disorder according to the *Diagnostic and Statistical Manual of Mental Disorders, Fifth Edition* (*DSM-5*; American Psychiatric Association [APA], 2013). First, an overview of the role of school counselors in addressing mental health is provided, followed by an overview of conduct disorder and the *DSM-5* criteria. Next, we provide three strategies that school counselors can use to work with students diagnosed with or showing symptoms of conduct disorder. These three strategies fall within a school-family-community partnership approach and are within the scope of school counselors' roles in schools and require school counselors to be proactive in developing interventions to address the needs of their students. These interventions include a group counseling approach to working with students, parent education, and collaborating with community partners.

Learning Objectives

By the end of this chapter, readers will accomplish the following:

- Understand the importance of the role of school counselors in working with students diagnosed with, or demonstrating symptoms of, conduct disorder.
- Understand the signs and symptoms of conduct disorder.
- Learn three strategies for working with students diagnosed with, or demonstrating symptoms of, conduct disorder.

Typically, school counselors are not trained to use the *DSM-5*; however, school counselors must be aware of the signs of any given mental disorder, as most students with mental disorders are also enrolled in and attending schools. Indeed, the American School Counselor Association's (ASCA) position statement (2015) on school counselors and mental health requires school counselors to

> recognize and respond to the need for mental health and behavioral prevention, early intervention and crisis services that promote psychosocial wellness and development for all students. School counselors are prepared to address barriers and to assess ways to maximize students' success in schools, communities and their family structure by offering education, prevention, and crisis and short-term intervention until the student is connected with available community resources. (p. 71)

This position statement also provides a list of action items for school counselors to address mental health in their schools, which include providing prevention, intervention, and services; in particular, providing "school-based prevention and universal interventions and targeted interventions for students with mental health and behavioral health concerns" (p. 71). Furthermore, the ASCA Code of Ethics (2016) stipulates that although school counselors do not diagnose mental disorders, they must be aware of how mental diagnoses can affect students' academic success. It is clear that ASCA considers the important role of school counselors in addressing the mental health needs of students.

However, although ASCA states that school counselors should be involved with meeting the mental health needs of their student populations, research suggests that school counselors may not be involved in working with students with mental health needs, and one reason for this is due to a lack of time or support to do so (Brown et al., 2006). In addition, role confusion continues to exist in the profession, causing some counselors to not view addressing mental health as a part of their job (Paisley et al., 2007; Walley et al., 2009). This role confusion is harmful to students because school counselors may be the first point of reference for any student with mental health disorders, and not addressing mental health disorders can negatively affect one's personal, social, and academic outcomes. Indeed, more than 75% of students in need of mental health services do not receive the help they need (Kataoka et al., 2002; Shatkin, 2015).

In addition to many students not receiving services for mental health diagnoses, disparities exist in who is diagnosed with a mental health disorder, especially when it comes to youth in schools and behavioral disorders. Many racial and ethnic minority populations, those living in low socioeconomic status (SES) and those living in rural environments are less likely to receive the mental health services they need (Shatkin, 2015). For example, youth living in poverty are 3 times more likely to be diagnosed with a conduct disorder than youth not living in poverty, and males of color are also more likely to be diagnosed as having conduct disorder (Shatkin, 2015). Indeed, cultural factors have a significant influence on how one judges students' behaviors and on who is seen as having behavioral problems (Auwarter & Aruguete, 2008; Nguyen et al., 2007; Sue, 2010). For example, referral rates for African American and Latino students from low SES environments have higher behavioral referral and discipline reports than other students (Bryan et al., 2012). This all speaks to the need for school counselors to be leaders and to take proactive measures to address the mental health needs of students, including those diagnosed with conduct disorders and those most at risk for being diagnosed as having conduct disorder.

Conduct Disorder Diagnostic Criteria

Disruptive behavior disorders are one of the most common disorders diagnosed in school-aged children (Shatkin, 2015). The *DSM-5* outlines conduct disorder with the following criteria:

A. A repetitive and persistent pattern of behavior in which the basic rights of others or major age-appropriate societal norms or rules are violated , as manifested by the presence of at least three of the following 15 criteria in the past 12 months from any of the categories below, with at least one criterion present in the past 6 months:

   Aggression to People and Animals

   1. Often bullies, threatens, or intimidates others.
   2. Often initiates physical fights.
   3. Has used a weapon that can cause serious physical harm to others (e.g., a bat, brick, broken bottle, knife, gun).
   4. Has been physically cruel to people.
   5. Has been physically cruel to animals.
   6. Has stolen while confronting a victim (e.g., mugging, purse snatching, extortion, armed robber).
   7. Has forced someone into sexual activity.

   Destruction of property

   8. Has deliberately engaged in fire setting with the intention of causing serious damage.
   9. Has deliberately destroyed others' property (other than by fire setting).

   Deceitfulness or Theft

   10. Has broken into someone else's house, building, or car.
   11. Often lies to obtain goods or favors or to avoid obligations (i.e., "cons" others).
   12. Has stolen items of nontrivial value without confronting a victim (e.g., shoplifiting, but without breaking and entering; forgery).

   Serious Violation of Rules

   13. Often stays out at night despite parental prohibitions, beginning before age 13 years.
   14. Has run away from home overnight at least twice while living in the parental or parental surrogate home, or once without returning for a lengthy period.
   15. Is often truant from school, beginning before age 13 years.

B. The disturbance in behavior causes clinically significant impairment in social, academic, or occupational functioning.

C. If the individual is age 18 years or older, criteria are not met for antisocial personality disorder.

Conduct disorder has three onset types specifiers: (1) childhood-onset type in which the characteristics appear before age 10, (2) adolescent-onset type in which characteristics do not appear before age 10, and (3) unspecified-onset type in which there is not enough information to determine if the first symptom appeared before or after age 10. Another specifier used in conduct disorder addresses the lack of prosocial emotions. A child can be diagnosed as having conduct disorder with limited prosocial emotions if they show at least two of the following characteristics: (1) lack of remorse or guilt, (2) callous, (3) unconcerned about their performance at school, or (4) shallow or deficient affect. Finally, a diagnosis of conduct disorder can be mild (few characteristics exist in excess of what is required to make a diagnosis, and the problems cause minor harm to others), moderate (the number of problems and the effects on others are intermediate and between more than a few but less than severe), or severe (many conduct problems exist in excess of those required to make a diagnosis, and the problems cause considerable harm to others) (*APA*, 2013).

In addressing conduct disorder, it is important to use a broad-based approach as opposed to simply focusing on direct interventions with the individuals (Shatkin, 2015). Mental health programming needs to include interventions geared toward helping children improve their prosocial engagement, self-efficacy, and behavioral competency skills, as well as an integrated school-family-community approach—offering strategies for the individual, the family, and the school and having community involvement (Catalano et al., 2004). To this end, we developed a three-pronged approach that includes an individual component, a parent education component, and a school-family-community partnership approach to working with youth identified with conduct disorder or at risk for identification with the conduct disorder.

Addressing Conduct Disorder in Schools—A Group Counseling Approach

The prevalence of conduct disorder in schools is more common in boys (6% to 16%) than girls (2% to 9%), with most displaying symptoms around the age of 10 or in adolescence (Mental Health America, 2019). Therefore, teaching and promoting self-regulation strategies can be a key part of a school counselor's role within a comprehensive school counseling program. Many studies support the development of self-regulation, especially for students with conduct disorder (Ohrt et al., 2015). Focusing on the students and interventions to build their internal beliefs about their ability to succeed and self-regulate will greatly affect them academically and in their careers, as well as socially and emotionally. Steinberg (2014) said that before students can master self-regulation, they must have three factors in place: (1) they must be emotionally secure to calm themselves, (2) behaviorally competent to know how to act responsibly, and (3) confident enough to take responsibility for their actions by developing a growth mindset. Students can change their mindset by viewing mistakes and failures as learning opportunities, embracing challenges, and putting in more effort through intrinsic motivation (Dweck & Blackwell, 2017). It is important to use interventions that focus on students' behavior but to also address the beliefs that underlie their behavior. Therefore, school counselors can support students with conduct disorder by providing direct services to the student by (a) teaching emotional vocabulary, behavior expectations within the school, and a growth mindset (Demanchick et al., n.d.) and (b) through cognitive behavior therapy (CBT), which has been noted as an effective approach for working with students with conduct disorder (Busari, 2013).

Because of the prevalence of conduct disorder in schools, chances are that multiple students have been diagnosed with or present symptoms of conduct disorder. The following section contains a psychoeducational group counseling approach that may be helpful in working with these students. This group is based on the CBT approach, which stresses the role of thinking and doing and is an action-oriented approach. When using CBT, group leaders combine empathy and sensitivity with technical competence in establishing their relationship with group members. The school counselor, as group leader, is to function as the content expert, create a safe environment so students will feel comfortable sharing, juggle content the with group process, and be sensitive to when group members are ready to address issues and engage in activities.

Objectives and Goals

The ASCA Mindsets and Behaviors for Student Success selected for this group support the desired outcomes of the student being able to successfully identify emotions within themselves, demonstrate appropriate behavior within a school setting, and develop a growth mindset. The school counselor's mindset will instill belief in the development of the whole self, including a healthy balance of mental, social/emotional, and physical well-being (M1) and self-confidence in the ability to succeed (M2). By the end of the group, the student will demonstrate self-discipline and self-control (B-SMS 2), as well as social maturity and behaviors appropriate to the situation and environment (B-SS 9) (ASCA, 2014). By the end of the final session, each participant will be able to do the following: (1) articulate at least five emotions in themselves and at least three strategies to support themselves, (2) identify at least three behavior expectations within the school, and (3) apply at least two growth mindset development techniques.

Group Composition

Group members should be selected, screened, and given take-home consent forms for parental/guardian signatures. Because of the average age of onset being around age 10 to adolescence, the group will focus on working with upper elementary students and middle school students with symptoms of conduct disorder to develop appropriate skills to successfully identify emotions within themselves, demonstrate appropriate behavior within a school setting, and develop a growth mindset. Groups tend to be most successful with more than three individuals, but because of the behaviors of conduct disorder, no more than six students should be in the group. The group is created to run 60 minutes once a week for 6 consecutive weeks.

Group Sessions Outline

Presession

The group leader should meet individually with each group member to introduce themselves and conduct a presurvey to obtain perception data for the group. Other data to be collected includes attendance of group sessions and a self-report postsurvey, specifically for the group members, which they will complete one week after the final group session (process data). Outcome data to be collected include behavior referral data pre and post group within the school. Other outcome data to collect are staff and parental/caregiver progress reports before and after the group sessions.

Session 1: Forming and Norming

The procedures for the first session are used to introduce members, go over confidentiality, establish group norms and expectations, and discuss group leader and member roles. The group leader will introduce the feelings wheel (see Appendix A). Before each session, members will select and disclose to the group at *least* one feeling they identify having at the moment. If the member chooses many feelings, ask them to choose their biggest, hardest, or favorite feeling. The leader will moderate time and validate feelings by accepting students' feelings. Explain that all feelings are okay to feel, but it is how you handle them that matters. Example: "Feeling aggressive is okay; hitting a peer is not."

Help students label their feelings by encouraging the use of a wide range of feeling words (begin at the center wheel and expand out to more specific terms as developmentally appropriate—i.e., younger grades focus on the inner circle). The group leader should express their own feelings in the group. ("I feel proud when I see you all on task." "I'm feeling frustrated that we are not following directions.") The group leader should also empower the group members by asking them, "What would help you feel better?" Or, "How can I help you with this feeling?" Teach them to solve their own problems using empathy, compassion, and mutual respect for each other's feelings.

Session 2: Following Rules

Members will begin with confidentiality, reviewing group norms, and the feelings wheel. The group leader should address any concerns about sharing in a group. Then the group should be directed to compile a list of school rules and expectations on a large sheet of paper or board. The group leader should then discuss the reasons for school rules and expectations—for example, explore why rules are in place and why it is important to know and follow the rules. The group leader will give homework that instructs the group members to choose one or more of the rules discussed to work on over the next week. Incentives for participation or visual reminders to motivate the members should be created. At the subsequent session, have members discuss any difficulties with focusing on one or more rules.

Session 3: Identifying Triggers

Members will begin with confidentiality, reviewing group norms, and the feelings wheel. Members will discuss homework from the last session and any difficulties with following the rules. Group members will identify triggers that make it hard to self-regulate their emotions or actions, as well as identify specific provoking events that make it hard to follow rules and discuss exact feelings with the events and triggers using the feelings wheel. Members will fill out a worksheet with the following statements/questions (alter vocabulary if needed for age-appropriate use): "Think of an event that happened within the last 3 weeks for which you got into trouble. List any actions during the event that led to trouble." "What were you thinking just before you acted?" "What were you feeling just before you acted?" (Provide the feelings wheel for visual aid.) "What thoughts and feelings were linked to the event?" "Do you have any idea why this event made you think and feel the way it did?" "What could have happened that would have made you feel or think differently?" "Are there any other ways to make sense of what happened?" "What ways of thinking and feeling about the event would have helped you keep your behavior aligned with school rules and out of trouble?" "What statements can you use to keep calm and think clearly?" "What feelings or thoughts do you need to watch for (clues that you are heading for trouble)?" Support members by helping them come up with specific answers. Use the remaining time to share with the group for the promotion of group accountability and cohesiveness.

Session 4: Changing Mindset

Members will begin with confidentiality, reviewing group norms, and the feelings wheel. Give group members time to complete any discussions necessary from the previous session. Introduce the concepts of growth mindset and goal setting. Begin the activity by asking the group members to pick an easy observable behavioral goal to work on that relates to their behavior in school or at home. The group leader's focus should be on the intermediate steps to attain the goal and emphasizing that small changes lead to bigger changes. Discuss the small changes members choose to make and a build growth mindset by rewording steps so that they are positive and challenging. The homework is for members to share this process with a teacher or parent/guardian.

Session 5: Changing Our Mindset

Members will begin with confidentiality, reviewing group norms, and the feelings wheel. Give group members time to complete any discussions necessary from the previous session. The group leader will discuss the growth mindset by asking the group to answer true or false to the following statements:

1. "You are a certain kind of person, and there is not much that can be done to really change that."
2. "No matter what kind of person you are, you can always change substantially."
3. "You can do things differently, but the important parts of who you are can't really be changed."
4. "You can always change basic things about the kind of person you are."

Statements one and three show a fixed mindset and statements two and four show a growth mindset. This belief comes into play in situations that show personal qualities, such as how dependable, cooperative, caring, or socially skilled someone is. Ask members to see if they can identify someone they know in their school who has a growth mindset. How does that person confront obstacles? How are other students in their class able to follow rules? Can they identify any strategies others use? Have a discussion about how everyone makes mistakes and what matters is what we learn from the mistakes, as a growth mindset does not ensure perfection; it ensures progress. Ask members to talk about any lessons they learned from mistakes they have made. The group leader should focus on healthy strategies discussed by the group members. A growth mindset takes work and effort. It makes things easier in the long run but needs effort to be maintained. Be sure, as the group leader, to cheerlead and positively reinforce any growth mindset strategies the students are already using.

Session 6: Closing the Group

Summarize the group and discuss what the members have learned from the experience. Have members draw four columns on a sheet of blank paper. Ask the members to add the heading "Fact" at the top of column 1, "Question" at the top of column 2, "Aha!" at the top of column 3, and "Action" at the top of column 4. Members should take time to reflect on the group. In column 1, members will write one fact that they now know that they did not know before. In column 2, members will write one question they still have (if they still have a question). In column 3, members will write one "aha!" moment—one or more new ideas or strategies they now have. In column 4, members will write what action(s) they will take as a result of their work in the group (Haskell et al., 2007). The members will then share their thoughts with the group. Review any further questions. Afterward, the members will take the postsurvey. Table 8.1 shows examples of what a student's completed table might entail.

TABLE 8.1 Closing Reflections

FACT	QUESTION	AHA	ACTION
It's okay to feel angry.		I can't hit people because I'm angry.	I will ask to go see the school counselor when I am angry.
I can change my behavior.	How do I identify my triggers?	I can learn to keep calm.	I will count as high as I need to count to calm myself.
I am not a bad person.	What caused me to feel angry?	I can keep my hands to myself.	I will practice sitting on my hands when I want to hit someone.

Sometimes, needs arise that require intensive individual support. Students may need additional individual counseling to work on other skills. According to research, CBT can also be used in individual counseling, and the techniques and strategies used in this group counseling plan can be effective in individual settings. We must caution that because of the severity of the symptoms of those with conduct disorder, it is important to collaborate with school staff and parents so that everyone is aware of the action plan created to help students de-escalate.

Addressing Conduct Disorder With the Family: Parent Education

It is important that parents are also included in the treatment plan for students with conduct disorder. This is especially important as parents need to have a clear understanding of the disorder and what it means for their child. As mentioned in the case study of Mason, his grandmother is aware of his violent tendencies. When working with parents, it is important to help them to understand the difference between what is normal behavior for youth and what is not normal. For example, it is normal for youth to be defiant, have tantrums, lie and cheat, or be mean-spirited, and while these behaviors are problematic, it becomes even more so when they are demonstrated with regular consistency and without regard or concern for others (*APA*, 2013; Shatkin, 2015). When working with parents, it is also important to note that they need to be taught components of CBT so that they too can help promote positive and healthy interactions with their children. Parents need to be taught how to identify and reward appropriate behavior and implement positive and negative consequences (Shatkin, 2015).

Parents must also be taught how to control their own emotions. It is beneficial to validate parents' feelings of stress, frustration, sadness, anger, or any other emotions parents may have while dealing with a child with conduct disorder. Parents may also "lose control" and yell or apply physical punishment as a means of getting their child to listen and behave, so parents may need to be taught CBT techniques, particularly to focus on increasing their own self-control when addressing the disruptive behaviors of their child. Most importantly, a parent education program should include a component for helping parents manage resistant behavior. Maag (2000) wrote about ways to address resistant behavior in children. The strategies (summarized next) discussed in his article should be included in a parent education program.

> ***Strategy 1.*** Teach parents to be comprehensive and unrestricted in their thinking. Often, parents have preconceived notions about what they should do or say to a child. These preconceived notions can prevent parents from expanding their perspectives to consider alternative options.
>
> ***Strategy 2.*** Teach parents to avoid negative reinforcement traps, which consist of applying negative reinforcements to unwanted behaviors, thus reinforcing what the child wants.
>
> ***Strategy 3.*** Teach parents how to conduct a functional assessment, which is determining the intent of an inappropriate behavior. Parents need to ask themselves what the outcome their child is looking for with their behavior is and then help the child select a more appropriate behavior that can accomplish the same goal.
>
> ***Strategy 4.*** Teach parents how to reframe their child's behavior by addressing the intent through context and meaning. Context reframing assumes that every behavior is useful but just not in all contexts or situations. For example, parents can ask their child in which situations is it helpful to be aggressive. The hope is that once the child realizes that their behavior is not all bad, then they may be open to accepting a more appropriate behavior to use in the target setting or context (i.e., classroom). Meaning reframing provides the child with a more acceptable and positive meaning for their inappropriate behavior; for example, stubbornness is reframed as being independent.

Strategy 5. Teach parents that they must change their mindsets about the behavioral expectations they have for their child. Oftentimes, parents become frustrated and ask themselves, "Why can't my child just listen and follow my rules?" Parents need to show genuine unconditional positive regard and empathy.

Strategy 6. Teach parents how to embed instructions. Instead of demanding that their child engage in a behavior that the parents want the child to do (a high-probability request), the parents direct the child to do what they already doing while including the request for a desired behavior. For example, "Joe, while you're yelling at the top of the lungs, take your clothes to your room."

Strategy 7. Teach parents to accept the child's resistance, as then the resistance becomes cooperation. A parent should never fight with their child. Instead, the parent should focus on encouraging the child to produce the maladaptive behavior (compliance based) or avoiding trying to behave appropriately (defiance based). Compliance-based behavior requires the parents to tell the child to keep engaging in the inappropriate behavior. For example, a parent wants their child to stop arguing. Instead of telling their child to stop arguing, the parent should have the child continue to argue for 5 minutes. If their child does it, they are being compliant, but if they do not, they are also being compliant in that they are not arguing, which is the desired outcome. Defiance-based behaviors stipulate that to change, the child should stay the same or give up. The goal is to have the child oppose carrying out the directive in circumstances in which by doing so, the child is being compliant. There are three types of defiant-based behaviors: (1) Have the child delay changing their behaviors by having them move more slowly than expected: "Today, it is not important to do anything to change your behavior." (2) Forbid the child from changing their behavior: "To find out how bad your behavior is, just give in to it and let it happen." (3) Declare hopelessness: "It is impossible for you to finish your homework." All variations focus on joining the child's frame of reference by instructing them to do what they are already doing. However, defiant-based compliance must be avoided with children engaging in behaviors that are dangerous to themselves or others (p. 138).

In summary, when managing resistance, teach parents to remember that if what they are currently doing is not working, they need to try something else. Parents should not be afraid to take risks; there are different ways of looking at situations; they should be flexible and think creatively when coming up with ways to address their child's behavior. Anything new that parents do to address their child's resistance will cause their child to pause, as new techniques break up rigid patterns of responding (p. 139). Managing resistance is important information to teach parents, as a hallmark of conduct disorder is the lack of self-control over emotions and behaviors. Therefore, it does not behoove parents to try to control their child's behavior through direct confrontation but to find other methods of getting their child to be compliant.

Addressing Conduct Disorder in the Community: Creating a Culture of Care

The main method school counselors use to work with students with mental health needs is using community referrals. School counselors often refer students to mental health professionals in the community if the students display behaviors that are above and beyond the scope of the school counselor's role. Referrals to community mental health agencies are also necessary when the severity of conduct disorder includes a steady pattern of harming others or property and violating the rights of others. Indeed, Kaffenberger and O'Rorke-Trigiani (2013) stated that counselor advocacy includes collaborating with mental health professionals in and out of the school

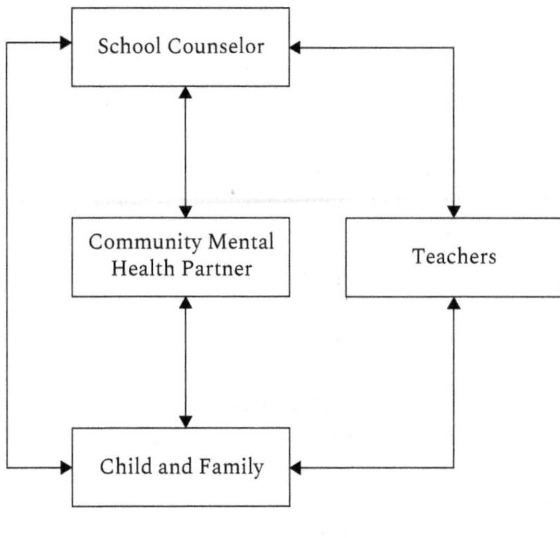

FIGURE 8.1. Culture of Care
A school counselor refers a student to a community mental health partner. The community mental health partner works with the child and family and communicates back to the school counselor, who in turn works with the child, the child's teacher, and the child's family. The family communicates with the school counselor and the child's teacher.

building. However, as stated by DeKruyf et al., (2013), the use of outside referrals to address the mental health needs of students will more likely than not result in several students not getting their mental health needs. As most students with conduct disorder will be suspended from school, school counselors may serve as the only source of intervention for these students. Furthermore, because of the increased prevalence of males of color and those in lower SESs being identified as having behavioral issues, school counselors must intervene and work with students whose behavior does not warrant a conduct disorder diagnosis but will ultimately see them pushed into the school-to-prison pipeline, where students' behavior leads them to be pushed out of school into a disciplinary practice that leads them to prison (American Civil Liberties Union, n.d.). In other words, school counselors must not think that their job is done simply by submitting a referral for a student. Even when the student does receive services outside of school, the student will still need to have services in place for when they are in school. Thusly, collaboration is warranted.

Creating a culture of care is vitally important, as coordinating with the community mental health professional to provide mental health services within the school is necessary for the academic success and social and emotional well-being of students (Whiston et al., 2011). Further, addressing the mental health needs of students requires the collaboration of family, school, and community stakeholders in the treatment process (Kiselica & Robinson, 2001). Doherty and Mendenhall (2006) stated that a reciprocal dynamic must exist among all stakeholders to address the mental health needs of students. A culture of care is a model of holistic care for students, meaning that communication streams are open between the school counselor, the community mental health professional, the teachers, and the family (see Figure 8.1).

Therefore, school counselors should view a referral as only the first step in addressing conduct disorder. Within this first step, school counselors should develop partnerships with community health professionals—developing alliances with those who are committed to creating a culture of care for students. This means that the community mental health partners are open to cultivating communication with the school counselor and the family. School counselors must take leadership in ensuring that the family members sign the requisite paperwork that allows for the sharing of medical information so that the community mental health partner can openly discuss the therapeutic plan of action with the student and even provide strategies for the school counselor to implement at school. The school counselor must also be able to share therapeutic strategies with the child's teachers, as, optimally, the student will be able to fully participate in all classroom activities.

Understanding What You Have Read: Comprehension Questions

Directions: Refer to what you learned in this chapter to answer the following questions.

1. What is conduct disorder?
2. What are the determining factors for a diagnosis of conduct disorder?
3. What is the role of school counselors in working with students with mental health diagnoses, such as conduct disorder?
4. What modalities of support can school counselors extend to students?
5. What are some ways that counselors can teach parents to manage their child's resistance?
6. How might you as a future counselor create a culture of care for students with conduct disorder?

Case Examples

Case Example One

As you read the case about Jessica, reflect on the strategies that we discussed earlier in the chapter. The questions that follow the case relate to the student's behavioral symptoms and accompanying responses.

Jessica is a 5-year old girl in a rural elementary school. Jessica's parents came to you because of their increasing concern about her temper tantrums at home. The parents indicated that Jessica often becomes enraged and argumentative with them, refusing to follow rules or take direction. In particular, they report difficulty getting her to transition from playing with her toys to coming to the dinner table. After Jessica ignored her parents' repeated prompts, her mother became frustrated and told her that she had lost her dessert privilege. Jessica became aggressive and destructive, breaking her toys and smashing food and water from the dinner table into the carpet. She even packed a bag and tried to run away. Her parents described similar scenarios at bedtime, bath time, and when getting her dressed in the morning. They described Jessica as irritable in these situations, and they felt that she was deliberately ignoring or trying to annoy them. You are the only counselor in the school, and Jessica has not been referred to you for behavioral concerns.

Case Example One: Questions for Processing and Reflection

Directions: Use what you have learned in this chapter to respond to Jessica's case.

1. What symptoms are being displayed by Jessica that *might* indicate that she may be experiencing symptoms of conduct disorder?
   a. Jessica becomes enraged and argumentative with her parents, refusing to follow rules or take direction.
   b. Jessica becomes aggressive and destructive after having a privilege taken away.
   c. Jessica tried to run away.
   d. Jessica's behaviors are persistent across multiple situations.
2. What information do you have regarding Jessica's situation?
   a. Jessica's parents are frustrated and feel that Jessica is deliberately ignoring them.
   b. Jessica's parents are asking for help.
   c. Jessica's behavior seems to happen in times of transition (at bedtime, bath time, getting dressed in the morning, and from play to dinner).

3. What additional information might you still need?
    a. Does Jessica display these behaviors at school and in other settings outside the home?
    b. How long have these behaviors been occurring?
    c. What other strategies have the parents used to manage Jessica's behavior?
    d. Does Jessica show any remorse after her outburst or tantrums?
4. How would you address concerns related to Jessica?
    a. Provide Jessica's parents with a referral source for mental health.
    b. Meet with Jessica's teachers to see if she has demonstrated any behavioral issues.
    c. Individual counseling support for Jessica to develop a trusting relationship, provide unconditional positive regard, and teach approaches to managing her own behavior. This is a proactive approach, as those with conduct disorder may display symptoms in more than one setting (i.e., home and school).

Case Example Two

As you read the case about Caleb, reflect on the strategies that we discussed earlier in the chapter. The questions that follow the case relate to the student's behavioral symptoms and accompanying responses.

Caleb is an 11-year-old African American male in the fifth grade. Caleb is from a rural town and has a 7-year old sister. You know that Caleb has a history of bullying, stealing, lying, and running away from home. His parents called and asked for additional help, as he has been coming home with items he has stolen from the classroom. They are concerned that as he gets older, he will get into more trouble. You try to talk to Caleb, but he ignores you. His teacher has given up on him and continually sends him to the office. What do you do?

Case Example Two: Questions for Processing and Reflection

Directions: Use what you have learned in this chapter to respond to Caleb's case.

1. What are the symptoms of conduct disorder that Caleb has demonstrated?
2. What is your next step when working with Caleb?
3. With whom within the school would you collaborate? Explain why.
4. What are the benefits of working with Caleb's parents when building a plan for Caleb?

Chapter Summary

School counselors can be change agents in addressing the mental health needs of their students. When working with conduct disorder specifically, school counselors may not be aware of the interventions that can be used to help meet the needs of their students. However, in taking a school-family-community approach to working with students with conduct disorder, school counselors can collaborate with families and community mental health workers to develop the appropriate strategies to meet the needs of students. The group counseling plan included in this chapter is helpful to teach students to understand their emotions and how to self-regulate. Finally, parents need information about the best practices they can use to work with their own children. The parent education information presented in this chapter provides parents with strategies that they can use with their children to address resistant behavior common in kids with conduct disorder.

Additional Recommended Readings and Resources

Grothaus, T. (2013). School counselors serving students with disruptive behavior disorders. *Professional School Counseling, 16*(4), 245–255.

Missouri Comprehensive Guidance Programs. (n.d.) *Missouri comprehensive guidance programs: Linking school success with life success.* Missouri Center for Career Education. https://dese.mo.gov/sites/default/files/RSSmallGroupUnitSelfControl3-5.pdf

References

American Civil Liberties Union. (n.d.). *School-to-prison pipeline.* https://www.aclu.org/issues/juvenile-justice/school-prison-pipeline

American Psychiatric Association (APA). (2013). *Diagnostic and statistical manual of mental disorders* (5th ed.).

American School Counselor Association (ASCA). (2014). *The ASCA mindsets and behaviors for student success: K–12 college-and career-readiness standards for every student.*

American School Counselor Association (ASCA). (2016). *ASCA ethical standards for school counselors.*

American School Counselor Association (ASCA). (2015). *ASCA position statements: The school counselor and student mental health.*

Auwarter, A. E., & Aruguete, M. S. (2008). Counselor perceptions of students who vary in gender and socioeconomic status. *Social Psychology of Education, 11*, 389–395.

Brown, C., Dahlbeck, D. T., & Sparkman-Barnes, L. (2006). Collaborative relationships: School counselors and non-school mental health professional working together to improve the mental health needs of students. *Professional School Counseling, 9*, 332–335.

Bryan, J., Day-Vines, N. L., Griffin, D., & Moore-Thomas, C. (2012). The disproportionality dilemma: Patterns of teacher referrals to school counselors for disruptive behavior. *Journal of Counseling & Development, 90*, 177–190.

Busari, A. O. (2013). *Cognitive behaviour therapy in the management of conduct disorder among adolescents.* IntechOpen. http://dx.doi.org/10.5772/53046. https://www.intechopen.com/books/mental-disorders-theoretical-and-empirical-perspectives/cognitive-behaviour-therapy-in-the-management-of-conduct-disorder-among-adolescents

Catalano, R. F., Berglund, M. L., Ryan, J. A. M., Lonczak, H. S., & Hawkins, J. D. (2004). Positive youth development in the United States: Research findings on evaluations of positive youth development programs. *Annals of the American Academy of Political and Social Science, 591*, 98–124.

DeKruyf, L., Auger, R. W., & Trice-Black, S. (2013). The role of school counselors in meeting students' mental health needs: Examining issues of professional identity. *Professional School Counseling, 16*(5), 271–282.

Demanchick, S. P., Rangan, M., & Douthit, K. (n.d.) *Addressing conduct disorder in elementary school children: An application of the ASCA National Model.* https://files.eric.ed.gov/fulltext/EJ901145.pdf

Doherty, W. J., & Mendenhall, T. J. (2006). Citizen health care: A model for engaging patients, families, and communities as co-producers of health. *Families, Systems, and Health, 24*, 251–263.

Dweck, C. S., & Blackwell, L. S. (2017). *Growth mindset tools & resources to transform school culture.* Mindset Works, Inc.

Haskell, J. E., Cyr, L. F., & McPhail, G. (2007). *Closing ideas: Facilitation tips, tools and techniques.* University of Maine and the U.S. Department of Agriculture Cooperating. https://www.uvm.edu/sites/default/files/closing-ideas.pdf

Kaffenberger, C. J., & O'Rorke-Trigiani, J. (2013). Addressing student mental health needs by providing direct and indirect services and building alliances in the community. *Professional School Counseling, 16*, 323–332.

Kataoka, S. H., Zhang, L., & Wells, K. B. (2002). Unmet need for mental health care among U.S. Children: Variation by ethnicity and insurance status. *American Journal of Psychiatry, 159*, 1548–1555. https://doi.org/10.1176/appi.ajp.159.91548

Kiselica, M. S., & Robinson, M. (2001). Bringing advocacy counseling to life: The history, issues, and human dramas of social justice work in counseling. *Journal of Counseling & Development, 79*, 37–397.

Maag, J. W. (2000). Managing resistance. *Intervention in School and Clinic, 35*(3), 131–140.

Mental Health America. (2019). *Conduct disorder.* https://www.mhanational.org/conditions/conduct-disorder

Nguyen, L., Huang, L. N., Arganza, G. F., & Liao, Q. (2007). The influence of race and ethnicity on psychiatric diagnoses and clinical characteristics of children and adolescents in children's services. *Cultural Diversity and Ethnic Minority Psychology, 13*, 18–25.

Ohrt, J., Webster, L., & Garza, D. L. (2015). The effects of a success skills group on adolescent's self-regulation, self-esteem, and perceived learning competence. *Professional School Counseling, 18*(1), 169–178.

Paisley, P. O. Ziomek-Daigle, J. Z., Getch, Y. Q., & Bailey, D. F. (2007). Using state standards to develop professional school counsellor identity as both counsellors and educators. *Guidance & Counseling, 21*, 143–151.

Shatkin, J. P. (2015). *Child & adolescent mental health: A practical, all-in-one guide.* W. W. Norton & Company.

Steinberg, L. (2014). *Age of opportunity.* Houghton Mifflin Harcourt Publishing Company.

Sue, D. W. (2010). *Microaggressions in everyday life: Race, gender, and sexual orientation.* John Wiley and Sons.

Walley, C., Grothaus, T., & Craigen, L. (2009). Confusion, crisis, and opportunity: Professional school counselors' role in responding to mental health issues. *Journal of School Counseling, 7*(36), 1–25. http://www.jsc.montana.edu/articles/v7n36.pdf

Whiston, S. C., Tai, W. L., Rahardja, D., & Eder, K. (2011). School counseling outcome: A meta-analytic examination of interventions. *Journal of Counseling & Development, 89*(1), 37–55. https://doi.org/10.1002/j.1556-6678.2011.tb00059.x

Credit

Fig. 8.2: G. Wilcox, The Feelings Wheel, from "The Feeling Wheel: A Tool for Expanding Awareness of Emotions and Increasing Spontaneity and Intimacy," *Transactional Analysis Journal*, vol. 12, no. 4.

Appendix A. The Feelings Wheel

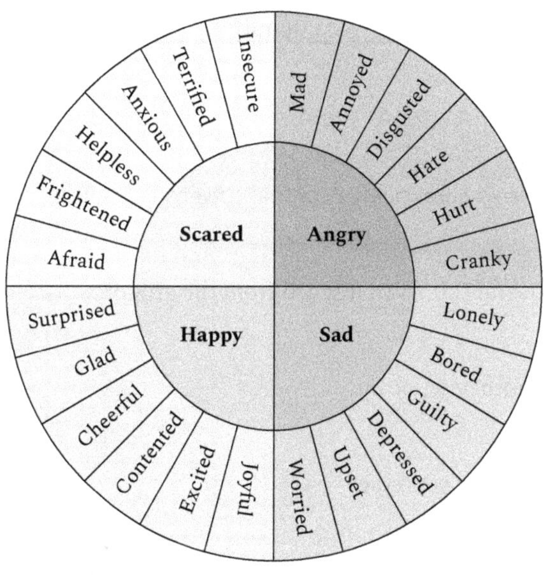

FIGURE 8.2.

Appendix B. Follow-Up Session Feedback Form for Students

Name: ______________________ Date: ______________

Questions:

1. What specific skills are you practicing now that the group is over?

2. What was the most useful thing you learned from the group?

3. What could you use more practice on?

4. How are things different for you now?

5. What progress have you made toward the goals you set for yourself at the end of our group meetings?

6. How are you keeping yourself accountable?

7. What suggestions do you have for future groups?

8. What specific "things" contributed to the ranking you gave your experience in the group?

9. What would have made it better?

10. Circle your overall experience in the group on a scale from 1 → 5 ______

1 = Most positive activity in which I have participated in for a long time
2 = Gave me a lot of direction with my needs
3 = I learned a lot about myself, and I am ready to make definite changes
4 = I did not get as much as I had hoped out of the group
5 = The group was a waste of my time

Additional Comments You Would Like to Share With the School Counselor:

Missouri Comprehensive Guidance Programs. (n.d.) *Missouri comprehensive guidance programs: Linking school success with life success.* Missouri Center for Career Education. https://dese.mo.gov/sites/default/files/RSSmallGroupUnitSelfControl3-5.pdf

CHAPTER NINE

Generalized Anxiety Disorder

Sean Finnerty

THE CASE OF SHELLY "Can I talk to you for a minute?" asks Shelly as she sticks her head in your door just as the tardy bell rings.

"Shelly, where are you supposed to be right now?" you ask.

"Well, math class, but I really need to talk to you first" implores Shelly with tears in her eyes.

"I can give you three minutes before I have to send you back to math, OK?" you reply.

Shelly is part of a group of students you have termed "frequent fliers." These are students who come down to your office multiple times during the day or week to seek out support. Your work with Shelly seems to be focused on a pervasive and at times overwhelming sense of anxiety. In Shelly's case, this anxiety manifests itself during everyday tasks, such as peer interactions and athletic and academic performance; in truth, there's seemingly nothing about Shelly's daily life that she doesn't feel some level of anxiety about. Today, she is in your office because she is worried about a math quiz that she has to take during class this period. After talking to Shelly briefly and practicing a minute or two of deep breathing, you send her back to class knowing that you will see her again soon.

Introduction to the Chapter

Anxiety is a normal part of life. Being nervous before a big sporting event, academic test, or performing in your school musical is understandable and completely normal. What Shelly and students like her experience is different. Her anxiety seems to be generalized into many, if not all, aspects of daily life. Relatively mundane tasks, such as choosing what to wear to school or having to play volleyball in gym class can cause Shelly anxiety. She seems continuously on edge and finds it hard to relax or enjoy situations because she is constantly thinking about what could go wrong or what she needs to do next. School staff, including school counselors, share that there seems to be an ever-increasing number of students like Shelly who are seeking support for anxiety-related issues.

Learning Objectives

By the end of this chapter, students will accomplish the following:

- Understand the signs and symptoms of generalized anxiety disorder (GAD).
- Develop increased knowledge of the educational and social effects of GAD on children and adolescents.
- Understand best practice strategies for supporting students diagnosed with GAD.

According to the *Diagnostic and Statistical Manual of Mental Disorders, Fifth Edition* (*DSM-5*; APA, 2013), the average onset age for GAD is around 30 years old. Yet there is no minimum age at which a child or adolescent can be diagnosed with GAD. It is also important to differentiate GAD from other anxiety disorders, including, separation anxiety disorder, social anxiety disorder, and obsessive-compulsive disorder. In many respects, GAD can be considered a "catchall" diagnosis in which a child is exhibiting signs of anxiety but does not meet the diagnostic criteria of other, more specific, anxiety disorders.

Signs and Symptoms of GAD

According to the *DSM-5*, the essential feature of GAD is an excessive amount of anxiety and worry about a number of different activities or events. In addition, the frequency, intensity, and duration of the worry and anxiety are out of proportion with either the likelihood of the event occurring or the effect that it would have. Most importantly, individuals with GAD find that they worry to the point that it negatively affects their quality of life. While adults with GAD tend to worry about everyday life circumstances—paying the bills, work performance, and family health—GAD in children shows up as a tendency to worry excessively about their performance in a wide variety of areas.

According to the *DSM-5*, diagnostic criteria for GAD include:

A. Excessive anxiety and worry (apprehensive expectation), occurring more days than not for at least 6 months, about a number of events or activities (such as work or school performance).
B. The individual finds it difficult to control the worry.
C. The anxiety and worry are associated with three (or more) of the following six symptoms (with at least some symptoms having been present for more days than not for the past 6 months):

   Note: Only one item is required in children.

   1. Restlessness or feeling keyed up or on edge.
   2. Being easily fatigued.
   3. Difficulty concentrating or mind going blank.
   4. Irritability.
   5. Muscle tension.
   6. Sleep disturbance (difficulty falling or staying asleep, or restless, unsatisfying sleep).

D. The anxiety, worry, or physical symptoms cause clinically significant distress or impairment in social, occupational, or other important areas of functioning.
E. The disturbance is not attributable to the physiological effects of a substance (e.g., a drug of abuse, medication) or another medical condition (e.g., hyperthyroidism).
F. The disturbance is not better explained by another mental disorder (e.g., anxiety or worry about having panic attacks in panic disorder, negative evaluation in social anxiety disorder [social phobia], contamination or other obsessions in obsessive-compulsive disorder, separation from attachment figures in separation anxiety disorder, reminders of traumatic events in posttraumatic stress disorder, gaining weight in anorexia nervosa, physical complains in somatic symptom disorder, perceived appearance flaws in body dysmorphic disorder, having a serious illness in illness anxiety disorder, or the content of delusional beliefs in schizophrenia or delusional disorder).

What is especially interesting in diagnosing GAD in children and adolescents is that they only need one item in criteria C to be present more days than not over a 6-month period. As a result, GAD may be overdiagnosed in children, especially when other anxiety disorders are taken into consideration. Over a 12-month period, 0.9% of adolescents are estimated to meet the diagnostic criteria for GAD, with females being twice as likely as males to experience the disorder (APA, 2013). Yet anxiety disorders as a whole are the most commonly diagnosed mental health issue for children and adolescents (Costello et al., 2003; Thompson et al., 2012). In fact, typical schoolchildren today, even those without an anxiety diagnosis, have higher baseline stress levels than psychiatric patients in the 1950s (Twenge, 2000). In many respects, the anxious frame of mind has now become the new normal (Chansky, 2014). The effects of GAD and other anxiety disorders include impaired social and academic skills; physical ailments, such as stomachaches and headaches, which in turn can affect attendance; and emotional well-being (Thompson et al., 2012).

There is not a singular view of what an anxious child or a child diagnosed with anxiety may look like; the signs and symptoms of anxiety and anxiety disorders can express and manifest in different ways. Chansky (2014) described several ways that children might express their anxiety:

- ***Verbal Anxious.*** These children talk openly, and at times endlessly, about their fears and worries. They want to tell you everything and can feel better when they explain their fears. However, often, their fears can build up, and they can get more worked up as they talk.
- ***Undercover Anxious.*** These children seem to have it all together in public and at times can put on a performance that makes it appear that everything is okay. Yet once they get home, they tend to fall apart. These are the students for whom you get a parent phone call seeking help in addressing the anxiety that they are not showing at school.
- ***The Somaticizer.*** These are children who can't tell you what they are worried about, and, truly, they may not have thoughts or images about what they are anticipating. Their anxiety is expressed through their bodies, as they may miss school with complaints of headaches and stomachaches.
- ***The Angry-Anxious Child.*** Walking on eggshells, prickly to the touch, the angry-anxious child is as much in need of your help, as they are insistent that they don't need or want help. This type of student may at first be resistant to help, wanting to go it alone, and are uncomfortable with a light being shone on their worst attribute.
- ***The Avoider.*** "I'm not anxious. I just don't want to go to parties." This is what you might hear from the child who solves their worry problems by simply avoiding situations that are difficult for them. These students would rather spend their lives working around anxiety-producing situations, no matter the consequences. Procrastination or staying home sick rather than going to school to give the oral presentation is perfectly acceptable in their minds.

Risk Factors

While there is no single risk factor that can account for GAD, there are several intrapersonal, environmental, and genetic factors that can be associated with anxiety in children and adolescents. On the intrapersonal level, traits such as behavioral inhibition, negative affectivity (neuroticism), and harm avoidance have been associated with GAD (APA, 2013). Studies over the past 2 decades have indicated that behavioral inhibition, or the tendency to withdraw or display fear around unfamiliar people, places, or situations, is a significant risk factor for the development of anxiety (Hirshfeld-Becker et al., 2008; Thompson et al., 2012). In looking at environmental risk factors, overprotective parenting plays a moderate role in the development of GAD (APA, 2013). It has been speculated that overprotective parents or anxious parents model the assumption that the world is a dangerous place and may selectively focus on negative outcomes (Thompson, et al., 2012). Research has found that children of anxious parents are up to 7 times more likely to develop anxiety than their peers who have nonanxious parents (Turner et al., 1987). On the genetic level, one third of the risk of experiencing GAD is genetic and overlaps with other anxiety and mood disorders, such as major depressive disorder, which is discussed in detail in Chapter 4 of this volume (APA, 2013).

Assessment

If a school counselor suspects that a student might be suffering from GAD or other related anxiety disorders, there is always an option to refer the student to get screened and possibly diagnosed. As discussed in the introduction to this book, the multi-tiered system of supports (MTSS), response to intervention (RTI), positive behavior interventions and supports (PBIS), and systematic procedures were developed within the educational system to address the academic, behavioral, and mental health needs of students in a collaborative format with other in-school stakeholders. If the student is not already diagnosed by an external mental health provider, these in-school processes serve as a vehicle to facilitate services for students both within the school setting and externally. Within school, there are also a number of brief anxiety assessments that are usable by school counselors. Thompson et al. (2012) summarized a number of different brief anxiety assessments that school counselors could use (Table 9.1).

Strategies for School Counselors

As a school counselor, you have a variety of interventions available to help you assist students dealing with anxiety. Individual counseling, especially cognitive behavioral therapy (CBT), has been found helpful in addressing the relationship between thoughts, feelings, and physiological symptoms of anxiety, thus helping the student to learn ways of reacting that result in better outcomes, especially

TABLE 9.1 Brief Anxiety Inventories

ANXIETY ASSESSMENT	AGE IN YEARS	TAKEN BY	COMPLETED IN MINUTES
Beck Anxiety Inventory for Youth	7–18	Student, parent counselor	5–10
Multidimensional Anxiety Scale for Children	8–19	Parent, student	15
Revised Children's Manifest Anxiety Scale	6–9	Student	10
Self-Report for Childhood Anxiety Related Emotional Disorders	8–18	Parent, student	5
Social Anxiety Scale-Child Adolescent Version	8–14	Parent, student counselor	20–30
Social Phobia and Anxiety Inventory for Children	8–14	Student	20–30
The Spence Children's Anxiety Scale	8–14	Parent, student	10
Behavioral Assessment System for Children, Second Addition	6–21	Parent, teacher student	10–20
The Child Behavior Checklist	6–18	Parent, teacher student	15

Source: Table 1: Thompson et al. (2012, p. 226)

when they first start to experience the anxiety. Individual work with students can include progressive muscle relaxation, guided imagery, changing negative self-talk, attentiveness training, and other problem-solving techniques (Thompson et al., 2012). Group counseling, including group CBT, is also an option when working with students dealing with anxiety. The advantage of group counseling is that it is generally more efficient than individual counseling since you are working with multiple students at the same time, thus encouraging normalization among students, as well as building a community for added support. For younger children, using play and play therapy might be more appropriate. Research has shown that play can reduce anxiety in children (Baggerly & Jenkins, 2009). However, as mentioned in other chapters, school counselors may not be trained or have the time and resources to conduct play therapy in schools. In situations in which this modality is most needed for the student, referrals to outside mental health agencies may be more appropriate. Instead, school counselors may choose to use some aspects of play and or expressive arts activities to support these students. School counselors may also use the core counseling curriculum (classroom guidance) to help provide students with strategies for dealing with anxiety. This would be especially important if a needs assessment indicated that anxiety was a concern for a significant part of the student body.

CBT

The effectiveness of CBT has been researched and documented for decades, with the majority of children, reported as high as 66%, no longer meeting the criteria for diagnosis once therapy was completed (Kendall, 1994). According to Chanskey (2014), CBT for reducing anxiety can be broken down into a framework that consists of the following:

- ***Psychoeducation.*** This is where the counselor normalizes the student's experiences by teaching them that anxiety is something that everyone experiences. The counselor also teaches the student the skills needed to manage their anxiety.
- ***Somatic Management Skills.*** These skills would include learning techniques, such as progressive relaxation and breathing, to counter the body's fight-or-flight response.
- ***Cognitive Restructuring.*** This skill enables the student to identify anxiety-producing thoughts and counter them with realistic thinking based on the evidence available.
- ***Exposure.*** This allows the student to replace the worry about what could happen with lived experiences. The student practices these new behaviors from easiest to most challenging one step at a time.
- ***Relapse Prevention.*** The counselor provides students with a "tool kit" that allows them to identify signs of relapse, thus giving them the skills and confidence to address future anxiety episodes.

A core part of Chanskey's model is the idea that we have a "worry brain" and a "thinking brain." The worry brain is seemly connected to our amygdala, which controls, among other things, the flight-or-right response, and in someone with GAD, it always seems to be active. The thinking brain is just that, the logical part of the brain that is connected to the "real" world. In this process, the goal isn't to make anxiety disappear but to change how the student responds to it by helping them connect and use their thinking brain instead of their worry brain. Additional suggestions include the following:

- ***Do the Side-by-Side Comparison to Outsmart the Worry Brain Trick.*** This means setting up a debate between the worry brain and the thinking brain. This can help enhance realistic thinking and generate alternatives to what the worry brain is telling the student.

- ***Separate Facts From Feelings.*** Teaching students how to do a risk assessment to counteract how the worry brain confuses facts with what we feel. Yes, there are things that we feel afraid of, but what is the likelihood of them actually happening?
- ***Schedule Worry Time.*** Students with GAD can have a running dialogue with their worry brain throughout the day. Scheduling a specific time to worry can help them gain more control.
- ***Imagine Taking Risks on Purpose and Then Take Them.*** One of the best ways to deal with fear is experience—the experience of doing something and not having the "worry" happen. Students with GAD need exposure to these harmless, yet undesirable, experiences to see that they can survive them.
- ***Use Getting Used to It Exercises to Move From What If to Wait and See.*** This means creating a worry hierarchy and starting with completing or experiencing the low anxiety items and working to the high anxiety ones.

These are but a few of the examples that are available to help students deal with anxiety by using CBT. Again, the goal is not to eliminate anxiety but to simply change how our students experience it. There is also nothing to prevent counselors from using the described CBT interventions in a group setting, as these techniques can be easily modified, as needed, for group work.

Breath Work

A simple intervention for supporting children and youth who are experiencing the signs and symptoms of general anxiety is to teach them how to breathe when they become anxious. When the amygdala is doing its thing and the fight-or-flight response is engaged, breathing is normally short and rapid. Having students do the four-fours can help short-circuit this response. The four-fours is simple: breathe slowly in for a four count, hold it for a four count, breathe out for a four count, hold the breath for a four count, repeat four times. This can also be used, once students understand what the worry brain is trying to do, to disengage the anxiety response even before it starts. In the case of Shelly, this breath work would be handy in situations like the one described in the vignette where she is anxious about her upcoming math test. The school counselor would teach Shelly the four-fours so that she is able to maintain some control over regulating her anxiety.

Strategies for Working With Teachers, Parents, and Other Stakeholders

School counselors are ideally positioned to help a school community deal with challenges related to GAD and anxiety in general. Yet school counselors should leverage the resources of the school community as a whole to help all students. Counselors should not try to deal with GAD in isolation. Outside of the direct interventions listed in the preceding paragraph, school counselors should engage in the use the indirect services outlined by the American School Counseling Association's (ASCA) National Model (ASCA, 2019). These services include the following:

1. ***Consultation.*** Consultation is the process of providing information, recommendations, and opinions to the stakeholders who can provide assistance to students. These stakeholders might include parents, teachers, administrators, coaches, and others. It is important to note that while school counselors may provide information to stakeholders, they also should be willing to seek out consultation with experts when needed, in this case an expert on helping students deal with anxiety. Yet school counselors could provide

professional development to faculty and staff on the basics of CBT and how the worry brain works. Consulting with faculty and staff to help push interventions into the classroom is an important way to address anxiety issues in the school population as a whole. In addition, these interventions can also benefit the faculty and staff in dealing with their own anxiety. If a student has GAD, working with an anxious teacher is only going to make things more challenging.
2. ***Collaboration.*** Collaboration is a process in which multiple individuals work toward a common goal. To address student needs related to anxiety, school counselors have a number of ways that they can collaborate within their school communities. Possible examples include forming community partnerships with outside agencies that have expertise in helping students deal with anxiety, working on school- or district-level committees to help generate support to address student anxiety needs, and providing parenting workshops to help educate families about both student anxiety needs and resources to address those needs.
3. ***Referrals.*** It is also important that school counselors recognize when a student's needs exceed their training or scope of practice. With the average student-to-counselor ratio approaching 500 to 1, many school counselors struggle to find time to meaningfully address all of their student needs. Knowing when to refer, especially to expert resources such as mental health counselors with specific training and experience working with clients with anxiety, is an important part of being effective as a school counselor. School counselors can keep a list of providers available either by request or posted on the school counseling page of the district/school website.

Understanding What You Have Read: Comprehension Questions

Directions: Refer to what you learned in this chapter to answer the following questions.

1. What is GAD?
2. What are the determining factors for a diagnosis of GAD?
3. What modalities of support can school counselors extend to students?
4. How might you as a future counselor support a student who is presented with anxiety episodes during your clinical experiences?
5. How might your personal experiences affect your ability to support students like Shelly?

Case Examples

Case Example One

As you read the case about Shelly, reflect on the strategies that we discussed earlier in the chapter. The questions that follow the case relate to the student's behavioral symptoms and accompanying responses.

Shelly is a 16-year-old student in the tenth grade in a small rural school district. Since the seventh grade, she has come to the counselor's office at least several times a week to express worry about a variety of aspects of daily life. She often expresses feeling "keyed up" or "on edge." This anxiety has also caused Shelly to miss school on a regular basis. She missed 30 days last year, and she spends a lot of time in the nurse's office complaining of headaches and stomachaches. A referral to her pediatrician found no medical issues. Shelly is a capable student, yet her missed classes and absences have caused her grades to fall from high Bs to solid Cs. You have tried a variety of interventions with Shelly, such as progressive relaxation and supportive counseling but with limited success. Shelly indicates that she does not take any drugs or medications other than an occasional aspirin for her headaches, and she was on medication for anxiety but stopped after 9 months when it didn't seem to help. Shelly's parents are supportive, yet at times, they seem overly concerned and anxious themselves.

Case Example One: Questions for Processing and Reflection

Directions: Use what you have learned in this chapter to respond to Shelly's case.

1. What symptoms are being displayed by Shelly that might indicate that she may be experiencing GAD?
   a. Shelly has been experiencing symptoms of anxiety, more days than not, for years. Well beyond the 6-month minimum.
   b. Shelly finds it difficult to control her worries.
   c. Shelly expresses feeling "keyed up" or "on edge."
   d. Shelly's anxiety is affecting her daily life, including grades and school attendance.
   e. Shelly's anxiety does not appear to be attributable to substance abuse or another psychological disorder.
2. What additional information might you still need?
   a. When did Shelly's "worries" actually start? You have been working with Shelly since she was in the seventh grade. Did these behaviors occur in elementary school?
   b. Are there days where Shelly is able to deal with her anxiety effectively? If so, how?
   c. Has Shelly received outside counseling for her anxiety? Has this helped? If so, what was helpful?
3. How would you address concerns related to Shelly?
   a. Using a brief anxiety assessment to track Shelly's anxiety over time could be helpful.
   b. Since the support that Shelly receives from the counseling office has not been fully successful in addressing her anxiety, a referral to the interdisciplinary team (CST, RTI, MTSS, etc.) might be helpful.
   c. Continue to provide individual counseling with a focus on interventions that Shelly finds most useful.
   d. Provide small-group counseling support.
   e. If student anxiety is a school-wide challenge, the core counseling curriculum addressing the needs of all students would be appropriate.

Case Example Two

As you read the case about Tyrone, reflect on the strategies that we discussed earlier in the chapter. The questions that follow the case relate to the student's behavioral symptoms and accompanying responses.

Tyrone is a 13-year-old eighth grader who is new to the school district. He just moved into his grandmother's house 3 months ago from out of state. Both of Tyrone's parents are in a National Guard unit that was just deployed to Afghanistan, which is why he had to move in with his grandmother. Tyrone is one of only a handful of students of color in the school district, and he has struggled to make connections with teachers, staff members, and students. When asked about the struggle to connect with people, he responds, "Why bother? I will be going home soon." Tyrone is seen in the counseling office a few times a month, as he struggles with the public speaking part of his English class, and he worries about the safety of his parents over in Afghanistan. His grades have gone down from what he received at his old school, and he is borderline failing several of his core classes. Tyrone's grandmother calls on a regular basis because she is worried about his happiness. According to his grandmother, Tyrone spends the majority of his free time playing games on the Internet with his friends from back home. He has connected well with the Junior Reserves Officers' Training Corps instructor at the school and is seen eating lunch with this teacher daily.

Case Example Two: Questions for Processing and Reflection

Directions: Use what you have learned in this chapter to respond to Tyrone's case.

1. What symptoms of GAD is Tyrone showing to the school and his grandmother?
2. Does Tyrone meet the clinical requirements for a GAD diagnosis? Why or why not?
3. What would be your next step in working with Tyrone?
4. How might you use a brief anxiety survey in your assessment?
5. Who might be helpful to collaborate with within the school? Why?
6. What are the benefits of working with Tyrone's grandmother when building a plan for Tyrone?

Chapter Summary

The focus of this chapter was on creating a better understanding of GAD and its effect on children and adolescents. GAD differs from other anxiety disorders in that it is generalized in nature. Students with GAD seem to worry about everything, and as a result, many, if not all, aspects of life are affected. Again, the goal of treating GAD isn't to make anxiety disappear but to change how the students react to it. Also discussed were specific diagnostic criteria, signs and symptoms, various assessment tools, and examples of appropriate interventions. As school counselors regularly work with students struggling with anxiety in many forms, this makes for a timely discussion. GAD, if left untreated, can have a long-term negative effect on a child's or adolescent's well-being.

Additional Recommended Readings and Resources

American School Counselor Association: https://www.schoolcounselor.org/magazine/blogs/september-october-2016/address-student-anxiety

American School Counselor Association. (n.d.). *Anxiety & stress management.* https://www.schoolcounselor.org/school-counselors/professional-development/asca-u-specialist-trainings/anxiety-stress-management-specialist

McCormac, M. (2016). Address student anxiety. *ASCA School Counselor.* https://www.schoolcounselor.org/asca/media/asca/ASCAU/Anxiety-Stress-Management-Specialist/AdressStudentAnxiety.pdf

National Institute of Mental Health. (2016). *Generalized anxiety disorder: When worry gets out of control.* https://www.nimh.nih.gov/health/publications/generalized-anxiety-disorder-gad/index.shtml

Turner, C. (2019, October 29). *How to help a child struggling with anxiety.* NPR. https://www.npr.org/2019/10/23/772789491/how-to-help-a-child-struggling-with-anxiety

References

American Psychiatric Association (APA). (2013). *Diagnostic and statistical manual of mental disorders* (5th ed.).

American School Counseling Association (ASCA). (2019). *ASCA national model—a framework for school counseling programs* (4th ed.).

Baggerly, J., & Jenkins, W. W. (2009). The effectiveness of child-centered play therapy on developmental and diagnostic factors in children who are homeless. *International Journal of Play Therapy, 18*(1), 45–55. https://doi.org/10.1037/a0013878

Chansky, T. E. (2014). *Freeing your child from anxiety, revised and updated edition: Practical strategies to overcome fears, worries, and phobias and be prepared for life—from toddlers to teens.* Harmony Books.

Costello, E. J., Mustillo, S., Erkanli, A., Keeler, G., & Angold, A. (2003). Prevalence and development of psychiatric disorders in childhood and adolescence. *Archives of General Psychiatry, 60*, 837–844. https://doi.org/10/1001/archpsyc.60.8.837

Hirshfeld-Becker, D. R., Masek, B., Henin, A., Blakely, L. R., Rettew, D. C., Dufton, L., Segool, N. & Biederman, J. (2008). Cognitive-behavioral intervention with young anxious children. *Harvard Review of Psychiatry, 16*(2), 113–125. https://doi.org/10.1080/10673220802073956

Kendall, P. C. (1994), Treating anxiety disorders in children: Results of a randomized clinical trial. *Journal of Consulting and Clinical Psychology, 62*, 200–210.

Thompson, E. H., Robertson, P., Curtis, R., & Frick, M. H. (2012). Students with anxiety: Implications for professional school counselors. *Professional School Counseling, 16*(2). https://doi.org/10.1177/2156759X12016002S06

Turner, S. M., Beidel, D. C., & Costello, A. (1987). Psychopathology in the offspring of anxiety disorders patients. *Journal of Consulting and Clinical Psychology, 55*, 229–235. https://doi.org/10.1037/0022-006X.55.2.229

Twenge, J. M. (2000). The age of anxiety? Birth cohort change in anxiety and neuroticism, 1952–1993. *Journal of Personality and Social Psychology, 79*(6), 1007–1021.

CHAPTER TEN

Obsessive-Compulsive Disorder

Carrie Lynn Bailey and Christie Jenkins

THE CASE OF HELEN Helen is in the fifth grade. She is a shy student who has recently appeared to be distant and preoccupied. Helen lives with her biological father because of sexual abuse allegations against her biological mother recently. Helen received a referral to see the school counselor because of excessive tardiness. Helen told the school counselor that she has to wash her hands for 4 minutes after each class. She stated that she only has 3 minutes in between classes. Helen reported feeling "out of control" and anxious when she can only wash her hands for 3 minutes. This has been going on for the past 2 months. It was during this period of time that Helen was removed from her mother's house and placed with her father. Helen admitted during one counseling session that she has a bad fear of germs and being dirty. Helen believes that if she counts out exactly 240 seconds while washing her hands, she will be "safe." The school counselor spoke with Helen about sharing his concerns with her father, but Helen does not want to burden her father with her "craziness." Helen feels like her father has already been through enough. The counselor told Helen that she may need to see an additional helper who may be able to provide a medical evaluation to assess any additional needs.

Introduction to the Chapter

Recognizing symptoms of obsessive-compulsive disorder (OCD) in students such as Helen can be complicated and difficult to pinpoint, as such students often become very adept at hiding their obsessive thoughts and compulsive behaviors from those around them. Most students have an awareness that others do not necessarily think about such issues in the same way. Often, because of teasing, shaming, and bullying they may have experienced related to similar behaviors in the past, these students may learn to hide their compulsions successfully until they finally reach a significant level of distress. Estimates indicate that OCD affects approximately 1%–4% of children and adolescents (Adams et al., 2007); however, there is limited research on how school personnel can best work to meet the needs of these students.

Learning Objectives

By the end of this chapter, readers will accomplish the following:

- Understand the signs and symptoms of OCD and build an increased awareness of how they may manifest in students.

- Develop an increased understanding of the complexities of OCD, along with how the disorder can affect students in the school setting.
- Review strategies for becoming an advocate for students facing the effects of this disorder in the school setting.
- Develop an awareness of the need for collaboration with parents and additional stakeholders in an effort to help the student explore treatment options.

OCD can manifest at varying levels of severity. Treatment often includes both psychopharmacological and ongoing therapeutic strategies. As such, it is vital that school counselors collaborate with other professionals, as well as caregivers, to support the student in managing this disorder. Adams (2004) noted that educators are often in a unique position to help identify issues related to OCD as they are familiar with the norms of children of the same age and background and may more readily recognize behavior patterns and responses that are markedly different.

OCD has been reported in students as young as 4 years of age (Chansky, 2011), but the most likely timing of onset falls between either the ages of 8 and 11 or during a student's adolescent and young adult years (Wertlieb, 2008). It is estimated that at 1 in 200 children experience clinical levels of OCD symptoms, but these symptoms are often underreported because of challenges in recognizing and diagnosing the disorder (March & Mulle, 1998). Gender differences have been identified, with boys being diagnosed twice as often as girls during the prepubescent years but then leveling out across gender following puberty. One of the challenges in identifying OCD symptoms in younger children lies in the fact that it is developmentally normal for children to have a number of rituals that help them stay on task throughout the day (such as morning routines, nighttime rituals, or magical thinking relayed in childhood rhymes like "don't step on a crack"). It can be difficult to differentiate the point at which those routines and rituals move from serving a developmental purpose into a more dysfunctional domain. OCD symptoms generally persist across the life span but may wax and wane in severity depending on a number of factors (Leininger et al., 2010).

At the end of this chapter, you will accomplish the following:

1. Identify symptoms of OCD in school-aged youth.
2. Learn to advocate for students in securing additional mental health support beyond the school setting.
3. Learn to advocate for appropriate accommodations for students within the school setting.
4. Understand how to support students through a variety of resources and strategies.

Diagnostic Criteria for OCD

OCD is characterized by recurrent obsessions and/or compulsions that cause marked distress and impairment in one's day-to-day activities (American Psychological Association [APA], 2013). *Obsessions* are defined as repetitive and persistent thoughts, ideations, impulses, urges, or images that cause fear, worry, and/or anxiety. In the school setting, this may manifest in intrusive thoughts related to germs and/or contamination, fears of harm to self or others, symmetry urges, religiosity/scrupulosity, and persistent doubts, among others. *Compulsions* are defined as stereotypical and repetitive behaviors or mental acts performed to alleviate fear, worry, and anxiety caused by obsessions (APA, 2013). In the school setting, compulsions may be observed as rituals of frequent washing or cleaning, checking and/or repeating behaviors, touching, counting, or ordering. Mental compulsions may also be present, such as praying, counting, and internal repetition of words, which are not observable but can take a significant amount of the student's mental focus and energy and be as distressing or disruptive as more overt behaviors (Adams, 2004). It is believed that there is a neurobiological basis for OCD that may include a chemical imbalance related to serotonin or malfunctions in the area of the brain that convert sensory information into thoughts and actions (Wilmshurst, 2011).

While OCD was previously categorized under the anxiety disorders umbrella in the *Diagnostic and Statistical Manual of Mental Disorders, Fourth Edition Text Revision* (APA, 2000), our understanding of the complexity of this and related disorders has evolved. In the revised and updated *Diagnostic and Statistical Manual of Mental Disorders, Fifth Edition* (*DSM-5;* APA, 2013), OCD has been moved to a category all its own, obsessive-compulsive and related disorders, with the primary rationale that while anxiety can certainly play a role in the disorder, the obsessions and compulsions are the fundamental features of the disorder. The function of the compulsions is to minimize the discomfort caused by the obsessions, and the obsessions and compulsions are time-consuming or cause clinically significant distress or impairment (APA, 2013).

Obsessions and compulsions can take a significant amount of the student's time and energy, although it will not always be evident to others when the obsessions are playing out for the student. When we consider OCD, we often think of stereotypical compulsions, such as hand washing or germ avoidance; however, those are truly only the tip of the iceberg. While the specific obsessions and compulsions typically change over time, there are some common themes that are seen in children and adolescents (Wertlieb, 2008).

Common Obsessions in Children and Adolescents

Contamination obsessions are likely the most well-recognized OCD symptom/obsession and the most common. In the school setting, this may be evident in students who are "germaphobes" and worry about other's sneezing and/or coughing or those students who avoid touching things that might be considered dirty. Magical thinking is akin to taking a superstition to the extreme. Students may worry that their thoughts or feelings can cause harm to others. For example, if a student has had negative thoughts toward a classmate, they may fear that this will somehow cause that child to become sick.

Catastrophizing is not unique to students with OCD but is a common obsession focus for these students who are prone to moving quickly to a worst-case scenario for a given situation, which for students with OCD will additionally lead to some form of compulsive behavior in an attempt to manage the issue. Excessive concerns related to a fear of harm, illness, death, or a need for things to be "just so" may manifest with a seemingly endless stream of questions or repetitive urges to check and recheck work and their belongings or consistent requests for validation and confirmation that they are okay (Adams, 2004). Other students may have obsessions related to perfectionism, fear of forgetting important information, or losing things, or they have recurrent intrusive thoughts related to sexual or aggressive impulses, thoughts, or images (Chaturvedi et al., 2014; Dotson, 2014).

Scrupulosity is a term used to describe the intense integrity-related concerns that students with OCD may experience. They are sometimes religious in nature and may involve an extreme struggle to ensure that they are always following directions or making the best choices. Checking and counting related obsessions involve students needing to repeat a task a set number of times to be able to move forward or to have things arranged in a specific manner to avoid overwhelming distress (Child Mind Institute, 2016; Wertlieb, 2008).

Common Compulsions in Children and Adolescents

As these obsessions grow in intensity and overwhelm the student, they turn to compulsions, rituals, and/or repetitive behaviors to try to soothe the distress that they are experiencing. As outlined earlier, some of the compulsions are behavioral, such as hand washing, cleaning rituals, ordering and arranging items, repeating routine activities or body movements, tapping or touching, or questioning and counting behaviors aloud. Others are more internal and may not be apparent to others. The student may "just" appear to be distracted or not paying attention. These may include a need to reread or rewrite work a set number of times; mental compulsions, including reviewing events, praying to prevent harm, counting while performing a task; or "canceling" or "undoing" actions that can involve having to mentally replace what is perceived as a "bad" word with a "good" word to cancel out the perception of harm (Dotson, 2014).

Additional compulsions may involve a need to tell or confess to get reassurance or simply avoiding situations that might trigger the student's obsessions. In a school setting, behaviors such as frequent and/or lengthy bathroom requests, constant reassurance seeking, getting stuck on tasks, retracing, and obsessive erasing or redoing work may be indicators of potential compulsive behaviors and should be explored with students who are frequently exhibiting some of these patterns (Child Mind Institute, 2016).

Some of these behaviors may be more easily recognized as coping strategies, but some may be perceived as oppositional if the underlying obsession is not something that others are aware of (Child Mind Institute, 2016). It is important to understand that these compulsions are powerful and not behaviors that the student can simply "turn off." For many individuals with OCD, prevention from engaging in these compulsions may escalate the anxiety and distress experienced to extreme levels (Chaturvedi et al., 2014).

Related and Comorbid Disorders

As outlined earlier, OCD is now classified in the *DSM-5* in its own category, along with "related disorders," including body dysmorphic disorder, hoarding disorder, trichotillomania (hair pulling), excoriation (skin picking), substance/medication-induced OCD, unspecified obsessive-compulsive and related disorder (such as body-focused repetitive behavior disorder), and obsessive-compulsive and related disorder because of another medical condition (APA, 2013).

It is interesting to note that obsessive-compulsive and related disorders because of another medical condition include two variations, which are important to have an awareness of when working with children and adolescents. Pediatric acute-onset neuropsychiatric syndrome (PANS) and pediatric autoimmune neuropsychiatric disorder associated with streptococcus (PANDAS) are relatively new and poorly understood disorders in which it is theorized that children develop rapid-onset obsessive-compulsive symptoms, in addition to a number of other psychiatric disturbances, following a childhood infection, most notably with the bacteria that causes strep throat. While obsessive-compulsive behaviors not associated with these variations may build slowly over time, in children with PANS or PANDAS, the symptoms come suddenly, causing significant difficulties in social, behavioral, and academic areas and impairing a student's functioning (Swedo et al., 2012). It is important to note that treatment for these disorders has markedly different components than that for OCD on its own and includes medication such as antibiotics to continue fighting the underlying infection in addition to treatments focused on behaviors (Wilmshurst, 2011). Much more research is needed to better understand the mechanism of onset for these students; however, the role of the school counselor in supporting the students is much the same as in supporting those with obsessive-compulsive and related disorders.

Across the life span, individuals with OCD often exhibit comorbid anxiety disorders, including generalized anxiety disorder, panic disorder, and social anxiety disorder and may also experience depressive disorder. Those with OCD are also more likely to have a comorbid tic disorder, and attention deficit hyperactivity disorder is often seen in these students (APA, 2013). Finally, the other disorders outlined earlier that fall within the category of "related disorders" can be additional challenges that individuals diagnosed with OCD may encounter.

Risk and Prognostic Factors

The *DSM-5* (APA, 2013) outlines temperamental factors, such as greater internalizing symptoms, higher negative emotionality, and behavioral inhibition, as potential risk factors, along with environmental risk factors, such as physical and emotional abuse or traumatic experiences. There are significant genetic and physiological factors that can contribute to OCD disorder as well.

Effects on Children and Adolescents (Academic/Social/Family, etc.)

OCD may affect students' cognitions, emotions, behaviors, and physical health and can have tremendous effects on student's development across the span of their school experience. Most students with OCD have average to above-average intelligence, but OCD can "exact a heavy toll on academic performance" (Adams, 2004, p. 50). Obsessions can be extremely intrusive and thus interfere with a student's focus, energy, and ability to process information. Students may be perceived as having challenges with motivation or attention when they are instead "stuck" or fixated on trying to process both their academic work and the competing internal obsessions and compulsions they are experiencing.

For many students with OCD, concern with how others perceive them or their need for affirmation can lead to them being very skilled at masking their symptoms, making it harder to identify these students and respond to their needs. This same behavior can also interfere with the time and energy that they are able to put toward their academic work, resulting in lower academic outcomes in the classroom. The most frequently reported school-related difficulties that students with OCD express are staying focused on classwork and being able to complete their homework (Piacentini et al., 2003). In addition to challenges related to focusing on the work in the classroom, students may have compulsions that are related to perfectionism that will greatly increase the amount of time even a "simple" assignment can take. The student may miss large amounts of class time because of the nature of the compulsions that are central to their manifestation of the disorder or because of the need to schedule therapy or medical appointments during school time.

Some students experience obsessions and compulsions that are self-harming or focus on suicidal ideation, which can be traumatizing for the student to manage but also often very well guarded. Some students with OCD may also suffer from body-focused repetitive behaviors, such as skin picking or trichotillomania. Students can also be perceived as antagonistic and defiant when the rigidity of their rituals and compulsions is counter to the expectations of the school or classroom setting (Miglioretti, 2019). Students may display signs of anxiety, depression, and/or somatic concerns related to that internal stress, and those can be further exacerbated during times of stress, changes to routines, or transition stages.

Research has highlighted that students with OCD have a lowered sense of social competence and routinely experience reduced social interaction, whether by isolating themselves or being isolated and bullied by their peers. Teachers who do not have an understanding or awareness of a student's OCD challenges may contribute to this as well if overly harsh in their criticism of the student for their engagement in their obsessions or compulsions (Miglioretti, 2019). Students often try to hide their symptoms from both their teachers and their peers out of a sense of shame, embarrassment, or fear of being misunderstood or ridiculed. This can lead to lowered self-esteem and increased avoidance of social situations, which then tends to exacerbate feelings of anxiety and depression, leading to increased self-criticism and a lack of a sense of belonging (Chaturvedi et al., 2014).

Strategies for School Counselors

Advocacy and Information

As is true for all students with disabilities or complex medical needs, No Child Left Behind (2002) and the Individuals with Disabilities Education Act (2004) outline schools' responsibility for providing support for these students. Specialized services may be provided through the implementation of appropriate individual education plans (IEPs) or through a Section 504 plan (1973). These plans serve to protect students with disabilities from discrimination and provide a setting in which the challenges presented by their illnesses are taken into account for best meeting their learning needs. School counselors who are knowledgeable of the effects that OCD can have on a student's learning are an essential part of ensuring that these plans are well-defined and tailored to the unique manifestation of symptoms that each child or adolescent presents. The American School Counselor Association (ASCA, 2015) National Model outlines how effective school counseling programs should address the needs of all students and specifically identifies the role of the school counselor in advocating for students at IEP and student study team meetings (ASCA, 2012). ASCA further supports the role of the school counselor in providing programming that enhances awareness of mental health issues and seeks to reduce associated stigma, including school-based prevention and interventions for students with mental health concerns, and collaborates with school and community stakeholders to ensure access to mental health services for students and their families (ASCA, 2015).

School counselors can serve in a psychoeducational role as educators of the interdisciplinary team concerning the symptoms that students may be experiencing within the school setting and help those who work with the students on a daily basis to better recognize potential OCD behaviors and issues. Identifying OCD tendencies can be one of the most critical steps in supporting the student and connecting them with services to have their social, emotional, and academic needs met within the school setting (Adams, 2004).

Working With Teachers and an Interdisciplinary Team

Often, teachers who have concerns about students in their classrooms will consult with the school counselor for recommendations about how to best proceed. If OCD appears to be a potential area of concern, school counselors will want to then consult with the school psychologist and child study team to explore a more formal psychoeducational assessment that can inform the next steps to explore. This psychoeducational assessment should include an interdisciplinary team that will consist of the student, family members or guardians, school counselor, school psychologist, teachers, and other relevant school personnel. A referral to the students' physician, as well as a mental health professional, may be warranted for additional medical and psychological assessments and as a part of the ultimate treatment team (Doran, 2016).

Once a student has been identified as needing accommodations, the school counselor can support the process in tailoring those accommodations to the current presenting challenges. It is important that student accommodation plans remain fluid, as the intensity and focus of the student's obsessions and compulsions may shift over time (Adams et al., 2007). The school counselor can help in providing resources that outline effective classroom strategies that can often easily be implemented to support not only the student with OCD but also other students in the classroom. One such example is the establishment of clear rules and expectations; as a common struggle for many students with OCD is the frequent worry that they are not meeting expectations, or "doing something wrong," a positive and nonpunitive approach to discipline can be instrumental to students' sense of comfort and security. Providing clear and supported transitions between tasks, assisting students in setting realistic and achievable goals, and promoting self-awareness and self-regulation are strategies that are helpful for all students but can be essential components of structure for those with OCD (Leininger et al., 2010).

More specific strategies that the school counselor can assist the teacher in implementing, or perhaps facilitate in group settings, are guided stress-reduction experiences, mindfulness techniques, and self-calming strategies. Finally, the school counselor can also serve as a liaison between outside treatment providers and the teachers who may be tasked with extending some of those strategies into the classroom. Most essential to the support that the teacher will provide for the student is an understanding of the unique challenges that OCD brings for both the student and the classroom.

The school counselor can be instrumental in educating teachers or, at best, provide resources to teachers about the effect of OCD on students' functioning in the classroom. Teachers should be made aware that even though students may be displaying obsessive and compulsive behaviors, they may most often be trying to do their best to manage their symptoms, and they are not intentionally being antagonistic. A positive and supportive attitude and an accepting classroom environment are important so that the student does not experience further distress because they perceive themselves to be an annoyance or nuisance to the teacher or the classroom (Leininger et al., 2010).

Working With Students

School counselors are in a unique role relative to their work with students in the school setting. Depending upon the grade level of the school that the counselor is in, the overarching philosophy of the school counseling program, and the availability of access to students throughout the day, the school counselor's work with students managing OCD may vary widely. However, a collaborative and multifaceted approach is central to supporting the student and coordinating the various professional and family supports that may be needed at various times in the student's school experience. Students with OCD are affected emotionally, socially, behaviorally, and cognitively, thus a comprehensive treatment strategy will address each of these areas both within the school setting and at home.

Adams (2004) outlined a number of excellent general strategies for helping students manage problems with OCD, some of which the school counselor can assist the student with or help the student practice self-advocacy skills. The school counselor should collaborate with the student to set a plan of support that is minimally disruptive but scheduled regularly, providing a consistent place to check in on how they are managing and to process the challenges that may arise. This may be structured with individual meetings or group support but should include a focus on building the student's strengths and providing opportunities for them to highlight them. In addition, the school counselor, student, and teacher should work together in providing opportunities for a sanctuary should a student begin to feel overwhelmed in class so that they can take the time and space to process those emotions, interrupt the OCD cycle, and reset (Wertlieb, 2008).

Ensuring that the student has opportunities to build their social competence and helping place the student with teachers who are more empathic and knowledgeable of the challenges of OCD can assist in reinforcing their self-esteem and efficacy in the classroom. Working to build awareness of differences for not only OCD but also related challenges that many students experience and building an environment of acceptance within the school setting and students' day-to-day environments can be instrumental for students' sense of belonging. Child Mind Institute (2016, p. 6) outlines a "Peer Understanding Program," which includes a classroom presentation on how disorders such as OCD may affect people in different ways. The presentation is then followed with a question-and-answer period to develop a broader understanding and acceptance of the differences that OCD can bring. School counselors and teachers using this approach should be mindful to maintain confidentiality about students' conditions should there be a student with OCD in the classroom. Other opportunities for building social skills and connections could be the implementation of "lunch bunch" type groups or after-school, interest-based group activities that provide a supportive space for developing that social competence. Bibliotherapy can be an excellent adjunct to this work as well.

Working With Families

Having a child who is diagnosed with OCD can be overwhelming, and parents may not know where to start in exploring all of the information that may soon be coming their way. In addition, because of the high genetic and physiological risk factors, OCD may be a component of one or more of the parents' struggles as well. Helping to connect parents with supportive resources can be key to the school counselor's role in nurturing the growth of students with this diagnosis. There are a few national support resources for parents provided at the end of this chapter, but the school counselor will want to also explore what is available in the local community. Children's hospitals and local branches of organizations, such as the National Alliance for Mental Illness, can be great starting points.

In addition, school counselors can provide referrals to families for additional counseling support outside of the school setting, ideally not only for the student with the diagnosis but also for the family as a whole. Building strong communication between parents and children can be an essential component of effective treatment strategies, as parents may be unintentionally contributing to continuing behaviors in their attempts to help their children manage the distress experienced. Providing parents with an understanding space where they can process what may be a new and frightening diagnosis can be an essential component of helping them to accept and seek out additional support (Chansky, 2011). Educating parents on the key challenges, as well as providing a brief introduction to the treatment strategies that are available in addition to offering hope and information regarding the efficacy of those strategies, can abate some of the anxiety that they may be experiencing in addition to that of their children (Wertlieb, 2008). Finally, as highlighted previously, school counselors can serve as liaisons or central points of contact between the family and the various professionals in the school setting who are working collaboratively to support the child (Adams, 2004).

Understanding What You Have Read: Comprehension Questions

Directions: Refer to what you learned in this chapter to answer the following questions.

1. What is OCD?
2. What are the determining factors for a diagnosis of OCD?
3. What techniques can school counselors use with students suffering from OCD?
4. How might you handle a student presenting with OCD during your field experience?
5. How will your own life experience affect your ability to help students like Helen?
6. What ethical and multicultural considerations would you examine when working with a student with OCD?

Case Examples

Case Example One

As you read the case about Ricky, reflect on the strategies that we discussed earlier in the chapter. The questions that follow the case relate to the student's behavioral symptoms and accompanying responses.

Ricky is a 12-year-old student in the seventh grade at a suburban middle school. Ricky is a stickler for details. His friends like to work with him on group projects, and teachers often ask for his help when organizing their classrooms. Ricky was recently referred to the school counselor because he has been worried about something bad happening to his parents. Ricky reported to a teacher that if he does not complete the exact same daily routine, his parents may die. Ricky has struggled with doing things in the exact same order for the past month since his parents were taken to jail on drug charges. Ricky's daily tasks must be completed in the exact same order all day, every day. Ricky has become so rigid that he is now counting his walking steps from one activity to another, which is causing him to frequently be late to class. Ricky's grandparents, with whom he resides, do not report any health conditions. Ricky met with the school counselor and reports that he knows that his thoughts and habits do not make sense, but he cannot make himself stop. Ricky reports that he is extremely anxious about what is happening with his parents. Ricky states that his grades are starting to fall because he is obsessed with keeping his parents safe through his rituals.

Case Example One: Questions for Processing and Reflection

Directions: Use what you have learned in this chapter to respond to Ricky's case.

1. What are the symptoms Ricky is exhibiting that *may* indicate that he has OCD?
   a. Ricky has been worried that something bad will happen to his parents.
   b. Ricky is doing the exact same rituals every day.
   c. Ricky is counting his steps from one activity to another.
   d. Ricky does not feel that he has control over his thoughts/behaviors/actions.
   e. Ricky's grades are starting to fall because of the new behaviors.
2. What information have you gathered regarding Ricky's situation?
   a. He does not have any known medical issues that could account for his behaviors.
   b. Ricky's grandparents have not recognized any issues.
   c. Ricky knows that his thoughts and habits do not make sense.
3. What additional information would you like to gather?
   a. The Obsessive-Compulsive Inventory—Revised.
   b. Information regarding any noted behavioral changes.
   c. Ricky's last exam by his pediatrician.
   d. Is Ricky partaking in healthy habits (i.e., eating well, sleeping well, exercise)
   e. Has Ricky experienced any trauma?
3. How would you address concerns for Ricky?
   a. Individual sessions to support Ricky in a safe space
   b. Meeting with Ricky's grandparents to process family support and available mental health services
   c. Multidisciplinary meeting with additional providers to determine the next steps
   d. Group counseling

Case Example Two

As you read the case about Clemente, reflect on the strategies that we discussed earlier in the chapter. The questions that follow the case relate to the student's behavioral symptoms and accompanying responses.

Clemente is an 8-year-old boy in the third grade. He is from a large urban city. You notice that Clemente has gone from a happy and outgoing child to a child who is constantly aware of his blinking, breathing, and other tactile sensations. You witness him blinking his eyes in a pattern and tapping his fingers under his desk to match the pattern. If this pattern gets disrupted, he will start over and appears incredibly fearful. He also refuses to touch the doorknob without wrapping his sweatshirt around his hand. Also, once when you asked him to turn the light on, he turned it on and off 11 times. He yelled, "Darn it!" and switched the light on and off exactly 10 times before leaving it on for good. Fellow students thought that it was funny, but you could tell it was incredibly stressful for him. You try to speak with Clemente about these new behaviors. He reports that he does not understand your concerns because his whole family does these types of things. He states that the only time that it bothers him is when he does not get the number exactly right. You reach out to this family, and they confirm it is just something that they have always done. What do you do?

Case Example Two: Questions for Processing and Reflection

Directions: Use what you have learned in this chapter to respond to Clemente's case.

1. What symptoms of OCD is Clemente exhibiting at school?
2. What is your next step when working with Clemente?
3. Would you do the Obsessive-Compulsive Inventory—Revised with Clemente? How would you use any information you gained from the assessment?
4. What community resources would you employ to help Clemente? Why did you choose those resources?
5. How will you work with Clemente's family? What will you do if they do not see this as an issue?
6. How will you collaborate with his teacher when building a plan for Clemente?

Chapter Summary

Much as Helen, Ricky, and Clemente have experienced, many students struggle with the effects of OCD and obsessive-compulsive tendencies with significant ramifications for their social, emotional, and academic development. School counselors are in a unique position to build awareness of this disorder and assist with identifying students in the schools who may be struggling with these challenges. In recognizing the signs and symptoms and working collaboratively with the student, family, teachers, and those providing additional care, the school counselor can play a vital role in helping these students develop positive coping strategies, connect with additional outside supports, better manage their symptoms, and have more success both in the classroom and their day-to-day lives.

Additional Recommended Readings and Resources

Child Mind Institute: https://childmind.org/topics/disorders/obsessive-compulsive-disorders/

International OCD Foundation (IOCDF): http://www.iocdf.org

IOCDF for Educators: https://anxietyintheclassroom.org/school-system/

National Alliance for Mental Illness: https://www.nami.org/learn-more/mental-health-conditions/obsessive-compulsive-disorder

OCD Youth: https://ocdyouth.org/about/

Bibliotherapy

Doran, P. R. (Ed.) (2016). *PANDAS and PANS in school settings: A handbook for educators*. Jessica Kingsley Publishers.

Huebner, D. (2007). What to do when your brain gets stuck: A kid's guide to overcoming OCD. Magination Press.

Film

UNSTUCK: An OCD Kids Movie: https://www.ocdkidsmovie.com/

References

Adams, G. B. (2004). Identifying, assessing, and treating obsessive-compulsive disorder in school-aged children: The role of school personnel. *Teaching Exceptional Children, 37*(2), 46–53.

Adams, G. B., Smith, T. J., Bolt, S. E., & Nolten, P. (2007). Current educational practices in classifying and serving students with obsessive-compulsive disorder. *Contemporary School Psychology, 12*, 93–105.

American Psychological Association (APA). (2000). *Diagnostic and statistical manual of mental disorders* (4th ed., text rev.).

American Psychological Association (APA). (2013). *Diagnostic and statistical manual of mental disorders* (5th ed.).

American School Counselor Association (ASCA). (2012). *The ASCA national model: A framework for school counseling programs* (3rd ed.).

American School Counselor Association (ASCA). (2015). The professional school counselor and student mental health. https://www.schoolcounselor.org/asca/media/asca/PositionStatements/PositionStatements.pdf

Chansky, T. E. (2011). *Freeing your child from obsessive compulsive disorder: A powerful, practical program for parents of children and adolescents.* Three Rivers Press.

Chaturvedi, A., Murdick, N. L., & Gartin, B. C. (2014). Obsessive compulsive disorder: What an educator needs to know. *Physical Disabilities: Education and Related Services, 33*(2), 71–83.

Child Mind Institute (2016). *A teacher's guide to OCD.* https://childmind.org/downloads/Teachers-Guide-to-OCD-v1.pdf

Doran, P. R. (2016). *PANDAS and PANS in school settings: A handbook for educators.* Jessica Kingsley.

Dotson, A. (2014). *Being me with OCD: How I learned to obsess less and live my life.* Free Spirit Publishing.

Individuals with Disabilities Education Act, 20 U.S.C. § 1400 (2004).

Leininger, M., Dyches, T. T., Prater, M. A., & Heath, M. A. (2010). Teaching students with obsessive-compulsive disorder. *Intervention in School and Clinic, 45*(4), 221–231.

March, J. S., & Mulle, K. (1998). *OCD in children and adolescents: A cognitive-behavioral treatment manual.* Guilford Press.

Miglioretti, M. (2019). *School-based services for children with pediatric acute-onset neuropsychiatric syndrome (PANS)* [Unpublished doctoral dissertation] Duquesne University. https://dsc.duq.edu/etd/1808

No Child Left Behind Act of 2002, 20 U.S.C.A. § 6301 et seq. (2002).

Piacentini, J., Bergman, R. L., Keller, M., & McCracken, J. (2003). Functional impairment in children and adolescents with obsessive-compulsive disorder. *Journal of Child and Adolescent Psychopharmacology, 13*(Supplement 1), 61–69.

Section 504 of the Rehabilitation Act of 1973, Pub. L. No. 93–112, et seq., 87 Stat. 394 (1973).

Swedo, S., Leckman J, & Rose N. (2012). From research subgroup to clinical syndrome: Modifying the PANDAS criteria to describe PANS (pediatric acute-onset neuropsychiatric syndrome). *Pediatric Therapeutics, 2*, 1–8.

Wertlieb, E. (2008). Obsessive compulsive disorder and the school counselor. *Journal of School Counseling, 6*(28). http://jsc.montana.edu/articles/v6n28.pdf

Wilmshurst, L. (2011). *Child and adolescent psychopathology: A casebook.* Sage Publications.

CHAPTER ELEVEN

Separation Anxiety Disorder

Pamela Harris and Amy E. Williams

THE CASE OF JAMAR Jamar is a fifth-grade student in a suburban elementary school. His family recently moved to the area at the beginning of the school year, and his transferred records indicate that he's typically an honor roll student. Jamar lives at home with his mom, dad, and younger sister, who is a third-grade student at the same school. This is the third elementary school that Jamar has attended since kindergarten, as his dad is in the military, and they have had to move on several occasions. One day, Jamar's mom requests to see the school counselor in the main office. This is the fourth day in a row that Jamar has had difficulty getting out of the car to come into the school. In fact, Jamar's teacher expressed concern about Jamar's absences and tardiness negatively affecting his grades. Jamar's mother admits that she has kept him home twice in the previous week because of his complaints about stomach pains. It usually takes about 10 minutes to get him into the school building after a lot of coaching from his mother. Later that day, Jamar comes to the school counselor's office to ask to call and check on his mom. He asks if the school counselor would call home first, as Jamar is worried his dad might answer the phone. According to Jamar, his dad often tells him to "toughen up and stick it out," but he cannot help it if his stomachaches are so "bad" that he needs to be at home.

Introduction to the Chapter

Although it is often believed that students like Jamar are only found in elementary schools, there are also cases of students experiencing separation anxiety in secondary school settings. Teachers commonly express concern about these students falling behind because of absences. Even when they are in school, they may pay frequent visits to the school nurse because of complaints of stomach pains and other aches, as well as asking other school officials for permission to call home. Often, these students are labeled as "needy," "sensitive," or "faking sick." Separation anxiety disorder (SAD) consists of more than just missing home. Yet this misconception results in students with SAD being met with frustration as opposed to the support they need.

Learning Objectives

By the end of this chapter, readers will accomplish the following:

- Understand the signs and symptoms of separation anxiety.
- Improve comprehension of the academic and socioemotional effects of SAD on both elementary and secondary students.
- Learn best practices for supporting students with SAD.

According to the *Diagnostic and Statistical Manual of Mental Disorders, 5th Edition* (*DSM-5*; American Psychiatric Association [APA], 2013), approximately 4% of children are affected by SAD within a 6- to 12-month period, and 1.6% of children are affected within a 12-month period. Although SAD may occur at any point throughout the life span, SAD is most prevalent in children aged 12 and younger and decreases in prevalence throughout adolescence (APA, 2013), with the peak window of onset being between ages 7 and 9 (Hanna et al., 2006). In fact, SAD is the most prevalent anxiety disorder observed in children 12 and younger (APA, 2013), which suggests a likelihood that school counselors will encounter children with this disorder, especially within elementary and middle school settings. SAD is diagnosed with equal frequency in males and females within a clinical sample; however, the disorder is observed more frequently in females in a nonclinical sample (APA, 2013). SAD may also occur in adults, with between 0.9% and 1.9% of adults meeting the diagnostic criteria of this disorder within a 12-month span (APA, 2013). This may be relevant for school counselors if an adult is struggling to separate from the child when the child is sent to school.

Separation anxiety is a normal response within the context of early childhood development, and this developmentally appropriate response to being separated from a caregiver during early life may actually suggest a secure attachment with the caregiver (APA, 2013). In fact, up to 50% of 8-year-olds may experience one or more symptoms of SAD without an associated negative effect on overall functioning (Hanna et al., 2006). SAD exists when anxiety in response to separation from a caregiver falls outside of the normal developmental range or creates excessive distress that exceeds typical separation anxiety as observed within normal developmental processes (APA, 2013). Symptoms of SAD may wax and wane over time, and for some young people, symptoms may recur throughout adulthood. For a majority of youth with SAD, however, the symptoms of this disorder do not increase later in life (APA, 2013).

Signs and Symptoms of SAD

The most obvious sign of SAD in young people is the presence of excessive anxiety, fear, or worry when faced with separation from an attachment figure (APA, 2013). This reaction to separation is excessive and beyond what is considered developmentally appropriate based on the child's age. In addition, symptoms occur for at least 4 weeks in children and adolescents (and at least 6 months in adults) and create "clinically significant distress or impairment in social, academic, occupational or other areas of functioning" (APA, 2013, p. 191).

To diagnose SAD, the following criteria must be met (APA, 2013):

A. Developmentally inappropriate and excessive fear or anxiety concerning separation from those to whom the individual is attached, as evidenced by at least three of the following:

1. Recurrent excessive distress when anticipating or experiencing separation from home or from major attachment figures.
2. Persistent and excessive worry about losing major attachment figures or about possible harm to them, such as illness, injury, disasters, or death.

3. Persistent and excessive worry about experiencing an untoward event (e.g., getting lost, being kidnapped, having an accident, becoming ill) that causes separation from a major attachment figure.
4. Persistent reluctance or refusal to go out, away from home, to school, to work, or elsewhere because of fear of separation.
5. Persistent and excessive fear of or reluctance about being alone or without major attachment figures at home or in other settings.
6. Persistent reluctance or refusal to sleep away from home or to go to sleep without being near a major attachment figure.
7. Repeated nightmares involving the theme of separation.
8. Repeated complaints of physical symptoms (e.g., headaches, stomachaches, nausea, vomiting) when separation from major attachment figures occurs or is anticipated.

B. The fear, anxiety, or avoidance is persistent, lasting at least 4 weeks in children and adolescents and typically 6 months or more in adults.
C. The disturbance causes clinically significant distress or impairment in social, academic, occupational, or other important areas of functioning.
D. The disturbance is not better explained by another mental disorder, such as refusing to leave home because of excessive resistance to change in autism spectrum disorder; delusions or hallucinations concerning separation in psychotic disorders; refusal to go outside without a trusted companion in agoraphobia; worries about ill health or other harm befalling significant others in generalized anxiety disorder; or concerns about having an illness in illness anxiety disorder.

The prognosis of SAD varies, although many young people recover without experiencing long-term adverse effects of the disorder on functioning (Hanna et al., 2006). For children who experience recurrent symptoms across time, stress and transitions may trigger a return of symptoms. Younger children are less likely to report worries about the risk of harm to themselves or their attachment figures (Hanna et al., 2006). The ability to anticipate separation, along with associated worries about the impending separation, is more likely to emerge in middle childhood (Hanna et al., 2006). Adolescents may be less likely to disclose worries about separating from an attachment figure and may be more likely to verbalize physical symptoms or avoid leaving home (Hanna et al., 2006). As a result, school counselors should familiarize themselves with the symptoms most likely to be expressed for the specific age group of students with whom they work to ensure that they are accurately assessing and supporting these students.

To diagnose SAD, it is important to ensure that the distress is not a result or by-product of another mental disorder (APA, 2013). Some disorders that may produce similar symptoms include autism spectrum disorder, in which an underlying reaction to changes in the environment may produce similar symptoms; psychotic disorders, in which symptoms of psychosis, such as delusions or hallucinations, may produce similar symptoms; agoraphobia, in which a fear of being in an open space without support may produce similar symptoms; and generalized anxiety disorder (GAD), in which a fear about the health or well-being of others may produce similar symptoms (APA, 2013). Other potential differential diagnoses that should be considered when a child presents with symptoms of SAD include panic disorder, conduct disorder, social anxiety disorder, post-traumatic stress disorder, illness anxiety disorder, bereavement, depressive and bipolar disorders, oppositional defiant disorder, and personality disorders (APA, 2013). Some children may also experience co-occurring separation anxiety and GAD or specific phobia (APA, 2013), so it would be appropriate to assess for these disorders alongside SAD. School counselors who suspect that a child may be experiencing separation anxiety based on that child's behaviors should communicate concerns about the symptoms to the parents; however, as with other mental health disorders, school counselors do not diagnose students with SAD.

Risk Factors and SAD

Several risk factors exist that increase the likelihood of developing SAD and encompass environmental and biological domains (APA, 2013). Environmental antecedents to the development of SAD in children include a major stressor or life transition. These may include events such as the death of a loved one, school change, divorce, serious illness in the child or another family member, moving or immigrating, or a disaster that separates the child from an attachment figure (APA, 2013). School refusal, in particular, may occur after the child is absent from school for some time because of illness or vacation (Hanna et al., 2006). Research also suggests that insecure attachment and insensitivity of the child's mother to the child's needs in infancy may predispose children to experiencing symptoms of SAD in childhood (Dallaire & Weinraub, 2005). Paternal absence was also demonstrated to be a risk factor for the later development of SAD in girls (Cronk et al., 2004). Research also demonstrated an association between low-income status and SAD, with between 50% and 75% of young people with the disorder residing in homes that have limited financial resources (Dallaire & Weinraub, 2005).

Studies with twin siblings demonstrate a potential genetic link to SAD, with twins demonstrating a 73% shared inheritance of the disorder and even higher rates of heritability observed in the twin girls involved in the study (APA, 2013). In addition, the characteristic of behavioral inhibition that is associated with the development of anxiety disorders, including SAD, is an inheritable temperamental disposition (Hanna et al., 2006). SAD is also found more frequently in siblings of children who have had SAD, as well as in children of mothers with a history of anxiety or depression (Hanna et al., 2006). Of particular note is the finding that children of mothers who have a history of co-occurring panic disorder and major depressive disorder are 10 times more likely to be at risk of experiencing SAD when compared to children with mothers who do not have those co-occurring disorders (Hanna et al., 2006). Because there are genetic links that may predispose some children to experiencing SAD, it is important to consider these factors within the context of assessment and early intervention.

Effects on Children and Adolescents

Of the many potential effects of SAD on children, absence from school may be the first and most likely impact to come to the attention of school counselors. This likelihood is also supported by research focusing on school refusal in children with SAD. Refusing to attend school is a consequence of SAD symptoms in approximately 75% of young people who have the disorder; among students who refuse to go to school, 80% meet the diagnostic criteria for SAD (Masi et al., 2001). Absence from school has an effect on academic achievement, and students who frequently miss school fare worse on state-administered standardized exams than peers who attend school regularly (Ginsburg et al., 2014). Avoiding separation from the attachment figure by failing to attend school may perpetuate the cycle of SAD symptoms, which may, therefore, perpetuate absenteeism. Unfortunately, absenteeism may result in further difficulties in addressing the disorder, as failure to attend school for a year or more may make children with SAD especially unresponsive to treatment and/or in-school interventions (Hanna et al., 2006).

For students who do attend school, unaddressed symptoms of SAD may affect their ability to actively engage in and attend to learning experiences. Research suggests that students with SAD demonstrate poorer academic achievement than their peers, especially when the SAD symptoms are chronic and increase in intensity over time (Battaglia et al., 2017). Because poor school performance is another indicator that is likely to come to the attention of school counselors, it is important for school counselors working with students who have poor academic achievement to consider SAD as a potential underlying concern that may be affecting academic functioning.

The presence of SAD may increase the likelihood of experiencing some other mental disorders, including other anxiety disorders (GAD, obsessive-compulsive disorder, panic disorder, social anxiety disorder, and specific phobia), depressive disorders, attention deficit hyperactivity disorder, enuresis, oppositional defiant disorder, and learning disorders (Eisen & Schaefer, 2005). Each of these disorders stands to affect the child's functioning within and outside of school in even more pronounced ways alongside SAD. When a child experiences a comorbid disorder with SAD, school counselors should ensure that they are carefully attending to supporting the student across the affected domains of functioning for each disorder. Of particular importance is the fact that children with SAD have an increased risk of suicide, especially when it occurs alongside another disorder that also increases suicide risk, such as depression, anxiety, or substance use disorders (APA, 2013). As a result, school counselors should be especially diligent in assessing for suicidality in children with SAD, specifically for those who have a comorbid disorder.

In addition to the academic and psychological effects on functioning, SAD may also affect a child's relationship with important others in the student's life. Children who have SAD may react poorly when facing separation from an attachment figure, at times demonstrating anger and potentially becoming physically aggressive (Hanna et al., 2006). These children may be perceived by teachers, peers, and family members as demanding, attention seeking, and intrusive (Hanna et al., 2006), thus increasing the possibility of negative reactions from others. The difficulty with the separation process for children with SAD may be frustrating to parents and school staff members alike, which may increase conflict within the family and school, perpetuate inconsistent sensitivity to the child's needs, heighten insecure attachment patterns, and inadvertently perpetuate the child's experience with SAD symptoms (Hanna et al., 2006). In addition, the child's avoidance of environments where the attachment figure is not present may hinder their social development, as the child may avoid spending time with peers when the attachment figure is not present (APA, 2013). Symptoms of SAD may also lead the child to avoid participating in extracurricular activities or becoming involved in community activities (APA, 2013), which may also limit engagement in recreational activities, hobbies, and other interests that necessitate leaving the attachment figure to participate.

Strategies for School Counselors

School counselors are likely to encounter students with SAD during the course of their careers, given the prevalence rates and affect SAD has on school attendance, academic performance, and psychosocial functioning. As a result, it is important for school counselors to assess themselves for any potential biases or reactions to the behaviors of students who have SAD that may inadvertently alienate these students or perpetuate the symptoms of SAD. Because fear of separation from an attachment figure is a primary driver of symptoms of SAD and because consistent exposure to separation and positive reunifications with the attachment figure help the child habituate and extinguish reactions to the separation (Hanna et al., 2006), school counselors must be aware of and attentive to the student's experience within the school when the separation event takes place. If the child separates from the attachment figure and is thrust into a hostile, rejecting, uncaring environment, it is likely that management of the SAD symptoms will be more challenging than if the child experiences acceptance, care, and sensitivity that supports a safe transition away from the attachment figure. As a result, the school counselor should advocate for an overall school climate that promotes acceptance, care, and empathy for all students; such an environment may not only support students with SAD but also all students who attend the school.

The first step toward addressing SAD within a school setting lies in accurately assessing the presence and severity of SAD symptoms. Ideally, the school counselor, in collaboration with the child's family and other school staff, will assess for and accurately capture the effect of the symptoms of SAD on the child's functioning to better inform interventions and approaches that reduce distress and promote improved functioning within the school environment. Assessment approaches may include formal and informal assessment processes and attend to symptoms related to the disorder, environmental factors, and risk of harm to ensure the safety of the child. These assessments may be conducted by the school counselor, school psychologist, or other members of the child study team who hold appropriate qualifications for conducting the assessment procedures.

There are several standardized assessment measures that may help school counselors assess for SAD. Table 11.1 summarizes the important elements of several of these assessment tools.

In addition to the use of formal assessments to measure the symptoms of SAD, school counselors would also benefit from assessing contextual dimensions that may affect the onset and severity of SAD. Given that SAD may emerge as a result of stressful transition- or loss-related events (APA, 2013), school counselors may choose to informally assess whether students have recently experienced a major transition, loss, or other stressful events, such as divorce or relocation. Assessment of

TABLE 11.1 Assessments for Separation Anxiety Disorder

ASSESSMENT NAME	ASSESSMENT TYPE	OTHER DISORDERS ASSESSED	ADMINISTRATION TRAINING REQUIREMENTS	TIME TO COMPLETE	OTHER INFORMATION
Diagnostic Interview Schedule for Children (Fisher et al., 2006)	Structured Interview	Thirty-four mental health disorders commonly observed in children and adolescents	May be administered by individuals with or without formal clinical training	70–120 minutes	Computer-based and paper-pencil versions available, training in administration strongly recommended, based on *DSM-IV-TR*
Multidimensional Anxiety Scale for Children, 2nd ed. (March, n.d.)	Test	Other anxiety disorders	Level B, school counselors can administer	15 minutes	Can be completed by child or parent
Screen for Child Anxiety Related Disorders (Birmaher, n.d.)	Test	Other anxiety disorders, school avoidance	School counselors can administer	Not reported	Can be completed by child or parent, freely available online
Achenbach System of Empirically Based Assessment (ASEBA, n.d.; Portico Network, n.d.)	Test	Internalizing and externalizing symptoms, six *DSM*-related diagnoses	School counselors can administer	10 minutes	Includes Child Behavior Checklist (two versions based on age) completed by parents, Teacher Report Form, and Youth Self-Report
Spence Children's Anxiety Scale (SCAS, n.d.)	Test	Six anxiety disorders	School counselors can administer	10 minutes	Freely available online for individual use

other environmental factors, such as the child's feelings about the school environment, the child's relationship with peers and family members, and the child's feelings about his or her academic performance and potential may also be helpful for contextualizing and better understanding any underlying effects of SAD on the child's perceptions and functioning. It may also be helpful to triangulate data obtained from the child by exploring these topics with family members and teachers and consulting academic records (for attendance and grades, for example) to create a well-rounded formulation of the child's current strengths, needs, and symptoms.

Once a school counselor has determined that a student is experiencing symptoms that may be a by-product of SAD that affect the child's functioning within the school setting, the counselor can begin formulating a plan for how to work with the student, support the family, and engage with the school and community to advocate for and with the student. Research supports the use of cognitive behavioral therapy (CBT) along with psychoeducation, parent support and education, family therapy, and, in some cases, medication, to help children with SAD (Eisen & Schaefer, 2005; Hanna et al., 2006; Masi et al., 2001). Within the scope of practice for school counselors, it is most likely that the counselor will work within the realms of individual support for the student and family consultation, education, and referral, as well as providing education and support to teachers and other school staff members who work with the child. The next sections explore options and approaches for working with children with SAD that are appropriate for use within the school setting.

Working With Students

CBT is an evidence-based practice that has demonstrated efficacy with SAD (Hanna et al., 2006; Masi et al., 2001) and, as a result, should be an approach school counselors take when working with students who have this disorder. The primary focus of CBT is to help the child develop coping skills for managing distressing reactions to separation (Hanna et al., 2006). CBT for separation anxiety may be provided in individual, family-based, or group settings and has demonstrated efficacy in each of these environments (Hanna et al., 2006). The key components of CBT for working with SAD are described in more detail next.

Psychoeducation

Psychoeducation is used to help the child develop the ability to identify the physiological states, cognitions, and actions associated with feeling afraid and develop ways of differentiating appropriate from excessive reactions. Psychoeducation may take the form of providing and applying information; using metaphors, stories, or images; or modeling (Hanna et al., 2006). For example, a school counselor could draw an illustration of the CBT model that indicates how thoughts, feelings, and behaviors all influence each other.

Self-Monitoring

Self-monitoring involves helping the child identify physiological states, cognitions, and actions that manifest because of anxiety as they are experienced and typically serves as a first step toward changing these reactions to anxiety. Coping strategies such as engaging in alternative behaviors; employing techniques that arrest physiological overarousal, such as relaxation-focused interventions; and challenging faulty cognitions in response to noticing these thoughts are typically employed in response to these excessive responses to anxiety (Hanna et al., 2006). A school counselor could help the student create a worry chart in which the student lists when they have a worry related to being separated from their caretaker, as well as what events led to the worry. Eventually, the worry chart can include other related emotions, as well as ways the student can cope with the worry.

Cognitive Strategies and Restructuring

Cognitive strategies challenge distorted thinking patterns and reactions to anxiety and encourage the child to identify alternative, realistic cognitions in response to anxiety rather than those that perpetuate and heighten anxiety (Hanna et al., 2006). For example, a school counselor could ask a student to list all of the possible worst outcomes of what would happen upon separating from their caretaker and then rank the likelihood of each outcome occurring. Common cognitive distortions that may be a focus of intervention include the following (Kress et al., 2019):

- ***Overgeneralizing.*** Taking one data point and generalizing it to be true in all situations
- ***Jumping to Conclusions.*** Making assumptions about another person's thoughts or feelings or about future events without evidence to support these conclusions
- ***Polarized Thinking.*** Viewing things as all-or-nothing without acknowledging the possibilities that exist within these two extremes
- ***Filtering.*** Focusing on only the negative elements of a situation, event, or interaction
- ***Personalizing.*** Believing that an individual is focusing on you or targeting you negatively
- ***Blaming.*** Either believing you are personally responsible for others' problems or that others are responsible for your problems
- ***Emotional Reasoning.*** Interpreting emotional reactions as factual information and using emotion-based reasoning in place of logic
- ***Labeling.*** Creating a generalized label that is applied to oneself or others to explain a situation or reaction rather than interpreting each circumstance or reaction as unique
- ***Should-ing.*** Blaming oneself or others for what "should" be done or has been done (Kress et al., 2019)

Graded Exposure

Graded exposure involves supporting the child in facing distressing situations in a systematic way to help the child habituate and reduce the anxiety response to being separated from an attachment figure. Effectively implementing this intervention requires that the exposures to anxiety-provoking separations occur with enough frequency for habituation to occur, that the child is able to remain engaged for the entirety of the exposure experience, and that the exposure does not involve a distraction from the experience that circumvents natural de-escalation of the emotional experience (e.g., video on a cell phone, toy, candy) (Hanna et al., 2006). Because coming to school represents an exposure opportunity for students with SAD, it may be helpful for the school counselor to collaborate with parents and the child to facilitate this process. This can be accomplished by creating routines that allow the child to separate from the parent or guardian in consistent, predictable ways, thus promoting decreased separation anxiety over time. Generally, when this process occurs at school, the parent brings the child to the school, leaves immediately, and those in the school support the child in using coping strategies to manage the subsequent anxiety response (Hanna et al., 2006).

Relaxation Training

Relaxation training is used to help the child develop the ability to manage physiological overarousal through the tensing and releasing of muscles while also paying attention to the physical responses. The overall goal of this process is to contrast muscle tension with relaxation and replace tension with relaxation when it is observed in anxiety-provoking situations (Hanna et al., 2006). Relaxation training includes deep breathing exercises, along with muscle relaxation.

Positive Reinforcement and Contingency Management

Positive reinforcement and contingency management are used to promote ongoing engagement in the processes described earlier. Rewards may be delivered by parents, teachers, and school counselors; the focus should be on rewarding the child's engagement in effective coping strategies that promote anxiety management (Hanna et al., 2006).

An evidence-based program focusing on using CBT to reduce anxiety disorders in children, called *Coping Cats* (Kendall & Hedtke, 2006), exists as a resource for implementing CBT with children who have anxiety disorders. *Coping Cats* consists of 16 sessions that help children developing coping skills through a structured implementation of the processes described earlier. For school counselors who are working with youth with anxiety disorders, including SAD, *Coping Cats* may be a useful resource for implementing an effective CBT-based program in schools.

Working With Families

A primary goal of family consultation for school counselors working with children who experience SAD is helping parents to understand the strategies being implemented in the school, as well as promoting separation rituals that facilitate a reduction in anxiety. Families can be provided with the CBT resources that are being used to work with the child, and they can also be encouraged to support the child in using these strategies at home and in the community. With regard to the school drop-off routine, explaining to parents the importance of having a consistent, predictable routine; familiarizing them with the role of graded exposure in the CBT process; and connecting them with resources that they can use to help them manage their own emotions surrounding their child's SAD may all facilitate a successful home-to-school transition for the child. It may also be helpful to provide referral resources to families who may need more specialized intervention, particularly if the child's refusal to attend school makes it impossible for the school counselor to work with the child in any capacity or if the child has a co-occurring mental health disorder that exacerbates his or her response to separation.

Working With the Community and Opportunities for Advocacy

It is important for school counselors to promote a positive school climate in which each child feels welcome, connected, and cared about. In addition, the school counselor may provide professional development and consultation to teachers and other school staff members regarding attachment, trauma, and the role of environmental stressors in triggering symptoms of SAD. The school counselor may also play a special role in starting the academic year by helping teachers of students with SAD proactively plan for and manage potentially difficult separations early in the school year. This may be especially valuable for students who are new to the school, either because of moving or first-year attendance in the school setting (e.g., kindergarten in an elementary school, sixth grade in a middle school). School counselors may be actively involved in the orientation, registration, and first-day procedures for these students to support their successful transition to their new environment.

School counselors may also benefit from collaborating with social service agencies and foster parents given the compounded stressors many young people who have experienced parental loss may endure that precipitate SAD. In addition, school counselors may initiate after-school programs that target children who are at risk of SAD and advocate for resources to support opportunities for these children in the community. This stands to increase both the accessibility of recreational and social activities outside of the home for these children and to support children with SAD by having understanding, supportive community partners who can help them connect with others while also developing the ability to manage SAD symptoms in the larger community.

Understanding What You Have Read: Comprehension Questions

Directions: Refer to what you learned in this chapter to answer the following questions.

1. What is SAD?
2. What are at least three symptoms of SAD?
3. What effects could SAD have on students with regard to school?
4. How can a school counselor best meet the needs of a student with SAD? How can a school counselor assist the family of a student with SAD?
5. What is your first impression of students like Jamar? How might this impression affect your work with students like Jamar?
6. What are ethical and multicultural considerations when working with a student with SAD?

Case Examples

Case Example One

As you read the case about Tia, reflect on the strategies that we discussed earlier in the chapter. The questions that follow the case relate to the student's behavioral symptoms and accompanying responses.

Tia is a 6-year-old kindergartener in a rural school. Prior to the start of the school year, Tia's grandmother passed away. Tia's parents inform the school counselor that the grandmother was Tia's "best friend"; the grandmother was a major caretaker for Tia from birth through prekindergarten. For the past month, Tia has been irritable during morning drop-offs. She screams whenever her mother tries to take her out of the car and tries to run out of the school building after being carried through the main entrance. The school counselor is able to meet with Tia one morning after one of these struggles. Once Tia calms down, she draws a picture for the school counselor of a woman in a casket. Tia tells the school counselor that the woman in the picture is not her grandmother but actually Tia's mother.

Case Example One: Questions for Processing and Reflection

Directions: Use what you have learned in this chapter to respond to Tia's case.

1. What symptoms are being displayed by Tia that *might* indicate that she may be experiencing separation anxiety?
    a. Tia is worried about potential harm to one of her caretakers.
    b. Tia has recurring nightmares about losing one of her caretakers.
    c. Tia is distressed whenever she has to leave her caretaker.
    d. Tia complains of being sick.
    e. Tia has been experiencing symptoms for more than 4 weeks.
2. What information do you have regarding Tia's situation?
    a. Tia has lost her grandmother, whom she considered her best friend.
    b. Tia was very close to her grandmother.
    c. Tia is fearful of leaving her mother to attend school.
3. What additional information might you still need?
    a. How is Tia performing academically?
    b. Does Tia have any friends at school?
    c. How did Tia perform on the Screen for Child Anxiety Related Disorders (Birmaher, n.d.)?

    d. Has Tia recently seen a physician about physical complaints?
4. How would you address concerns related to Tia?
    a. Complete an observation and informal assessment.
    b. Individual counseling to practice relaxation techniques.
    c. Collaboration and consultation with Tia's teachers and parents.
    d. Parent education sessions.

Case Example Two

As you read the case about Rafael, reflect on the strategies that we discussed earlier in the chapter. The questions that follow the case relate to the student's behavioral symptoms and accompanying responses.

Rafael is an 11-year-old in sixth grade in an urban school. Over the summer, Rafael's mother lost her job, and Rafael's parents separated. Rafael now lives with his father and grandmother. Teachers have reported that Rafael frequently skips class to hide out in one of the bathrooms; he has not turned in several assignments and has yet to make up a major test that he missed while absent. During a meeting with the school counselor, Rafael admits that he texts his father while in the bathroom to let him know he has a headache. Rafael says that he gets a headache at least once a day, and it's hard for him to concentrate in class. When the school counselor calls Rafael's father, the father blames Rafael's mother for the child's behavior. According to the father, Rafael's mother "suffers from depression" and "has passed on all that stuff" to Rafael. He wants the school counselor to "fix" Rafael. What should the school counselor do?

Case Example Two: Questions for Processing and Reflection

Directions: Use what you have learned in this chapter to respond to Rafael's case.

1. What are the symptoms of SAD that Rafael is showing?
2. How can the school counselor assess whether Rafael may be experiencing SAD?
3. What should the school counselor prioritize during individual counseling with Rafael?
4. What kind of information would be helpful for Rafael's father to know?
5. What strategies should the school counselor recommend to Rafael's teachers?
6. Outside of the school and Rafael's family, who else might the school counselor collaborate with to better support this student?

Chapter Summary

This chapter focused on symptoms and behaviors related to students experiencing SAD. The authors described the prevalence of this diagnosis, as well as the effects that SAD may have on children and adolescents academically and interpersonally. Methods of screening for SAD, as well as interventions for school counselors to use with students diagnosed with SAD, were presented. In addition, suggestions for collaborating with family, school personnel, and community members were detailed. SAD is one of the most common anxiety disorders diagnosed in children and youth; if left untreated, it can have a negative effect on academic and social functioning, as well as lead to additional diagnoses, such as phobias and depression. School counselors can play an integral role in meeting the needs of students with SAD by implementing evidence-based interventions, as well as educating caretakers and school personnel in reinforcing these interventions outside of the school counselor's office.

Additional Recommended Readings and Resources

Preschool Plan It: https://www.preschool-plan-it.com/separation-anxiety.html

Coping Cat Parents: https://www.copingcatparents.com/Separation-anxiety-disorder

Help Guide: https://www.helpguide.org/articles/anxiety/separation-anxiety-and-separation-anxiety-disorder.htm

References

Achenbach System of Empirically Based Assessment (ASEBA). (n.d.). ADEBA: *Integrated multi-informant evidence-based assessment for ages 1½ to 90+.* https://aseba.org/wp-content/uploads/2019/04/catalog.pdf

American Psychiatric Association (APA). (2013). *Diagnostic and statistical manual of mental disorders* (5th ed.).

Battaglia, M., Garon-Carrier, G., Cote, S. M., Dionne, G., Touchette, E., Vitaro, F., Tremblay, R. E., Boivin, M. (2017). Early childhood trajectories of separation anxiety: Bearing on mental health, academic achievement, and physical health from mid-childhood to preadolescence. *Depression and Anxiety, 34*(10), 918–927.

Birmaher, B. (n.d.). *The screen for child anxiety related disorders (SCARED).* MIDSS. http://www.midss.org/content/screen-child-anxiety-related-disorders-scared

Cronk, N. J., Slutske, W. S., Madden, P. A. F., Bucholz, K. K., & Heath, A. C. (2004). Risk for separation anxiety disorder among girls: Paternal absence, socioeconomic disadvantage, and genetic vulnerability. *Journal of Abnormal Psychology, 113*(2), 237–247.

Dallaire, D. H., & Weinraub, M. (2005). Predicting children's separation anxiety at age 6: The contributions of infant–mother attachment security, maternal sensitivity, and maternal separation anxiety. *Attachment & Human Development, 7*(4), 393–408. https://doi.org/10.1080/14616730500365894

Eisen, A. R., & Schaefer, C. E. (2005). *Separation anxiety in children and adolescents: An individualized approach to assessment and treatment.* Guilford Press.

Fisher, P., Lucas, L., Lucas, C. Sarsfield, & Shaffer, D. (2006). *Columbia University DISC Development Group interviewer manual.* CDC. https://www.cdc.gov/nchs/data/nhanes/limited_access/interviewer_manual.pdf

Ginsburg, A., Chang, H., & Jordan, P. (2014). Absences add up: How school attendance influences student success. Retrieved from https://www.attendanceworks.org/wp-content/uploads/2017/05/Absenses-Add-Up_September-3rd-2014.pdf

Hanna, G. L., Fischer, D. J., & Fluent, T. E. (2006). Separation anxiety disorder and school refusal in children and adolescents. *Pediatrics in Review, 27*(2), 56–63.

Kendall, P. C., & Hedtke, K. A. (2006). *The coping cat workbook* (2nd ed.). Workbook Publishing.

Kress, V. E., Paylo, M. J., & Stargell, N. A. (2019). *Counseling children and adolescents.* Pearson.

March, J. S. (n.d.). *Multidimensional anxiety scale for children (MASC 2)* (2nd ed.). https://www.mhs.com/MHS-Assessment?prodname=masc2

Masi, G., Mucci, M., & Millepiedi, S. (2001). Separation anxiety disorder in children and adolescents: Epidemiology, diagnosis and management. *CNS Drugs, 15*(2), 93–104. https://doi.org/10.2165/00023210-200115020-00002

Portico Network (n.d.). *Child behavior checklist (CBCL).* https://www.porticonetwork.ca/documents/489955/494758/Child+Behavior+Checklist+%28CBCL%29%20PDF/b02af15e-d378-4fe9-870b-9aef6489202c

Spence Children's Anxiety Scale (SCAS). (n.d.). *Spence children's anxiety scale: Overview.* https://www.scaswebsite.com/index.php?p=1_12

CHAPTER TWELVE

Social Anxiety Disorder

Taqueena Quintana

THE CASE OF KENNEDY Kennedy is an eighth-grade student who attends school in a suburban school district. Most of her classmates would describe Kennedy as shy and quiet. Kennedy is an only child and resides with her mother, a homemaker, and her father, a truck driver. She has two friends she has known for several years but rarely interacts with others. Although Kennedy has the potential to perform academically well, she has a history of chronic absenteeism that has placed her at risk of repeating the eighth grade. In addition, her teacher has expressed concerns regarding Kennedy's social functioning and has referred her to the school counselor. The teacher reports that Kennedy avoids social situations and does not engage with the teacher or her peers. When asked to participate or called upon in class, the teacher shares that Kennedy seems fearful and worried, often responding in a soft, shaky voice or asking to use the restroom, usually leaving for an extended period of time. The teacher also mentioned that Kennedy does not eat lunch, nor does she engage with peers during recess, opting to sit on the bench outside instead.

During her initial session with Kennedy, the school counselor noticed that the child trembled when she spoke, avoided eye contact, and continuously rubbed her hands together. Kennedy briefly discussed her discomfort with speaking to others she doesn't know, including the school counselor, and participating in class. She reported her fear of being called on, even when she knew the correct response. She also mentioned symptoms of rapid heartbeat, dizziness, and feeling "sick" when her teacher asked her to share in class. The school counselor also spoke with Kennedy's mother, who shared that Kennedy stays in her room most of the time and struggles to meet new people. She explained that Kennedy has always hated school and cried often when she was younger because she did not want to attend.

Introduction to the Chapter

Students in schools who exhibit behaviors like Kennedy may sometimes go unnoticed, as these behaviors may be less disruptive in comparison to students with behavioral disorders and/or concerns. In addition, parents may neglect to share information with the school related to these students' social development, as they themselves may not recognize concerns. Social anxiety disorder is often misdiagnosed and/or left untreated in children and adolescents because of differential diagnoses and lack of knowledge of symptomology by school personnel and family. In schools, social anxiety disorder can negatively affect academic achievement, cognitive development, and social relationships. It is, therefore, critical for school counselors to be able to assess symptoms and implement interventions to support students with social anxiety disorder.

Learning Objectives

By the end of this chapter, readers will accomplish the following:

- Understand the signs and symptoms of social anxiety disorder.
- Enhance their knowledge of the academic and social effects of social anxiety disorder on children and adolescents.
- Identify strategies for supporting students diagnosed with social anxiety disorder.

Anxiety disorders are the most frequently diagnosed mental health concerns in children and adolescents but are often the least treated (Chavira et al., 2004). The *Diagnostic and Statistical Manual of Mental Disorders, Fifth Edition* (*DSM-5*; APA, 2013) states, "The median onset of social anxiety disorder in the United States is 13 years of age although 75% of individuals have an age of onset age range between 8 and 15 years" (p. 205). It is important to note that compared to younger children, adolescents and youth may be at a higher risk of developing social anxiety–related symptoms because of social engagements, such as dating, preparing for college, and career expectations. The *DSM-5* also mentions that prevalence rates are higher in females than in males, with females reporting a higher number of social fears and comorbid depressive, anxiety, and bipolar disorders (APA, 2013). In understanding these statistics, it is likely that school counselors in elementary, middle, and high schools will support children and adolescents with social anxiety disorder. It is critical that school counselors are adequately prepared to address the needs of these students.

What Is Social Anxiety Disorder?

It is common for children and adolescents to experience moments of discomfort, shyness, nervousness, and even avoidance in social situations, especially if they are new (e.g., the first day of school, asking a question of someone who is unfamiliar). When these experiences become persistent, however, and begin to interfere with daily functioning, despite attempts to provide support, this may be a cause for concern. The *DSM-5* defines social anxiety disorder (or social phobia) as "a marked, or intense fear or anxiety of social situations in which the individual may be scrutinized by others" (APA, 2013, p.203). APA (2013) further mentions that the criteria for social anxiety disorder in children must occur in peer settings (e.g., schools) and not just with adult interactions. Individuals with social anxiety disorder tend to avoid dreaded situations to prevent distress. This is important for school counselors to note, as social anxiety disorder in children and adolescents often manifests in schools, an inherent social environment (Kashdan & Herbert, 2001). Other criteria for social anxiety disorder include (a) a disproportion between the fear/anxiety and the actual threat posed by the social situation, (b) significant distress and impairment in important areas of functioning, (c) fear/anxiety is not attributed to substances (e.g., medication, drug abuse), and (d) fear/anxiety are unrelated to a medical condition and/or another mental health disorder (APA, 2013). Symptoms related to social anxiety disorder are persistent and typically last for at least 6 months.

The *DSM-5* discusses two types of social anxiety disorder: (1) *performance* (e.g., public speaking in front of other students, reading aloud, participating in sports-related activities) and (2) *social interaction* (e.g., eating in front of others in the cafeteria, asking a teacher or peer for help when needed)—both of which are activities that are integral to the school experience. Exposure to the feared situation may trigger a panic attack and sometimes anticipatory anxiety occurring in advance of an upcoming situation. For example, the student becomes anxious even before lunch period, as they are fearful of potential social interactions. Because social anxiety disorder may interfere with daily functioning at school, including academic success and peer relationships, school counselors should be knowledgeable about its signs and symptoms.

Signs and Symptoms of Social Anxiety Disorder

The *DSM-5* (APA, 2013) states that children with social anxiety disorder may express fear and anxiety through "crying, tantrums, freezing, clinging, shrinking, or failing to speak in social situations" (p. 202). Other physical indicators include shaky voice, flushing, palpitations, abdominal discomfort, trembling, nausea, and excessive sweating" (National Institute of Mental Health [NIMH], 2019). Cognitive signs may include excessive fear of embarrassment or humiliation, poor eye contact, decreased coping and social skills, sensory distortions, difficulty verbalizing feelings, and performance anxiety (NIMH, 2019). In identifying signs and symptoms, school counselors can help to educate stakeholders and provide appropriate student support.

Misdiagnosis and Societal Perceptions

Misidentification of social anxiety disorder is common in children and adolescents (Kashdan & Herbert, 2001). As previously mentioned, school personnel, parents, and even peers may misinterpret its symptoms. Children with social anxiety disorder are sometimes viewed as rude or shy based on their quietness. They may experience peer rejection because of their nonreciprocal nature during social interactions. This is especially detrimental to the inclusion in peer and social groups at school. With the prevalence of belongingness and acceptance in childhood and adolescence, the misinterpretation of social anxiety disorder can increase one's vulnerability to other mental health illnesses.

The *DSM-5* outlines various differential diagnoses—that is, other disorders that share similar signs and symptomology. Social anxiety disorder may be misinterpreted as disorders prevalent in childhood, including separation anxiety disorder, selective mutism (because of a failure to speak), oppositional defiant disorder, and autism spectrum disorder. See Table 12.1, which displays the similarities and differences between the diagnoses.

TABLE 12.1 Differential Diagnoses

DIFFERENTIAL DIAGNOSIS	SIMILARITY	DIFFERENCE
Separation Anxiety Disorder	Exhibit discomfort in social settings	With separation anxiety disorder, the discomfort is only present in the absence of the attachment figure. With social anxiety disorder, the absence of an attachment figure has no bearings on the symptoms.
Selective Mutism	Refusal to speak because of negative evaluation from others	With selective mutism, the fear is not present in social environments where speaking is not required.
Oppositional Defiant Disorder	Refusal to speak	With oppositional defiant disorder, individuals may refuse to speak to authority figures. In contrast, individuals with social anxiety disorder may fail to speak because of negative evaluation.
Autism Spectrum Disorder	Social interaction anxiety	Although social anxiety is common in individuals with autism spectrum disorder, individuals with social anxiety disorder normally have age-appropriate social relationships and social communication capacity.

Although school counselors do not diagnose, it is imperative that they are aware of the specific characteristics and symptoms of social anxiety disorder when supporting the academic, social/emotional, and career development needs of children and adolescents. The school counselor's role encompasses direct and indirect student services through collaboration with stakeholders, including students, parents, teachers, and, possibly, mental health providers. Through these collaborative partnerships, school counselors may seek to educate stakeholders about the identification of warning signs of social anxiety disorder, along with screening and interventions, which are discussed later in the chapter.

Risk Factors Related to Social Anxiety Disorder

The *DSM-5* (APA, 2013) highlights risk factors that may increase the likelihood of social anxiety disorder. The risk factors are listed in Table 12.2.

Anxiety or mood disorders, including depression, may also coexist with social anxiety disorder. School counselors should be aware of these risk factors, as it may help to identify a student who is potentially struggling with social anxiety disorder. If ignored or untreated, social anxiety disorder can lead to social/emotional and academic issues that interfere with a child/adolescent's educational success as they transition into adulthood (Thompson et al., 2013).

Impact on Children and Adolescents

Academic

Academically, social anxiety disorder can lead to school refusal (Ybañez-Llorente, 2014), which may lead to poor grades and/or dropping out of school (APA, 2013). Although school refusal has an immediate negative effect on academic success, students with social anxiety disorder are also at risk of facing various issues during their adult years, including marital discord, work-related stress, and decreased well-being (APA, 2013). Chronic absenteeism, tardiness, and early dismissals can serve as warning signs of social anxiety disorder; therefore, it is essential that school counselors attendance of students who demonstrate increased behavioral risks for this disorder.

Social/Emotional

Children and adolescents with social anxiety disorder often have trouble with peer and adult interactions. Kashdan and Herbert (2001) explained, "Children and adolescents with social anxiety disorder demonstrate sensitivity to rejection experiences, reporting fewer friendships, fewer close

TABLE 12.2 Risk Factors for Social Anxiety Disorder

RISK FACTORS	DESCRIPTIONS
Temperamental	• Behavioral inhibition • Fear of negative evaluation • Emotional self-efficacy (Thompson et al., 2013)
Environmental	• Childhood maltreatment and adversity • Parenting practices—e.g., children with parents who display anxiety-related symptoms (Muris & Broeren, 2009) • Maladaptive family environments—high levels of parental criticism and overcontrol (Kashdan & Herbert, 2001)
Genetic	• Heritable—First-degree relatives have a 2 to 6 times greater chance of having social anxiety disorder

relationships, and less social support and acceptance from peer classmates" (p. 43). With the school setting serving as an environment where students often thrive in social groups among their peers, constant social isolation and avoidance can be key indicators of social anxiety disorder. Students who often sit alone during lunch and recess, have difficulty participating in class, and struggle with making friends may be demonstrating symptoms related to social anxiety. In monitoring student social and emotional development, school counselors can work with other school stakeholders, including teachers, parents, and mental health providers, to support students within these developmental areas.

Evidenced-Based Treatment Modalities

The NIMH (2019) stated that cognitive behavioral therapy (CBT) is an effective intervention in treating social anxiety disorder. CBT techniques, such as gradual social exposure, cognitive restructuring, and relaxation techniques, have been reported as effective approaches in the treatment of social anxiety disorder (Kashdan & Herbert, 2001). Psychoeducation on social anxiety disorder can also be beneficial for children, adolescents, and their parents/guardians. For example, education about the benefits of relaxation techniques (e.g., deep breathing exercises, visualization, stretching/physical activity) can be helpful for students both in school and at home (Thompson et al., 2013). Medication, including antianxiety medicine, anti-depressants, and beta-blockers, can also be used in combination with psychotherapy (NIMH, 2019). These medications can help to decrease anxiety-related symptoms and reduce physical responses to anxiety-provoking stimuli.

Strategies for School Counselors

Within their scope of practice, school counselors address the academic, social/emotional, and career development needs of all students through a comprehensive school counseling program (American School Counselor Association [ASCA], 2019). Although school counselors do not diagnose, prescribe medication, or provide therapy, they play an integral role in the lives of their students. As students with social anxiety disorder are at risk for developing other mental health illnesses, including depression, it is essential that school counselors are active in ensuring that these students receive the support necessary to attain educational success. School counselors provide both direct and indirect student services through assessment, intervention, and consultation/collaboration with stakeholders. The following are best practice procedures that school counselors may find useful in identifying the needs and deficiencies of their students.

Working With Students

Assessment

As data-driven school counselors, we know that the role of assessment in schools is essential in guiding interventions and their outcomes. The assessment process includes collecting information to identify, analyze, evaluate, and address student concerns. School counselors do not diagnose during this process; however, assessment results can be beneficial to teachers, parents, and mental health providers in identifying and addressing the needs of the student.

Thompson et al. (2013) recommend the use of brief screenings to allow school counselors to promptly identify students who may be at risk of anxiety-related symptoms. This is especially helpful for students with social anxiety disorder, as their symptoms are often unnoticed or misinterpreted. The authors also mention various measures that allow school counselors to assess for social anxiety–related symptoms, cognitions, and behaviors. These assessments include the Liebowitz Social Anxiety Scale-Child Adolescent version and the Social Phobia and Anxiety Inventory for Children. As with any assessment, it is imperative that school counselors adhere to professional standards and operate within the scope of the profession when selecting, administering, and interpreting assessment measures (ASCA, 2016). As a matter of fact, best practice would dictate that school counselors consult with other professionals within the school when interpreting even brief screening assessments.

Classroom Lessons

School counselors develop lesson plans and facilitate classroom instruction to all students as a core element of their comprehensive school counseling program. Along with instruction that focuses on academic and career readiness, school counselor–facilitated lessons should allow students to develop an awareness of mental health, promote positive behaviors, and help to remove stigma and barriers associated with mental illness (ASCA, 2015). Research supports classroom guidance lessons as effective prevention and intervention tools for reducing anxiety-related symptoms in students (Thompson, et. al, 2013). In a study that examined the effects of an anxiety-reduction classroom guidance intervention on third-grade students' level of anxiety and self-concept, the researcher reported that after 10 weeks of instruction and support, there was a measurable decrease in physical symptoms and separation/panic related to anxiety (Ybañez, 2010). Supporting students with social anxiety disorder through classroom lessons can be beneficial to their academic success.

When supporting students with social anxiety disorder through classroom instruction, school counselors can

1. provide structured lessons that educate students about the nature and symptoms of social anxiety disorder and its effect on cognition, behavior, and emotions;
2. differentiate instruction to support various learning styles (e.g., integrating visual tools within the lesson, assigned partner and small group activities);
3. provide rewards to support social interaction and participation efforts; and
4. teach coping skills that empower students and promote confidence and resilience.

Group Counseling

Group counseling is another core intervention within the comprehensive school counseling program. For students with social anxiety disorder, group counseling provides them with a smaller setting in which to communicate their emotions, gain a sense of normalcy, and experience universality among their peers. Because students with social anxiety disorder may demonstrate difficulty with social interactions, it is important for school counselors to conduct a group screening to ensure that the setting is appropriate (Curtis et al., 2004).

There are various approaches to group counseling that can promote social and emotional wellness within the school setting for students with social anxiety disorder. Bibliocounseling, otherwise known as bibliotherapy, is one approach that can be beneficial. Bibliocounseling uses literature and other media to address social/emotional concerns to meet the goals of counseling (Pehrsson & McMillen, 2007). It is a natural fit within schools, where school counselors have easy access to books, and students are already familiar with reading and storytelling. Through bibliocounseling, students with social anxiety disorder have the opportunity to connect with characters, view concerns similar to their own from various perspectives, and learn ways to address these concerns (Thompson et. al, 2013). As a cautionary note, however, students with social anxiety disorder should not be asked to read orally to others without proper preparation and practice, as this may exacerbate symptoms (Pehrsson & McMillen, 2007).

Role-playing is another strategy that can be used within group counseling to support students with social anxiety disorder. Role-playing allows students to rehearse scenarios, model behaviors, and use coping skills while receiving support from their peers (Zyromski & Joseph, 2008). The tools learned during group counseling can support students with social anxiety disorder in the real world. Role-playing can also be used in individual counseling.

Individual Counseling

With individual counseling, school counselors provide short-term, one-on-one support to students during times of transition, stress, crisis, and other issues that may impede student success (ASCA, 2019). Individual counseling can be preventative or responsive and can be an alternative to group counseling for students with social anxiety disorder who require support separate from their peers. School counselors should be mindful to use theoretical approaches that they are familiar with and have been reported as supportive in addressing the behavioral symptoms of social anxiety disorder.

Play Approaches

Research shows that therapeutic play has positive effects on elementary-aged students and can reduce anxiety in children (Baggerly & Jenkins, 2009; Lindsey & Colwell, 2003; Russ & Schafer, 2006; Shen, 2002). Play-based interventions can be especially beneficial for students with social anxiety disorder who do not have the vocabulary or are uncomfortable with expressing their thoughts and feelings through words. With play, students can practice various coping strategies, address and adjust negative thinking, and enhance social skills and relationships (Echterling et al., 2010). For school counselors with limited space, Echterling and colleagues recommended a tote bag of toys and other items for play-based interventions. Note that there is a professional difference between being a registered play therapist and using aspects of play during individual counseling. What is being proposed in this chapter is the latter. Most recently, the Association for Play Therapy developed a school-based play therapist certificate that school counselors may find useful. Additional information on this credential can be found at https://cdn.ymaws.com/www.a4pt.org/resource/resmgr/credentials/sb-rpt_faq_aug_2018.pdf.

Technology-Based Approach

Thompson et. al (2013) discussed computer-based CBT (CCBT) as an efficient and accessible intervention option for students with anxiety-related disorders. This approach may be especially beneficial to older students and those more developmentally advanced for play interventions. CCBT focuses on preventing and reducing anxiety-related symptoms through online interventions in the school setting. The authors provide a table of recommendations that lists several evidence-based CCBT programs, including Cool Teens, Camp Cope-a-Lot, and the Brave Program. Research conducted on these programs reports improvement in anxiety-related symptoms in children and adolescents (Khanna & Kendall, 2010; March et al., 2009; Wuthrich et al., 2006). CCBT program and purchase information can be found online, with links to several programs provided at the end of this chapter.

Working With Stakeholders

In addition to direct student services, school counselors work on behalf of students through indirect services (ASCA, 2019). Indirect services include collaboration and consultation with school stakeholders. School counselors serve on various teams/committees with stakeholders as advocates for students' needs. Stakeholders include parents, teachers, administrators, and mental health professionals.

Administrators

The school counselor–administrator relationship is one of great importance, as it is often the principal who sets the tone for the school counselor's role (Paolini & Topdemir, 2013). ASCA (2019) suggested an annual administrative conference: a formalized discussion between the school counselor and administrator that allows for the increase of administrator's knowledge regarding the school counselor's program priorities, services to be delivered, and use of time. School counselors can use this time to educate administrators about diagnostic issues that affect students' learning process. It is vitally important to educate the school administration about student experiences, as they are often the first line of contact for students who are deemed noncompliant. New knowledge may influence disciplinary decisions that more appropriately address students' needs.

Teachers

School counselors and teachers work together in various ways to contribute to student growth and achievement. Kashdan and Herbert (2001) mentioned that students with social anxiety disorder "tend to be invisible and neglected in the classroom and often do not come to the attention of school personnel unless the disorder progresses to a point where they refuse to attend school" (p. 39). In the classroom setting, school counselors and teachers can co-teach lessons on topics that lend themselves to identifying and addressing the symptomologies related to social anxiety disorder and other disorders that are prevalent among children and youth. School counselors and teachers also collaborate as part of student success teams, Section 504 committees, and individualized education program teams (ASCA, 2016). This is important, especially as students with social anxiety disorder may need this additional support. School counselors engage in consultation with teachers in the assessment process, as teachers are key components in data collection (e.g., attendance and academic data) and can speak to student development because of longer periods of time spent in the classroom. In addition, school counselors can provide teacher education through workshops and presentations on social anxiety–related symptoms and ways to employ strategies to create an environment that helps to alleviate these symptoms (ASCA, 2016; Ybañez, 2010).

Parents/Guardians

Parents/guardians are key stakeholders in supporting students' educational success. For students with social anxiety disorder, their concerns often go unrecognized by parents, who may assume that the student is shy or quiet. In addition, "parents are unlikely to know how to obtain treatment for their child, even if they recognize that he or she has a treatable disorder" (Kashdan & Herbert, 2001, p. 40). For students with social anxiety disorder, parent-school counselor partnerships are critical in addressing behavioral and academic needs. The literature provides recommendations that lend themselves to school counselor and parent partnerships that support students with social anxiety disorder. Recommendations are as follows:

1. Parents/guardians should always be informed of their legal rights, including informed consent, Family Educational Rights & Privacy Act (FERPA), and confidentiality (ASCA, 2016).
2. School counselors should consistently collaborate with parents/guardians when student assistance is required, including the identification of early warning signals of student stressors (ASCA, 2016). School counselors should regularly engage in consultation meetings with the parent/guardian to discuss the student's concerns related to anxiety and techniques that can support the student at home (Thompson et. al, 2013, Ybañez, 2010).
3. Parents/guardians should be a part of the assessment process, including data collection, analysis, evaluation, and intervention. In addition, parents/guardians should have a voice within

the assessment process, as their perspective of the student concerns can help to shed light on the data (Ybañez, 2010). Pertinent data may include attendance and behavioral information.

4. School counselors should provide parent education that includes information about warning signs, symptoms, and risk factors of social anxiety disorder and the effect of social anxiety disorder on student learning, parental anxiety, parenting, family environment, diet, referrals, and involvement in treatment. School counselors can collaborate with community mental health agencies in providing information sessions and workshops at school to support all families (ASCA, 2016; Ybañez, 2010).
5. Parents/guardians should be educated about the scope of the school counselor's role and be made aware of when students' needs are beyond the training of the school counselor. Parents/guardians should be provided a list of district and community resources for additional support. Counselors should not be biased toward one provider over another and should support parents in interviewing referral sources to make the best possible decision for their students (ASCA, 2016).
6. When supporting parents/guardians who may have difficulty obtaining external counseling services for students, school counselors should "recognize and address barriers to access mental health services and the associated stigma" (ASCA, 2015, p.72).

Mental Health Providers

When students present issues that require long-term counseling and these needs are determined to be beyond the scope of the school counselor, it is imperative that counselors direct students and parents/guardians to school and community mental health resources for additional support (ASCA, 2016, 2019). For students with social anxiety disorder, this is especially important, as some mental health providers can diagnose and may be well equipped to discuss both symptoms and clinical treatment options, including therapy and medication. The ASCA Ethical Standards for School Counselors (ASCA, 2016) provide guidance on how school counselors can link students and their families to referral sources. The standards (2016) stress the following:

1. Connecting students to services provided by the school district and community resources can be beneficial for students who require more intensive support. School counselors should establish a professional, collaborative relationship with internal and external providers to help address students' needs (Standard A.6.a).
2. Maintaining an awareness of school policies and the law is crucial when working with referral sources. This is especially important when working with students with a formal diagnosis (Standard A.6.c).
3. A release of information authorizes a treating entity (usually health related) to share (or release) the protected health information of a client/patient. School counselors should request a release of information form from the provider that is signed by the student and parent/guardian prior to collaborating with the provider. If available, school counselors may also have the student and parent/guardian sign a district release of information form that authorizes them to share student educational information with the provider. This allows the school counselor to share "accurate, objective, meaningful data necessary to adequately assess, counsel and assist the student" through consultation with the provider (Standard A.6.g).
4. Creating a plan in collaboration with the provider for the transfer of counseling support allows for a structured, smooth transition of services for the student and their family. Students and their parents/guardians have the right to opt to continue services with the school counselor, along with the external provider, or to discontinue counseling services with the school counselor while still preserving a relationship with the school counseling office in other areas of support (Standard A.6.d).

Understanding What You Have Read: Comprehension Questions

Directions: Refer to what you learned in this chapter to answer the following questions.

1. What is social anxiety disorder?
2. What are the determining factors for a diagnosis of social anxiety disorder?
3. What modalities of support can school counselors extend to students?
4. How might you as a future counselor support a student who demonstrates symptoms of social anxiety during your clinical experiences?
5. How might your personal experiences affect your ability to support students like Kennedy?
6. What are some of the ethical and multicultural considerations that should be examined when working with a student with social anxiety disorder?

Case Examples

Case Example One

As you read the case about Lauren, reflect on the strategies that we discussed earlier in the chapter. The questions that follow the case relate to the student's behavioral symptoms and accompanying responses.

Lauren is a 10-year-old student in the fifth grade at a rural elementary school. Lauren has attended this school for 3 years, as she transferred in the middle of the second grade. Lauren has a history of attendance issues, which is believed to have caused academic deficits. Lauren is frequently tardy to school, sometimes several hours after school has already started, and is failing major subjects because of missed classroom instruction. Her classroom teacher reports that Lauren appears quiet and shy in class, often speaking in a low and soft tone when addressed by the teacher individually. She does not like to engage in partner or group work and hates to be called on, visibly shaking and crying when asked a question in front of her peers. In addition, her previous teachers report similar classroom behaviors and chronic absenteeism, with one teacher stating, "At least she comes to school now." In a meeting with the school counselor, Lauren's father shared that Lauren has always been shy and was bullied several times in her previous school. He believes that Lauren's reluctance to attend school is due to her experiences with being bullied. Lauren's father did not report any existing medical or mental health concerns. Following the parent discussion, the school counselor attempted to speak with Lauren; however, during their session, Lauren barely engaged in conversation, asked to use the restroom, and never returned to the counseling office.

Case Example One: Questions for Processing and Reflection

Directions: Use what you have learned in this chapter to respond to Lauren's case.

1. What are the symptoms that Lauren is exhibiting that may be related to social anxiety disorder?

   Lauren's symptoms include difficulty verbalizing feelings, shaking, and crying when prompted to engage in social interactions.
2. What additional information would be helpful to understand Lauren's concerns?

   Additional information that would be helpful to understand Lauren's concerns include the history of her symptoms, specific triggers, and previous coping strategies.
3. What roles do assessment and interventions play in identifying and addressing Lauren's needs?

   Assessment allows the school counselor to collect data through brief screenings and other tools to pinpoint Lauren's issues and develop appropriate interventions that will support Lauren's overall success. Through this process, the school counselor may also learn whether Lauren requires additional services.

4. Specifically, how would you collaborate with stakeholders to support Lauren?

   In supporting Lauren, the school counselor can work with the classroom teacher as a consultant to assist the teacher in developing/using best practices in the classroom to meet Lauren's needs. The school counselor can also collaborate with Lauren's mother by educating her about Lauren's concerns and modeling various coping strategies to support Lauren at home.
5. How would you have responded to these questions? How similar or different are your responses?

Case Example Two

As you read the case about Derik, reflect on the strategies that we discussed earlier in the chapter. The questions that follow the case relate to the student's behavioral symptoms and accompanying responses.

Derik, a 16-year-old student in an urban high school, has been identified as at risk for academic failure. Derik, who is in his second year of the ninth grade, has had several home visits from the school counselor and attendance coordinator because of absences and skipping school (mainly in the afternoon during lunch, physical education, advisory, and other elective courses). In Derik's county, the law mandates that school personnel file a report with child protective services when students are absent from school for at least 10 consecutive days. Despite calls to the local child welfare agency and several investigations over the years, Derik continues to miss school. In speaking with teachers, the school counselor found that Derik is often described as "rude and defiant" because he does not engage with peers or faculty. His math teacher states that when called on during lessons, Derik refuses to respond, often freezing like "a deer in headlights," and she believes that this happens because he doesn't pay attention. Derik's biology teacher shares that he refuses to work with his peers during lab, often leaving for extended periods of time and returning once lab is over. Several teachers also reported that when Derik did attend school, he sat in the back of his classes with his head down and a jacket draped over him, even during the warmer months, so he often went unnoticed. In addition, a few students mentioned that Derik sometimes smelled of marijuana before entering class. The school counselor addressed these concerns in a brief counseling session with Derik, who shared that marijuana helps him to "zone out," as he is uncomfortable being around people and would prefer to be alone at all times. Derik also shared that since he was a child, he disliked being called on in class and would have "stomach issues and sweats" whenever he was called on or paired with other students. He now says when he turns 17 years of age, he's going to leave school completely to obtain a GED and will get his own apartment to get away from his "controlling, overprotective" mother.

Case Example Two: Questions for Processing and Reflection

Directions: Use what you have learned in this chapter to respond to Derik's case.

1. What are some warning signs presented in this case that lend themselves to social anxiety disorder?
2. Describe the risk factors associated with Derik's case. How do they contribute to Derik's issues?
3. What additional information is needed to identify Derik's concerns accurately? What steps should be involved?
4. What are some ethical and legal issues to consider regarding Derik's case?
5. As a school counselor, how would you collaborate with Derik's mother and teachers to address his concerns?

Chapter Summary

This chapter focused on symptoms and behaviors related to social anxiety in children and adolescents. The author presented relatable descriptors of the varying behaviors that may be observed of a child who either has been diagnosed with social anxiety disorder or may be demonstrating related symptoms. Strategies have been provided for school counselors regarding best practices in understanding social anxiety disorder and supporting students through collaborative strategies with administrators, parents, and other stakeholders. Social anxiety disorder can negatively affect overall functioning in children and adolescents. If left unaddressed, social anxiety disorder may lead to other mental health illnesses, including depression. School counselors, while working within their professional scope of practice, are qualified to advocate for and provide support services to students with social anxiety disorder.

Additional Recommended Readings and Resources

Anxiety and Depression Association of America: https://adaa.org/resources-professionals

BRAVE Self-Help: http://brave.psy.uq.edu.au/index.html? site= public&page=about

Social Anxiety Disorder Basics: https://childmind.org/guide/social-anxiety-disorder/

Social Anxiety Disorder: More Than Just Shyness: https://www.nimh.nih.gov/health/publications/social-anxiety-disorder-more-than-just-shyness/index.shtml

Stress Free Kids: https://stressfreekids.com/

References

American Psychiatric Association (APA). (2013). *Diagnostic and statistical manual of mental disorders* (5th ed.).

American School Counselor Association (ASCA). (2015). *The school counselor and student mental health.* https://www.schoolcounselor.org/asca/media/asca/PositionStatements/PS_StudentMentalHealth.pdf

American School Counselor Association (ASCA). (2016). *ASCA ethical standards for school counselors.* http://www.schoolcounselor.org/asca/media/asca/Ethics/EthicalStandards2016.pdf

American School Counselor Association (ASCA). (2019). *The ASCA national model: A framework for school counseling programs* (4th ed.).

Baggerly, J., & Jenkins, W. W. (2009). The effectiveness of child-centered play therapy on developmental and diagnostic factors in children who are homeless. *International Journal of Play Therapy, 18*(1), 45–55. https://doi.org/10.1037/a0013878

Chavira, D. A., Stein, M. B., Bailey, K., & Stein, M. T. (2004). Child anxiety in primary care: Prevalent but untreated. *Depression and Anxiety, 20*, 155–164.

Curtis, R. C., Kimball, A., & Stroup, E. (2004). Understanding and treating social phobia. *Journal of Counseling & Development, 82*, 3–9. https://doi.org/10/1002/j.1556-6678.2004.tb00279.x

Echterling, L., Stewart, A., & Budash, D. (2010). *Suddenly military: Play-based interventions for deployed National Guard and Reserve families.* Counseling Outfitters. http://counselingoutfitters.com/vistas/vistas10/Article_19.pdf

Kashdan, T. B. & Herbert, J. D. (2001). Social anxiety disorder in childhood and adolescence: Current status and future directions. *Clinical Child and Family Psychological Review, 4*, 37–61

Khanna, M. S., & Kendall, P. C. (2010). Computer-assisted cognitive behavioral therapy for child anxiety: Results of a randomized clinical trial. *Journal of Consulting and Clinical Psychology, 78*(5), 737–745. https://doi.org/10.1037/a0019739

Lindsey, E. W., & Colwell, M. J. (2003). Preschoolers' emotional competence: Links to pretend and physical play. *Child Study Journal, 33*, 39–52.

March, S., Spence, S. H., & Donovan, C. L. (2009).The efficacy of an internet-based CBT intervention for child anxiety disorders. *Journal of Pediatric Psychology, 34*(5), 474–487. https://doi.org/10.1093/jpepsy/jsn099

Muris, P., & Broeren, S. (2009). Twenty-five years of research on childhood anxiety disorders: Publication trends between 1982 and 2006 and a selective review of the literature. *Journal of Child and Family Studies, 18*, 388–395. https://doi.org/10.1007/s10826-008-9242-x

National Institute of Mental Health (NIMH). (2019). Social anxiety disorder: More than shyness. https://www.nimh.nih.gov/health/publications/social-anxiety-disorder-more-than-just-shyness/index.shtml

Paolini, A. C. & Topdemir, C. M. (2013). Impact of accountability on role confusion: Implications for school counselor practice. *VISTAS Online*, Article 93. https://www.counseling.org/docs/default-source/vistas/impact-of-accountability-on-role-confusion.pdf

Pehrsson, D. E., & McMillen, P. (2007). *Bibliotherapy: Overview and implications for counselors* (ACAPCD-02). American Counseling Association.

Russ, S. W., & Schafer, E. D. (2006). Affect in fantasy play, emotion in memories, and divergent thinking. *Creativity Research Journal, 18*, 347–354. https://doi.org/10.1207/s15326934crj1803_9

Shen, Y. (2002). Short-term group play therapy with Chinese earthquake victims: Effects on anxiety, depression, and adjustment. *International Journal of PlayTherapy, 11*(1), 43–63. https://doi.org/10.1037/h0088856

Thompson, E. H., Robertson, P., Curtis, R., & Frick, M. (2013). Students with anxiety: Implications for professional school counselors. *Professional School Counseling, 16*(4), 222–234. https://doi.org/ 10.5330/PSC.n.2013-16.222

Wuthrich, V. M., Rapee, R. M., Cunningham, M. J., Lyneham, H. J., Hudson, J. L., & Schniering, C. A., (2006). A randomized controlled trial of the CoolTeens CD-ROM computerized program for adolescent anxiety. *Academy of Child and Adolescent Psychiatry, 51*(3), 261–270. https://doi.org/10.1016/j.jaac.2011.12.002

Ybañez, K. (2010). Effects of an anxiety reduction classroom guidance intervention for elementary students. *New York State School Counseling Journal, 7*(2), 40–49.

Ybañez-Llorente, K. (2014). Addressing anxiety in school settings: Implications for counselors. *VISTAS Online*, Article 62. https://www.counseling.org/docs/default-source/vistas/article_62.pdf?sfvrsn=20677d2c_10

Zyromski, B., & Joseph, A. E. (2008). Utilizing cognitive behavioral interventions to positively impact academic achievement in middle school students. *Journal of School Counseling, 6*(15). http://www.jsc.montana.edu/articles/v6n15.pdf

CHAPTER THIRTEEN

Panic Disorder

Seungbin Oh

THE CASE OF OLIVER Oliver is a 16-year-old male 11th-grade student at a Title I school. He is a diligent student yet very shy and reticent. He lives with his parents and one younger brother and has been sent to see the school counselor by his teachers because he has been seen as overly anxious and worried in class. He shared with the counselor that he was extremely anxious about his performance in school during the past 4 months. He reported that during that time, he has experienced acute palpitations, shortness of breath, nausea, chest pain, and the fear that he was about to die. He also shared with the counselor that these symptoms began suddenly and peaked within minutes, leaving him convinced that he'd experienced a heart attack. He said that he experienced a total of two or three such attacks in the past 4 months, specifically at school. Oliver revealed that since that experience, he persistently worried about having other attacks, which led him not to want to go to school. When the counselor asked him if there were any specific situations or places in the school that triggered such attacks, he reported that they began spontaneously without any warning. However, he also revealed that he experienced a feeling of dread more often before taking tests or exams. Oliver's parents reported that he sometimes used herbal supplements to manage his anxiety. The parents also shared that they think that Oliver was just anxious in general and stressed out about his homework.

Introduction to the Chapter

Students like Oliver may present as shy, introverted, and even the "typical" anxious students who tend to worry too much about schoolwork. Oliver's mental health concern remained unnoticed because symptoms of panic disorder are easily disguised as emotional and physical distress or some other medical condition. Panic disorder is often not recognized, particularly in youth, because there is a lack of training or guideline to help counselors identify panic symptoms in school-aged youth. Given the anxiety epidemic in schools, it can be difficult to decipher whether students' panicky symptoms are "normal" or clinically defined panic attacks. This difficulty often leads to misdiagnosis among youth, especially between ages 13 to 17. Moreover, this is also an important developmental stage where youth are expected to experience emotional and social changes, which provokes deep anxiety in them. Unfortunately, because of these aforementioned challenges, panic disorder in youth is often unnoticed until they have made frequent runs to the emergency room or harmed themselves.

Learning Objective

By the end of this chapter, readers will accomplish the following:

- Understand the signs and symptoms of panic disorder.
- Recognize the educational and social effects of panic disorder on adolescents and youth.
- Develop increased knowledge of best practice strategies for supporting students diagnosed with panic disorder or experiencing the symptoms of panic disorder.

Although the median age of onset for panic disorder is 20 to 24 years old, first experiences with a "panicky feeling" often begin in childhood or adolescence. It is often during the adolescent years that an increased number of students start to experience panic attacks and become diagnosed with panic disorder. As such, it is becoming more likely that middle school and high school counselors are working with students experiencing the symptoms of panic disorder. According to the National Institute of Mental Health (NIMH, 2017), "An estimated 2.3% of adolescents aged 13 to 18 had panic disorder, and 2.3% had severe impairment" (Prevalence of Panic Disorder among Adolescents section, para. 3). The rate of adolescents diagnosed with panic disorder gradually increases year to year, with 1.8% of 13-year-olds to 3.3% of 17-year-olds (NIMH, 2017). Panic disorder in adolescence is more likely to have a chronic course if not treated earlier, and it is often combined with major depressive disorder. Although studies vary widely, the rate of major depressive disorder in individuals with panic disorder can be as high as 65% (APA, 2013). There is also a high possibility of other anxiety disorders in individuals with panic disorder. Rates of coexisting agoraphobia in panic disorder can be as high as 30%, specific phobia 20%, and OCD 10% (Shatkin, 2015). Panic disorder is also highly related to other medical conditions, such as dizziness, asthma, irregular heartbeat, abdominal pain, and progressive lung diseases. An increased number of students with panic disorder may also engage in substance use and abuse to manage their anxiety (APA, 2013).

Signs and Symptoms of Panic Disorder

Anxiety disorders commonly developed in childhood and adolescence fall into five categories: (1) separation anxiety disorder, (2) selective mutism, (3) specific phobia, (4) social anxiety disorder, and (5) panic disorder (APA, 2013). The most common anxiety disorders in childhood are separation anxiety disorder, selective mutism, and specific phobia, whereas social anxiety disorder commonly emerges in adolescence. Although panic disorder rarely occurs in childhood, the first incidence of unexpected "panicky feeling" is often traced back to childhood. In addition, the incidence rate of panic disorder begins to increase from the adolescent years, and such a disorder developed in adolescence tends to persist throughout one's life span unless it is treated. This chronic disorder can result in severe problems in many areas of youth's lives, including absence from school, poor academic performance, lack of socialization with peers, and dropping out of school. In this chapter, we will focus on the general signs and symptoms of panic disorder.

According to the *DSM-5*, panic disorder refers to the experience of unexpected and repeated panic attacks (at least more than one). A youth can experience unexpected and recurrent panic attacks and/or show symptoms of a panic attack as signs of panic disorder. The panic attack symptoms are the essential features for a diagnosis of panic disorder but may be caused by other emotional states, such as anger and grief. Panic attacks may also result from other medical conditions, such as asthma and irregular heartbeat. Being intoxicated with substances and stimulants (e.g., marijuana, cocaine, alcohol, and caffeine) may cause some symptoms of a panic attack. Panic attacks can also be caused by the other anxiety disorders. If a child or adolescent encounters a specific social situation or phobic object that is anxiety provoking, that may trigger symptoms of panic disorder. Panic

TABLE 13.1 Symptoms of Panic Disorder

SYMPTOMS	DESCRIPTION
Physiological symptoms	Sweating, heart palpitations, shortness of breath, chest discomfort, nausea, dizziness, and migraine headaches Example: A student's parents report that their child suddenly wakes up during the night sweating, with shallow breath, and experiencing dizziness. At school, the student consistently complains about chest discomfort, nausea, and headaches.
Cognitive symptoms	Pervasive physical, social, and daily task concerns Example: A student consistently worries about their physical health, has fears about being negatively judged by peers, and is afraid of being unable to complete daily tasks, such as assignments, or cope with daily stressors.
Behavioral symptoms	Avoidance, poor social skills, reduced activity, restricted daily routine, and extreme use of drugs Example: A student consistently avoids participating in normal activities with peers and restrict their daily activities and food consumption. The student may also avoid certain situations, such as leaving home and using school buses.
Emotional symptoms	Fear of losing control, fear of dying, feeling of choking, uneasiness, and feelings of unreality Example: A student feels like they are going crazy and losing their mind. This student expresses that they feel like they are living in a dream or movie.

attacks can also be a proponent of post-traumatic experience. Reexperiencing intrusive thoughts and flashbacks of a traumatic event may foster the symptoms of a panic attack.

Broadly speaking, we can categorize symptoms into four different categories in relation to associated features, which give us a developmental point of view. These different categories are shown in Table 13.1.

Misdiagnosis and Societal Perceptions

To better understand panic disorder, we will break down the symptoms based on the diagnostic criteria of the *DSM-5*. Table 13.2 shows 13 symptoms associated with panic disorder that school counselors can observe. Please bear in mind that for a diagnosis of panic disorder, more than one unexpected panic attack should occur with at least **four** of the 13 panic symptoms and must be followed within 1 month by consequential symptoms of either *persistent concern* about another panic attack or a *significant change in behavior* to avoid triggers of another panic attack. Note that a panic attack is *not* a mental disorder *nor* equivalent to panic disorder. Instead, it serves as the building block for a diagnosis of panic disorder, and it can co-occur in the context of intense emotional states, other mental disorders, and any anxiety disorders. In general, panic attacks initially occur out of the blue without any cue or trigger but later attacks can be triggered by a specific situation

TABLE 13.2 Common Social Misconceptions

SYMPTOM	MISCONCEPTION
Palpitations and pounding heart	These days, the student does not engage in outdoor activities but spends a lot of time on their phone. Maybe this student did strenuous outdoor exercise today. Or this student is a typical "anxious" kid.
Sweating	The student is another typical teen who does not like outdoor activities. This kid did outdoor activities today. Or the student is coming down with a cold.
Shaking	The student is just an emotionally and mentally unstable kid. Maybe the student needs to take an attention deficit hyperactivity disorder (ADHD) test.
Shallow or shortness of breath	Maybe the student has asthma or is allergic to something.
Choking feeling	The student is just another "too worried" or "high-strung" kid.
Chest pain or discomfort	This student is overly stressed out about exams. This student needs to overcome this normal "exam anxiety."
Nausea or abdominal distress	The student has a highly sensitive stomach. Or this student is having food poisoning.
Feeling dizzy or light-headed	The student stayed up too late watching TV shows, playing video games, and being on social media. Or this student is coming down with a severe cold.
Feeling overheated or chills	The student is just overly sensitive to the temperature in the classroom.
Sensations of numbness or tingling	Maybe this student is experimenting with alcohol and drugs.
Derealization	This student is another typical teenager who spends too much time on social media. These days, the student has multiple realities online and less experience with in-person social interactions.
Fear of losing control or going crazy	There goes another mentally unstable student. Let the student take a test for ADHD.
Fear of dying	This student is just an attention seeker. The best way to deal with this student is not to give them the attention that they want.

or object, such as school tests, arrival of the school bus, and extracurricular activities. In Table 13.2, we have added to each symptom societal misconceptions that may obscure the understanding and judgment of adults.

At the surface level, we may look at these symptoms as the result of the student being highly anxious, sensitive, unstable, and digitally dependent. These misconceptions and unfair stereotypes may result in the misdiagnosis of children and youth. It is, therefore, important to be aware of implicit biases or preconceived ideas about youth that may cloud our judgment and lead to the misdiagnose of our students. One example is the misconception that Generation Z or iGeneration youth are lazy and unaware. School counselors working with Generation Z students may find the following book helpful: *iGen: Why Today's Super-Connected Kids Are Growing Up Less Rebellious, More Tolerant, Less Happy—and Completely Unprepared for Adulthood—and What That Means for the Rest of Us,* written by Jean Twenge.

Risk Factors and Panic Disorder

Extensive research highlights various factors that increase the risks of youth experiencing panic disorder. Risk factors include increases in societal violence and hostility, social problems at school, and dysfunction and violence in the family system.

Societal Violence and Hostility

Increased violence and hostility in society is one factor that has contributed to panic disorder in youth and young adults. Societal hostility and violence, from deportation of immigrants to sexual harassment to mass shootings, have caused significant stress among youth. When students are exposed to societal hostility through either experience or from witnessing traumatic events, they are more likely to develop mental health issues (APA, 2008; Little & Akin-Little, 2013). After reviewing the current literature, Little and colleagues reported that exposure to societal or community violence increases the risks of youth experiencing fear, anxiety, and elevated heart rates. Moreover, the American Psychological Association (APA, 2019) recently revealed that Generation Z youths (15 to 21 years old) report more mental health concerns because they are more stressed about such societal violence than all other generations. As such, school counselors and teachers need to be more attentive to the negative effects of social violence on youths who are witnessing the increased level of violence within society through news and social media.

Social Life in School

Social problems in school is another risk factor for panic attacks, which may lead to the development of panic disorder in children and adolescents. Poor social skills and difficulties in peer relations in schools (e.g., not being able to get along with other children, getting teased a lot, or not being liked by other children) are significant predictors of panic attacks in adolescents that can progress to panic disorder (Mathyssek et al., 2012). Social problems (e.g., poor interaction with peers, fear of talking in a group or class, avoidance of social activities) may be the result of certain personality traits that children have inherited from their parents. Asselmann and colleagues (2016) reported that adolescents with harm avoidance personalities, as characterized by shyness, self-doubt, consistent worry, and inhibiting behaviors, were at significantly higher risk of panic disorder. Here we can see that such personality traits, which are transmitted from their parents, may lead to less developed social skills, eventually resulting in social problems in school.

Family System

Family dysfunction and violence are other factors that may increase the risk for the development of panic disorder in children and youth (Asselmann et al., 2016; Goodwin et al., 2005). Asselmann and colleagues reported that parental anxiety and depression are significant predictors of panic disorder in youth. Moreover, they also explored the association of parenting styles with the likelihood of panic attacks and panic disorder in youth. The authors reported that parental overprotection and parental affectionless control (i.e., high protection without emotional support) were significant predictors not only of panic disorder in youth but also of panic attacks, which can later progress to panic disorder and other anxiety disorders. Moreover, Goodwin and colleagues (2005) investigated the relationship between familial violence (e.g., childhood physical or sexual abuse) and the subsequent development of panic disorder. The authors indicated that childhood physical abuse (e.g., physical punishment) and sexual abuse were significantly associated with the later development of panic disorder.

Strategies for School Counselors

School counselors do not clinically diagnose; however, school counselors may work with children and youth in schools who are already diagnosed, are presenting with high-level anxiety, or are demonstrating symptoms of anxiety disorders, such as panic disorder. In all cases, school counselors have an ethical and professional mandate to address the symptoms that influence students' functioning in various areas of life, including academic, social/emotional/personal, and career development. Children and youth with anxiety disorders, such as panic disorder, are not only at a higher risk of suicidal attempts and suicidal ideation but also have increased levels of avoidance behaviors, a higher rate of dropping out of school, and a decreased level of academic productivity and social interaction in school (APA, 2013; Reichenberg & Seligman, 2016). Given the psychosocial and physical effects of panic disorder, it is vital for school counselors to provide comprehensive and appropriate care to these students. Next, we introduce practical strategies for school counselors to use when working with these students within the scope of available training and resources.

Reichenberg and Seligman (2016) addressed several practical strategies that can be adapted in school settings. The first step is *to develop a therapeutic relationship through an affirmative counseling approach*. In general, students experiencing the symptoms of panic disorder or diagnosed with panic disorder have several experiences with failing to control their panic attacks. They may feel defeated by the unsuccessful treatment and even angry about having panic symptoms that seem to be out of control. Thus these students will benefit from school counselors affirming and normalizing these reactions and reassuring that interventions can be effective. Second, *psychoeducation about symptoms of panic attacks* is recommended. These students often do not understand the difference between what is a "normal" and "not normal" level of anxiety that they should experience at school. Therefore, these students will benefit from receiving psychoeducation about panic disorder and its physiology. Third, *teach calm breathing exercises and muscle relaxation* as a way of providing students with a toolbox of strategies to manage their anxiety and panic attacks. Calm breathing and muscle relaxation can be particularly helpful strategies that these students can use to calm down quickly as they face their fears of future panic attacks. Lastly, provide necessary accommodations with school-related work through collaboration with other stakeholders. For example, school counselors can consider making recommendations to have IEP and/or Section 504 Plans revised and adjusted as needed to provide students extra time to complete assignments and more frequent breaks.

Assessment

School counselors should play an active role in assessing students' therapeutic needs. Assessments are the cornerstone of effective school counseling and should be a process of gathering information from both family and school personnel about students' academic performance and psychosocial functioning. It is especially critical to assess students who may contemplate suicide. In the context of working with a student at risk of attempting suicide, school counselors can use the SLAP method to complete a suicide assessment. Details in the SLAP method can be found in Chapter 4, "Major Depressive Disorder").

Another important component that should be included in the assessment of students is avoidance behaviors. Out of fear of future panic or anxiety attacks, students may often develop a pattern of unhealthy behaviors to avoid specific situations or objects that trigger panic attacks, such as taking school exams, getting on school buses, completing particular subject assignments, and engaging in outside activities with their peers. The avoidance behavior may result in the impairment of students' ability to study, exercise, socialize, or engage in daily activities, and they may even drop out of school (Reichenberg & Seligman, 2016). Therefore, it is critical for school counselors to measure the severity of the avoidance behavior in relation to specific triggering situations or objects. To assess avoidance behaviors, school counselors can use the fear ladder method.

THE FEAR LADDER

Please create a list of feared situations and rank other them using the following scale.

1	2	3	4	5	6	7	8	9	10
No panic or avoidance									**Extreme anxiety and avoidance**

Step	Feared Situations	Panic and Avoidance Rating

There are other factors that may play a role in students experiencing panic attacks and panic disorder. School counselors would benefit from exploring the possibility of serious medical conditions (e.g., cancer, asthma, diabetes, and chronic pain) that may foster panic. Youths with chronic illness may react to the condition with internal mental turmoil by being excessively worried, anxious, and sad, which may mimic symptoms of panic disorder. In addition, it would be beneficial to explore a history of substance or drug use (e.g., alcohol, tobacco, or marijuana) that may cause panic attacks. Recently, there was a high school junior who was considered to be panicky for months because of his pounding heart, shortness of breath, and feeling dizzy. After a comprehensive test, it was found that he was vaping nicotine and marijuana with his peers. In fact, a recent survey on drug use among eighth, 10th, and 12th graders reported a **significant increase in vaping** nicotine and marijuana in all grades (National Institute of Health on Drug Use [NIH], 2018). Therefore, it is critical to assess other medical or mental health conditions that may co-occur with panic attacks or panic disorder.

Individual Counseling

Once comprehensive assessments are complete, school counselors should decide the best therapeutic approach for helping students who need psychological help. It has been well documented that cognitive behavior therapy (CBT) is an effective individual treatment for youth experiencing panic disorder (Barlow et al., 2015; Seligman & Ollendick, 2012). Reichenberg and Seligman (2016) also emphasized the benefits and effectiveness of CBT in treating panic disorder. Specifically, a combination of CBT, psychoeducation, and interoceptive exposure reduced the symptoms of panic disorder. For example, psychoeducation about normal or non-normal bodily sensations is an important first step in the CBT treatment process. In addition, a combination of CBT and medication, especially selective serotonin reuptake inhibitors (SSRIs), is considered to be effective for treating panic disorder or any anxiety-related disorder. Although SSRIs are generally viewed as safe for children and adolescents, it is important to be attentive to the recent concerns about the side effects of inducing suicidal thoughts and depression. Note that school counselors should not make recommendations for the use of psychotropic medications to parents or students. However, a consultation focused on the child's medical history may be warranted.

School counselors can use CBT in both individual and small-group counseling. In any counseling setting, the school counselor should adapt traditional CBT methods to the child's or adolescent's developmental level. When traditional talk CBT is developmentally inappropriate, the counselors will benefit from tailoring talk CBT with another therapeutic modality that is developmentally appropriate or refer the student out to other helping professionals who can provide therapeutic inventions that are developmentally appropriate, such as expressive art and play therapy. For example, parent-child interaction play therapy was shown to significantly reduce symptoms of anxiety disorders in children (Brendel et al., 2014). In addition, cognitive behavioral art therapy was found to be an effective intervention for a significant reduction in panic frequency and other symptoms of panic attacks (Morris, 2014). Hence a developmental approach to working with students is important to provide the best therapeutic service.

Group Counseling

Research indicates the benefits of group counseling in reducing some symptoms of panic disorder, especially anxiety, in both children and adolescents. Specifically, as both a preventive and treatment intervention, CBT group counseling has shown to reduce anxiety symptoms significantly in children and adolescents (Wolgensinger, 2015). For example, the FRIENDS program is considered to be an effective school-based CBT program for children. Research has shown that the program helped children between 9 and 12 years old to reduce anxiety symptoms significantly up to 12 months after the program experience (Wolgensinger, 2015). In addition, as a CBT group-based treatment, the Coping Cat Program was found to be advantageous for reducing anxiety symptoms in children between 8 and 17 years old until the 1-year follow-up (Flannery-Schroeder et al., 2005). Lastly, it was found that group play therapy was an effective intervention for reducing anxiety symptoms in children (Fathalipouri et al., 2013).

Other Treatment Modalities

Acceptance-based therapeutic modalities, such as mindfulness and meditation, have received increased attention for treating symptoms of panic attacks and panic disorder. Although more research is needed, few studies have shown a significant correlation between mindfulness and meditation and a reduction in panic symptoms (Crowley et al., 2018; Kraemer et al., 2015). For example, a recent study on group mindfulness therapy in a school setting reported a significant reduction in the anxiety symptoms of adolescents (Crowley et al., 2018). In addition, it was found that school-based cognitive mindfulness intervention significantly decreased symptoms of panic disorder in students between 9 and 13 years old (Lam, 2016). School-based cognitive mindfulness was a group training program to help students be aware of the thought patterns that keep them susceptible to anxiety and depression. As for other important sources, the National Institute of Mental Health (2016) highlighted the importance of a healthy lifestyle to combat panic disorder, including maintaining good sleep hygiene, participating in exercise, eating a healthy diet, and having the support of family and friends. School counselors can also help students experiencing the symptoms of panic disorder by using aerobic activity, specifically running (Sabourin et al., 2015). Such aerobic activity could be incorporated into small groups, parental training, and school wellness activities.

Strategies for Working With Parents/Guardians of the Student

It is also critical to collaborate with parents/guardians to provide maximum support for students in a state of panic. There are several factors for school counselors to be aware of when collaborating with parents/guardians. First, as discussed earlier, the family system, particularly family dysfunction and violence, can have a big influence on mental health in youth. When working with youth living with panic symptoms, school counselors should address the patterns of the parent-child dyad or family dynamics, such as parenting and communication styles. While working with parents, we must teach them that the goal of the parent-counselor collaboration is not to blame parents but rather to understand the big picture and provide their children with the best coping strategies to deal with their panic symptoms.

In addition, parental involvement is vital to the school-home collaboration for providing counseling interventions to their children (Shillingford et al., 2018). School counselors may find parents to be critical to therapeutic interventions for panic disorder, such as the CBT-based systematic exposure intervention to help children gradually become desensitized to panic-provoking situations or objects. As such, school counselors should provide parents/guardians with sufficient information regarding therapeutic interventions offered at school without breaching confidentiality. Furthermore, school counselors can provide parents with psychoeducation about useful communication skills, such as good modeling to help their children learn healthy coping mechanisms for dealing with their panic symptoms. Patterns of a child's responses to anxiety- or panic-provoking situations are often learned behaviors, especially from parents. Therefore, parents' appropriate modeling behaviors in regard to anxiety can play a significant role in helping their children reduce their anxiety and learn new coping strategies.

Strategies for Working With Teachers and Other Stakeholders

Because panic symptoms are internalized behaviors and can be hidden in the features of other health conditions, it is crucial to collaborate with teachers, parents, nurses, and administrators to maximize the probability of identifying students living with panic symptoms and providing comprehensive care for students. Given the multiple roles in the school setting, it is important for school counselors to clarify their roles and duties when working with teachers and other stakeholders.

According to the ASCA National Model (2019), school counselors can take the following five roles in partnership with teachers and administrators: (1) communication, (2) consultation, (3) collaboration, (4) education, and (5) advocacy. The well-developed strategy to maintain a balance in the first two roles, communication and consultation, can be found in Chapter 4, "Major Depressive Disorder." This chapter will focus on the remaining three roles of school counselors in the partnerships formed for helping students living with panic symptoms.

1. ***Collaborate.*** One way to collaborate with the teacher is to develop a lesson plan together on topics such as anxiety, de-stressing, and building supportive friendships. For example, teachers and school counselors can both deliver de-anxiety activities in the classroom, such as coloring mandalas, mindfulness, stress balls, and blowing bubbles (McCormac, 2016). In addition, school counselors can collaborate with the school nurse who can provide a safe space for students to practice new coping strategies to deal with panic symptoms. School nurses are often the first people in a school to identify students who make frequent visits to the health office for their physical symptoms (e.g., chest pain), which in reality are panic symptoms. Additional collaboration may include a community mental health provider

involved with students' care, if available. It is beneficial to discuss with the professionals the possibility of therapeutic service being offered at school or a referral to the community mental health provider.

2. ***Education.*** School counselors can provide teachers, administrators, and other stakeholders with psychoeducation about the signs of panic disorder. As discussed earlier, adults often misunderstand or underrecognize students' behaviors that may indicate panic symptoms. Teachers would benefit from psychoeducation about the common signs of panic disorder in academic, affective, and behavioral areas, such as difficulty concentrating, lack of interest, or decline in participation; missed deadlines for homework; and absenteeism and tardy arrivals. In addition, school counselors can help teachers, school nurses, and administrators through workshops, training programs, and the school newsletter.
3. **Advocate**. School counselors can take a leadership role in advocating for their students. One way to advocate for students living with panic symptoms may include speaking up for change in the school culture that places unnecessary pressure on students at a cost to their mental health. For example, school counselors can advocate for the modification of a school calendar that is overcrowded with demands but has no downtime for students, which may lead to increases in anxiety across the school. Another way to advocate may include raising one's voice in support of school-wide special events that focus on the wellness of the students. The school counselor can serve as an advocate for a mental health day or anxiety-awareness week by looking at the school calendar and identify the peak times of anxiety or stress (e.g., the period during statewide testing). Lastly, school counselors can advocate for the rights of students, particularly when special accommodations for students are necessary in the classroom in light of the affective, behavioral, and academic effects that this disorder can have on children.

Understanding What You Have Read: Comprehension Questions

Directions: Refer to what you learned in this chapter to answer the following questions.

1. What is panic disorder?
2. What are the key factors for a diagnosis of panic disorder?
3. What modalities of support can school counselors offer to students?
4. As a future school counselor, how would you support a student who is presenting with symptoms of panic disorder during your clinical experience? What would your counseling approach be?
5. What are some of the ethical and multicultural considerations that should be examined when working with a student with panic disorder?

Case Examples

Case Example One

As you read the case about Amelia, reflect on the strategies that we discussed earlier in the chapter. The questions that follow the case relate to the student's behavioral symptoms and accompanying responses.

Amelia is a 17-year-old female who is a 12th-grade student at an urban school. When she was in the 10th grade, she was a kind and composed student who was favored by many friends and teachers. However, in the past 3 months, Amelia made several visits to the school health office with complaints of chest pain. Amelia's teachers later shared that she has been very uneasy and even sometimes restless in class. The teachers also reported seeing Amelia trembling whenever she was about to take an exam and that she was not interested in participating in outside activities with her peers. When talking with her parents, they shared that Amelia would sometimes wake suddenly during the night while sweating profusely. She complained of not wanting to go to school and not engaging in activities that she once enjoyed. Her parents also shared that she does not have any other medical conditions. Amelia met with the school counselor and expressed that she was apprehensive about not being able to complete all school works and felt a lot of pressure on her chest when thinking about her future.

Case Example One: Questions for Processing and Reflection

Directions: Use what you have learned in this chapter to respond to Amelia's case.

1. What symptoms are being demonstrated by Amelia that might suggest that she may be experiencing panic attacks?
    a. Amelia is experiencing disturbing physical symptoms (chest pain or discomfort).
    b. Amelia presents with anxiety-appearing symptoms (uneasiness, restlessness, trembling).
    c. Amelia suddenly wakes up during the night sweating.
    d. Amelia feels extremely anxious about school-related work and the future.
    e. Amelia feels like she is losing control over her life.
2. What information do you have regarding Amelia's situation?
    a. She does not have any known medical or health conditions that could be responsible for her behaviors.
    b. Her parents and teachers are aware of her anxious behaviors and are concerned.
    c. She has worries about school-related work and her future.
    d. She has a sense of powerlessness.
3. What additional information might you need?
    a. A fear ladder assessment should be completed to identify specific situations or events that foster panicky feelings
    b. History of substance use or stimulants (alcohol or caffeine) from parents and teachers
    c. Information about parenting styles and family relationships from the parents and Amelia
    d. The results of Amelia's last visit with her physician
    e. Details about her daily diet
    f. Information about any recent traumatic events
4. How would you address concerns related to Amelia?
    a. Individual sessions to normalize and validate her experience with panicky symptoms in an affirmative manner
    b. Psychoeducation to discuss "normal" and "non-normal" symptoms of panic attacks
    c. Parent consultations to discuss available resources outside of school (e.g., mental health counseling services, art therapy, or play therapy)
    d. Collaboration with teachers and other stakeholders to provide systemic support and the necessary accommodations for Amelia
    e. Small-group counseling support (if applicable)

Case Example Two

As you read the case about Katie, reflect on the strategies that we discussed earlier in the chapter. The questions that follow the case relate to the student's behavioral symptoms and accompanying responses.

Katie is a 15-year-old girl in the 10th grade. She has one older sister and lives with her parents in a small rural town. You have noticed that Katie has started to lose interest in outdoor activities with peers, and the normally composed child has become overly anxious; in fact, you often see her fidgeting with her hands. During lunchtime, you run into the school nurse who tells you that Katie visited the health office for extreme chest pain, along with numbness in her arms. The nurse says Katie told her that the chest pain made her feel like she was going to die. After lunch, you reach out to Katie's teacher, and he is also very concerned about the student. He shares that she not only looks very worried about participating in in-class activities but also is very scared about the minor homework he assigns. When he encourages her to engage in in-class activities, she asks to be excused from participating and says she does not feel well. He has also noticed a big difference in her interactions with her peers. She avoids contact (e.g., conversation) with the other students and spends a lot of time sitting in her chair alone. The teacher has called her home, and her parents are also concerned about Katie not wanting to go to school. Her parents asked him for advice on how to help their daughter, but he couldn't think of a good approach for helping her. Now the teacher asks you for your advice on the next steps. What do you tell him?

Case Example Two: Questions for Processing and Reflection

Directions: Use what you have learned in this chapter to respond to Katie's case.

1. What are the symptoms of panic attacks that Katie is demonstrating to her counselor, teacher, and parents?
2. What would your next step be to support Katie? What would your focus be for her?
3. Would you use the fear ladder assessment? What would these steps entail? What purpose would this assessment serve when working with Katie?
4. With whom would you collaborate within the school setting to support Katie? Explain why.
5. What are the benefits of having Katie's parents' involvement in developing a plan for Katie?
6. How would you collaborate with her teacher to develop a plan for Katie?

Chapter Summary

This chapter addressed symptoms and behaviors associated with panic disorder in children and adolescents. The author provided practical descriptors of the various verbal and nonverbal behaviors that can be recognized in school-aged youth who either have been diagnosed with panic disorder or may be experiencing the symptoms of panic disorder. This chapter also offered practical strategies for the best practices that school counselors can use to support their students at the individual, family, school, and societal levels. Panic disorder is detrimental to the wellness of children and adolescents in various areas of their lives. Youth experiencing panic disorder may live with the symptoms for the rest of their lives unless it is treated earlier. Therefore, school counselors are professionally mandated to provide comprehensive care to these students within the scope of their practice and roles in schools.

Additional Recommended Readings and Resources

Panic Disorder and Agoraphobia: https://anxietycanada.com/disorders/panic-disorder-and-agoraphobia/

Teen Mental Health for Panic Disorder: http://teenmentalhealth.org/learn/mental-disorders/panic-disorder/

Twenge, J. (2017). *iGen: Why today's super-connected kids are growing up less rebellious, more tolerant, less happy—and completely unprepared for adulthood—and what that means for the rest of us* (2nd ed.). Atria Books.

References

American Psychological Association (2008). Children and trauma: Update for mental health professionals. Washington, DC: Author.

American Psychological Association (2019). Gen Z more likely to report mental health concerns. Retrieved from https://www.apa.org/monitor/2019/01/gen-z

American Psychiatric Association (2013). *Diagnostic and statistical manual of mental disorders* (5th ed.). Arlington, VA: Author.

Asselmann, E., Wittchen, H., Lieb, R., & Beesdo-Baum, K. (20116). Risk factors for fearful spells, panic attacks and panic disorder in a community cohort of adolescents and young adults. *Journal of Affective Disorders, 193*, 305–308.

Barlow, D. H., Conklin, L. R., & Bentley, K. H. (2015). Psychological treatments for panic disorders, phobias, social and generalized anxiety disorders. In P.E. Nathan and J. M. Gorman (Eds.), *A guide to treatments that work* (p. 409–461). Oxford University Press.

Brendel, K. E., & Maynard, B. R. (2014). Child–parent interventions for childhood anxiety disorders: A systematic review and meta-analysis. *Research on Social Work Practice, 24*(3), 287–295.

Crowley, M. J., Nicholls, S. S., McCarthy, D., Greatorex, K., Wu, J., & Mayes, L. C. (2018). Innovations in practice: Group mindfulness for adolescent anxiety—results of an open trial. *Child Adolescent Mental Health, 23*, 130–133.

Fathalipouri, P., Makvandi, B., & Heidarie, A. (2013). Effectiveness of group play therapy in reducing generalized anxiety in female elementary students. *International Journal of Psychology and Behavioral Research, 2*, 231–239.

Flannery-Schroeder, E., Choudhury, M. S., & Kendall, P. C. (2005). Group and individual cognitive-behavioral treatments for youth with anxiety disorders: 1-year follow-up. *Cognitive Therapy and Research, 29*, 253–259

Goodwin, R., Fergusson, D., & John-Horwood, L. (2005). Childhood abuse and familial violence and the risk of panic attacks and panic disorder in young adulthood. *Psychological Medicine, 35*, 881–890.

Kraemer, K. M., McLeish, A. C., & Johnson, A. L. (2015). Associations between mindfulness and panic symptoms among young adults with asthma. *Psychology, Health & Medicine, 20*, 322–331.

Lam, K. J. (2016). School-based cognitive mindfulness intervention for internalizing problems: Pilot study with Hong Kong elementary students. *Journal of Child and Family Study, 25*, 3293–3308.

Little, S. G., & Akin-Little, A. (2013). Trauma in children: A call to action in school psychology. *Journal of Applied School Psychology, 29*, 375–388.

McCormac. (2016). Address Student Anxiety | American School Counselor Association (ASCA). Retrieved from https://www.schoolcounselor.org/magazine/blogs/september-october-2016/address-student-anxiety

Mathyssek, C. M., Olino, T. M., Verhulst, F. C., & van Oort, F. V. A. (2012). Childhood internalizing and externalizing problems predict the onset of clinical panic attacks over adolescence: The TRAILS study. *PLoS ONE, 7*, e51564.

Morris, F. J. (2014). Should art be integrated into cognitive behavioral therapy for anxiety disorders? *The Arts in Psychotherapy, 41*(4), 343–352.

National Institute of Health on Drug Use. (2018). *Monitoring the future survey: High school and youth trends.* https://www.drugabuse.gov/publications/drugfacts/monitoring-future-survey-high-school-youth-trends

National Institute of Mental Health (2017). Panic Disorder. Retrieved from https://www.nimh.nih.gov/health/statistics/panic-disorder.shtml

National Institute of Mental Health (2016). Panic Disorder: When fear overwhelms. Retrieved from https://www.nimh.nih.gov/health/publications/panic-disorder-when-fear-overwhelms/index.shtml

Sabourin, B. C., Stewart, S. H., Watt, M. C., & Krigolson, O. E. (2015). Running as Interoceptive Exposure for Decreasing Anxiety Sensitivity: Replication and Extension. *Cognitive Behaviour Therapy*, 44(4), 264–274. https://doi.org/10.1080/16506073.2015.1015163

Seligman, L., & Ollendick, T. H. (2012). Cognitive behavioral therapy for anxiety disorder in youth. *Child Adolescent Psychiatric Clinic of North America*, 20(2), 217–238.

Reichenberg, L. W. & Seligman, L. (2016). *Selecting effective treatments: A comprehensive, systemic guide to treating mental disorders*. Hoboken, NJ: Wiley & Sons.

Shatkin, J. P. (2015). Child & adolescent mental health: A practical, all-in-one guide. New York, NY: W.W. Norton & Company.

Shillingford, A., Oh, S., & Finnell, L. R. (2018). Perceptions of parents of color towards STEM professions: A school counselor leadership engagement. *Special Issue in Professional School Counseling Journal*, 21(1b), 1–11.

Wolgensinger L. (2015). Cognitive behavioral group therapy for anxiety: recent developments. *Dialogues in Clinical Neuroscience*, 17(3), 347–351.

CHAPTER FOURTEEN

Post-Traumatic Stress Disorder

Richelle Joe

THE CASE OF BRIAN As a rising senior, Brian should be excited about the beginning of another school year and being the "big man on campus." Instead, he's terrified of returning to school and hesitant to even leave the townhouse where he lives with his parents and younger sister. Brian is a 17-year-old African American male who earns above-average grades and has a solid group of friends in his neighborhood and school. However, 4 months ago, he witnessed the violent death of his best friend who was hit by a stray bullet as the two walked home from school. Although Brian was not hurt in the incident, he often zones out and relives the moment. Immediately following the shooting, Brian had nightmares every night, but now those nightmares occur about once a week. He is easily startled by loud noises and has difficulty feeling relaxed or safe when anywhere other than home. He spent most of the summer alone in his room. As the first day of school gets closer, Brian is irritable, fidgety, and avoids interactions with his family members and friends. He rarely leaves the house, and when he does, he feels anxious and returns home quickly, sometimes stating that he was sure he saw his deceased friend walking down the street. When his parents mention the upcoming school year, Brian states emphatically that he is not going to school and shuts down any further discussion on the topic.

Introduction to the Chapter

A significant number of children and adolescents have experienced trauma in their homes, schools, and communities. Some have suffered abuse and neglect, while others, like Brian, have been affected by gun violence. In Brian's case, his exposure to trauma has resulted in symptoms characteristic of post-traumatic stress disorder (PTSD)—namely, avoidance, recurring and intrusive images of the trauma, and persistent fear. In addition, his hypervigilance and refusal to return to school present as signs of PTSD, although they may be misconstrued as attention concerns or defiance. Treatment for PTSD requires ongoing therapy that goes beyond the scope of practice for professional school counselors. However, school counselors possess counseling, collaboration, and consulting skills that, coupled with knowledge of PTSD, can be used to support children and adolescents who are at risk for or diagnosed with PTSD.

Learning Objectives

By the end of this chapter, readers will accomplish the following:

- Understand the neurological, psychological, social, and academic effects of trauma on children and adolescents.
- Identify the signs and symptoms of PTSD.
- Understand the professional school counselor's role in supporting students with PTSD through direct and indirect services.

Trauma Exposure and Its Effects on Children and Adolescents

Trauma exposure includes "actual or threatened death, serious injury, or sexual violence" that an individual either experiences directly, witnesses as it occurs to another, or learns that it occurred to a close family member or friend (American Psychiatric Association [APA], 2013a, p. 271). Prevalence estimates for trauma experiences among children and adolescents are difficult to establish given the multiple challenges associated with gathering this data. Oftentimes, trauma events involving children and adolescents occur in private settings, resulting in the underreporting of incidents because of fear, internalized stigma, guilt, and shame (Saunders & Adams, 2015). In addition, although young children (less than age 7) constitute approximately 56% of victims of maltreatment, there has been a lack of focus on trauma in this age group because of misconceptions about infant/toddler mental health (De Young et al., 2011).

Despite challenges in determining accurate prevalence statistics for children and adolescents who have experienced trauma, research indicates that young people are experiencing traumatic events that are adversely affecting their growth and development. The Centers for Disease Control and Prevention (CDC)-Kaiser Permanente Adverse Childhood Experiences (ACE) Study found that two thirds of participants reported at least one ACE, which includes emotional, physical, or sexual abuse, as well as neglect, domestic violence, substance abuse or mental illness within the household, parental separation or divorce, and incarceration of a household member (CDC, 2019). In a study of the lifetime prevalence of mental health diagnoses, Merikangas et al. (2010) reported that in a sample of more than 10,000 adolescents, 31.9% met the criteria for severe anxiety disorders, including PTSD. McLaughlin et al. (2013) reported a prevalence rate of 61.8% for exposure to traumatic events among adolescents and a lifetime prevalence of PTSD ranging from 4.7% to 7.3%. Demonstrating the differential exposure to trauma associated with community context, Breslau et al. (2004) reported that 82.5% of youth in a large sample from an urban setting had experienced one or more traumatic events, and 71% met the criteria for PTSD in their lifetime. Among children in the child welfare system, Beal et al. (2019) found that an average of 10 out of 26 traumatic events were endorsed within this group, including complex trauma that is severe and pervasive (Lawson, 2009; National Child Traumatic Stress Network, n.d.). Sadly, childhood trauma is common and has adverse effects on an individual's physical and mental wellness over their lifetime.

Childhood trauma can affect an individual's psychological, social, emotional, and physiological development and well-being. Abuse, neglect, and sexual exploitation can lead to multiple mental health concerns, including attachment difficulties, depression, suicidality, and PTSD (Lawson, 2009). For children who are not mistreated but who experience a parental loss, grief can be prolonged, and PTSD can develop (Melhem et al., 2011). Trauma can also have significant effects on the brain and cognitive functioning (Bremner, 2006; Bremner et al., 2008; Olff et al., 2005). Experiences of trauma are associated with stress and increased cortisol levels, as well as a reduction in brain volume in children (Bremner, 2006). In addition, children and adolescents who experience traumatic events can experience memory deficits, dissociation, and an attentional bias toward trauma-related material (Bremner, 2006; Bremner et al., 2005). In the school setting, these effects can impair students' ability to engage with teachers and peers, focus in class, and cognitively process information taught to them.

Children and adolescents who have been exposed to traumatic events will likely be affected by these experiences in some way, yet not all will develop symptoms of PTSD. Smith et al. (2019) reported that the prevalence of PTSD diagnoses among children is 4%–5% and 16%–21% among adolescents. Protective factors for youth who have experienced trauma include a positive self-concept, a secure attachment, a supportive environment, and coping skills, (Lawson, 2009; Olff et al., 2005). Specifically, children and adolescents who can employ adaptive coping strategies (e.g., positive thinking) and who are empowered and feel a sense of control regarding the trauma may be less likely to be diagnosed with PTSD compared to youth with maladaptive coping strategies (e.g., avoidance) (Olff et al., 2005). In addition, time matters in that treatment delivered promptly following trauma exposure can address traumatic memories and facilitate neurogenesis (or nerve growth) to reduce the likelihood of the onset of PTSD (Bremner, 2006). Herein lies the challenge for children and adolescents who experience complex or prolonged trauma. The lack of protection from future trauma within a safe and supportive environment makes youth vulnerable for the onset of PTSD, as well as other mental health conditions (Beal et al., 2019; McLaughlin et al., 2013; Melhem et al, 2011; Szymanski et al., 2011). In addition, preexisting psychological concerns and poor family functioning are risk factors for the development of PTSD in children and adolescents (Smith et al., 2019).

PTSD: Diagnosis and Misconceptions

Significant changes were made to the diagnostic criteria for PTSD in the fifth edition of the *Diagnostic and Statistical Manual of Mental Disorders* (*DSM-5*; APA, 2013a) to address the age-related and developmental aspects of the disorder (APA, 2013b; APA, 2013c; Wheeler & Jones, 2015). In addition, the *DSM-5* now includes criteria specifically for children age 6 and younger to account for the unique ways in which children in this age group manifest symptoms of trauma (APA, 2013b; Wheeler & Jones, 2015). *DSM-5* criteria for PTSD address both the exposure to a traumatic experience and an individual's reaction to that experience (APA, 2013a). Exposure includes directly experiencing the trauma, witnessing the trauma occurring to another person, learning that a traumatic event has occurred to a close family member or friend, and repeated or extreme exposure to details of a traumatic event (e.g., work-related exposure for law enforcement officers and first responders). Reactions to trauma include intrusive symptoms (e.g., recurring dreams, memories, flashbacks), avoidance of both internal (e.g., memories and thoughts) and external (e.g., people and places) reminders of the traumatic event, changes in cognitions and mood, and changes in arousal and reactivity. Symptoms must occur for more than 1 month and must cause "clinically significant distress or impairment in social, occupational, or other important areas of functioning" (APA, 2013a, p. 272).

The *DSM-5* (APA, 2013a) notes that for children, the symptoms for PTSD may manifest in repetitive play that incorporates elements of the traumatic event or reenacts the trauma with specificity. In addition, children may experience flashbacks and nightmares that include less specific or recognizable content but are associated with the trauma. For children under age 6, intrusive symptoms include memories and flashbacks that appear in play reenactment, distressing dreams where the connection to the traumatic event may be difficult to determine, and marked psychological and physiological reactions to internal or external reminders of the trauma. Other symptoms for this age group include regression; subtle avoidance, such as turning away (Wheeler & Jones, 2015); increased frequency of negative emotions; hypervigilance; and sleep disturbance (APA, 2013a). Table 14.1 provides specific examples of age-related signs and symptoms of PTSD in children and adolescents. In addition, Putman (2009) provides some specifics about how PTSD manifests in children who have

TABLE 14.1 Age-Related Signs and Symptoms of PTSD in Children and Adolescents

CHILDREN OVER AGE 6 AND ADOLESCENTS	
SYMPTOM CATEGORY	**EXAMPLES**
Intrusive symptoms	Child has distressing memories of the traumatic event (recurrent and involuntary) Child has nightmares (recurrent) associated with the trauma Child dissociates, experiences flashbacks in which the child feels the event is occurring again Child reenactments trauma during play
Avoidant symptoms	Child avoids bad memories, thoughts, or feelings associated with the traumatic event Child avoids people, places, situations, and objects associated with the trauma
Changes in cognition and mood	Child is unable to recall aspects of the traumatic event Child holds exaggerated negative beliefs about people and the world Child internalizes blame because of distorted beliefs about the cause or consequences of the trauma Child experiences a persistent negative emotional state marked by fear, horror, anger, guilt, or shame Child is unable to experience positive emotions, such as happiness, satisfaction, or love Child is disinterested, detached, or estranged from other people and activities that were once significant
Changes in arousal and reactivity	Child is irritable, angry, and verbally or physically aggressive toward others Child is reckless or self-destructive Child is hypervigilant or easily startled Child has difficulty concentrating Child has trouble falling asleep or staying asleep
CHILDREN UNDER AGE 6	
SYMPTOM CATEGORY	**EXAMPLES**
Intrusive symptoms	Child expresses intrusive memories through play that may not appear distressing Child experiences frightening dreams, although the content may be difficult to connect to the trauma Child experiences flashbacks that manifest as a trauma-specific reenactment during play
Avoidance symptoms	Child turns away or disengages from people or situations that arouse memories of the traumatic event Child avoids activities, places, and other physical reminders of the traumatic event
Changes in cognition	Child experiences negative emotions, such as fear, sadness, guilt, and shame, more frequently Child expresses fewer positive emotions Child is socially withdrawn
Changes in arousal and reactivity	Child has outbursts of unprovoked anger or extreme temper tantrums Child is easily startled and hypervigilant Child has difficulty concentrating Child is restless or has difficulty sleeping

experienced sexual abuse. In addition to fearfulness, nightmares, and avoidance, child survivors of sexual abuse may hold a self-image of badness or unworthiness, accompanied by increased guilt and hyperarousal. This internalized shame reflects the negative alterations in cognition outlined in the *DSM-5* criteria for the disorder (APA, 2013a).

PTSD Screening and Assessment

Assessment for PTSD in children and adolescents is comprehensive and multifaceted, incorporating information from multiple data points (Kisiel et al., 2014). Brief screening tools universally administered to children and adolescents help to identify trauma-exposed youth and determine if symptoms of a trauma response are evident (Kisiel et al., 2014). The purpose of such screenings is identification rather than diagnosis; hence, professional school counselors can use these screening tools to identify students who may need referrals to mental health professionals in the community. In addition to screenings, a comprehensive assessment includes details about the nature and severity of trauma exposures and symptoms and reports on the child's level of functioning (Kisiel et al. 2014). Multiple instruments can be used to gather information about a child's experiences, including the Clinician-Administered PTSD Scale for Children and Adolescents, the Child PTSD Symptom Scale, the Impact of Events Scale, the Trauma Play Scale, and the UCLA PTSD Reaction Index (Perron & Pender, 2015). In addition to these objective measures, mental health professionals also rely on clinical interviews, behavior observations, and input from caregivers and educational professionals in conducting a complete assessment of a child or adolescent for PTSD (Kisiel et al., 2014). Parents, guardians, and other caregivers can provide critical insight into the trauma experiences and responses of children and adolescents at risk for PTSD. When appropriate and safe for the client, an assessment includes input from parents and guardians, who typically interact with children most often (APA, 2013b; Wheeler & Jones, 2015). Professional school counselors who have established strong partnerships with parents can help facilitate referrals to mental health professionals and support parents, guardians, and other caregivers as they prepare to share their observations of their child with a clinician.

Professional school counselors can also help dispel misconceptions about PTSD that conflate its symptoms with attention deficit hyperactivity disorder (ADHD). Both the avoidance and hyperarousal symptoms of PTSD mirror those of ADHD, resulting in dual diagnoses of both conditions and PTSD being underdiagnosed (Szymanski et al., 2011). Children and adolescents experiencing PTSD often seek to guard themselves against cognitively and emotionally overwhelming remembrances of a traumatic event in ways that can appear to others as inattentiveness and distractibility. Similarly, traumatized children or adolescents may employ protective mechanisms to prevent threats and potential trauma to their bodies, and this hypervigilance or irritability may appear as fidgeting and restlessness. As a result of these similarities, Syzmanski et al. (2011) suggested that all children and adolescents diagnosed with ADHD be screened for PTSD. Even if this is not feasible, an awareness of how the symptoms of PTSD and ADHD overlap can change how parents, guardians, caregivers, and school personnel perceive the behaviors of children and adolescents who have experienced trauma.

Treatment for PTSD

Treatment for PTSD requires ongoing, comprehensive care, especially in children and adolescents who present with unique vulnerabilities. Best practice guidelines for practitioners treating PTSD address diagnosis, treatment strategies, and other treatment issues, such as lack of responsiveness to treatment (Marotta, 2000). Comprehensive care includes psychotherapy, parental involvement, and medication when developmentally appropriate (Lawson, 2009; Marotta, 2000; Wheeler & Jones,

2015). Psychotherapeutic treatment models for PTSD typically include four common elements: (1) a solid, safe therapeutic relationship; (2) cognitive restructuring; (3) self-regulation and relaxation; and (4) exposure to desensitize or narrative to integrate experiences (Gentry et al., 2017). Because of the age and cognitive development of children, parent-child interaction therapy and child-parent psychotherapy are appropriate interventions when caregivers are safe and appropriate individuals in a child's life (Wheeler & Jones, 2015). Parents and other caregivers can operate as co-counselors to build solid relationships with children through play with the desired outcome being changes in both internalized cognitions and externalized behaviors.

Most common among treatment modalities for PTSD is cognitive behavior therapy (CBT), which has been used in varying ways with consistent effectiveness across client populations (Gutermann et al., 2016; Gutermann et al., 2017; Lenz et al., 2017; Morina et al., 2016). CBT approaches to PTSD broadly address cognitions surrounding the traumatic experience and aim to rewire the brain regarding the safety of the world and one's place in it (Makinson & Young, 2012). Prolonged exposure therapy incorporates talk therapy and psychoeducation with relationship techniques and imaginal exposure to traumatic events to help clients gain control of their reactions. Trauma-focused CBT (TF-CBT) integrates CBT with attachment, person-centered, and family therapies to help clients change negative personal meanings and reduce the reexperiencing of trauma. Other approaches, such as eye-movement desensitization and reprocessing and mindfulness-based cognitive therapy, are experiential and intrapersonal modalities that decrease the vividness of distressing memories and allow clients to engage in moment-to-moment awareness that focuses on existence and acceptance (Makinson & Young, 2012).

For children and adolescents experiencing PTSD, TF-CBT has demonstrated effectiveness in reducing trauma symptomology among diverse populations of young children (ages 3–6) and youth ages 7–17 (Nixon et al., 2012; Scheeringa et al., 2011). TF-CBT begins with establishing safety and stability, then moves to processing traumatic experiences, and, finally, reconnecting with self and others (Myrick et al., 2017). Integrating play into this approach, particularly during the third phase, makes it developmentally appropriate in that it allows children to nonverbally express themselves in an environment of unconditional acceptance and safety (Myrick et al., 2017).

Strategies for Professional School Counselors

Although licensed mental health counselors will provide the ongoing therapy that is needed to treat PTSD effectively, professional school counselors can support the healing of students with this diagnosis while still operating within the scope of practice for the profession. Professional school counselors are equipped with the knowledge and skills to engage in individual and group counseling, classroom guidance curricula, collaboration, and consultation to provide both direct and indirect services to students, caregivers, and families. In addition, as advocates and leaders in their schools, professional school counselors can ensure that trauma-exposed students are assessed and supported properly regardless of the presence or absence of a PTSD diagnosis.

Indirect Services

Recognizing and Reporting Child Mistreatment

Because of the prevalence of child mistreatment, professional school counselors will report suspected child abuse or neglect multiple times throughout a school year. Legal statutes and ethical standards require this reporting, and by upholding these expectations, professional school counselors may help to prevent a child's prolonged exposure to trauma. Children often hesitate to reveal mistreatment at home because of feelings of guilt, shame, and fear. Hence professional school counselors must demonstrate trust and safety and be visible and approachable to students. School districts typically require school personnel to complete training regarding the signs of child abuse and neglect, and professional school counselors must be committed to ongoing professional development in this area so that they remain aware of new information regarding how trauma responses manifest in children and adolescents.

Collaboration and Consultation

As the most accessible mental health professional in schools, professional school counselors can share their expertise with teachers, administrators, and parents and act as a bridge that connects schools and families with mental health professionals in the community. Parents of children experiencing PTSD might ask professional school counselors for guidance regarding treatment options and providers. Professional school counselors can engage parents in psychoeducation about treatment types, explaining the efficacy of CBT and the value of engaging safe, stable adult figures in the treatment process. In addition, professional school counselors can provide community resources to parents and families, including the contact information for mental health practitioners who specialize in PTSD treatment. It is important to note that there may be varying degrees of comfort among parents when they receive information about mental health services for their children. Hence professional school counselors must first work to build trust with parents and families before referring them to another provider. When making referrals, a "warm handoff" is preferred. With parental consent, the professional school counselor might contact a mental health professional to directly refer a student, providing the parent's contact information and the presenting concerns. Or, as a means of empowering the parent, the professional school counselor might invite the parent to contact the community provider while in the school counselor's office so that the parent can receive support and assistance with answering any intake questions or setting up an appointment.

For students who are engaged in treatment for PTSD, professional school counselors can collaborate with treatment providers and school personnel to support these students throughout the school day. Once they have ensured that the appropriate consent forms have been signed by parents or guardians, professional school counselors can check in with students and their teachers to assess their progress in the school setting. Students can report on their PTSD symptomology while in school, and teachers can report their observations of students' performances in the classroom. This information can help both the treatment provider and the professional school counselor assess students' progress. When engaging in such collaboration and consultation, professional school counselors must ensure that their interactions with other professionals align with the ethical standards for the profession in that students' personal information is safeguarded to the greatest extent possible.

Direct Services

Individual Counseling

When supporting individual students who are experiencing PTSD, professional school counselors want to be mindful not to interfere with the treatment provided by other mental health professionals. Still, there may be instances when students need to meet with the professional school counselor either when triggered at school or if treatment is not accessible to them. Although long-term therapy is often not feasible or appropriate for professional school counselors, ignoring the immediate psychosocial needs of students on their caseloads is unethical. Hence school counselors should be prepared for the moments when they will need to counsel students individually. For young children experiencing PTSD, professional school counselors can use play to connect with the students and help them feel safe enough to communicate in a developmentally appropriate manner (Myrick et al., 2017). When working with older children, professional school counselors might also use play with consideration to the age and development of the student.

In addition to CBT, professional school counselors might consider the value of grounding their work in relational cultural theory (RCT) to address trauma experiences, such as abuse and sexual assault, which are relational in nature (Kress et al., 2018). Complex trauma, such as abuse and neglect, is prolonged, repetitive, and often occurs at developmentally vulnerable moments; hence, it affects attachment and development (Kress et al., 2018). In addition, sexual assault and abuse disrupt relationships, resulting in isolation, shame, and distrust (Haiyasoso & Schuermann, 2018). RCT focuses on helping clients heal through growth-fostering relationships; the healing is in the relationship (Kress et al., 2018). Professional school counselors using RCT can provide radical empathy and reduce the isolation felt as a result of traumatic experiences and PTSD symptomology. In addition, through the lens of RCT, professional school counselors can facilitate relational competency in students to help them better navigate interpersonal relationships and find trusted adults within their school or community (Haiyasoso & Schuermann, 2018).

Group Counseling

Because of high rates of trauma exposure among children and adolescents, professional school counselors might find group counseling to be an effective approach when significant numbers of students are affected by PTSD or trauma symptomology. School and community violence can affect groups of students who might need a safe place to process their feelings and experiences. In addition, natural disasters, such as tornadoes, hurricanes, and floods can have catastrophic effects on the psychological and emotional wellness of children and adolescents who may need the community and connection that a counseling group provides. Following hurricanes Katrina and Rita, Herbert and Ballard (2007) shared counseling interventions that helped children heal from those environmental traumas. Based on their suggestions, school counselors might form groups of students to engage them in expressive arts and grief activities, such as memory books and scrapbooks. Similar groups could be helpful for children and adolescents who are affected by school and community violence. Such groups reduce the isolation that these students might feel and help them to process their feelings of fear, anger, and anxiety within a safe and empathic context.

Groups for children and adolescents who have experienced interpersonal trauma can be efficacious as well. Auslander et al. (2017) outlined and assessed a TF-CBT group for adolescent girls in child welfare and found that PTSD symptoms among the girls decreased following the intervention. Because of privacy concerns and the need for sensitivity to the girls' lived experiences, this group was facilitated in a community agency by a licensed mental health counselor. Although it may not be feasible or appropriate to facilitate such a group in the school setting where confidentiality in the group cannot be guaranteed, especially regarding deeply personal experiences, professional school counselors can collaborate with community agencies to organize such a group, again providing the linkage to appropriate care in the community.

Additional Approaches

In addition to individual and group counseling, professional school counselors can engage students in classroom guidance lessons and whole-school activities that address trauma and encourage psychological healing. Classroom guidance lessons and professional development workshops can focus on mental health literacy so that students and teachers understand what trauma symptomology looks like in children and adolescents. Such psychoeducation will empower students to understand and empathize with their peers and even encourage their peers to ask for help. In addition, professional development for faculty and staff can help them to identify children who may need to be screened for PTSD, while also encouraging educators to employ trauma-informed teaching and interventions with students. Professional school counselors might also conduct more focused psychoeducation, such as workshops focused on healthy discipline strategies and alternatives to corporal punishment or sessions that guide parents in effective ways of discussing abuse and other forms of trauma with children (Brown et al., 2008). To encourage a school-wide commitment to wellness, professional school counselors might implement a large-scale mindfulness program, such as that described by Campbell et al. (2019). Their 6-week intervention taught staff and students about mindful eating, body scans, mind-body activities, and feelings. Although it was not a trauma-focused intervention, such a school-wide program can equip all students with coping tools that can prove useful when they encounter traumatic events. Large-scale programming, as well as individual and group counseling in schools, can contribute to the psychosocial healing necessary for children and adolescents who have been affected by trauma whether or not they have been officially diagnosed with PTSD.

Understanding What You Have Read: Comprehension Questions

Directions: Refer to what you have learned in this chapter to answer the following questions.

1. What are some examples of traumatic events experienced by children and adolescents?
2. What are some symptoms of PTSD according to the *DSM-5*?
3. Describe common and effective clinical treatments for PTSD in children and adolescents.
4. What are some ways that professional school counselors can support students experiencing trauma and/or PTSD?
5. What ethical and cultural considerations might arise in addressing PTSD in schools?
6. What personal challenges might you have when working with students experiencing trauma and/or PTSD?

Case Examples

Case Example One

As you read the case about Christopher, reflect on the strategies that we discussed earlier in the chapter. The questions that follow the case relate to the student's behavioral symptoms and accompanying responses.

Christopher is an 8-year-old student who has been retained and is repeating the second grade. He recently came to live with an aunt after he and his older sister were removed from their home because of severe neglect and violence occurring within their home over several months. When child protective services investigated reports of abuse and neglect, it was discovered that Christopher had only been eating condiments for several weeks because no other food was available in the home. In addition, Christopher had witnessed his mother being physically abused by her partner. In school, Christopher angers easily when playing with peers and is hypervigilant in class. He has difficulty sitting still, fidgets often, and is impulsive both physically and verbally. At home, he has trouble sleeping and reports that he does not sleep much because he is afraid of the dark. He fears that something will happen while he is asleep. Christopher fantasizes often, and typically these fantasies involve violent encounters where he is the hero. When he talks about why he is now living with his aunt, he expresses intense guilt and shame.

Case Example One: Questions for Processing and Reflection

Directions: Use what you have learned in this chapter to respond to Christopher's case.

1. What are the symptoms Christopher is displaying that indicate that he may be experiencing PTSD?

   a. Christopher is experiencing changes in arousal and reactivity that indicate PTSD. He seems to be holding on to the trauma in his physical body, which then manifests in fidgeting, physical impulsivity, and sleeplessness. In addition, changes in his mood and cognition are apparent, as he is experiencing a mixture of emotions, including anger, fear, guilt, and shame. His fantasies may also be manifestations of intrusive bad memories associated with the trauma.
2. What information do you have regarding Christopher's situation?
   a. Christopher has experienced multiple ACE, including neglect, abuse, domestic violence, and separation from his parents. He also may be experiencing an ambiguous loss now that he is no longer living with his parents. Adjusting to a new household might be challenging for him, and he may have difficulty making friends as a result of his anger and physical impulsivity.
3. What additional information might you still need?
   a. Now that Christopher is in a new home, it would be helpful to know what the relational dynamics are within this new family structure. Who lives within the household and what family members can provide support to Christopher? In addition, it may be helpful to know who, if anyone, at school has a positive connection with Christopher. Identifying trusted adults and peers at school, as well as trusted family members can help to establish a solid support network for Christopher as he heals from his traumatic past.
4. How would you address the concerns you have regarding Christopher?
   a. Collaboration with Christopher's classroom teacher and guardian will be critical. Through this collaboration, the school counselor can help identify what mental health supports would be most appropriate for him. Christopher will likely need therapy from a mental health professional in the community, so the school counselor can help his guardian identify an appropriate provider to address his needs. In addition, the school counselor can include Christopher in a small group where he can learn coping skills to help him identify and appropriately express his emotions. This group will reduce the sense of isolation he may feel and can help him connect to his peers. Finally, the school counselor can do periodic check-ins with Christopher to gauge how he is progressing in his classes and with his behaviors at school.
5. How would you collaborate and consult with other professionals to support Christopher?
   a. To best help Christopher, the school counselor will need to collaborate and consult with his teacher given that there are concerns about his behaviors in the classroom. This collaboration and consultation might include information gathering from the teacher to get a sense of the frequency and severity of his impulsivity or other behaviors of concern. Further, the school counselor can provide information about trauma-informed teaching to help Christopher's teacher learn to interact with him differently to reduce the likelihood of his behaviors escalating and resulting in disciplinary action.

Case Example Two

As you read the case about Alyssa, reflect on the strategies that we discussed earlier in the chapter. The questions that follow the case relate to the student's behavioral symptoms and accompanying responses.

Alyssa is a 12-year-old student who previously performed well in school. However, halfway through her seventh-grade year, she began to have poor attendance, and her grades began to drop. Her teachers have noted a change in her behavior: she has become loud, boisterous, and disruptive in class. She has also begun making inappropriate sexual comments to classmates. Despite these external behaviors, Alyssa reports feelings of deep self-loathing when in one-on-one situations with friends or the school counselor. Recently, she mentioned to a friend in passing that her stepdad was being "weird." Although she did not explain what she meant by "weird," she told her friend that she hates being around him, especially when no one else is home.

Case Example Two: Questions for Processing and Reflection

Directions: Use what you have learned in this chapter to respond to Alyssa's case.

- What concerns do you have about Alyssa?
- What information do you have about Alyssa's situation?
- What do you not yet know?
- What is your next step in working with her?
- What might collaboration with Alyssa's family look like? What challenges to collaboration might you face as a school counselor trying to support Alyssa?

Chapter Summary

Sadly, trauma exposure among children and adolescents is common and, in some cases, PTSD can develop, resulting in hypervigilance, intrusive memories, and dissociation. Developmental considerations require professional school counselors to be aware of how PTSD manifests differently among children and adolescents so that they can properly engage in the identification and treatment of youth with PTSD. Although ongoing therapy for PTSD is most appropriately delivered by licensed mental health professionals, professional school counselors can support children and adolescents who have been exposed to trauma and/or who are experiencing PTSD by collaborating with their colleagues within the schools, as well as with other mental health professionals in the community. Professional school counselors can coordinate services, provide psychoeducation to parents, and engage in direct service provision through individual and group counseling, classroom guidance, and whole-school activities to encourage social and emotional well-being.

Additional Recommended Readings and Resources

Helping Students During Crisis: https://www.schoolcounselor.org/school-counselors/professional-development/learn-more/helping-kids-during-crisis

Adverse Childhood Experiences: https://www.cdc.gov/violenceprevention/childabuseandneglect/acestudy/index.html

The National Child Traumatic Stress Network: https://www.nctsn.org/

References

American Psychiatric Association (APA). (2013a). *Diagnostic and statistical manual of mental disorders* (5th ed.).

American Psychiatric Association (APA). (2013b). *DSM-5 and diagnoses for children.* https://www.psychiatry.org/File%20Library/Psychiatrists/Practice/DSM/APA_DSM-5-Diagnoses-for-Children.pdf

American Psychiatric Association (APA). (2013c). *Highlights of changes from DSM-IV-TR to DSM-5.* https://www.psychiatry.org/File%20Library/Psychiatrists/Practice/DSM/APA_DSM-5-Diagnoses-for-Children.pdf

Auslander, W., McGinnis, H., Tlapek, S., Smith, P., Foster, A., Edmond, T., & Dunn, J. (2017). Adaptation and implementation of a trauma-focused cognitive behavioral intervention for girls in child welfare. *American Journal of Orthopsychiatry, 87*(3), 206–215. https://doi.org/10.1037/ort0000233

Beal, S. J., Wingrove, T., Mara, C. A., Lutz, N., Noll, J. G., & Greiner, M. V. (2019). Childhood adversity and associated psychological function in adolescents with complex trauma. *Child & Youth Care Forum, 48*, 305–322. https://doi.org/10.1007/s10566-018-9479-5

Bremner, J. D. (2006). Traumatic stress: Effects on the brain. *Dialogues in Clinical Neuroscience, 8*(4), 445–461.

Bremner, J. D., Elzinga, B., Schmahl, C., & Vermetten, E. (2008). Structural and functional plasticity of the human brain in posttraumatic stress disorder. *Progress in Brain Research, 167*, 171–186. https://doi.org/10.1016/S0079-6123(07)67012-5

Breslau, N. Wilcox, H. C., Storr, C. L., Lucia, V. C., & Anthony, J. C. (2004). Trauma exposure and posttraumatic stress disorder: A study of youths in urban America. *Journal of Urban Health: Bulletin of the New York Academy of Medicine, 81*(4), 530–544. https://doi.org/10.1093/jurban/jth138

Brown, S. D., Brack, G., & Mullis, F. Y. (2008). Traumatic symptoms in sexually abused children: Implications for school counselors. *Professional School Counseling, 11*(6), 368–379. https://doi.org/10.5330/PSC.n.2010-11.368

Campbell, A. J., Lanthier, R. P., Weiss, B. A., & Shaine, M. D. (2019). The impact of a schoolwide mindfulness program on adolescent well-being, stress, and emotion regulation: A nonrandomized controlled study in a naturalistic setting. *Journal of Child and Adolescent Counseling, 5*(1), 18–34. https://doi.org/10.1080/23727810.2018.1556989

Centers for Disease Control and Prevention (CDC). (2019). *About the CDC-Kaiser ACE study.* https://www.cdc.gov/violenceprevention/childabuseandneglect/acestudy/about.html

De Young, A. C., Kenardy, J. A., & Cobham, V. E. (2011). Trauma in early childhood: A neglected population. *Clinical Child and Family Psychology Review, 14*, 231–250. https://doi.org/10.1007/s10567-011-0094-3

Gentry, J. E., Baranowsky, A. B., & Rhoton, R. (2017). Trauma competency: An active ingredients approach to treating posttraumatic stress disorder. *Journal of Counseling and Development, 95*, 279–287. https://doi.org/10.1002/jcad.12142

Gutermann, J., Schreiber, F., Matulis, S., Schwartzkopff, L., Deppe, J., & Steil, R. (2016). Psychological treatments for symptoms of posttraumatic stress disorder in children, adolescents, and young adults: A meta-analysis. *Clinical Child and Family Psychology Review, 19*, 77–93. https://doi.org/10.1007/s10567-016-0202-5

Gutermann, J., Schwartzkopff, L., & Steil, R. (2017). Meta-analysis of the long-term treatment effects of psychological interventions in youth with PTSD symptoms. *Clinical Child and Family Psychology Review, 20*, 422–434. https://doi.org/10.1007/s10567-017-0242-5

Haiyasoso, M., & Schuermann, H. (2018). Application of relational-cultural theory with adolescent sexual abuse survivors. *Journal of Child and Adolescent Counseling, 4*(2), 164–177. https://doi.org/10.1080/23727810.2017.1381933

Herbert, B. B., & Ballard, M. B. (2007). Children and trauma: A post-Katrina and Rita response. *Professional School Counseling, 11*(2), 140–144. https://doi.org/10.1177/2156759X0701100209

Kisiel, C., Conradi, L., Fehrenbach, T., Torgersen, E., & Briggs, E. C. (2014). Assessing the effects of trauma in children and adolescents in practice settings. *Child and Adolescent Psychiatric Clinics of North America, 23*, 223–242. https://doi.org/10.1016/j.chc.2013.12.007

Kress, V. E., Haiyasoso, M., Zoldan, C. A., Headley, J. A., & Trepal, H. (2018). The use of relational-cultural theory in counseling clients who have traumatic stress disorders. *Journal of Counseling and Development, 96*, 106–114. https://doi.org/10.1002/jcad.12182

Lawson, D. M. (2009). Understanding and treating children who experience interpersonal maltreatment: Empirical findings. *Journal of Counseling and Development, 87*, 204–215. https://doi.org/10.1002/j.1556-6678.2009.tb00569.x

Lenz, A. S., Haktanir, A., & Callender, K. (2017). Meta-analysis of trauma-focused therapies for treating the symptoms of posttraumatic stress disorder. *Journal of Counseling and Development, 95*, 339–353. https://doi.org/10.1002/jcad.12148

Makinson, R. A., & Young, J. S. (2012). Cognitive behavioral therapy and the treatment of posttraumatic stress disorder: Where counseling and neuroscience meet. *Journal of Counseling and Development, 90*, 131–140. https://doi.org/10.1111/j.1556-6676.2012.00017.x

Marotta, S. A., (2000). Best practices for counselors who treat posttraumatic stress disorder. *Journal of Counseling and Development, 78*, 492–495. https://doi.org/10.1002/j.1556-6676.2000.tb01933.x

Mclaughlin, K. A., Koenen, K. C., Hill, e. D., Petukhova, M., Sampson, N. A., Zaslavsky, A. M., & Kessler, R. C. (2013). Trauma exposure and posttraumatic stress disorder in a national sample of adolescents. *Journal of the American Academy of Child & Adolescent Psychiatry, 52*(8), 815–830. https://doi.org/10.1016/j.jaac.2013.05.011

Melhem, N. M., Porta, G., Shamseddeen, W., Payne, M. W., & Brent, D. A. (2011). Grief in children and adolescents bereaved by sudden parental death. *Archives of General Psychiatry, 68*(9), 911–919. https://doi.org/10.1001/archgenpsychiatry.2011.101

Merikangas, K. R., He, J-P., Burstein, M., Swanson, S. A., Avenevoli, S. Cui, L., Benjet, C., Georgiades, K., & Swendsen, J. (2010). Lifetime prevalence of mental disorders in US adolescents: Results from the National Comorbidity Study-Adolescent Supplement (NCS-A). *Journal of the American Academy of Child & Adolescent Psychiatry, 49*(10), 980–989. https://doi.org/10.1016/j.jaac.2010.05.017

Morina, N., Koerssen, R., & Pollet, T. V. (2016). Interventions for children and adolescents with posttraumatic stress disorder: A meta-analysis of comparative outcome studies. *Clinical Psychology Review, 47*, 41–54. https://doi.org/10.1016/j.cpr.2016.05.006

Myrick, A. C., Green, E. J., & Fazio-Griffith, L. (2017). Fostering reconnection and resilience in complexly traumatized youth: Integration of play into empirically supported treatment. *Journal of Child and Adolescent Counseling, 3*(2), 120–128. https://doi.org/10.1080/23727810.2017.1320623

National Child Traumatic Stress Network. (n.d.). *Complex trauma*. https://www.nctsn.org/what-is-child-trauma/trauma-types/complex-trauma

Nixon, R. D. V., Sterk, J., & Pearce, A. (2012). A randomized trial of cognitive behavior therapy and cognitive therapy for children with posttraumatic stress disorder following single-incident trauma. *Journal of Abnormal Child Psychology, 40*, 327–337. https://doi.org/10.1007/s10802-011-9566-7

Olff, M., Langeland, W., & Gersons, B. P. R. (2005). The psychobiology of PTSD: Coping with trauma. *Psychoneuroendocrinology, 30*, 974–982. https://doi.org/10.1016/j.psyneuen.2005.04.009

Perron, N. C., D., & Pender, D. A. (2015). Meeting the need: Applying concepts for assessment and planning with child and adolescent trauma. *Journal of Child and Adolescent Counseling, 1*(1), 37–49. https://doi.org/10.1080/23727810.2015.1023607

Putman, S. E. (2009). The monsters in my head: Posttraumatic stress disorder and the child survivor of sexual abuse. *Journal of Counseling and Development, 87*, 80–89. https://doi.org/10.1002/j.1556-6678.2009.tb00552.x

Saunders, B. E., & Adams, Z. W. (2015). Epidemiology of traumatic experiences in childhood. *Child and Adolescent Psychiatric Clinics of North America, 23*, 167–184. https://doi.org/10.1016/j.chc.2013.12.003

Scheeringa, M. S., Weems, C. F., Cohen, J. A., Amaya-Jackson, L., & Guthrie, D. (2011). Trauma-focused cognitive-behavioral therapy for posttraumatic stress disorder in three through six-year-old children: A randomized clinical trial. *Journal of Child Psychology and Psychiatry, 52*(8), 853–860. https://doi.org/10.1111/j.1469-7610.2010.02354.x

Smith, P., Dalgleish, T., & Meiser-Stedman, R. (2019). Practitioner review: Posttraumatic stress disorder and its treatment in children and adolescents. *Journal of Child Psychology and Psychiatry, 60*(5). https://doi.org/ 10.1111/jcpp.12983

Szymanski, K., Sapanski, L., & Conway, F. (2011). Trauma and ADHD—Association or diagnostic confusion? A clinical perspective. *Journal of Infant, Child, and Adolescent Psychotherapy, 10*, 51–59. https://doi.org/10.1080/15289168.2011.575704

Wheeler, N., & Jones, K. D. (2015). DSM-5 PTSD in children six years and younger: Implications for assessment and treatment. *Journal of Child and Adolescent Counseling, 1*(2), 119–134. https://doi.org/10.1080/23727810.2015.1090289

CHAPTER FIFTEEN

Self-Harm

Huan-Tang Lu

THE CASE OF ERICA Erica is a ninth-grade Caucasian female student who rarely shows up to the counseling department. Erica lives with her parents and one younger brother. To her school counselor, Erica is a quiet student with decent peer support in school. One day, her friend Veronica reported to the school counselor that she glimpsed several cuts on Erica's wrist. Because of the school policy, the school counselor sent Erica to the school nurse for screening. The school nurse shared that these cuts were old, and there was no imminent danger presented. Upon following up with Erica, she reported dealing with a mix of family, peer, and academic issues a few months ago during which she experienced an extreme level of anxiety. She struggled in silence and developed a strategy to cope with her worries and emotions. Although Erica reported that the last cutting was 3 months ago, for her safety, the school counselor explained the need to contact her parents. Concerned, Erica's parents promised to take her to see a therapist.

Introduction to the Chapter

Self-harm in this chapter is defined as nonsuicidal self-injury (NSSI) performed without suicidal intent. Methods of self-harm vary among children and adolescents, and cases like Erica's may go unnoticed sometimes. Professionals often hold misconceptions about self-harm, which ultimately lowers the efficiency of the service provided to students (Haskin et al., 2016), and may cause harm unconsciously. As school counselors working with many students and with the high prevalence of self-harm in this population, we have an obligation to prepare ourselves to support students on this matter.

Learning Objectives

By the end of this chapter, readers will accomplish the following:

- Understand the signs and symptoms of self-harm.
- Develop increased knowledge of risk factors of self-harm in children and adolescents.
- Understand best practice strategies for supporting students with self-harm behaviors.

Students, especially adolescents, appear to perform self-harm behaviors more frequently than adults (DiCorcia et al., 2017). A range of 7% to 18% of adolescents has experienced self-harm at least once (Hawton et al., 2005), which is alarming to middle school and high school counselors. In a more recent study, researchers examined data from the Centers for Disease Control and Prevention's Youth Risk Behavior Surveillance System in 2015 (Monto et al., 2018). The results showed that rates of high school–age boys reporting self-harm behavior ranged from 6.4% to 14.8% in 11 US states, and rates for high school–age girls ranged from 17.7% to 30.8%. Although the rates declined with age, these numbers imply that each high school counselor, based on the 250:1 ratio (American School Counselor Association [ASCA], 2018), may have about 60 to 114 students once purposefully hurting themselves without suicidal intent. With this high prevalence, it is especially difficult for school counselors to target self-harm behavior, as it has been linked to many risk factors, such as mood disorders, substance use disorders, and parental relationships. To provide better support, school counselors will also need to understand signs of self-harm as students who engage in this behavior may keep it hidden. School counselors working with this population should develop a plan and collaborate with stakeholders. Because of the nature of self-harm, school counselors will have to pay attention to the ethical and legal aspects of this behavior when working with students.

Signs and Symptoms of Self-Harm

Despite its prevalence among and effect on children and adolescents, self-harm behavior only appeared as part of the criteria for the manic episode of bipolar I disorder in the *Diagnostic and Statistical Manual, Fourth Edition, Text Revision* (*DSM-IV-TR*; American Psychiatric Association; APA, 2000). In its fifth edition, the *DSM* included NSSI in Section 3, "Disorders Requiring Further Research," with the following descriptions (APA, 2013):

A. In the last year, the individual has, on 5 or more days, engaged in intentional self-inflicted damage to the surface of his or her body of a sort likely to induce bleeding, bruising, or pain (e.g., cutting, burning stabbing, hitting, excessive rubbing), with the expectation that the injury will lead to only minor or moderate physical harm (i.e., there is no suicidal intent).
Note: The absence of suicidal intent has either been stated by the individual or can be inferred by the individual's repeated engagement in a behavior that the individual knows, or has learned, is not likely to result in death.

B. The individual engages in the self-injurious behavior with one or more of the following expectations:
1. To obtain relief from a negative feeling or cognitive state.
2. To resolve an interpersonal difficulty.
3. To induce a positive feeling state.

Note: The desired relief or response is experienced during or shortly after the self-injury, and the individual may display patterns of behavior suggesting a dependence on repeatedly engaging in it.

C. The intentional self-injury is associated with at least one of the following:
1. Interpersonal difficulties or negative feelings or thoughts, such as depression, anxiety, tension, anger, generalized distressed, or self-criticism, occurring in the period immediately prior to the self-injurious act.
2. Prior to engaging in the act, a period of preoccupation with the intended behavior that is difficult to control.
3. Thinking about self-injury that occurs frequently, even when it is not acted upon.

D. The behavior is not socially sanctioned (e.g., body piercing, tattooing, part of a religious or cultural ritual) and is not restricted to picking a scab or nail biting.

E. The behavior or its consequences cause clinically significant distress or interference in interpersonal, academic, or other important areas of functioning.

F. The behavior does not occur exclusively during psychotic episodes, delirium, substance intoxication, or substance withdrawal. In individuals with a neurodevelopmental disorder, the behavior

TABLE 15.1 Differential Diagnoses and Behaviors

DIAGNOSIS	SELF-HARM
Borderline personality disorder (BPD) Students often manifest hostile behaviors	Students present phases of closeness and are more willing to collaborate with others
Suicidal behavior disorder	The goal of the behavior is to experience relief. The goal of the behavior is a wish to die
Trichotillomania (hair-pulling disorder) To sense or feel the behavior	To harm oneself
Stereotypic self-injury Usually associated with developmental delay or intense concentration in some psychotic episodes	Less frequent and intense
Excoriation (skin-picking disorder) This occurs mainly in females. Picking is more frequent, unconscious, and typically at areas that students feel are unpleasant to look at	To harm oneself to experience relief

is not part of a pattern of repetitive stereotypies. The behavior is not better explained by another mental disorder or medical condition (e.g., psychotic disorder, autism spectrum disorder, intellectual disability, Lesch-Nyhan syndrome, stereotypic movement disorder with self-injury, trichotillomania [hair-pulling disorder], excoriation [skin-picking] disorder).

According to the *DSM-5* (APA, 2013), self-harm behavior often begins in the early teenage years, yet the age of onset remains unclear. The fact that students may keep the self-harm behavior hidden, and the behavior is often in the shadow of inaccurate presentations or other conditions hinders further understanding of its onset and development, especially among the K–12 population. Common methods of self-injury include cutting, scratching, burning, or other forms of damaging one's own skin tissue, which rarely causes severe injuries that require advanced medical service (Klonsky, 2017).

Although self-harm behavior or NSSI was listed as a diagnosable disorder, the *DSM-5* provided ways to distinguish such behavior from other disorders (APA, 2013). Table 15.1 summarizes these differential diagnoses.

One must note that, although there is a fundamental difference between suicidal behavior disorder and self-harm, a check of the history of suicidal behavior and an investigation of any recent significant changes in stress and mood are imperative (APA, 2013). School counselors must be aware that students with self-harm behaviors can also attempt suicide. In addition, Klonsky (2017) pointed out some most common misconceptions about self-harm. Table 15.2 illustrates these misconceptions, as well as their counterparts.

Associated Factors and Conditions

Many factors and associated conditions have been discussed. Table 15.3 summarizes the factors discussed in the literature (e.g., APA, 2013; Virginia Commission on Youth, 2017; Xavier et al., 2016). These categories can be viewed through environmental, biological, cognitive, affective, and behavioral dimensions. Regardless of the dimension, the common theme among these factors is the triggered emotions, feelings, behaviors, or further interpersonal challenges, which are later coped with through self-harm behavior.

TABLE 15.2 Common Misconceptions Related to Self-Harm

MISCONCEPTIONS	FACTS
Self-harm behavior is the most important symptom of BPD	One with self-harm behavior does not need to be labeled as having BPD
Individuals engage in self-harm behavior to seek attention from others	The intention is to get relief (self) instead of on social functions (others)
Self-harm behavior is caused by childhood sexual abuse	There is only a modest correlation, which does not imply a causal relationship
Self-harm behavior or NSSI is a form of suicidal behavior	Self-harm behavior is more common, frequent, and is likely to involve different methods, which result in less severe damage

Note that the factors listed in Table 15.3 are not for labeling purposes. Rather, they can help counselors recognize the existence of self-harm behavior. Knowing these factors can also enable counselors to better conceptualize cases among students. There are many models to help counselors understand the causes of self-harm. For example, the Explanatory Models for NSSI in Youth and a Functional Model of NSSI listed in the book by Miller and Brock (2010). According to Miller and Brock, when working with students exhibiting self-harm behavior, a holistic model should be employed to make the conceptualization.

TABLE 15.3 Potential Factors Associated with Self-Harm

CATEGORY	FACTOR
Traumatic event	Childhood abuse Neglect Domestic violence Childhood separation Childhood loss Bullying
Familial cause	Missing parent(s) (e.g., parental illness, single-parent family, low quality of relationship with attachment figures) Family devaluation/invalidation/involvement
Feelings	Hopelessness Loneliness Hostility/anger Emotion dysregulation
Psychiatric disorders	Anxiety Depression Substance use disorders (Followed by) suicidal behavior Eating disorders/body dissatisfaction Dissociative disorders BPD

Strategies for School Counselors Working With the Student

Assessment

Although school policies may vary, school counselors should be instrumental in assessing students with evidence of self-harm, as they are often the first contact in these situations. Many available assessment tools for self-harm include suicidal behavior, for example, Suicidal Behavior Questionnaire (SBQ)—14 for adolescents, SBQ-C for children, and Self-Injurious Thoughts and Behaviors Interview. Prior to adopting these assessment tools, school counselors have to ensure (a) an intervention plan is developed and in place, (b) these measures are within the scope of practice, and (c) their professional competency (ASCA, 2016). These three assessments look at both suicidal and nonsuicidal aspects of behavior (Virginia Commission on Youth, 2017). However, it is recommended that school counselors follow up with a more detailed assessment of self-harm when necessary (Cloutier & Humphreys, 2009)

Several suggestions for first responding to students with self-harm behavior were made in the literature. For example, it is imperative to distinguish the student's self-harm behavior from suicidal behavior (Walsh, 2006). If there is no suicidal intent, school counselors should avoid using suicide terminology in the follow-up actions. Moreover, using the student's own language would show respect and help conceptualize the context. One must note that this suggestion does not apply to situations where the student's words do not reflect the truth, such as exaggeration of the wounds or when a psychotic episode is present (Walsh, 2006). Lastly, school counselors must choose their words and tone of voice carefully not only to convey respect for the student but also to appear nonjudgmental.

Another assessment that comes highly recommended as an applicable reference for school counselors is the SOARS model (**S**uicidal ideation; **O**nset, frequency, and method; **A**ftercare; **R**easons; and **S**tage of change) by Westers et al. (2016). This model includes an initial suicidal ideation screening component that school counselors use to ensure the safety of the student. An example of one of the screening questions is, "Self-harm is not always about suicide, but sometimes people may have the idea about suicide when they self-harm. Have you ever thought about ending your life when you hurt yourself?" If the risk is identified, the school counselor should follow the school policy for suicidal cases. The next step using the SOAR model involves gathering information about the onset, frequency, and methods of self-harm. Knowing these details not only helps conceptualize the case but also allows the counselor to determine the student's level of safety, as a higher frequency of self-harm (e.g., between 20 and 50 lifetime) may lead to increased risk for suicide. Although school counselors are not medical providers, asking about aftercare, for example, "How do you typically handle your wounds," will allow the school counselor to determine whether an immediate referral to medical service is needed. Such a question also serves to gather information about the context, including the student's support system.

After these steps, the school counselor should have a relatively good rapport with the student. It is then that the work begins exploring the reasons for self-harm. According to the *DSM-5*, reasons can be to (a) get relief from negative emotions, (b) solve an interpersonal difficulty, and/or (c) obtain a positive feeling. After identifying the reason for self-harm, it is imperative to also assess the student's stage of behavioral change, particularly because, oftentimes, students are involuntarily sent to the school counselor. Knowing whether the student is ready to make a change or not will heavily influence the choice of intervention strategies afterward.

Treatment Modalities

Before considering the treatment modalities, school counselors must determine their professional competency to provide service (e.g., individual counseling, group counseling), especially when complicated treatment planning is involved (ASCA, 2016; Kress et al., 2006). A referral may be needed in such cases. However, in most cases, when imminent danger is not found to be present, the school counselor may provide immediate, brief intervention to explore alternate coping strategies based on the identified reasons for self-harm. Some basic goals for students in such cases are (1) to learn ways to tolerate the present moment, (2) to identify and accept their feelings, and (3) to adopt positive behaviors or social skills to manage emotions and stress. For example, reflective questions can be asked, such as, "What are some other strategies that have helped you manage when you are feeling hopeless?" Or, "What are some other ways to help you start the conversation with you dad?" With the counselor speaking to the student in an encouraging manner, we hope to see the student adopt another strategy to obtain the relief they seek.

As mentioned earlier, it is crucial to identify the student's motivation to change early in intervention. For that concept, motivational interviewing has been considered an effective technique to work with a student with self-harm behavior (e.g., Hoffman & Kress, 2010; Kamen, 2009). In addition, cognitive behavior therapy (CBT) and dialectical behavior therapy, as well as interpersonal psychotherapy, have been demonstrated as effective intervention modalities for this population (e.g., Gonzales & Bergstrom, 2013; Lovell & Clifford, 2016). Interested school counselors may check the "Additional Recommended Reading and Resources" section at the end of this chapter for more practical guidelines.

The literature has discussed group counseling in various formats (e.g., CBT, support group) for students who have been observed to engage in self-harm. However, studies have shown mixed outcomes in relation to small-group counseling and reduction in the frequency of self-harm behavior. For example, a study showed the efficacy of a group counseling program for adolescents to reduce the repetition of self-harm behavior (Wood et al., 2001). Participants who received group counseling in the study were less likely to have two or more episodes of self-harm behaviors. However, in a later replication study (Hazell et al., 2009), the researchers could not prove the same efficacy of the program. Instead, some results even showed that a greater portion of the experimental group had engaged in self-harm behaviors during the study. In addition, as suggested by Kress et al. (2006), school counselors consider the intensity and complexity of the behavior before providing such service in schools. Moreover, school counselors should also be cautious about social contagion when running groups (c.f. Hasking et al., 2016; Richardson et al., 2012). Given the previous contradictory findings and statements, school counselors should exercise extreme caution when developing and conducting small groups for this population in schools.

Confidentiality

According to the ASCA Ethical Standards for School Counselors (ASCA, 2016), school counselors must "keep the information confidential unless legal requirements demand that confidential information be revealed or a breach is required to prevent serious and foreseeable harm to the student" (Standard A.2.e), and school counselors should consult with other relevant professionals when in doubt about further action. As previously stated, a thorough assessment of both suicidal risk and self-harm behavior will help school counselors determine whether the student is in imminent danger. Because of protected parental rights, it is suggested that school counselors to consider reporting self-harm behavior even when there is no perceived imminent danger (Kress et al., 2006). Given potential liability issues, school counselors should consult with their school administrators and/or the school district attorney, especially when feeling hesitant about reporting the behavior to parents (ASCA, 2016, Standard A.9.a). Lastly, as in other confidential student issues, school counselors should be mindful of record-keeping practices as other school personnel who do not have the same obligations to confidentiality have access to student files (Kress et al.).

Strategies for School Counselors Working With Parents/Guardians of the Student

Working with parents and guardians is an integral part of post-intervention with students exhibiting self-harm behavior, not only because of the ethical and legal considerations but also because of the potential causes of the development of self-harm behavior. In addition to the suggestions made in other chapters (e.g., major depressive disorder), here we discuss some salient points specific to this topic.

As mentioned earlier, potential risk factors include childhood sexual/physical abuse, neglect, parental involvement, parental devaluation, and family invalidation. When working with the family to address the student's self-harm behavior, school counselors should put these risk factors on their radar, as these may provide some context of the family dynamics and help with navigating the conversation. Knowledge of potential adverse experiences of students does not automatically mean that the parents/guardians are to be blamed or are the perpetrators. Instead, school counselors should focus on the current issue (i.e., self-harm) and work with caregivers to explore available plans to support the student.

One study examined the psychosocial profile of parents who attended a support program because their children were engaged in self-harm behavior (Morgan et al., 2013). The results indicated that most of these parents reported considerable emotional challenges (e.g., minor psychological distress, lower parental well-being, and lower social support). Moreover, lower well-being was associated with poorer family communication, poorer parenting satisfaction, and more perceived difficulties for the child. The results did not imply that these factors caused the students' self-harm behavior. However, they help in the development of a plan to work with the families effectively.

The previous passage indicates the importance of maintaining meaningful connections with the family. In addition, school counselors should be transparent and clear about their thoughts and goals for working with the family to support the student. For example, "My hope is that we as a team can come up with a plan to provide emotional support and to help Erica identify other ways to manage her negative emotions." In the meantime, it is also crucial for school counselors to be encouraging and to install hope that this team effort (parents and school) will be meaningful to the student. Most importantly, because of the stigma and misconceptions about self-harm, school counselors should provide psychoeducation on this topic to parents/guardians to ensure that everyone is on board and on the same page. School counselors may choose to consult with parents in person and/or direct parents to other useful information online. Topics may include understanding self-harm and learning effective strategies to support the student. In situations where the needs of the student surpass the training and/or resources available to the school counselor, other community resources should be made available to parents/guardians for additional treatment options. Lastly, regardless of whether the school counselor is the primary source of support to the student or not, it is important to follow-up with both the student and caregiver to support the wellness of the student and to maintain a sense of meaningful collaboration.

Strategies for Working With Teachers and Other Stakeholders

Teachers are an important part of the collaborative team for student support. However, school counselors should be mindful of how much information they share with these professionals. Even when working with teachers, the confidentiality of the students' situation should remain paramount. The school counselors should communicate with teachers to gather more information to conceptualize the students' situation and develop an action plan. Considering that students spend most of their days with their teachers, the input of these stakeholders should be an important part of the conversation. One example of a conversation with a teacher follows: "I am working with Erica to help her learn to identify her emotions and stressors. She and I have agreed that if she feels overwhelmed during your class, she will excuse herself and report to my office. I wanted to check in with you about this plan."

To promote collaborative services within schools, several researchers have discussed best practices and the importance of addressing self-harm at the systemic level (e.g., Hasking et al., 2016; Riggi et al., 2017; Toste & Heath, 2010). One crucial component is to have a school protocol ready to respond to self-harm. A comprehensive protocol should address (a) roles and responsibilities of stakeholders, (b) self-harm assessment and suicide assessment, (c) resources and referrals, (d) parents/guardians notifications, and (e) management of social contagion (Hasking et al., 2016). Detailed suggestions for developing a school protocol for self-harm can be found in the "Additional Recommended Reading and Resources" section in this chapter. As advocates for students, school counselors can provide psychoeducational workshops to teachers and stakeholders on the topic of self-harm to (1) correct misconceptions, (2) improve stakeholders' attitudes toward self-harm, and (3) prepare stakeholders' to identify and respond to students with self-harm behavior (Townsend et al., 2018). The "Additional Recommended Reading and Resources" section also provides a comprehensive overview of addressing this topic in schools through a multitiered approach.

Understanding What You Have Read: Comprehension Questions

Directions: Refer to what you learned in this chapter to answer the following questions.

1. What is self-harm?
2. How is self-harm different from suicidal behavior?
3. What are the risk factors and conditions associated with self-harm?
4. What modalities of support can school counselors provide to students?
5. What are some ethical and legal considerations when working with students on the issue of self-harm?

Case Examples

Case Example One

As you read the case about Daniel, reflect on the strategies that we discussed earlier in the chapter. The questions that follow the case relate to the student's behavioral symptoms and accompanying responses.

Daniel is a quiet and brilliant high school student in his freshman year. He belongs to the most academically advanced group in the school. As students started to know each other better during the beginning of the freshman year, his peers noticed that Daniel has avoided showing his wrists and arms and always covered them with long-sleeve shirts or jackets. During an incident, one of his peers witnessed several burn scars on Daniel's arms and then reported this to the school counselor. Daniel stated that he had used this coping strategy since the age of 12 to make him "feel better" and had always carried a lighter with him. He could not name the emotions he had dealt with, but based on his descriptions, those feelings included emptiness, depression, and hopelessness. He did not even know where those feelings came from and seemed resistant to reflect more. Upon further exploring his developmental history, Daniel indicated that his father, who lived with alcohol abuse disorder and physically abused him when he was young, left when he was 10. Daniel had lived with his mother since then. Daniel reported that his mother was unaware of his self-harm behavior.

Case Example One: Questions for Processing and Reflection

Directions: Use what you have learned in this chapter to respond to Daniel's case.

1. What information do you have regarding Daniel's situation?
    a. Daniel uses burning as a coping strategy to deal with his emotions.
    b. Daniel has difficulties identifying his emotions.
    c. Daniel has experienced traumatic events in the past.
    d. Daniel keeps this self-harming behavior secret.
2. What additional information might you still need?
    a. A suicide and self-harm assessment
    b. Information about concerns/symptoms that might otherwise indicate additional mental health conditions
    c. Details about his social support system, specifically regarding the self-harm behavior
3. What do you want to consider before moving to treatment planning?
    a. If there is any imminent danger
    b. Confidentiality
    c. Stigma and potential labeling (since his peer reported it)
    d. Consultation with school administrations and/or the school district attorney if needed
4. How would you address concerns related to Daniel?
    a. Explain his privacy rights and my obligations as a school counselor
    b. Develop a plan to address potential issues with his peers based on his will
    c. Parent consultation to discuss the situation and provide support as a team
    d. Provide individual sessions to work with Daniel on identifying feelings, managing emotions, and replacing the self-harm behavior
    e. Suggest referrals to address the past trauma

Case Example Two

As you read the case about Jennifer, reflect on the strategies that we discussed earlier in the chapter. The questions that follow the case relate to the student's behavioral symptoms and accompanying responses.

Jennifer is a seventh-grade female student who just transferred to the school a month ago. The initial impression about her is that she is a person who rarely speaks up and appears rather stoic. Upon reviewing her records from the previous school, you, the school counselor, found that there was no significant issue that stood out. Jennifer's teachers have reported that she is skipping classes. Her behavior, as well as noted scars on her arms, brought her to your office. Now you are in the initial contact (or first session) with her. Jennifer explained that she cut her arms with a blade, and these cuts were shallow and "not a big deal." When asked about skipping classes, she explained that sometimes she felt numb and just did whatever she wanted. She could not articulate information about these cuts, especially when she started and how frequently she cuts herself. Jennifer indicated that she was adopted when she was 4. Her middle-upper class family, although strict, had provided great support to her. Jennifer did not seem to be resistant to talking with you. Instead, she seemed confident but lost. What would you do to support Jennifer?

Case Example Two: Questions for Processing and Reflection

Directions: Use what you have learned in this chapter to respond to Jennifer's case.

1. What other information would you gather during the rest of the session?
2. What information would you share with her?

3. Do you suspect other mental health conditions? If so, what would you do about that?
4. Will you contact the parents? What are your goals and rationale for this communication?
5. Will you consult with other stakeholders? What are the goals and rationale?
6. What is your next step in working with Jennifer?

Chapter Summary

This chapter focused on self-harm behavior in the student population, which exists in many contexts. If left untreated, it may lead to suicide, as suggested in the literature. In this chapter, you were presented with the definition of self-harm according to the *DSM-5* and risk factors and conditions associated with self-harm based on the literature. Strategies for school counselors to work with students exhibiting self-harm behavior were provided, as well as the ethical and legal considerations. Because of the common misconceptions and stigma associated with self-harm, it is imperative to address this issue with parents/guardians, teachers, and stakeholders through consultation and psychoeducational workshops as suggested. Both reactive and proactive services from school counselors are needed.

Additional Recommended Readings and Resources

Hamza, C. A., & Heath, N. L. (2019). Nonsuicidal self-injury: What schools can do. In A. W. Leschied, D. H. Saklofske, & G. L. Flett (Eds.), *Handbook of school-based mental health promotion* (pp. 237–260). Springer.

Hasking, P. A., Heath, N. L., Kaess, M., Lewis, S. P., Plener, P. L., Walsh, B. W., Whitlock, J., & Wilson, M. S. (2016). Position paper for guiding response to non-suicidal self-injury in schools. *School Psychology International, 37*(6), 644–663.

Kress, V. E., & Hoffman, R. M. (2008). Non-suicidal self-injury and motivational interviewing: Enhancing readiness for change. *Journal of Mental Health Counseling, 30*(4), 311–329.

Miller, D. N., & Brock, S. E. (2010). *Identifying, assessing, and treating self-injury at school.* Springer.

Wells, A., & Axe, J. B. (2013). A three-tiered approach for addressing nonsuicidal self-injury in the classroom. *Beyond Behavior, 22*(2), 35–43.

References

American Psychiatric Association (APA). (2000). *Diagnostic and Statistical Manual* (4th ed., text rev.).

American Psychiatric Association (APA). (2013). *Diagnostic and Statistical Manual* (5th ed.).

American School Counselor Association (ASCA). (2016). *ASCA Ethical Standards for School Counselors.*

American School Counselor Association (ASCA). (2018). *ASCA national model: A framework for school counseling programs* (4th ed.).

Cloutier, P., & Humphreys, L. (2009). Measurement of nonsuicidal self-injury in adolescents. In M. K. Nixon & N. L. Heath (Eds.), *Self-injury in youth: The essential guide to assessment and intervention* (pp. 115–142). Routledge.

DiCorcia D. J., Arango A., Horwitz A. G., & King C. A. (2017). Methods and functions of non-suicidal self-injury among adolescents seeking emergency psychiatric services. *Journal of Psychopathology Behavioral Assessment, 39*(4), 693–704.

Gonzales, A. H., & Bergstrom, L. (2013). Adolescent non-suicidal self-injury (NSSI) interventions. *Journal of Child and Adolescent Psychiatric Nursing, 26*, 124–130.

Hasking, P. A., Heath, N. L., Kaess, M., Lewis, S. P., Plener, P. L., Walsh, B. W., Whitlock, J., & Wilson, M. S. (2016). Position paper for guiding response to non-suicidal self-injury in schools. *School Psychology International, 37*(6), 644–663.

Hawton K., James A., & Viner R. (2005). Suicide and deliberate self-harm in young people. *BMJ, 330*(7496), 891–894

Hazell, P. L., Martin, G., McGill, K., Kay, T., Wood, A., Trainor, G., & Harrington, R. (2009). Group therapy for repeated deliberate self-harm in adolescents: Failure of replication of a randomized trial. *Journal of the American Academy of Child and Adolescent Psychiatry, 48*(6), 662–670.

Hoffman, R. M., & Kress, V. E. (2010). Adolescent nonsuicidal self-injury: Minimizing client and counselor risk and enhancing client care. *Journal of Mental Health Counseling, 32* (4), 342–347.

Kamen, D. G. (2009). How can we stop our children from hurting themselves? Stages of change, motivational interviewing, and exposure therapy applications for non-suicidal self-injury in children and adolescents. *International Journal of Behavioral Consultation and Therapy, 5*(1), 106–123.

Klonsky, D. E. (2017). Nonsuicidal self-injury: Separating fact from fiction. *Visions: BC's Mental Health and Substance Use Journal, 13*(2), 8.

Kress, V. E. W., Drouhard, N., & Costin, A. (2006). Students who self-injure: School counselor ethical and legal considerations. *Professional School Counseling, 10*(2), 203–209.

Lovell, S., & Clifford, M. (2016). Nonsuicidal self-injury of adolescents. *Clinical Pediatrics, 55*(11), 1012–1019.

Miller, D. N., & Brock, S. E. (2010). *Identifying, assessing, and treating self-injury at school.* Springer.

Monto, M. A., McRee, N., & Deryck, F. S. (2018). Nonsuicidal self-injury among a representative sample of US adolescents, 2015. *American Journal of Public Health, 108*(8), 1042–1048.

Morgan, S., Rickard, E., Noone1, M., Boylan, C., Carthy, A., Crowley, S., Butler, J., Guerin, S., & Fitzpatrick, C. (2013). Parents of young people with self-harm or suicidal behaviour who seek help—a psychosocial profile. *Child and Adolescent Psychiatry and Mental Health, 7*(13), 1–10.

Richardson, B. G., Surmitis, K. A., & Hyldahl, R. S. (2012). Minimizing social contagion in adolescents who self-injure: Considerations for group work, residential treatment, and the internet. *Journal of Mental Health Counseling, 34* (2), 121–132.

Riggi, M. E., Moumne, S., Heath, N. L., & Lewis, S. (2017). Non-suicidal self-injury in our schools: A review and research-informed guidelines for school mental health professionals. *Canadian Journal of School Psychology, 32*(2), 122–143.

Toste, J., & Heath, N. L. (2010). School response to non-suicidal self-injury. *Prevention Researcher, 17*(1), 14–17.

Townsend, M. L., Gray, A. S., Lancaster, T. M., & Grenyer, B. F. S. (2018). A whole of school intervention for personality disorder and self-harm in youth: A pilot study of changes in teachers' attitudes, knowledge and skills. *Borderline Personality Disorder and Emotion Dysregulation, 5*(17), 1–9.

Virginia Commission on Youth. (2017). *Nonsuicidal self-injury.* http://vcoy.virginia.gov/documents/collection/025%20Nonsuicidal%20self%20injury2.pdf

Walsh, B. (2006). *Treating self-injury: A practical guide.* Guilford Press.

Westers, N. J., Muehlenkamp, J. J., & Lau, M. (2016). SOARS model: Risk assessment of nonsuicidal self-injury. *Contemporary Pediatrics,* 25–31.

Wood, A., Trainor, G., Rothwell, J., Moore, A., & Harrington, R. (2001). Randomized trial of group therapy for repeated deliberate self-harm in adolescents. *Journal of the American Academy of Child and Adolescent Psychiatry, 40*(11), 1246–1253.

Xavier, A., Cunha, M., Pinto-Gouveia, J. (2016). The indirect effect of early experiences on deliberate self-harm in adolescence: Mediation by negative emotional states and moderation by daily peer hassles. *Journal of Child and Family Studies, 25*(5), 1451–1460.

CHAPTER SIXTEEN

Grief and Bereavement

Naomi J. Wheeler and Autumn Cabell

THE CASE OF KARA Kara and William are African American ninth- and 11th-grade students at a Title I high school located in an urban community. Kara and William live with their mother, a single parent who works more than 50 hours a week between her two part-time jobs. Although they only get to see their mom for short periods of time before and after school, the family is close-knit. Their mother encourages them to go to school and keep their grades up. Kara is a quiet, high-achieving student who is academically thriving in her first year of high school. Kara has a small diverse group of friends with whom she is regularly seen in the hallways and at lunch. Although Kara is new to high school, she is actively involved in Key Club and other student organizations. William is a varsity football player on his high school team. He is a rising star player on the football team, outspoken, friendly, and widely adored by his peers. Although his grades are not as high as his sister's, he has maintained a 2.8 grade point average and hopes to get into a state school to play football in college. The community that surrounds the school is small and impacted by economic disadvantage and frequent gang-related violence.

After a Friday night varsity football game, William is struck by a stray bullet during a drive-by shooting near his home. The next morning, the administration, staff, teachers, and school counselors are notified about the shooting, which resulted in William's death. The school and community are shocked and devastated, but the school swiftly acts to provide support to students and staff. A couple of days later, Kara returns to school because her mother cannot continue to take off more time from work. Over the course of the next few weeks, the school counselor is informed that Kara has begun skipping her favorite classes and she has not been responsive to her peers in Key Club. Kara also fails most of her midterm exams. The school counselor attempts to reach out to Kara's mother several times but does not receive a response. The school counselor calls Kara into her office to check in. The school counselor begins the conversation by letting Kara know that she is not in trouble. The counselor empathizes and conveys her understanding that the loss of her brother has been difficult for Kara, her family, and the school community. At first, Kara is silent, but after the school counselor asks Kara how she has been doing, she breaks down sobbing.

Introduction to the Chapter

Loss is an inevitable and inherent reality of human existence. We will all experience a loss at some point in our lives and may also encounter a wide range of losses—including the death of a family member, loved one, friend, classmate, or pet; non-death-related losses, such as a home, job, health/ability, status; or normal transitions between phases and stages of life. Grief associated with a loss is a natural part of the healing process. Moreover, how a person grieves is often influenced by their age, developmental stage, culture, identity, and resources for coping and adaptation, as well as the context surrounding the loss. For instance, children and adolescents who experience the loss of a loved one through traumatic circumstances (e.g., suicide, homicide, natural disaster, an act of terrorism, or community violence), such as the case with Kara, may demonstrate grief that reflects the traumatic stress of the situation in addition to the loss itself. Kara may feel sadness associated with the loss of her brother, as well as fear for her and her mother's safety given the unpredictable nature of the events surrounding his death. Similarly, grief is experienced at the individual and systemic levels. In the case of Kara and William, grief and loss are likely felt at the individual, family, school, and community levels. Students and teachers are affected by the loss of a peer, teammate, and student. Neighbors are affected by the loss of a neighbor and friend. And, overall, the journey toward healing can look different for each of these relationships and systems within which William will be remembered. There is no one pattern or time line for grief; however, symptoms that become more extreme or last longer than 12 months after a loss could meet the criteria for persistent complex bereavement disorder (PCBD; American Psychiatric Association [APA], 2013). Therefore, school counselors should be aware of the common and less common reactions to grief and loss as a part of their comprehensive care for the school community.

Learning Objectives

By the end of this chapter, readers will accomplish the following:

- Identify symptoms and criteria associated with typical grief processes, as well as criteria to distinguish PCBD or childhood traumatic grief.
- Understand the developmental and cultural influences of grief and bereavement.
- Identify best practices and strategies for interventions in school settings.

Grief can apply to a wide range of experiences and losses. In this chapter, we will focus on death-related losses. Researchers estimate that 1 in 14 children will experience the death of a parent or sibling by the time they are 18 years of age (JAG Institute, 2018). In addition, studies suggest that about half (Rheingold et al., 2004) to three quarters (Jenkins et al., 2014) of African American children experience the death and loss of a close family member. African American children report disparate rates of early and multiple losses as a consequence of disparities in health and illness, as well as a greater likelihood of exposure to community violence and victimization; therefore, all children, but African American children, in particular, are likely to experience death and the loss of a significant other. Grief is strongly related to social, emotional, and academic well-being. Therefore, school counselors will also likely encounter bereaved students who display a variety of related behaviors and should be prepared to support the grief-related needs of a student population. Identification and intervention are important contributions that school counselors make. In this chapter, we will use the term *bereavement* to refer to a person's state after the death of a loved one. The term *grief* will refer to the psychological response to bereavement, identifiable through changes in a person's thoughts, feelings, and behaviors.

An Overview of Death and Grief

Following a death, a child's stage of development will influence their emotional reaction and ability to understand the situation. For example, very young children or children with developmental disabilities may have difficulty grasping the permanency of death and will respond instead to the emotional reactions of the adults/caregivers around them. School-aged children are better able to comprehend the universality and inevitability of death. As a result, they may also experience death-related anxiety or fear about their own deaths or what occurs after they die, even if they are currently in good health. Finally, adolescents understand death and may have past experiences that influence their thoughts and feelings about death. Teenagers also tend to take risks and believe that although death is inevitable, they are exempt. Therefore, age and developmental levels influence a young person's response to and experience of loss and death.

In the past, researchers suggested that grief followed a linear and uniform process of adaptation that was applicable to all grievers. You may have even heard people talk about the stages of grief developed by Kübler-Ross (1969)—a chronological pattern of learning to live with the loss of a loved one that included stages of denial, anger, bargaining, depression, and acceptance. Different models for grief now exist (e.g., Rando, 1984; Rubin, 1999), and each varies slightly in how it incorporates the tasks commonly associated with bereavement (Worden, 2018), such as (a) acceptance of the reality of the loss, (b) processing of the pain (emotional, behavioral) associated with grief, (c) adjustment (external, internal, spiritual) to a world without the deceased, and (d) identification of a connection to and memory of the deceased that endures as the individual reinvests in life. One particular model, the dual-process model, highlights how mourners fluctuate between stress and coping related to the loss, as well as restoration or adjustment to life changes associated with the loss (Stroebe & Schut, 1999). In sum, grief is a uniquely individualized experience (e.g., Holland et al., 2009) such that the exact symptoms, frequency, intensity, and duration may differ between individuals.

Observable Behavioral Changes Related to Grief

There are some more typical grief reactions that may be observable and discernable by age. In general, young children may regress to old habits or behaviors (e.g., tantrums, bed-wetting, clinging to a caregiver) and seem more irritable, tearful, anxious, or distressed. Children may have more physical complaints of aches and pains or have notable changes in their eating patterns. Some children may avoid talking about the loss because they blame themselves, feel different than others, or are more fearful overall since the loss. Other children will have lots of questions and want to talk often about death and details of the loss or seem preoccupied with ideas of mortality more generally. Children in middle childhood or adolescence may also work hard to please the caregivers in their lives and take on typically adult responsibilities. In school, their behavior may present as difficulty concentrating in class, reduced participation in classroom assignments, frequent absences, or decreased quality and reliability of assignments. Students who experienced the loss of a parent also reported "premature school withdrawals and diminished interests in college attendance" (Feigelman et al., 2016, p. 133). Counselors should be aware of the potential to misinterpret these areas of difficulty as signs of another mental health issue or a behavioral problem and miss their connection as expressions of grief altogether. In addition, children and adolescents might also begin to examine their religiosity and spirituality. For example, young people undergoing the grief process might express *anger* toward God or a Higher Power and may struggle using spirituality to make meaning of their loss (Andrews & Marotta, 2005). Overall, children and adolescents can experience a wide range of emotional and cognitive responses to bereavement that often include feelings of emptiness and loss. Grief reactions vary from day-to-day and can even resurface well after the initial loss as individuals encounter reminders, have thoughts of the deceased, or experience important milestones in life.

Influencing Factors of Grief

Factors that influence the grief process include (Worden, 2018) the type of relationship with the deceased, attachment to the deceased, context of the death itself, historical experience of grief, personality, social support, or concurrent changes/loss/stress. For instance, one study found that although boys and girls were both affected by grief following the loss of a loved one, it was a stronger predictor of depression, post-traumatic stress disorder (PTSD), acting out behaviors, and lower academic achievement among boys (Jenkins et al., 2014). To expand upon a few other factors influential to grief in more detail, let's start by considering the context surrounding William's death from our case example. William's death was unexpected, violent, preventable, and the result of an accident. Grieving his loss would likely look differently if his death were natural, the result of intentional homicide, or even an ambiguous loss, such as in the case of missing children. Similarly, consider if William was one of several who died in the same event or if the death was more proximal where the shooting happened at school or during school hours. Each of these factors would influence Kara's grief process, as well as the process of others in the school and community. As another example, consider how Kara's personality might play a part in her grief in association with her age, gender, coping style, attachment style, cognitive style, or ego strength. We briefly discussed developmental nuances to grief earlier, which shows how aspects of our identity, culture, and experience will affect our grief.

William's death was unexpected and traumatic. Kara had a close relationship with William and had not experienced the death of a loved one before this loss. Yet Kara has a lot of support from her mom and internal resources who have contributed to her academic and personal success thus far. Therefore, Kara's grief process will likely differ when compared to students in the school who knew of William but maybe did not know him personally. However, a school counselor would also want to monitor Kara's well-being, be attentive to changes in her grief, and also be aware of the potential for challenges in adaptation. Most individuals adapt to the loss of a loved one naturally over time. However, about 10%–15% of people who are bereaved experience longer and atypical grief reactions (Shear et al., 2011). Furthermore, some studies suggest that African Americans experience more traumatic forms of loss, which can also complicate the grief process (Laurie & Neimyer, 2008). Therefore, knowledge of diagnostic criteria and symptoms of grief-related disorders is important to adequately address student needs.

Diagnostic Criteria for Grief/Bereavement

Little agreement exists for what "normal" grief should look like. In fact, during the most recent revision to the *Diagnostic and Statistical Manual of Mental Disorders, Fifth Edition* (*DSM-5*; APA, 2013), experts engaged in a fierce debate over this very idea (Zachar et al., 2017). Some argued that all grief is normal, and symptoms of grief should not be pathologized through diagnosis. Yet others pointed to cases of intense, prolonged, and unresolved forms of grief to suggest a distinct mental disorder for some bereaved individuals. Evidence supports the distinction of intense, enduring, and impairing forms of grief as symptoms distinguishable from other diagnoses, such as depression, anxiety, or PTSD. In fact, prior editions of the *DSM* and criteria for depression included a "bereavement exclusion rule" or criteria that ruled out a diagnosis of a major depressive episode for the bereaved unless symptoms related to bereavement were highly severe (e.g., psychotic, suicidal) or lasted more than 2 months. The latest version of the *DSM* removed the bereavement exclusion rule. Interestingly, in the *DSM-5*, you'll see a note and footnote in the section about major depressive episodes that encourages practitioners to apply clinical judgment and carefully distinguish normative grief responses and symptoms indicative of a diagnosis. Counselors must use clinical judgment and assess an individual's history, culture, and associated norms related to the expression of grief and loss. The footnote provides further elaboration for how feelings and thoughts may be distinguishable between grief and a major depressive episode. For example, thoughts about death and dying may relate to a desire to join the deceased, whereas thoughts of suicide as in a major depressive episode are usually about a sense of worthlessness or the inability to cope with the pain. Likewise, grief reactions can also parallel symptoms associated with a diagnosis of PTSD, such as emotional numbing or avoidance of reminders. Thus although somewhat controversial, grief that yields intense reactions that persist across a longer period of time may meet preliminary criteria for a diagnosis.

The chronic experience of grief symptoms that impair functioning is, therefore, known by many names, depending on who you ask. The International Classification of Diseases (ICD), 11th revision, a diagnostic tool of the World Health Organization (2018), refers to such symptoms as *prolonged grief disorder* (PGD). Also known as *traumatic* (Mannarino & Cohen, 2011), *disturbed*, or *complicated bereavement or grief* in the literature, the *DSM-5* refers to such symptoms as PCBD. PCBD is referenced in Section III of the *DSM-5* as "a condition for further study," while researchers attempt to establish agreement of the exact criteria, timing requirements, and most appropriate nomenclature. Both PGD and PCBD account for normative grief symptoms that have become protracted, include a 6-month timing criterion, and emphasize separation distress or longing or yearning for the deceased. Yet PCBD requires more symptoms to be present for diagnosis, such as intense sorrow and emotional pain in response to the loss, bitterness, or excessive avoidance of reminders of the loss. Researchers also found lower rates of diagnosis among bereaved children (i.e., > 6 months after the loss) when compared to criteria for PGD (Boelen et al., 2019).

The *DSM-5* criteria commonly reported by children and adolescents include persistent yearning/longing for the deceased, difficulty accepting the death, bitterness or anger, feeling alone or detached from other persons, difficulties pursuing interests or plans for the future, confusion about one's role and diminished identity, preoccupation with the deceased person, and difficulty trusting other people. Other criteria that are less commonly reported (i.e., less than 10% of children; Boelen et al., 2019) include intense sorrow and emotional pain, preoccupation with the deceased person, preoccupation with the circumstances of the death, disbelief or numbness, maladaptive appraisals about the "self" associated with the loss, a desire to die to be with the deceased, feeling that life is empty or meaningless or that one is unable to function without the deceased, and difficulty positively reminiscing about the deceased. Researchers continue to debate which criteria are best to assess, diagnose, and treat individuals with risks associated with chronic and impairing symptoms of grief. In practice, counselors can begin to identify prolonged and acute grief reactions that may require additional support and intervention. Furthermore, counselors need to continue to stay abreast of research and look for future revisions within the *DSM* and ICD related to PCBD and grief.

Strategies for School Counselors

During periods of bereavement, familiar routines, comfort, and attention from supportive figures can offer reassurance for some (not all) young people and mitigate the secondary losses often associated with the death of a loved one. It is important to individualize your approach to work with all students, including those who are grieving. In addition, counselors should avoid well-intended but stereotypical statements like, "I know how you feel," or "It will get better with time." Likewise, counselors should match the mode of intervention to students' needs. Students experiencing an uncomplicated grief process might benefit from support for the typical tasks of mourning, also known as *grief counseling.* In some situations, *grief therapy* or specialized techniques to help individuals with complicated or abnormal grief reactions may be warranted. When symptoms or needs of the student exceed the time or competence of the school counselor, referrals to specialized counseling services are an important and ethical decision.

In general, school counselor intervention for uncomplicated grief can include talking about the loss and verbalizing memories of the deceased as a way to help actualize the loss. Counselors can encourage identification, expression, and experience of feelings associated with the loss. For example, negative-only feelings, such as excessive bitterness, anger, or a desire to die, can create challenges in the grief process. Thus individuals may benefit from the expression of feelings of affection (i.e., nostalgia, meaning-making), as well as processing anger, guilt, anxiety, helplessness, loneliness, or sadness about the loss. Counselors can assist students in adapting to the loss, for example, through the development of problem solving. When a student is ready, it may also be helpful to support their process to find meaning in the death. (Why did this happen? Why did this happen to me? How am I different because of the loss?) Similarly, when individual students are ready, it may be helpful to develop ways to remember the deceased. Counselors can provide time to grieve, recognize times that may be more difficult for the student, and allow for the natural process of accommodation to all the changes in a student's life. Counselors should be able to normalize grief behaviors while also taking individual differences into consideration. Finally, school counselors can play an important role in identification for when more serious needs occur and provide referrals.

Interventions

According to Heath and colleagues (2008), younger children may benefit from basic information and concrete details regarding grief and loss, while adolescents may appreciate more detail, other people's perspectives, and peer support. Therefore, when being responsive to a student's developmental needs, school counselors can consider individual and group formats for intervention. In comparison to younger students, older students (i.e., middle and high school students) may also have had more experience with loss and death and may be better able to place their loss in context with past events. Grief interventions should be flexible and developmentally appropriate for the student's maturity level and understanding of loss. Therefore, counselors would benefit from the inclusion of play-based intervention or training and the application of play therapy skills to address the grief needs of students and nonverbal expressions of loss. There are few empirically supported forms of grief counseling intervention; however, strong evidence exists for manualized forms of intervention, such as trauma-focused cognitive behavioral therapy for children who have experienced traumatic grief (Cohen & Mannarino, 2011) and cognitive-behavioral intervention for trauma in schools (CBITS; Jaycox, 2004). In addition, researchers have conceptually identified the potential fit for play therapy to address grief in children and adolescents (e.g., Webb, 2011) in ways that honor a family's traditions and beliefs. Next, we will present commonly used interventions for grief counseling in the school setting; however, counselors are encouraged to ensure fit with their theoretical approach to intervention, as well as the needs of the individual student and their family. Furthermore, the establishment of a solid therapeutic relationship is the foundation for any type of intervention to be effective. Grief interventions for elementary, middle, and high school students may include experiential and expressive arts, bibliotherapy, and group interventions.

Expressive Arts Interventions

Expressive arts often include interventions that allow students at different developmental stages to process their feelings. Guidry et al. (2013) explained that school counselors' facilitation of expressive arts interventions can provide students with the opportunity to freely express their grief process. School counselors can help students create memory boxes, drawings, collages, and writings related to their loss and grief. For example, counselors can provide students with acrylic paints and rocks to create "*memory rocks.*" On these large rocks, school counselors can work with students to draw pictures or messages and encourage students to place them in places that are important to them. During this activity, school counselors allow students to create something in memory of their loved one while also giving students the opportunity to process their experience and express their feelings associated with the loss. Throughout any grief intervention, it is important for school counselors to create safe spaces for students that promote emotional expression (Heath et al., 2008).

Bibliotherapy

Bibliotherapy includes the use of text and other media sources (e.g., music, poetry, movies) that can facilitate understanding and problem solving. Stories can be used to normalize feelings of grief and loss and to provide a character with whom a student may be able to identify in terms of their experience or coping. Bibliotherapy should also include discussion and processing of the activity, whether verbally or through creative forms of self-expression (e.g., art, role-playing, creative writing, music), to translate the medium to a student's experience of loss and coping. For example, school counselors can make book recommendations and provide grief-related activities that support students' emotional processing and expression (Heath et al., 2008). For example, *The Bridge to Terabithia* by Katherine Paterson (1977) may be appropriate for older children and adolescents dealing with loss. It is the story of two friends, Jess and Leslie, who go on an adventure in an imaginary kingdom. After Leslie's accidental drowning, Jess learns to cope with his friend's death. As a student reads books like *The Bridge to Terabithia*, school counselors can ask the student to keep a journal to describe the similarities and differences between their experience with loss and the experience of the characters in the book. Counselors should aim to incorporate media that closely matches the student's age and experience. Some additional books and movies related to grief and loss are provided next:

Invisible String by Patrice Karst (general death of a loved one)

I Miss You: A First Look at Death by Pat Thomas (general death and grief facts)

Ida, Always by Caron Levis and Charles Santoso (terminal illness of a loved one)

The Memory Box: A Book About Grief by Joanna Rowland (death)

Tear Soup by Pat Schwiebert (death)

Nana Upstairs and Nana Downstairs by Tomie dePaola (grandmother death)

The Scar by Charlotte Moundlic (mother death)

I'll Always Love You by Hans Wilhelm (pet loss)

The Tenth Good Thing About Barney by Judith Viorst (pet loss)

Middle and High School Readers

If Only by Carole Geithner (mother death)

Toning the Sweep by Angela Johnson (grandparent loss)

Fire in My Heart, Ice in My Veins by Enid Traisman (general death)

Saying Goodbye When You Don't Want To by Martha Bolton

Speak of Me As I Am by Sonia Belasco (mother, friend death)

We Are Okay by Nina LaCour (grandparent loss)

Goodbye Days by Jeff Zentner

Movies with grief-related themes include *The Lion King* (1994, 2019), *Big Hero 6* (2014), *Coco* (2018), *Harry Potter and the Sorcerer's Stone* (2001), *Fly Away Home* (1996), *Hugo* (2011), *My Dog Skip* (2011), *Up* (2009), *We Bought a Zoo* (2011), or *Charlotte's Web* (1973).

Group Counseling

To help students gain a sense of peer support, school counselors can lead grief group interventions. Although grief groups may be challenging to coordinate with teachers' and students' class schedules, groups are best held during the school day rather than before or after school because of possible transportation issues for students (Openshaw, 2011). Thus school counselors need to be flexible and corporative when trying to develop small-group interventions for grief.

Grief groups, particularly those related to cognitive-behavioral interventions and trauma, are showing promising effectiveness in the literature regarding grief interventions for children and adolescents (Brown et al., 2008; Lang et al., 2010; Openshaw, 2011). For children and adolescents who are exhibiting externalizing behaviors after experiencing loss, group interventions can be helpful in grief symptom reduction. In Cohen et al. (2004) 16-week, trauma-focused cognitive behavioral therapy–childhood traumatic grief (CBT-CTG) group intervention pilot study that included 22 children ages 6–17 who had experienced CTG, participants showed improvements in their externalizing behaviors. Increases in externalizing behaviors, such as outbursts in class or aggression toward self or others (see the additional case examples that follow), are a common response for children and adolescents who have experienced loss. In Cohen et al.'s (2004) trauma-focused, CBT-CTG group intervention, the participants completed several grief- and loss-related activities, including learning coping skills, developing a narrative surrounding the loss they experienced, receiving grief and loss psychoeducation, processing unresolved emotions and ambivalent feelings, creating positive memories of the person they lost, and making new meaning from their traumatic loss. School counselors can build from and adapt these activities based on the developmental maturity of the students in their grief group intervention.

In addition, trauma grief component therapy for adolescents (TGCT-A) is a cognitive-behavioral based group model that includes five modules that address (1) traumatic experiences, (2) trauma and loss reminders, (3) post-traumatic stress and adversities, (4) the interplay of trauma and grief, and (5) resumption of developmental progression. These TGCT-A groups are typically provided in school settings and have been shown to be more effective than classroom-based psychoeducation and skill intervention alone (Layne et al., 2008). In addition, the CBITS format was developed for school staff members working with adolescent students ages 10 to 14 years old (Openshaw, 2011). Training for CBITS can be found online. The CBITS program consists of 10 group sessions, one to three individual sessions, two parent psychoeducational sessions, and one teacher educational session. In addition, the CBITS program and activities have been translated into multiple languages and have been shown effective when working with economically disadvantaged students, students from a variety of faiths and cultures, ethnically diverse students, and non-English-speaking students.

Understanding What You Have Read: Comprehension Questions

Directions: Refer to what you have learned in this chapter to answer the following questions.

- What are the similarities and differences between CTG and PCBD?
- What are some common symptoms that students may exhibit after experiencing a loss?
- How will you as a future counselor help advocate for the needs of a student who has experienced a loss?

- What are some multicultural concerns to consider when addressing grief and loss?
- How might your own experiences with grief and loss affect your interactions with a student who has experienced an impactful loss?

Case Examples

Case Example One

As you read the case about Mark, reflect on the strategies that we discussed earlier in the chapter. The questions that follow the case relate to the student's behavioral symptoms and accompanying responses.

Mark is a third-grade student who lost his mother to breast cancer last year. Mark, his classmates, and the school had known about his mother's breast cancer for several months. His second-grade teacher even had the class make a card for Mark's mother when she was first diagnosed. Mark did not understand what cancer was, but he knew that it was making his mother very sick. His teacher would always know when Mark's mother got chemo treatment because shortly after, Mark would begin to act out in class—sometimes hitting his classmates when he got frustrated or yelling at his teacher when she wouldn't let him do something. However, when Mark's mother was getting better or when she had good days, his teacher noticed a decrease in his externalizing behaviors. You have been close to Mark throughout the ups and downs of his mother's illness. Last school year, Mark was a member of your lunch groups for anger. However, after his mother's death, Mark began to shut down. Over this school year, you've noticed Mark keeping to himself during recess. His teacher reported to you that he has not been turning in his homework, and he has been struggling throughout the school year. One day, Mark asks his teacher if he can go talk with you. When Mark comes into your office, he says he's really sad that his mom is an angel now, and he really misses her. He tells you that sometimes he wishes he could be with her.

Case Example One: Questions for Processing and Reflection

Directions: Use what you have learned in this chapter to respond to Mark's case.

1. What are some indicators that Mark may be experiencing PCBD?
   a. Mark has been struggling with the day-to-day activities in school for a prolonged amount of time (i.e., < 1 year).
   b. Mark is showing a continuous yearning for his mother.
   c. Mark has begun to shut down emotionally.
   d. Depending on the context, Mark may be expressing a desire to also die.
2. How would you advocate for Mark to receive more specialized counseling services? Who would be the key stakeholders in your advocacy efforts?
   a. It might be helpful to refer Mark to school-based therapeutic services.
   b. Key stakeholders might include a school social worker or clinician, his teacher, or community agencies that support children and families who have experienced a loss.
   c. Collaboration between the school counselor and Mark's guardian may be needed to ensure that Mark can receive outside support.
3. How would you address concerns related to Mark?
   a. Mark may be a good candidate for an in-school grief group depending on his interest in joining a group, his ability to open up about the loss he has experienced, and how well his needs align with the needs of other group members.

b. Engaging Mark in developmentally appropriate expressive arts interventions might help him process his emotions. For example, having Mark draw his feelings might help him to talk about his loss in a meaningful way.
c. Fostering the therapeutic alliance is important to help Mark feel safe and comfortable discussing his feelings.

Case Example Two

As you read the case about Jennifer, reflect on the strategies that we discussed earlier in the chapter. The questions that follow the case relate to the student's behavioral symptoms and accompanying responses.

It has been 1 month since Lori, a high school senior at a small school in a rural community, passed away. She died in a car accident after the car she was riding in was struck by a drunk driver. Two other people were in the car with her and survived the accident. One of the people in the car was an alumna of the high school who had graduated last school year. The driver of the car was Jennifer, also a senior at the high school. Jennifer has been struggling with the death of her best friend, Lori. She has expressed to friends that she feels responsible for Lori's death. After an outburst in her English class, Jennifer's teacher recommends that she go visit the school counselor. You welcome Jennifer into your office and ask her about what happened in class, but Jennifer ignores you. You've been Jennifer's counselor since the ninth grade, and you know how close she was to Lori. Jennifer was not a student who frequented your office, but you had developed a relationship with her over the years. What do you say to Jennifer to help her start to process her emotions with you?

Case Example Two: Questions for Processing and Reflection

Directions: Use what you have learned in this chapter to respond to Jennifer's case.

1. After Jennifer's outburst in her English class, how would you respond to her teacher, who may not understand the full scope of grief and bereavement?
2. What interventions would you use when working with Jennifer?
3. How could you incorporate expressive arts interventions into your work with Jennifer?

Chapter Summary

This chapter focused on the symptoms associated with bereavement and grief. The authors discussed the differences between uncomplicated grief and more long-term symptoms typically associated with PCBD. In addition, this chapter explained the lack of consensus surrounding diagnostic criteria related to grief and the need for more empirically supported interventions. Focusing specifically on death-related loss, this chapter provided school counselors with developmentally appropriate strategies and interventions for working with students who are experiencing uncomplicated grieving symptoms. When students have experienced a loss, school counselors are of critical importance because of their ability to provide referrals when grief responses become prolonged, severe, and a barrier to academic achievement. Lastly, this chapter provided relatable case scenarios for school counselors to reflect on, process, and consider their responses to students at various developmental stages who have experienced loss.

Additional Recommended Readings and Resources

Training for Cognitive-Behavioral Intervention for Trauma in Schools: https://cbitsprogram.org/

Training for Trauma-Focused Cognitive Behavioral Therapy for Traumatic Grief: https://ctg.musc.edu

Uplift Center for Grieving: http://grievingchildren.org/

The Dougy Center: https://www.dougy.org/

References

American Psychiatric Association. (2013). *Diagnostic and statistical manual of mental disorders* (5th ed.). Arlington, VA: Author.

Andrews, C. R., & Marotta, S. A. (2005). Spirituality and coping among grieving children: A preliminary study. *Counseling and Values, 50*(1), 38–50. https://doi.org/10.1002/j.2161-007x.2005.tb00039.x

Boelen, P. A., Spuij, M., & Lenferink, L. I. M. (2019). *Journal of Affective Disorders, 250*, 71–78. https://doi.org/10.1016/j.jad.2019.02.046

Brown, E. J., Amaya-Jackson, L., Cohen, J., Handel, S., De Bocanegra, H. T., Zatta, E., Goodman, R. F., & Mannarino, A. (2008). Childhood traumatic grief: A multi-site empirical examination of the construct and its correlates. *Death Studies, 32*(10), 899–923. https://doi.org/10.1080.07481180802440209

Cohen, J. A., & Mannarino, A. P. (2011). Supporting children with traumatic grief: What educators need to know. *School Psychology International, 32*(2), 117–131. https:doi.org/10.1177/0143034311400827

Cohen, J. A., Mannarino, A. P., and Knudson, K. (2004). Treating childhood traumatic grief: A pilot study. *Journal of the American Academy of Child and Adolescent Psychiatry, 43*(10), 1225–1233. https://doi.org/10.1097/01.chi.0000135620.15522.38

Feigelman, W., Rosen, Z., Joiner, T., Silva, C., & Mueller, A. S. (2016). Examining longer-term effects of parental death in adolescents and young adults: Evidence from the national longitudinal survey of adolescent to adult health. *Death Studies, 41*(3), 133–143. https://doi.org/10.1080/07481187.2016.1226990

Guidry, K., Simpson, C., Test, T., & Bloomfield, C. (2013). Ambiguous loss and its effect on children: Implications and interventions for school counselors. *Journal of School Counseling, 11*(15), 1–19.

Heath, M. A., Leavy, D., Hansen, K., Ryan, K., Lawrence, L., & Sonntag, A. G. (2008). Coping with grief: Guidelines and resources for assisting children. *Intervention in School and Clinic, 43*(5), 259–269. https://doi.org./10.1177/1053451208314493

Holland, J. M., Neimeyer, R. A., Boelen, P. A., & Prigerson, H. G. (2009). The underlying structure of grief: A taxometric investigation of prolonged and normal reactions to loss. *Journal of Psychopathology and Behavioral Assessment, 31*, 190–201. https://doi.org/10.1007/s10862-008-9113-1

JAG Institute. (2018). *Understanding childhood grief in the U.S.: Childhood bereavement estimation model.* https://www.judishouse.org/cbem

Jaycox, L. H. (2004). *Cognitive behavioral intervention for trauma in schools.* Sopris West.

Jenkins, E. J., Wang, E., & Turner, L. (2014). Beyond community violence: Loss and traumatic grief in African American elementary school children. *Journal of Child and Adolescent Trauma, 7*, 27–36. https://doi.org/10.1007/s40653-014-0001-4

Kübler-Ross, E. (1969). *On death and dying.* Macmillan.

Lang, J. M., Ford, J. D., & Fitzgerald, M. M. (2010). An algorithm for determining use of trauma-focused cognitive-behavioral therapy. *Psychotherapy Theory, Research, Practice, Training, 47*(4), 554–569. https://doi.org/10.1037/a0021184

Laurie, A., & Neimeyer, R. A. (2008). African Americans in bereavement: Grief as a function of ethnicity. *Omega, 57*, 173–193.

Mannarino, A. P., & Cohen, J. A. (2011). Traumatic loss in children and adolescents. *Journal of Child and Adolescent Trauma, 4*(1), 22–33.

Openshaw, L. L. (2011). School-based support groups for traumatized students. *School Psychology International, 32*(2), 163–178. https://doi.org/10.1177/0143034311400830

Paterson, K. (1977). *Bridge to Terabithia*. Harper Collins.

Rando, T. A. (1984). *Grief, dying, and death*. Research Press.

Rheingold, A. A., Smith, D. W., Ruggiero, K. J., Saunders, B. E., Kilpatrick, D. G., & Resnick, H. S. (2004). Loss, trauma exposure, and mental health in a representative sample of 12–17-year-old youth: Data from the National Survey of Adolescents. *Journal of Loss and Trauma, 9*, 1–9.

Rubin, S. S. (1999). The two-track model of bereavement: Overview, retrospect, and prospect. *Death Studies, 23*, 681–714. https://doi.org/10.1080/074811899200731

Shear, M. K., Simon, N., Wall, M., Zisook, S., Neimeyer, R., Duan, N., ... Keshaviah, A. (2011). Complicated grief and related bereavement issues for DSM-5. *Depression and Anxiety, 28*, 103–117. https://doi.org/10.1002/da.20780

Stroebe, M. & Schut, H. (1999). The dual process model of coping with bereavement: Rationale and description. *Death Studies, 23*, 197–224. https://doi.org/10.1080/074811899201046

Webb, N. B. (2011). Play therapy for bereaved children: Adapting strategies to community, school, and home settings. *School Psychology International, 32*(2), 132–143. https://doi.org/10.117/0143034311400832

Worden, W. (2018). *Grief counseling and grief therapy: A handbook for the mental health practitioner* (5th ed.). Springer Publishing Company.

World Health Organization. (2018). *International classification of diseases* (11th ed.). https://icd.who.int/en/

Zachar, P., First, M. B., & Kendler, K. S. (2017). The bereavement exclusion debate in the DSM-5: A history. *Clinical Psychological Science, 5*(5), 890–906. https://doi.org/10.1177/2167702617711284

CHAPTER SEVENTEEN

Selective Mutism

Jung H. Hyun and Tiphanie Gonzalez

THE CASE OF JEREMY Jeremy is a nine-year-old Caucasian boy who attends public school. He is shy and petite compared to his peers. Jeremy lives with his mom and dad. His parents are both college educated; his father works for a tech company, and his mother is a housewife. Jeremy's parents are complete opposites when it comes to their personalities. His mother is lively and talkative, whereas his dad is much quieter. Jeremy was referred by his teacher to the school counselor because the teacher was concerned that Jeremy did not speak in class at all. His teacher contacted his parents and surprisingly learned that he was considered to be a "chatterbox" at home. In fact, after hearing the news, they chose to share a home movie that showed a snapshot of Jeremy's typical day at home where he is talking and laughing with his family.

Introduction to the Chapter

The prevalence of selective mutism is reported as 7.1 per 1,000 in the United States (Bergman et al., 2013). While some professionals have reported a higher percentage of the population with selective mutism, the *Diagnostic and Statistical Manual of Mental Disorders, Fifth Edition* (*DSM-5*; American Psychiatric Association [APA], 2013) states that approximately 1% of the population lives with the disorder. As a school counselor, you may not meet a student like Jeremy often. Students like Jeremy may easily go unnoticed unless a teacher pays particular attention to the student. These students usually stay quiet, and their behavior issues are more internalized (i.e., anxiety or social phobia) rather than externalizing behavior problems, such as oppositional behaviors (Cunningham, McHolm, & Boyle, 2004). Students like Jeremy are able to easily blend in with their peers unseen, essentially becoming invisible in plain sight. Although some students with selective mutism may begin to talk over time, without treatment, selective mutism can result in academic or educational impairment. For example, teachers often find it difficult to assess reading skills or other study areas that require verbal responses during evaluation. In addition, students with selective mutism may lose out on opportunities to interact with peers and falter on age-appropriate experiences common for social and emotional development (APA 2013).

Learning Objectives

At the end of this chapter, you will accomplish the following:

- Understand the characteristics of selective mutism.
- Increase knowledge of the effects of selective mutism on children.
- Learn the research-based strategies for supporting students with selective mutism, families, and teachers in the school system.

Definition of Diagnosis

Previously categorized as "other disorders of infancy, childhood, or adolescence" (APA, 2000), the nature of selective mutism was not clearly understood among scholars. More recently, though, selective mutism has become understood as a disorder in which a child does not speak in one or more situations, such as in school or with strangers, particularly in situations where the student feels anxious. These are situations that are not otherwise caused by language or vocal deficit. While the onset of selective mutism usually occurs before the age of 5, professional school counselors may encounter a student with this disorder who has yet to be diagnosed at the elementary school level. School counselors working with students with selective mutism may find that these students are also commonly diagnosed with other anxiety disorders (*DSM-5*; International Classification of Diseases-9 code 313.23). In fact, Vecchio and Kearney (2005) conducted a study on selective mutism and found that all 15 children involved with a diagnosis of selective mutism had also received a comorbid diagnosis of social anxiety disorder, and at least 53% of these children received a diagnosis of some other type of anxiety disorder.

According to the *DSM-5*, the diagnostic criteria for selective mutism include (a) consistent failure to speak in specific social situations in which there is an expectation for speaking (e.g., at school) despite speaking in other situations; (b) the disturbance interferes with educational or occupational achievement or with social communication; (c) the duration of the disturbance is at least 1 month (not limited to the first month of school); d) the failure to speak is not attributable to a lack of knowledge of, or comfort with, the spoken language required in the social situation; and (e) the disturbance is not better explained by a communication disorder (e.g., childhood-onset fluency disorder) and does not occur exclusively during the course of autism spectrum disorder, schizophrenia, or another psychotic disorder.

Etiology and Characteristics

Although the literature on selective mutism has not reached a consensus on causality, Scott and Beidel (2011) suggested multiple factors, including genetics, poor reinforcement strategies, unresolved internal conflicts, and family dysfunctions. While the etiology is not clearly understood among scholars (see Table 17.1; Wong, 2010), studies on selective mutism over the past 2 decades have demonstrated that common etiologies exist with generalized social phobia (Chavira et al., 2007; Hua & Major, 2016). Consistent with these studies, selective mutism was moved to the anxiety disorders section of the *DSM-5* (APA, 2013) and characterized by "extreme shyness, fear of social embarrassment, compulsive traits, withdrawal, clinging behavior, and temper tantrums." (p. 159)

Effect on Children and Adolescents

As students with selective mutism usually fail to speak at school or in other social environments, some parents are told that the child will grow out of it. Other parents may not see the necessity of treatment, thinking this disorder as a rite of developmental passage for those who are extremely shy

TABLE 17.1 Theories on the Etiology of Selective Mutism

ETIOLOGY	DESCRIPTION
Psychodynamic theory	Based on the concept of unresolved conflict. Underlying oral or anal fixation persists. Mutism represents a coping mechanism for anger and anxiety and a means for punishing parents.
Behavior theory	Learned behavior for manipulating the environment in response to triggers. An adaptive response to the sympathetic nervous system arousal that affects behavior, including speech.
Social anxiety and phobia	Association between selective mutism and excessive social anxiety. Selective mutism falls on the extreme end of the spectrum of social anxiety disorders.
Family systems perspectives	Intense attachments to parents lead to extreme interdependency and distrust of the outside world.
Respond to trauma	Association with post-traumatic stress disorder as a potential, albeit uncommon, cause. Case studies of children exposed to extreme trauma or abuse reveal mutism as an avoidance reaction to trauma.
Dissociative identity disorder	Possessing multiple identities inhibits individuals from talking to other people out of fear of revealing traumatic conflicts and experiences.

(*Wong, 2010*)

(Cline & Baldwin, 2004). In addition, in a few studies comparing academic abilities and activities that include teachers' and parents' ratings of students with selective mutism and their counterparts, the authors found there were no significant differences in overall academic performance (Cunningham et al., 2004). However, selective mutism may result in significant social and academic impairment if left untreated (Keen et al., 2007). Selective mutism limits opportunities for "social interactions and growth, delays the development of appropriate oral reading and word attack skills, and curtails involvement in normal school activities, thus limiting the roles the child can play at school" (Giddan et al., 1997, p. 127). Because of the effects on the social engagement of children, selective mutism should be diagnosed early so that students can receive appropriate treatment and develop proper coping skills.

Strategies for School Counselors

According to the American Speech-Language-Hearing Association (ASHA, n.d.), selective mutism should be treated in conjunction with the support of a speech-language pathologist, pediatrician, and psychologist or psychiatrist (Jackson et al., 2005; Keen et al., 2008). School counselors can play an integral part in recognizing a student with selective mutism and providing systemic support for not only the student with selective mutism but also teachers, staff, and parents through consultation, education, and advocacy. The following sections detail step-by-step, research-based strategies that school counselors may use to support students with selective mutism.

Working With Teachers and Staff

Most of the time, teachers are the first to identify students with selective mutism, differentiating these students from those who just refuse to speak in class. The students' lack of vocalization may cause teachers to become frustrated. Subsequently, teachers may not know how to appropriately evaluate these students in necessary academic areas, such as reading and language development, and may, therefore, reach out to the school counselor to brainstorm best practices for success and/or to initiate a Section 504 plan.

Students diagnosed with selective mutism do not qualify for an individualized education plan. Students, however, may qualify for a 504 educational plan. The plan will include modifications and accommodations so that students can have an opportunity to perform at the same level as their peers. Examples of accommodations that the teacher may find helpful include the use of nonverbal communication techniques, such as gestures, nodding, and writing; giving students extra time to answer questions, either nonverbally or verbally; and avoiding eye contact when awaiting a response. As students with selective mutism speak in selected circumstances, taping verbal homework, writing for oral communication, pairing with a "buddy," using communication cards, and using an "electronic communication device" (Kee et al., 2001, p. 389) are also recommended interventions.

School counselors can help educate teachers and staff by providing workshops and other resources related to selective mutism. Sheely-Moore (2013) recommended workshops for parents, teachers, and school staff to increase awareness. The workshop can include characteristics of selective mutism and related anxiety issues, as well as clarification of symptoms that differ from communicative and anxiety-related diagnoses. Lessons on demystifying selective mutism would also be helpful. According to the Child Mind Institute (2019), typical myths are as follows:

- Selective mutism is a form of oppositional behavior or being manipulative.
- Selective mutism will disappear with time.
- Students with selective mutism have been abused.
- Selective mutism is a form of autism.
- Students with selective mutism have speech problems.

Working With Students

Because of the limited number of reported cases of selective mutism, research conducted with a large sample size or a strong experimental control design has been sparse. In spite of the limited number of studies, behavioral approaches have shown to be effective in treating selective mutism (Jackson et al., 2005; Pionek Stone et al.; Serlin, 2002). Definitions and examples of common behavioral strategies for selective mutism were shared in the review of treatments for the disorder from 2005 to 2015 (see Table 17.2; Zakszeski & DuPaul, 2017). In addition, several researchers reported play therapy as an effective modality to use in supporting students with this disorder (Cohan et al., 2006; Pionek Stone et al., 2002). Narrative therapy has also been documented in the literature as a successful approach (Nafziger & DeKruyf, 2013) to rework the stories that affect students with selective mutism negatively, thus helping them to create a new story with their own meaning (Winslade & Monk, 2007).

It is important to note that the duration of treatment for selective mutism ranges from five sessions to more than 3 to 4 years (Cohan et al., 2006). As school counselors are limited in time, resources, and possibly training in selective mutism, the goals of individual and small-group counseling should be to decrease anxiety and increase confidence, self-esteem, and communication skills. It is also recommended that school counselors strategically incorporate strategies according to the student's characteristics, strengths, and difficulties with the comprehensive consideration of home and school factors (Zakszeski & DuPaul, 2017). Referrals to services external to the school setting should be made in conjunction with the supports provided by the school counselors.

TABLE 17.2 Definitions and Examples of Common Behavioral Strategies for Selective Mutism

STRATEGY	DEFINITION	EXAMPLE
Cognitive restructuring	Teaching the child to identify and challenge maladaptive thoughts and reasoning	Supporting the child in identifying their reason for not speaking and understanding how withholding speech may not be rational in the context of this reason
Contingency management	Providing positive reinforcement for appropriate behaviors (e.g., verbalization)	Offering the child praise, tangible reinforcers (e.g., stickers), or activity reinforcers (e.g., iPad time) for speaking
Defocused communication	Providing opportunities for communicating in a way that is comfortable to the child	Avoiding eye contact, sitting beside rather than across from the child, maintaining distance between oneself and the child
Goal setting	Identifying, communicating, and supporting behavioral goals, often in a progressive fashion	Collaborating with a child to have them establish a goal for speaking (e.g., speaking with one peer during a classroom activity) and helping the child identify what will need to occur for that goal to be met
Hierarchical exposure	Developing a gradient of feared situations and having the child encounter each situation sequentially, beginning with the least feared and ending with the most feared	Having the child practice speaking in the classroom (a) to the teacher with the parent present, (b) to the teacher with the parent in the hallway, (c) to the teacher alone, (d) to the teacher and a student, and (e) to the teacher and his or her class
Modeling	Displaying the desired behavior. In self-modeling, having the child repeatedly view themselves enacting the desired behavior	Video recording a child speaking in a classroom with their parent and playing this recording for the child to observe
Priming	Allowing the child to preview an activity or expectation prior to its occurrence	Informing the child that you will ask them to answer a certain question during large-group instruction
Role-playing	Creating a scenario and having the child take on a role in the scenario to practice a desired behavior	Asking the child to practice speaking to you as if you were a classmate
Shaping	Reinforcing progressive approximations of a behavior (e.g., volume or frequency of verbal response)	Offering the child praise, tangible reinforcers (e.g., stickers), or activity reinforcers (e.g., iPad time) for mouthing a response
Social skills training	Teaching the child skills to use in interpersonal situations	Instructing the child on how to initiate an interaction with a peer or how to ask the teacher for help
Stimulus fading	Gradually transitioning a comfortable context into a feared situation	Incrementally increasing the number of people present or reducing the distance at which people are located when the child is speaking

Behavioral Approaches

Sheely-Moore (2013) suggested contingency management, stimulus fading, and systematic desensitization as three behavioral techniques to be used in helping students with selective mutism. Contingency management is a reward system in which a student will be positively rewarded when an expected behavior is shown. Collaborating with the teacher by providing the same reward system in and out of class will be effective. In working with Jeremy, our student in the case study, the school counselor will need to build trust with him first, as trust is an essential attribute to productive therapy when working with children (O'Malley, 2002). After building rapport, the school counselor will want to find out his strengths, including learning about hobbies and activities that he enjoys. As Jeremy is not verbal in the counseling office, the use of creative expressions, such as drawing, may prove to be most beneficial. Another possible approach could be a reward chart system. For example, if Jeremy likes to read, a reward chart can be developed for him so that whenever Jeremy speaks (even whispers), a sticker is added to the chart, and once a predetermined number of stickers are collected, he is awarded a book of his choice.

Stimulus fading is a behavioral learning technique in which a new stimulus is introduced into the environment in small increments (Busses & Downey, 2011). When a school counselor observes Jeremy in the classroom and on the playground, Jeremy always sits with his friend Juan and plays with him, although still nonverbally. The school counselor may invite Juan to an individual counseling session with Jeremy. In the counseling office, Jeremy can play a board game or therapeutic game with Juan once a week. After a few sessions, the school counselor asks Jeremy to invite another friend to the counseling office to play once Jeremy feels more comfortable playing with Juan.

Finally, systematic desensitization involves structuring a hierarchy of behaviors from zero anxiety to full anxiety, reducing situations, and then guiding students to move from a low-anxiety-inducing behavior to fully speaking in class with relaxation techniques (Cohan et al., 2006). After careful observation of Jeremy's behaviors in the classroom, it is imperative that the school counselor create a list of targeted behaviors with the teacher and the parents. Using this list, the team of parent, teacher, counselor, and Jeremy may decide which behaviors they would like to address. For example, suppose Jeremy is observed to begin tapping his feet whenever the teacher suggests that the class is going to take turns reading. Although the teacher does not call on Jeremy, as she is aware of his condition, he still displays a strong level of anxiety through his tapping. The counselor would invite Jeremy to the counseling office and ask him to read a story of his choice, first silently, then in whispers, and then louder. Note that such a strategy, although beneficial, has the potential to cause harm to Jeremy. Therefore, interventions such as systematic desensitization should be used in consultation with the students' out-of-school mental health counselor and the parents. School counselors who are not trained in this method should not use it. For the untrained school counselor, stick with relaxation techniques.

Expressive Arts Approaches

Play is a natural language of children, and play therapy provides an environment in which students do not feel pressure to speak. Play and other forms of expressive arts can be useful in working with students with selective mutism. It is important to note that the use of play in counseling is different from play therapy. For school counselors who have additional training as licensed play therapists, play therapy has been documented as an effective modality to help children express their inner conflicts. School counselors who are trained in school-based play therapy can understand the underlying issues as symbolized and repeated in students' play, as well as assist students with sharing their thoughts and feelings using their play universe and mastering fears (Cohan et al., 2006)

The use of playing or building games or the use of art or other activities that focus on the use of nonverbal communication from student to school counselor can be an innovative intervention to build into the therapeutic relationship (Fernandez & Sugay, 2016). For example, when working with Jeremy in school, the school counselor asks if he would like to create a picture book. Jeremy can draw whatever he wants for a specific theme each session. The school counselor goes through the different parts of the pictures without the expectation that Jeremy needs to reply to any questions. For example, the school counselor comments on Jeremy's color choices and the structure and design of the house he has drawn, giving voice to easily identifiable elements. The use of art in a session is a commonly used activity across age groups. Like play therapy, it important to differentiate between the use of art in counseling and being an art therapist.

Narrative Counseling

Students with selective mutism may experience feelings of isolation and feel excluded in settings where they are unable to communicate verbally. Walker and Tobbel (2015) found their participants with selective mutism experienced "dissociation of identity" (p. 461), where selective mutism took over their own sense of identity, and they felt distressed and uncomfortable. Walker and Tobbel further shared that the expectation of others regarding speaking led these children to feel even more isolated and excluded. Aligned with the school counselor's tenets of strength-based approach, narrative counseling was found powerfully helpful in assisting students with selective mutism to externalize the issue contributing to the disorder and to strategize skills to challenge the underlying issue (Nafziger & DeKruyf, 2013). As narrative counseling is about re-storying and creating a new reality based on the reworked story by the narrator (Winslade & Monk, 2007), the school counselor can influence the student's school experience more positively and create concrete ways to change behaviors in the classroom by using this intervention. In a case study (Nafziger & DeKruyf, 2013), the school counselor used narrative counseling in working with a student diagnosed with selective mutism. First, the school counselor listened to the student's story (the student in the case study by Nafziger and DeKruyf didn't talk in class but was verbal with the school counselor) and helped the student with externalizing the problem by naming selective mutism through a variety of strategies, such as drawing, playing with play dough, and using the student's native language. This externalizing the problem process separated the student from the problem. Next, the school counselor asked questions, such as, "How has this problem controlled relationships in your life" (Nafziger & DeKrruyf, 2013, p. 292) to assist the student in seeing where and how selective mutism affects her life. Then the school counselor helped the student recognize her strengths by discussing the exceptions in the story—that is, places and times when the problem doesn't exist. Moving forward, the school counselor and the student created a preferred story and practiced what the student could do to make the story real. Finally, the school counselor encouraged the student to share and celebrate her new story with others.

Small-Group Counseling

Although it is summarized that behavioral or cognitive-behavioral interventions and pharmacotherapy with selective serotonin reuptake inhibitors are considered to be the most effective treatments for reducing anxiety related to selective mutism (Muris & Ollendick, 2015), some scholars reported using and recommended small-group counseling (Kearney, 2010; Sharkey et al., 2008; Skedgell et al., 2017). School counselors can provide small-group counseling with the purpose of reducing the anxiety associated with selective mutism and modeling appropriate social behaviors (Kearney, 2010). Topics such as social skills, self-esteem, and communication skills interventions may be the most beneficial in small-group settings. It should be noted that the goal is not to encourage students with selective mutism to speak verbally but to provide a safe and less anxious environment where they can express their underlying issues and learn and practice skills and strategies to use in situations where their silence prevails. Kearny (2010) recommended that members of the group be carefully selected based on the needs of the students. The school counselor should promote an atmosphere in which the more vocal students serve as role models for students with selective mutism by expressing their thoughts and emotions through open verbal communication. However, it is also important that school counselors create a setting in which students do not feel forced to speak if they are not ready or if uncomfortable. Kearney (2010) also suggested forming a group with students of similar age, cognitive functioning, and speech levels.

Strategies for Working With Families

Parents of students who are vocal at home may be shocked when they hear their children are not vocal at school or other settings. This information can be difficult to accept, and its effect can be tremendous. In an in-depth interview with a pair of twins diagnosed with selective mutism and their parents 2 years after recovery (Albrigtsen et al., 2016), the parents shared, "The silence outside the house filled the home with worries and blame" (p. 314). With care, school counselors can share an assessment of a student's symptoms. School counselors can inform guardians of etiology, general characteristics, and the importance of having guardians' involvement in the treatment process (Albrigtsen et al., 2016). For caregivers who may be in denial about their child not speaking verbally at school, school counselors may want to invite them to observe the student in different settings at school (e.g., classroom, lunch, physical education).

Ethically, school counselors, cannot and should not diagnose. If parents/caregivers report that the student communicates successfully at home, then the school counselor can refer the family to a speech-language pathologist (SLP). An SLP may screen the student using a comprehensive assessment, including norm-referenced parent/caregiver and teacher report measures; competency-based tools, such as interviews and observations; and hearing screening (ASHA, n.d.). In helping the family to move on in supporting the student, emphasize that the longer they wait to intervene, the more severe the anxiety about speaking is likely to become.

As explained in Albrigtsen and his colleagues' (2016) case, the parents felt helpless when their twins did not show progress and ended up using ineffective strategies, such as forcing them to answer and answering for them outside the home. Instead, school counselors should encourage caregivers to focus on easing students' anxiety and reinforcing verbal communication as opposed to coercing them to speak. School counselors should advise parents/caregivers against forcing students with selective mutism to speak up, disciplining them for failure to verbalize, or speaking for their children when they fail to communicate verbally. Instead, school counselors should consult with parents on effective relaxation techniques to reduce anxiety. Family therapy or counseling, as well as a comprehensive list of resources, may be most helpful in supporting families and caregivers. An example of such a resource list is provided at the end of this chapter.

Multicultural Concerns

When working with children diagnosed with selective mutism and their families, it is important to consider cultural backgrounds and influences. For example, a higher prevalence of selective mutism was reported among immigrant children than nonimmigrant children (Elizur & Perednik, 2003; Toppelberg et al., 2005). Although it is understood that diagnosis of selective mutism in this population can be challenging because second language learners may go through a "silent period" (Toppelberg et al., 2005), researchers suggested that an early selective mutism diagnosis should be made through a school's multidisciplinary team or an external practitioner. Second language learners are more likely to be underserved in the school system. Therefore, advocating in-time evaluations and providing appropriate interventions will be helpful in supporting the social skills learning, second language acquisition, and educational achievement of immigrant students (Toppelberg et al., 2005).

Understanding What You Have Read: Comprehension Questions

Directions: Refer to what you learned in this chapter to answer the following questions.

1. What is selective mutism?
2. What are the most common causes of selective mutism?
3. What approaches are available for supporting students with selective mutism?
4. What suggestions can school counselors make when developing the 504 plan?
5. What are multicultural considerations for students with selective mutism?

Case Examples

Case Example One

As you read the case about Julia, reflect on the strategies that we discussed earlier in the chapter. The questions that follow the case relate to the student's behavioral symptoms and accompanying responses.

During one of your monthly classroom guidance sessions, you noticed that Julia is still not responding to your questions verbally. This has gone on for a few months now. At first, you thought she was just being shy. However, you remember seeing Julia talking to her dad when she was dropped off in the morning in front of the school. You became curious and you stayed and observed Julia in her kindergarten classroom. She was quiet but engaged in nonverbal classroom activities. On the playground, she played only with Sonia. She whispered to Sonia when she talked.

Case Example One: Questions for Processing and Reflection

Directions: Use what you have learned in this chapter to respond to Julia's case.

1. Now you are concerned about Julia but don't want to jump to conclusions. What do you do next?
   a. Interview Julia's teacher and get more information on Julia's classroom behaviors.
   b. Contact Julia's parents/caregivers and gather information about Julia's home behaviors.
   c. Inform the school's multidisciplinary team of your concerns.
2. If Julia's diagnosis is confirmed as selective mutism, what is your plan to support Julia at school?
   a. Through individual counseling using a play and/or expressive arts approach, provide a less anxiety-provoking environment in which Julia can feel relaxed, and find out the themes and possible underlying issues causing the selective mutism.
   b. Create a behavioral chart with the teacher and parents/caregivers with rewards.
   c. If appropriate, invite Julia to small-group counseling so that she can be exposed to social interactions and feel more confident using social skills.

Case Example Two

As you read the case about Jonathan, reflect on the strategies that we discussed earlier in the chapter. The questions that follow the case relate to the student's behavioral symptoms and accompanying responses.

Jonathan is an eighth-grader who has been diagnosed with social anxiety disorder and selective mutism. He receives specially designed instruction in the areas of social/emotional, adaptive, and communication skills. He does communicate verbally at home. He does not communicate verbally at school. He is bilingual and speaks both English and Spanish. He seems to make conversations with peers, but he has not been observed having conversations with adults at school. One of his individualized goals is to improve his ability to seek out and find information on his own. He wants to go to college and eventually work in a science-related field.

Case Example Two: Questions for Processing and Reflection

Directions: Use what you have learned in this chapter to respond to Jonathan's case.

1. As a school counselor, what kind of approaches do you want to try in assisting Jonathan with initiating conversations with adults?
2. What kind of resources would you provide for his parents/caregivers?
3. What are the multicultural concerns in his case?

Chapter Summary

This chapter focused on the prevalence and etiology of selective mutism and the recommended approaches for supporting students with this disorder. School counselors play a vital role in supporting students with selective mutism and providing individual and systemic support for these students. In supporting the student with selective mutism in the school-based counseling setting, school counselors may try a multimodal approach, including behavior approaches, play therapy, small-group counseling (if needed), and narrative counseling approaches. Through counseling sessions, school counselors will understand the underlying issues and help students with selective mutism to thrive through and over silence. School counselors can also help administrators, teachers, parents/caregivers, and other stakeholders by providing accurate knowledge about selective mutism and collaborating with them in supporting the student with selective mutism.

Additional Recommended Readings and Resources

American Speech-Language-Hearing Association: http://www.asha.org/

Anxiety Network: https://anxietynetwork.com/content/selective-mutism

Selective Mutism, Anxiety, & Related Disorders Treatment Center: http://selectivemutismcenter.org

Selective Mutism Association: http://selectivemutism.org

Selective Mutism Foundation, Inc.: https://www.selectivemutismfoundation.org/knowledge-center/articles/helping-a-child-with-selective-mutism

Bibliotherapy

Bos, E. (2013). *Lola's words disappeared.* Create Space.

Cheng, W-W. (2013). *Maya's voice.* Create Space.

Cline, T., & Baldwin, S. (2003). *Selective mutism in children* (2nd ed.). Wiley.

Joffe, V. (2007). *Sophie's story: A guide to selective mutism.* Create Space.

Longo, S. (2007). *My friend Daniel doesn't speak.* Routledge.

Schaefer, C. E. (1992). *Cat's got your tongue?: Story for children afraid to speak.* Magination Press.

Shipon-Blum, E. (2019). *Understanding Katie: Understanding a child with selective mutism.* Independently Published.

References

Albrigtsen, V., Eskeland, B., & Mæhle, M. (2016). Ties of silence—family lived experience of selective mutism in identical twins. *Clinical Child Psychology, 21*(2), 308–323. https://doi.org/10.1177/1359104515591225

American Psychiatric Association (APA). (2000). *Diagnostic and statistical manual of mental disorders* (4th ed., text rev.).

American Psychiatric Association (APA). (2013). *Diagnosis and statistical manual of mental disorder* (5th ed.).

American Speech-Language Hearing-Association (ASHA). (n.d). *Selective mutism.* https://www.asha.org/PRPPrintTemplate.aspx?folderid=8589942812

Bergman, R. L., Gonzalez, A., Piacentini, J., & Keller, M. L. (2013). Integrated behavior therapy for selective mutism: A randomized controlled pilot study. *Behaviour Research & Therapy, 51*(10), 680–689. http://dx.doi.org/10.1016/j.brat.2013.07.003

Busses, R. T., & Downey, J. (2011). Selective mutism: A three-tiered approach to prevention and intervention. *Contemporary School Psychology, 15*(1), 53–63.

Chavira, D. A., Shipon-Blum, E., Hitchcock, C., Cohan, S., & Stein, M. B. (2007). Selective mutism and social anxiety disorder: All in the family? *Journal of the American Academy of Child & Adolescent Psychiatry, 46*(11), 1464–1472.

Child Mind Institute (2019). Myths about selective mutism. Retrieved from https://childmind.org/article/myths-about-selective-mutism/

Cline, T., & Baldwin, S. (2004). *Selective mutism in children.* Whurr Publisher Ltd.

Cohan, S. L., Chavira, D. A., & Stein, M. B. (2006). Practitioner review: Psychosocial interventions for children with selective mutism: A critical evaluation of the literature from 1990–2005. *Journal of Child Psychology and Psychiatry, 47*(11), 1085–1097. http://dx.doi.org/10.1111/j.1469-7610.2006.01662.x

Cunningham, C. E., McHolm, A., Boyle, M. H., & Patel, S. (2004). Behavioral and emotional adjustment, family functioning, academic performance, and social relationships in children with selective mutism. *Journal of Child Psychology and Psychiatry, 45*(8), 1363–1372. http://dx.doi.org/10.1111/j.1469-7610.2004.00327.x

Elizur, Y., Perednik, R. (2003). Prevalence and description of selective mutism in immigrant and native families: A controlled study. *Journal of the American Academy of Child and Adolescent Psychiatry, 42*, 1451–1459.

Fernandez, K. T. G., & Sugay, C. O. (2016). Psychodynamic play therapy: A case of selective mutism. *International Journal of Play Therapy, 25*(4), 203–209. https://doi.org/10.1037/pla0000034

Giddan, J. J., Ross, G. J., Sechler, L. L., & Becker, B. R. (1997). Selective mutism in elementary school: Multidisciplinary interventions. *Language, Speech & Hearing Services in Schools, 28*(2), 127–133. http://dx.doi.org/10.1044/0161-1461.2802.127

Hua, A., & Major, N. (2016). Selective mutism. *Current Opinion in Pediatrics, 28*(1), 114–120. http://dx.doi.org/10.1097/MOP.0000000000000300

Jackson, M. F., Allen, R. S., Boothe, A. B., Nava, M. L., & Coates, A. (2005). Innovative analyses and interventions in the treatment of selective mutism. *Clinical Case Studies, 4*(1), 81–112. http://dx.doi.org/10.1177/1534650103259676

Kearney, C. (2010). *Helping children with selective mutism and their parents: A guide for school-based professionals.* Oxford University Press.

Kee, C. H., Fung, D. S., & Ang, L. K. (2001). An electronic communication device for selective mutism. *Journal of the American Academy of Child and Adolescent Psychiatry, 40*(4), 389. http://dx.doi.org/10.1097/00004583-200104000-00004

Keen, D., Fonseca, S., & Wintgens, A. (2008). Selective mutism: A consensus based care pathway of good practice. *Archives of Disease in Childhood, 93*(10), 838–844.

Muris, P., & Ollendick, T. H. (2015). Children who are anxious in silence: A review on selective mutism, the new anxiety disorder in DSM-5. *Clinical Child and Family Psychology Review, 18*(2), 151–169. https://doi.org/10.1007/s10567-015-0181-y

Nafziger, J., & DeKruyf, L. (2013). Narrative counseling for professional school counselors. *Professional School Counseling, 16*(5), 290–302. http:dx.doi.org/10.1177/2156759X1201600502

O'Malley, P. (2002). Raising Martin. In L. Golden (Ed.), *Case studies in child and adolescent counseling* (pp. 142–152). Merrill/Prentice Hall.

Pionek Stone, B., Kratochwill, T., Sladezcek, I., & Serlin, R. (2002). Treatment of selective mutism: A best-evidence synthesis. *School Psychology Quarterly, 17*(2), 168–190. http://dx.doi.org/10.1521/scpq.17.2.168.20857

Scott, S., & Beidel, D. C. (2011). Selective mutism: An update and suggestions for future research. *Current Psychiatry Reports, 13*(4), 251–257. http://dx.doi.org/10.1007/s11920-011-0201-7

Sharkey, L., Mc Nicholas, F., Barry, E., Begley, M., & Adhern, S. (2008). Group therapy for selective mutism—A parents' and children's treatment group. *Journal of Behavior Therapy and Experimental Psychiatry, 39*, 538–545. https://doi.org/10.1016/j.jbtep.2007.12.002

Sheely-Moore, A. (2013). Finding their voice: Empowering students with selective mutism. In J. R. Curry & L. J. Fazio-Griffith (Eds.), *Integrating play techniques in comprehensive school counseling programs* (pp. 67–80). IAP Information Age Publishing.

Skedgell, K., Fornander, M., & Kearney, C. A. (2017). Personalized individual and group therapy for multifaceted selective mutism. *Clinical Case Studies, 16*(2), 166–181. https://doi.org/ 10.1177/1534650116685619

Toppelberg, C. O., Tabors, P., Coggins, A., Lum, K., & Burgers, C. (2005). Differential diagnosis of selective mutism in bilingual children. *Journal of American Academy of Child Adolescent Psychiatry, 44*, 592–595.

Vecchio, J. L., & Kearney, C. A. (2005). Selective mutism in children: Comparison to youths with and without anxiety disorders. *Journal of Psychopathology and Behavioral Assessment, 27*(1), 31–37. http://dx.doi.org/10.1007/s10862-005-3263-1

Walker, A. S., & Tobbell, J. (2015). Lost voices and unlived lives: Exploring adults' experience s of selective mutism using interpretative phenomenological analysis. *Qualitative Research in Psychology, 12*, 453–471. https://doi/10.1080/14780887.2015.1054533

Winslade, J. M., & Monk, G. D. (2007). *Narrative counseling in schools: Powerful & brief* (2nd ed.). Corwin Press.

Wong, P. (2010). Selective mutism: A review of etiology, comorbidities, and treatment. *Psychiatry, 7*(3), 23–31.

Zakszeski, B. N., & DuPaul, G. J. (2017). Reinforce, shape, expose, and fade: A review of treatments for selective mutism (2005-2015). *School Mental Health, 9*, 1–15. https://doi.org/10.1007/s12310-016-9198-8

About the Editors

Tiphanie Gonzalez is an assistant professor of mental health counseling at the State University of New York at Oswego. She has earned both her bachelor's in psychology and master's in counseling services from the State University of New York at Oswego. She earned her doctorate in counselor education at the University of Central Florida. She is an active member of several state and national organizations in the fields of counseling, counselor education, and counselor supervision. Her service to the field of counseling has included leadership positions with both the American Counseling Association of New York, where she most recently served as President through July of 2018, and the Association of Multicultural Counseling and Development where she has served as the North Atlantic Regional Chair since 2013. She continues to be an active voice in the field of counseling through both service and scholarship. Dr. Gonzalez has published and presented in local, regional, national, and international settings.

M. Ann Shillingford, Ph.D. is an associate professor of counselor education at the University of Central Florida in Orlando, Florida. She currently serves as coordinator of the counselor education Ph.D. program at UCF. She has several years of experience as a professional school counselor prior to completing her doctorate at the University of Central Florida. Dr. Shillingford has written several articles and book chapters on multicultural issues, particularly focused on disparities among of color. She has a keen interest in exploring measures to deconstruct educational, social, and health disparities among marginalized communities. Dr. Shillingford is currently conducting research exploring the effects of media exposure to police and community violence on the physical and mental health of African American mothers raising young black men. She also facilitates a study abroad program with counseling students to the island of Dominica, exploring the multicultural competence of counseling students through a cultural immersion experience. Dr. Shillingford also serves as coordinator for the UCF National Holmes Scholar program (NHS). The NHS is a mentoring program to support students from underrepresented groups in higher education. Dr. Shillingford's co-edited book, *The Journey Unraveled: College and Career Readiness of African American Students,* was published Fall 2015.

About the Contributors

Carrie Lynn Bailey, PhD, is a core faculty member in the Clinical Mental Health Counseling Program at Walden University and a licensed professional counselor with clinical experience in family, school, and college counseling settings. With a strong grounding in humanistic perspectives that uphold the unique developmental potential of each individual, Dr. Bailey strives to facilitate such growth in both students and clients through creating environments of meaningful, self-directed learning and a balance of challenge and support. Dr. Bailey's clinical work focuses on the needs of college students navigating the transition to adulthood, social and emotional challenges of gifted individuals across the life span, affirmative counseling and advocacy for LGBTIQ+ clients, and supporting individuals coping with issues of anxiety, obsessive-compulsive disorder, and depression. Current research interests include experiential pedagogy, cognitive-developmental strategies, social-emotional needs of gifted and twice exceptional individuals, and positive social change.

Christopher Belser, PhD, NCC, is an assistant professor at the Counselor Education and Supervision Program at the University of New Orleans. He has worked as a middle school counselor and a high school career coach and provided career interventions for first-semester college students. Dr. Belser's research centers on science, technology, engineering, and math (STEM) career initiatives, career development across the life span, and school counseling practice. He holds a PhD in counselor education and supervision from the University of Central Florida, as well as an MEd in school counseling and a BA in English in secondary education, both from Louisiana State University.

Jon Borland, PhD is an assistant professor with the Division of Psychology and Counseling at Governors State University in University Park, Illinois. He has been a licensed professional school counselor in the state of Ohio since 2010 and has more than a decade of experience working with students and their families in educational settings. He earned his master's degree in counselor education with a specialization in school counseling at the University of Toledo and a PhD specializing in counselor education at the University of Central Florida. His research interests include school counselor training and competencies, trauma work in schools, youth mental health, and instrument development.

Autumn Cabell is a nationally certified counselor and resident in counseling (Virginia). She received her master's in school counseling at George Washington University and worked predominantly with black and Latinx high school students in the DC area. She received her PhD in counselor education and supervision at Virginia Commonwealth University. Currently, Autumn is an assistant professor in counseling at DePaul University. Her line of research centers on the career development and mental health of underrepresented K–12 and college students. To increase the representation of racial minorities in STEM and health sciences, she examines how career development interventions improve underrepresented students' persistence in those fields.

Erika Cameron, PhD, is an associate professor and chair of the Department of Counseling and Marital and Family Therapy at the University of San Diego. She has worked as a school counselor and career counselor in a variety of diverse settings, including a primary, middle, and secondary school; university; residential facility; and community agency in Hawaii, Missouri, and California. Dr. Cameron is an active counselor educator and enjoys learning and teaching in creative and innovative ways. Her scholarly interests include school counselor professional development, qualitative research methods, and treatment of adverse childhood experiences. She regularly trains school counselors and teachers on issues of assessing and treating trauma in schools.

Matt Dahlman is a graduate student specializing in school counseling at the University of San Diego. Before starting graduate studies, he worked in an inpatient child and adolescent psychiatric facility. While in graduate school, he has been able to work in a variety of school settings, such as juvenile county schools, charter high schools, private Catholic schools, and an international school.

Dalena Dillman Taylor, PhD, LPC, LMHC, RPT-S, QS, is an associate professor at the University of Central Florida in the Department of Counselor Education and School Psychology/Counselor Education Program. She earned her doctoral degree in counseling and completed her master's degree in counseling at the University of North Texas. Dr. Dillman Taylor's primary research interests include advancement of the Adlerian play therapy field toward evidence-based practice, counseling and educational services for high-need children and families, and counselor development and supervision. Dr. Dillman Taylor has more than 25 scholarly works in refereed and/or peer-reviewed dissemination outlets. Dr. Dillman Taylor is also the founder/director of the Center for Play Therapy Training and Research at the University of Central Florida. She is a certified child-centered play therapist supervisor, a certified child-parent relationship therapist supervisor, and a certified Adlerian play therapist.

Jason Duffy, PhD, is an Assistant Professor at SUNY Oswego and has been a counselor educator for nearly a decade. In addition, Jason has been a practicing counselor and counselor supervisor for nearly 10 years. Prior to this, Jason was a high school English teacher for 10 years in Rochester, New York, as well as an administrator for an innovative school-based program designed to help at-risk high school students find success in school socially and academically. Jason has presented nationally, lead many workshops, and published various articles and book chapters on topics dealing with creative pedagogy, counseling, and counselor supervision.

Sean Finnerty, PhD, has been an assistant professor and coordinator of the school counseling program at SUNY Oswego for the past 10 years. Dr. Finnerty also has more than 13 years of experience as a school counselor working in both the middle school and high school levels in New York and North Carolina.

Lauren Flynn is completing her master's degree in clinical mental health counseling at the University of San Diego. Her research interests include trauma resilience, suicide loss, and military sexual trauma. She has presented regionally at the Association for Counselor Education and Supervision—West Region Conference and nationally at the Association for Counselor Education and Supervision Conference. She is an active member of Chi Sigma Iota, American Counseling Association, Western Association for Counselor Education and Supervision, and Southern Association for Counselor Education and Supervision.

Vikki Gaskin-Butler, M.Div., PhD, is a visiting clinical associate professor and director of the University of Central Florida (UCF) Psychology Clinic. Prior to joining the Department of Psychology in the fall of 2019, Dr. Gaskin-Butler was a faculty member in the Counselor Education and School

Psychology Department at UCF. She served as a faculty member at the University of South Florida (USF) St. Petersburg for 12 years before coming to UCF. Dr. Gaskin-Butler also served as USF St. Petersburg's first chief diversity officer. Dr. Gaskin-Butler earned her PhD in clinical and health psychology from the University of Florida. She also earned a master's of divinity from the Candler School of Theology at Emory University. Dr. Gaskin-Butler's clinical, research, and academic interests focus on spiritual, psychological, and physical well-being in adolescents and adults. Her recent research and scholarly activities have focused on the development and piloting of the "Figuring It Out for the Child" co-parenting curriculum for first-time parents of African American children.

Dana Griffin, PhD, is an associate professor at the University of North Carolina at Chapel Hill. A former school counselor, Dr. Griffin teaches in the School Counseling, Human Development and Family Studies, and Applied Developmental Sciences and Special Education Programs in the School of Education. Among the courses she teaches in the School Counseling Program is the Mental Health and Well-Being course, which focuses on the school counselor's role in working with kids diagnosed with *Diagnostic and Statistical Manual of Mental Disorders, Fifth Edition* (*DSM-V*) disorders. Dr. Griffin strongly believes that school counselors should be aware of the *DSM-V* and evidenced-based strategies for working with students with various *DSM-V* diagnoses. Dr. Griffin also researches best practices for schools for working with culturally diverse families and communities. Further, Dr. Griffin has a strong commitment to social justice and advocacy and, as such, believes that school counselors are in a pivotal role to pave the way for bridging the gap between families, schools, and communities. She is also dedicated to the multicultural training of preservice and professional counselors in hopes that it may lead to better relationships, collaborations, and increased effectiveness when working with diverse families and students.

Whitney Hanley, PhD, is an assistant professor, American Association of Colleges for Teacher Education Holmes scholar, and LEAD IT scholar in the PhD Exceptional Education Program at the UCF. Whitney received her BS in special education from the University of Louisville in Louisville, Kentucky, and her teaching certificate in special education P–12 for students with learning and behavior disorders. She received her MEd from Georgia State University in Atlanta, Georgia. While teaching in Georgia, Whitney also completed her EdS in curriculum and instruction at Piedmont College in Demorest, Georgia. For 7 years, Whitney taught in three different classroom settings. For the first 6 years of her teaching career, she taught students with learning and behavior disorders in the elementary setting. During her seventh year of teaching, she taught eighth-grade students with learning and behavior disorders. Her research interests include the extent that gender and other confounds affect the achievement of culturally diverse females with or at risk of emotional and behavioral disorders (EBD) and evaluating systems and practices within our field that may perpetuate delinquency and poor achievement among young females with or at risk of disabilities.

Pamela Harris, PhD, is an assistant professor in the Department of Counseling at the University of the Cumberlands. She has worked as a professional middle school counselor for 7 years and has received training in family counseling. She has conducted research that involves school-family partnerships with families of color, college and career readiness for African American females, and culturally responsive counselor preparation. Dr. Harris enjoys teaching coursework in school counseling, counseling children and adolescents, and human growth and development, as well as supervising practicum students and interns.

Nicole S. Helton has a bachelor's of science degree in psychology and is currently a master's student in the School Counseling Program at the University of North Carolina at Chapel Hill and will be graduating in August 2020. She is currently completing her internship at an elementary school where she works closely with students with extreme behaviors. Prior to graduate school, she was working with students with various DSM-V diagnoses such as anxiety, autism, specific learning disorder, oppositional defiant disorder, and conduct disorder. Ms. Helton also presented a poster at the 2019 North Carolina School Counseling Association Conference on self-regulation strategies for students with behavior disorders. She believes school counselors can provide services for all students by forming school-family-community partnerships. Her research and advocacy interests include working with families from low-income backgrounds and children who struggle with behavior disorders.

Lèa Herbert is a PhD student in UCF's Counselor Education and Supervision Program. Lèa is an American Association of Colleges for Teacher Education (AACTE) Holmes Scholar and is an active member of the American Counseling Association, the Association for Counselor Education and Supervision, and the Association for Multicultural Counseling and Development. Lèa's work primarily focuses on wellness counseling and trauma literacy education, the influence of media on mental health, and feedback-informed psychotherapy.

Jung H. Hyun, PhD, LMHC, NCC, is an associate professor and chair of the School Counseling Program at Seattle Pacific University. Dr. Hyun teaches core school counseling courses, including multicultural counseling in schools, legal and ethical issues in schools, practicum, and internship. Her scholarly work and presentations cover multicultural counseling in K–12 schools; school counselor supervision; play therapy integration in schools; school, family, and community partnership; and promoting resiliency and a safe learning environment. She is also a licensed mental health counselor in Washington. She uses play therapy when working with K–5 graders and provides parenting workshops for Asian American populations in the greater Seattle area.

Kara Ieva, PhD, is currently an associate professor in the Counseling in Educational Settings Program at Rowan University. Kara's areas of research interest include counseling children and adolescents from underserved populations regarding college and career readiness, social-emotional development, and group counseling. She focuses on addressing the academic, behavioral, and mental health needs of all students simultaneously in schools. As such, she provides professional development to K–12 school counselors, teachers, and administrators on how to embed social-emotional development into curricula and creating a safe and welcoming mental health culture in schools.

Christie Jenkins, PhD, is core faculty in the Clinical Mental Health Counseling Program at Walden University and the CEO of Family and Child Abuse Prevention Center and the Children's Advocacy Center (FCAPC). FCAPC is the only agency in Northwest Ohio whose sole mission is dedicated to preventing, intervening, and eliminating interpersonal violence. Dr. Jenkins is an independently licensed counselor who is very active in service to counseling organizations and her community. She has received several honors for her work concerning domestic violence and sexual abuse and published several works on animal-assisted therapy and various other topics.

Richelle Joe, PhD, is an assistant professor in counselor education at the UCF in Orlando. She is a graduate of the College of William & Mary in Williamsburg, Virginia, where she earned her doctoral degree in counselor education and supervision. She has served as a professional school counselor in Virginia and is a nationally certified counselor and an approved clinical supervisor. Her research focuses on culturally responsive services for underserved and marginalized clients and communities and specifically includes an emphasis on effective school-family relationships, the experiences of individuals of color, and the mental health needs of individuals and families affected by HIV/AIDS.

Huan-Tang Lu, PhD, LSC, LPC, NCC, is an assistant professor in the Counseling in Educational Settings Program at Rowan University. Dr. Lu has taught courses such as assessment, research, practicum, and internship, with an emphasis on working with P–20 students. He has provided counseling services to a wide range of populations, from children to older adults. His scholarly work specifically addresses professional issues in counseling, counselor education, group work, immigrants, and trauma.

Seungbin Oh, PhD., is an assistant professor in the Clinical Mental Health Counseling Graduate Program at Merrimack College where he is researching multicultural counseling competencies, particularly pursuing the development of culturally focused interventions for clients from diverse cultural backgrounds. He has written numerous articles and book chapters that focus on social justice and cultural issues in counseling, as well as made numerous professional presentations at international, national, regional, and state associations.

Taqueena Quintana EdD, LPC, NCC, BC-TMH, earned her doctorate in counselor education and supervision from Argosy University. She holds graduate degrees in special education and school counseling (with advanced graduate education in clinical mental health counseling) and has worked in K–12 education for more than a decade. Presently, Dr. Quintana serves as an assistant professor, supervisor, and mentor, supporting emerging and novice school counselors. Her research interests include advocacy for students with disabilities, school-based clinical mental health, and military-connected students and families.

Bethany Russell, MA, completed her master's degree in mental health counseling, with an emphasis on play therapy, from UCF. She is a registered mental health counselor intern, nationally certified counselor, and a certified child life specialist. Her research interests include Adlerian play therapy, therapeutic interventions with children who have faced trauma, and the effect of chronic illness on the mental health of children and adolescents.

Stacy Walkowitz, MEd, is a seventh-grade inclusion science teacher at Lindenwold Middle School in New Jersey. She holds a master's degree in school administration and has 20 years of experience in education in three states (Florida, Maryland, and New Jersey)—all Title 1 schools—that span a range of subjects and certifications: elementary education, English for speakers of other languages/ English-language learner, special education, and middle school science. Her expertise is in academic and behavior modifications simultaneously throughout classroom lessons. In addition, she teaches in the Rowan University ASPIRE program and trains alternate route teachers to help teachers learn to build executive functioning skills in their specific settings.

Naomi J. Wheeler, PhD, LMHC, NCC, is an assistant professor in the counselor education program at Virginia Commonwealth University. She has extensive clinical and administrative experience with children and families from predominantly low-income and historically marginalized backgrounds. Her research agenda builds from her professional experience to examine relational stress across the life span, including early life adversity and couples' stress as contributors to health disparities.

CPSIA information can be obtained
at www.ICGtesting.com
Printed in the USA
BVHW010212041022
648619BV00009B/212